The Windows NT Device Driver Book:
A Guide for Programmers

Art Baker

Cydonix Corporation

Prentice Hall PTR
Upper Saddle River, New Jersey 07458

http://www.prenhall.com

Library of Congress Cataloging-in-Publication Data

Baker, Art (Arthur H.)

The Windows NT Device Driver Book: A Guide for Programmerss / Art Baker
p.   cm.
Includes index.
ISBN 0-13-184474-1
1.)Microsoft Windows NT device drivers (computer programs)   I. Title.
QA76.76.D46B355   1996
005.7'126--dc20   96-22449
                                                       CIP

Editorial/production supervision and Interior Design: *Joanne Anzalone*

Manufacturing manager: *Alexis R. Heydt*

Acquisitions editor: *Mike Meehan*

Marketing Manager: *Stephen Soloman*

Editorial assistant: *Kate Hargett*

Cover design: *Design Source*

Cover design director: *Jerry Votta*

© 1997 by Prentice Hall PTR

Prentice-Hall, Inc.

A Simon & Schuster Company

Upper Saddle River, New Jersey 07458

The publisher offers discounts on this book when ordered in bulk quantities.

For more information, contact:

Corporate Sales Department
Prentice Hall PTR
1 Lake Street
Upper Saddle River, NJ 07458

Phone: 800-382-3419, Fax: 201-236-7141

E-mail: corpsales@prenhall.com

Printed in the United States of America

10 9 8 7 6 5 4

ISBN 0-13-184474-1

Prentice-Hall International (UK) Limited, *London*
Prentice-Hall of Australia Pty. Limited, *Sydney*
Prentice-Hall Canada Inc., *Toronto*
Prentice-Hall Hispanoamericana, S.A., *Mexico*
Prentice-Hall of India Private Limited, *New Delhi*
Prentice-Hall of Japan, Inc., *Tokyo*
Simon & Schuster Asia Pte. Ltd., *Singapore*
Editora Prentice-Hall do Brasil, Ltda., *Rio de Janeiro*

Contents

Preface

In case you haven't guessed, this book explains how to write, install, and debug kernel-mode device drivers for Windows NT. If you're in the process of designing or coding an NT driver, or if you're porting an existing driver from some other operating system, this book is a valuable companion to the Microsoft DDK documentation.

This book might also have something to say to you if you just need a little more insight into the workings of Windows NT, particularly the I/O subsystem. Perhaps you're trying to decide if NT is a reasonable platform for some specific purpose. Or you may be studying operating systems, and you want to see how theory gets applied in the real world.

And of course, we mustn't discount the power of morbid curiosity. The same fascination that forces us to slow down as we drive past a car accident can also motivate us to pull a volume off the bookstore shelf.

What You Should Already Know

Throughout this book, I make several assumptions about what you already know. First of all, you need to have all the basic Windows NT user skills such as logging in and running various utilities. Since driver installation requires you to have administrator-level privileges, you can trash things pretty badly if you don't know how to use the system.

Second, you'll need decent C-language programming skills. I've tried to avoid the use of "cleverness" in my code examples, but you still have to be able to read them.

Next, some experience with Win32 user-mode programming is helpful, but it isn't really required. If you haven't worked with the Win32 API, you might want to browse through volume two of the *Win32 Programmers Reference*. This is the one that describes system services. Take a look at the chapters on the I/O primitives (**CreateFile**, **ReadFile**, **WriteFile**, and **DeviceIoControl**) and the thread-model. See the bibliography for other books on Win32 programming.

Finally, you need to understand something about hardware in order to write drivers. It would be helpful if you already had some experience working with hardware, but if not, Chapter 2 will give you a basic introduction. Again, the bibliography will point you toward other, more-detailed sources for this kind of information.

What You'll Find Here

One of the most difficult choices any author has to make is deciding what to write about and what to leave out. In general, I've attempted to focus on core issues that are crucial to kernel-mode driver development. I've also tried to provide enough background information so that you'll be able to read the sample code supplied with the NT DDK, and make intelligent design choices for your own drivers.

The overall flow of the book goes from the theoretical to the practical, with earlier chapters providing the underpinnings for later topics. Here's what's covered:

Chapters 1–5   The first part of this book provides the basic foundation you'll need if you plan to write drivers. This includes a general examination of the Windows NT driver architecture, a little bit about hardware, and a rather detailed look at the NT I/O Manager and its data structures. This group of topics ends with some general kernel-mode coding guidelines and techniques.

Chapters 6–13   These eight chapters form the nucleus of the book and present all the details of writing kernel-mode NT device drivers. You'll also find discussions here of full-duplex driver architectures, handling timeout conditions, and logging device errors. Unless you're already familiar with NT's driver architecture, you should probably read these chapters in order.

Chapters 14 and 15   The next two chapters deal with alternative driver architectures supported by Windows NT. This includes the use of kernel-mode threads in drivers and higher-level drivers.

Chapters 16–18   The final part of the book deals with various practical details of writing NT drivers. Chapter 16 takes a look at all the things your mother never told you about the BUILD utility. Chapter 17 covers various aspects of testing and debugging drivers, including how to analyze crash dumps and how to *really* get WINDBG to work. If you're actually writing a driver while you read this book, you may want to read these chapters out of order. Chapter 18 examines the crucial issue of driver performance and how to tie your driver into NT's performance monitoring mechanisms.

Appendices The appendices cover various topics that people in my classes have asked about. The first one deals with the mechanics of setting up a driver development environment.

The second appendix contains a list of the bugcheck codes you're most likely to encounter, along with descriptions of their various parameters. Used in conjunction with the material in Chapter 17, this may help you track down the cause of a blue screen or two.

What You Won't Find

I excluded topics from this book for several reasons. Some subjects were just too large to cover. Others addressed the needs of too small a segment of the driver-writing community. Finally, some areas of driver-development are simply unsupported by Microsoft. Specifically, you won't find anything here about the following items:

File system drivers At the time this book went to press, Microsoft still hadn't released any kind of developer's kit for NT file system drivers. In fact, there seemed to be a great deal of resistance to the idea within Microsoft. Until this situation changes, there's not much point in talking about the architecture of file system drivers.

Net-card and network protocol drivers NDIS and TDI drivers are both very large topics — large enough to fill a book of their own. Unfortunately, there just wasn't enough room for all of it here. I can offer one bit of consolation: The material in this book will give you much of the background you need in order to understand what's happening inside the NDIS/TDI framework.

SCSI miniport and class drivers Although SCSI HBA miniport drivers are vital system components, the number of people actually writing them is (I suspect) rather small. Consequently, the only reference to SCSI miniports is the overview material in Chapter 1.

I would have liked to include a discussion of SCSI class drivers in this book, but unfortunately there just wasn't any time to write it. The material on developing intermediate drivers in Chapter 15 will give you much of the necessary background. From there, take a look at the sample SCSI class driver for CD-ROMs that comes with the NT DDK.

Video, display, and printer drivers This is another area where I had to make a tradeoff between the number of people writing these kinds of drivers and the time available to finish the book. Unfortunately, graphics drivers for video and hardcopy devices didn't make the cut this time. Perhaps in a later, expanded version of the book...

Virtual DOS device drivers In my opinion, the best way to run 16-bit MS-DOS and Windows applications under Windows NT is to port the source code to Win32. In any event, the Microsoft documentation does a decent job describing the mechanics of writing VDDs so I haven't included anything about them here.

About the Sample Code

There's a great deal of sample driver code scattered throughout this book. You'll find all of it on the accompanying floppy disk. I've created separate directories on the floppy for each chapter, and where appropriate, subdirectories for each component or driver in the chapter.

Coding style   Since the purpose of this book is instruction, I've done a couple things to improve the clarity of the samples. First, I've adopted a coding style that avoids smart tricks. Some of the examples could probably have been written in fewer lines of code, but I don't think they would have been as easy to understand.

Also in the name of clarity, I've eliminated everything except the bare essentials from each sample. For example, most of the drivers don't contain any error-logging or debugging code, although a real driver ought to include these things. These topics have their own chapters, and you shouldn't have too much trouble back-fitting the code into other sample drivers.

Naming conventions   You'll notice that almost all the sample drivers appearing in this book are called "XXDRIVER." (The only exception is the higher-level driver Chapter 15. Its name is "YYDRIVER.") This makes it somewhat easier to interchange the parts of different samples. It also reduces the amount of clutter that you'll be adding to the Registry while you're playing with these drivers.

Within any particular driver, I've also adopted the convention of adding the prefix, **Xx** to the names of any driver-defined functions. Similarly, device registers, driver structures, and constants are also prefixed with XX_. This makes it easy to see which things you have to write and which ones come from the folks at Microsoft.

Platform dependencies   It's worth mentioning that these samples have been targeted to run on Intel 80x86 platforms. In particular, the drivers all assume that device registers live in I/O space rather than being memory-mapped. This is relatively easy to fix with a little bit of coding and some modifications to each driver's hardware-specific header file.

To build and run the examples   You'll need several tools if you plan to do any driver development for Windows NT. First, get yourself a Level II subscription to the Microsoft Developer Network CDs. This is the only source for the NT DDK and the Win32 SDK.

You'll also need a C compiler. I've chosen to use the Microsoft compiler for developing and testing all the code in this book. Your mileage may vary if you're using some other vendor's tools. See Appendix A for more information on setting up your driver development environment.

Training and Consulting Services

The material in this book is based on classes that I've been delivering for several years through Cydonix Corporation — a training and consulting firm whose goal is to help its clients develop device drivers and other high-performance Windows NT software. Cydonix offers services that range from formal classroom training to direct participation in software design and coding.

For the past three years, Cydonix has been helping companies like Adaptec, AT&T, Compaq Computers, Hewlett-Packard, and Intel to learn more about the workings of Windows NT. We have training available in a number of areas including:

- Windows NT device driver programming
- Win32 system service programming
- Advanced server development techniques

Cydonix offers both onsite training at customer facilities and open enrollment classes that are available to the general public. The public classes are hosted by training vendors in several geographic areas.

For more information about training and consulting from Cydonix Corporation, visit our Web site at **http://www.cydonix.com** or send email to **info@cydonix.com**. You can also contact us through more earthbound means using this postal address:

Cydonix Corporation
Suite 304
2117 L Street, N.W.
Washington, DC 20037

Acknowledgments

Many people have kindly contributed to the creation of this volume. First and foremost, I want to thank David Lucas (to whom this book is dedicated) for his steadfast friendship and unfaltering faith in me over the years. David, so many things have been possible in my life only because of you...

My gratitude also goes to the editorial and production staff at Prentice Hall. Mike Meehan and Joanne Anzalone have shown infinite patience while I tried to balance my training and consulting schedule with the demands of writing a book. I'm sure you're glad it's over.

I would be remiss if I didn't acknowledge all the people who've been students in my various driver classes over the last twelve years. Your questions and insights have helped me understand how to communicate this kind of material to others, and I'm grateful.

Finally, I'm very pleased to say that all crash sequences were performed by stunt doubles and no programmers or other small animals were actually harmed.

Introduction to Windows NT Drivers

*T*radition demands that any book about writing device drivers starts out by answering the question, "What is a driver?" Unfortunately, asking this question in Windows NT is a little like asking "What color is plaid?" because there are at least a dozen different software components that can rightfully be called drivers. This chapter takes a roundabout look at the different kinds of drivers supported by Windows NT, and along the way, presents some of the design philosophy that makes this operating system such an intriguing beast.

1.1 OVERALL SYSTEM ARCHITECTURE

Windows NT drivers don't live in isolation, of course. Rather, they are just one part of a large and complex operating system. This section takes you on a quick tour of the Windows NT architecture and points out those features that will be of most interest to driver writers.

Design Goals for Windows NT

Like every other commercial operating system, Windows NT is the result of a complex interaction between idealized goals and market-driven realities. The Windows NT design team set their sights on the following:

- **Compatibility** — The operating system should support a wide range of existing software and legacy hardware.

- **Robustness and reliability** — The operating system has to resist the attacks of naive or malicious users, and individual applications should be as isolated from one another as possible.

1

- **Portability** — The operating system should be able to run on a wide variety of current and future hardware platforms.

- **Extendibility** — It should be possible to add new features and support new I/O devices without perturbing the existing code base.

- **Performance** — The operating system should be able to give reasonable performance on commonly available hardware. It should also be able to take advantage of features like multiprocessing hardware.

Trying to balance all these goals with a reasonable time to market was a complex process. The rest of this section describes the solution that the system designers came up with — beginning with a look at the protection mechanisms that keep the operating system safe.

Hardware Privilege Levels in Windows NT

There are any number of things that application programs shouldn't be allowed to do in a multitasking environment. Fooling with the memory management hardware or halting the processor are just two examples of actions that would cause serious problems. Rather than depending on the kindness of strange applications, Windows NT takes advantage of hardware-enforced privilege-checking mechanisms to guarantee system integrity.

To avoid hardware dependencies, Windows NT uses a simplified model to describe hardware privileges. This model then maps onto whatever privilege-checking mechanisms are available on a given CPU. A CPU must be able to operate in two modes if it's going to support the Windows NT hardware privilege model.

Kernel mode   Anything goes when the CPU runs in kernel mode. A task can execute privileged instructions, and it has complete access to any I/O devices. It can also touch any virtual address and fiddle with the virtual memory hardware. This mode corresponds to Ring 0 on an Intel 80x86.

User mode   In this mode, the hardware prevents execution of privileged instructions and performs access checks on references to memory and I/O space. This allows the operating system to restrict a task's access to various I/O operations, and trap any other behavior that might violate system integrity. Code running in user mode can't get itself into kernel mode without going through some kind of gate mechanism in the operating system. On an Intel 80x86 processor, this mode corresponds to Ring 3.

Base Operating System Components

The base components of Windows NT implement a general operating system platform on which to build more complex environments. As you can see from

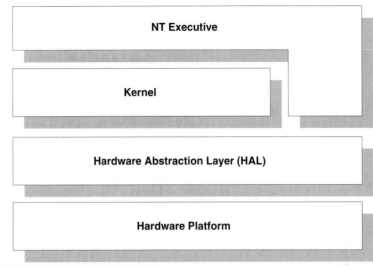

Figure 1.1   Overall architecture of the NT kernel-mode components

Figure 1.1, these base components consist of three major blocks of kernel-mode code.

Hardware Abstraction Layer (HAL)   The HAL is a thin layer of software that presents the rest of the system with an abstract model of any hardware that's not part of the CPU itself. The HAL exposes a well-defined set of functions that manage such items as:

- Off-chip caches
- Timers
- I/O buses
- Device registers
- Interrupt controllers
- DMA controllers

Various system components use these HAL functions to interact with off-CPU hardware. This essentially hides platform-specific details from the rest of the system and removes the need to have different versions of the operating system for platforms from different system vendors. In particular, the use of HAL routines makes the Kernel and device drivers binary-compatible across platforms with the same CPU architecture.

Kernel   Where the HAL is an abstraction of the platform, the Kernel presents an idealized view of the CPU itself. Among other things, the Kernel provides mechanisms for

- Interrupt and exception dispatching
- Thread scheduling and synchronization
- Multiprocessor synchronization
- Time keeping

By using these Kernel services, upper layers of the operating system can (for the most part) ignore the architecture of the underlying CPU. This makes it possible for drivers and higher-level operating system components to be source-code portable across different CPU architectures.[1]

An interesting feature of the Kernel is that it presents an object-based interface to its clients. When other parts of the operating system need help from the Kernel, they request its services by calling functions that create and manipulate various kinds of objects. These Kernel objects fall into two main categories:

- **Dispatcher objects** — These are used primarily for managing and synchronizing threads.

- **Control objects** — These objects affect the behavior of the operating system itself in some way.

Device drivers don't have much use for dispatcher objects. Those that do are described in Chapter 14. Control objects are another matter, however. In particular, device drivers make frequent use of Deferred Procedure Call objects and Interrupt objects (described in Chapters 3 and 4 respectively).

Executive   The Executive is by far the largest and most complex kernel-mode component in Windows NT. Its job is to implement many of the basic functions normally associated with an operating system. Like the Kernel, the Executive uses the HAL to interact with any off-CPU hardware and so becomes binary compatible across platforms from different system vendors. By relying on Kernel objects, the Executive gains the additional advantage of being source-code portable across different CPU architectures. Because it's such a key part of Windows NT, it's worth exploring the Executive a little more.

What's in the Executive

As you can see from Figure 1.2, the Executive actually consists of several distinct software components that offer their services both to user-mode processes and to one another. These Executive components are completely independent and communicate only through well-defined interfaces. This modularity

---

[1] It also means that much of the work of porting Windows NT to a new CPU is really a matter of rewriting the Kernel. To make this process easier, Microsoft has adopted a *microkernel* approach that tries to keep the Kernel as small as possible.

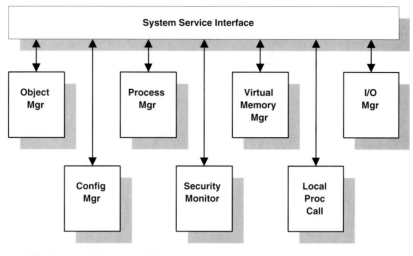

Copyright © 1994 by Cydonix Corporation. 940003a.vsd

Figure 1.2   Detailed view of the Executive

makes it possible to replace an existing Executive component without perturbing any other parts of the operating system. As long as the replacement exposes the same interface, the change will be transparent. The remainder of this subsection gives cursory descriptions of the various Executive modules.

System service interface   All operating systems have to give user-mode processes a limited ability to execute kernel-mode code. In particular, there must be a controlled path from user to kernel mode that applications can follow when they call system services. In Windows NT, the system service dispatcher uses a technique based on the CPU's hardware exception mechanism to give user-mode code access to Executive services.

Object Manager   The Executive offers its services to user-mode processes through an object-based interface. These Executive objects represent things such as files, processes, threads, and shared memory segments. This use of objects provides a unified mechanism for tracking resources and enforcing security.

 The Object Manager does all the grunt work of managing these Executive objects. This includes creating and deleting objects, maintaining the global object namespace, and keeping track of how many outstanding references there are to any given object.

Configuration Manager   From a driver writer's perspective, the main job of the Configuration Manager is to maintain a model of all the hardware and software installed on the machine. It does this using a database called the Registry. As you read through the rest of this book, you'll see that drivers are linked to the Registry through an intricate web of connections. Among other things, drivers use the Registry to

- Identify themselves as trusted system components
- Find and allocate peripheral hardware
- Set up error-logging message files
- Enable driver-performance measurement

Process Manager   A process is the unit of resource-tracking and security access checking in Windows NT. Along with any resources it might be holding, each process has its own virtual address space and security identity. A process also contains one or more executable entities called threads. It is the thread (and not the process) that receives ownership of a CPU and does actual work.

The Process Manager is the Executive component that handles the creation, management, and deletion of processes and threads. It also provides a standard set of services for synchronizing the activities of threads. Most of the features exposed by the Process Manager are just fancy versions of mechanisms implemented by the Kernel.

Security Reference Monitor   This Executive component enforces the system's security policies. The Security Reference Monitor doesn't actually define security policy; that job belongs to the Local Security Authority subsystem (described later in this chapter). Rather, the Security Reference Monitor simply provides a set of primitives that both kernel- and user-mode components can call to validate access to objects, check for user privileges, and generate audit messages. For the most part, device drivers don't concern themselves with security issues.

Device drivers normally don't do much with the Security Reference Monitor. The I/O Manager handles those kinds of details before it calls any routines in your driver.

Virtual Memory Manager   Under Windows NT, each process has a flat 4-gigabyte virtual address space. The lower half of this space contains process-private code and data along with the process's stack and heap space. It also holds any File Mapping objects and DLLs the process is using. The upper half of every process's address space contains nothing but kernel-mode code. One of the jobs of the Executive's Virtual Memory Manager is to maintain this illusion of a huge address space using demand-paged virtual memory management techniques.

From a driver writer's point of view, the Virtual Memory Manager is more important as a memory allocator because it maintains the system heap areas. The Virtual Memory Manager also builds and manipulates various buffer descriptors that are crucial to the operation of DMA drivers. Both these topics are covered in more detail later.

Local Procedure Call facility   The Local Procedure Call (LPC) facility is a message-passing mechanism used for communication between processes on the same machine. LPCs are used primarily by protected subsystems (described later) and their clients. Device drivers have no access to the LPC facility.

I/O Manager   This Executive component converts I/O requests from user- and kernel-mode threads into properly sequenced calls to various driver routines. Through the use of a well-defined formal interface, the I/O Manager is able to communicate with all drivers the same way. This makes it unnecessary for the I/O Manager to know anything about the underlying hardware managed by a given driver. The rest of this book describes the operation of the I/O Manager in gory detail.

Extensions to the Base Operating System

The Executive components of Windows NT present a fairly neutral face to the world. They don't implement a user interface nor do they define any external policies like security. They don't even offer a programming interface since the Executive's system service calls are not publicly documented. The base kernel-mode components simply provide a generic operating system platform.

Defining the look and feel of the operating system — both to users and programmers — is the job of some extended components known collectively as *protected subsystems*. Rather than dealing directly with the Executive, users and programmers of Windows NT interact with these subsystems.

In the original architecture of Windows NT, protected subsystems were implemented entirely as a group of privileged user-mode processes. This rather elegant design made it possible to extend the base operating system without risking any damage to the underlying kernel-mode components. For performance reasons, Windows NT 4.0 has moved away from this pure user-mode model and shifted some subsystem components into kernel mode.

Depending on the kind of work they do, all protected subsystems can be divided into two major categories. The following subsections describe each category in more detail.

Integral subsystems   An integral subsystem performs some necessary system function. The responsibilities of these subsystems actually cover quite a lot of territory. The following are just a few examples of what they do.

- Together with the Security Accounts Manager and the Logon process, the Local Security Authority defines security policy for the system.

- The Service Control Manager loads, supervises, and unloads trusted system components like services and drivers.

- The RPC Locator and RPC Service processes give support to distributed applications that use remote procedure calls.

Environment subsystems   The other kind of protected subsystem is called an environment subsystem. The job of an environment subsystem is to provide a programming interface and execution environment for application programs native to some specific operating system. Currently, Windows NT provides the following subsystems:

- The Win32 subsystem implements the native-mode programming interface for Windows NT. A more detailed description of this subsystem appears below.

- The Virtual DOS Machine (VDM) subsystem allows 16-bit MS-DOS applications to run under Windows NT. Unlike other subsystems, the VDM software is actually part of the process where the MS-DOS application is running.

- The Windows on Windows (WOW) subsystem supports the execution of 16-bit Windows applications. The default behavior of the WOW subsystem is to run all 16-bit Windows applications as separate threads within the address space of a single VDM process. This helps to mimic the 16-bit Windows environment more closely.

- The POSIX subsystem provides API support for programs conforming to the POSIX 1003.1 source-code standard. Because POSIX 1003.1 is not a binary standard, applications must be compiled and linked on Windows NT in order under this subsystem.

- The OS/2 subsystem creates an execution environment for 16-bit OS/2 applications. This subsystem is available only for the 80x86 version of Windows NT.

A given application is always tightly coupled to one specific subsystem and can use only the features of that subsystem. For example, a POSIX application can't make calls to Win32 API functions. Also keep in mind that applications running under any subsystem other than Win32 will experience some performance degradation. These other subsystems are provided mainly for compatibility.

More about the Win32 Subsystem

All environment subsystems are not created equal. In particular, the services provided by the Win32 subsystem are crucial to the operation of Windows NT. The duties of this subsystem include the following:

- As the owner of the screen, keyboard, and mouse, it manages all console and GUI I/O for the entire system. This includes I/O for other subsystems as well as user applications.

- The Win32 subsystem implements the GUI seen by programmers and users. As the screen and window manager for Windows NT, it defines GUI policy and style for the whole system.

- It exposes the Win32 API that both application programs and other subsystems use to interact with the Executive.

Because of its special status, the Win32 subsystem is implemented in a different way from any of the others. Figure 1.3 shows the organization of the Win32 subsystem.

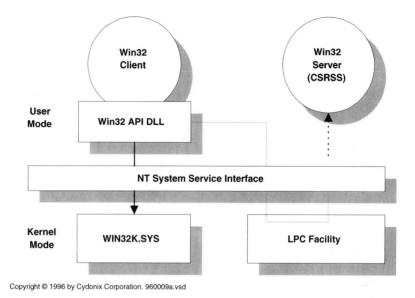

Copyright © 1996 by Cydonix Corporation. 960009a.vsd

Figure 1.3   The Win32 subsystem has both user- and kernel-mode components

Unlike its counterparts, the Win32 subsystem doesn't run entirely in user mode. Instead, it consists of both user- and kernel-mode components. To understand how it all fits together, you need to know a little bit about the organization of the Win32 API itself. Broadly speaking, you can divide Win32 functions into three categories:

- The USER functions manage GUI objects like menus and buttons.

- The GDI functions that perform low-level drawing operations on graphical devices like the displays and printers.

- The KERNEL functions manage such things as processes, threads, synchronization objects, shared memory, and files. They map very directly onto the system services provided by the Executive.

In the original design of Windows NT, one of the goals was to confine all GUI policy-making code to the Win32 server process, CSRSS. The developers believed this would make the system more robust and easier to modify. As a result, calls to many USER and GDI functions required some interaction with the CSRSS process. This is a rather expensive operation since it involves a process context switch between the Win32 client and the CSRSS server. By comparison, KERNEL functions could be handled in the context of the calling process. Their only overhead was the transition to and from kernel mode.

This architecture has been replaced in Windows NT 4.0 because of the performance limitations it put on graphically-based Win32 programs. Now, a new kernel-mode component called WIN32K.SYS has taken over most of the work formerly done by CSRSS. With this approach, calls to USER and GDI functions can execute in the context of the calling process. The result is that the speed of graphically intensive applications improves significantly.

This shift from user- to kernel-mode graphic support also had implications for the architecture of video and printer drivers under Windows NT. The next section of this chapter will provide some more details on this subject.

1.2   KERNEL-MODE I/O COMPONENTS

Here we're going to take a look at the general layered driver model used by the kernel-mode portions of Windows NT. We'll also be examining variations on this architecture that support specific kinds of I/O devices.

Design Goals for the I/O Subsystem

In addition to the general Windows NT design goals, there were several additional requirements that the I/O subsystem had to satisfy:

- **Ease of development** — It shouldn't take unreasonable amounts of work to provide support for a new device.

- **Portability** — It should be relatively easy to move drivers to new platforms. In the best case, this would mean simply compiling and linking the driver.

- **Extendibility** — It should be easy to add support for new devices and file systems without breaking anything that already works.

- **Robustness** — The I/O architecture should offer clean, well-defined interfaces and minimize the use of backdoor mechanisms.

- **Security** — It must be possible to allow or deny various kinds of access to I/O objects on a user-by-user basis.

- **Multithreaded operation** — Drivers should be able to handle overlapping requests from multiple threads, even if the threads are running simultaneously on multiple CPUs.

- **Performance** — I/O throughput must be consistent with the needs of large-scale client-server applications.

As if all this isn't enough, the I/O architecture has to work with all the legacy devices that people have been attaching to PCs for the last decade. Some of these devices have characteristics that don't blend well with modern, large-scale operating systems.

Layered Drivers in Windows NT

In most operating systems, the term *driver* refers to a piece of code that manages some peripheral device. Windows NT takes a more flexible approach which

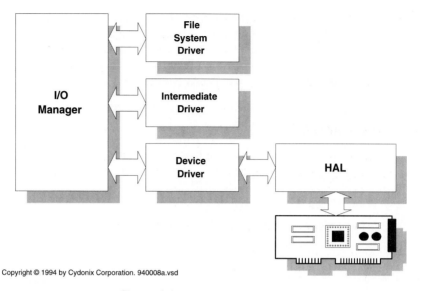

Copyright © 1994 by Cydonix Corporation. 940008a.vsd

Figure 1.4   Layered kernel-mode drivers

allows several driver layers (shown in Figure 1.4) to exist between an application program and a piece of hardware. This layering permits Windows NT to define a driver in much broader terms that include file systems, logical volume managers, and various network components as well as physical device drivers.

Device drivers   These are the drivers that manage actual data transfer and control operations for a specific type of physical device. This includes starting and completing I/O operations, handling interrupts, and performing any error processing required by the device.

Intermediate drivers   Windows NT allows you to layer any number of intermediate drivers on top of a physical device driver. These intermediate layers provide a way of extending the capabilities of the I/O system without having to modify the drivers below them. For example, the fault-tolerant disk driver in Windows NT Server is implemented as a layer that sits between the file system and the drivers for any physical disks.

Another use for intermediate drivers is to separate hardware-specific operations from more general management issues. In this kind of arrangement, the intermediate driver is referred to as a *class driver* and the hardware driver is called a *port driver*. For example, the keyboard class driver handles general keystroke processing while the keyboard port driver worries about the details of specific keyboard controllers. The use of separate class and port drivers makes it easier to target a wider range of hardware since only the port driver needs to be rewritten.

File-system drivers (FSDs)   This kind of driver is generally responsible for maintaining the on-disk structures needed by various file systems. For design reasons, some other system components are implemented as file-system drivers, even though they aren't file systems as such. Microsoft currently supplies the following FSDs:

- **FAT** — Windows 95 extended MS-DOS file system
- **NTFS** — Windows NT high reliability file system
- **HPFS** — OS/2 high performance file system
- **CDFS** — ISO 9660 CD-ROM file system
- **MSFS** — Mailslot file system
- **NPFS** — Named pipe file system
- **RDR** — LAN Manager redirector

Unfortunately, you can't develop file-system drivers using the standard NT DDK. Microsoft released a beta version of a file system developer's kit at a conference in 1994, but at the time of this writing, they hadn't committed to any release date for the final version of this kit.

SCSI Drivers

The Windows NT SCSI architecture uses layered drivers to separate the management of specific devices from the control of the SCSI host bus adapter (HBA) itself. Figure 1.5 shows the components of the Windows NT SCSI architecture.

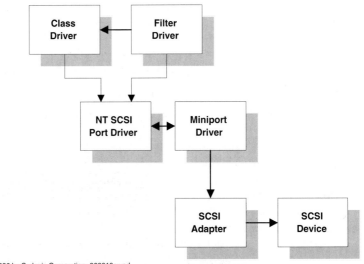

Figure 1.5   Architecture of Windows NT SCSI drivers

SCSI port and miniport drivers   The port driver is a Microsoft-supplied component that acts as an interface between a SCSI miniport driver and the operating system. By handling common SCSI grunt work and hiding the details of the local operating system, the SCSI port driver makes it easier to write drivers for new SCSI HBAs. It also reduces the overall size of a miniport and makes it easier to move the miniport to other operating systems (like Windows 95).

SCSI miniports supply the port driver with routines that perform any HBA-specific control operations. Generally, the only people writing SCSI miniport drivers are HBA vendors who want to sell their products in the Windows NT marketplace.

SCSI class drivers   Class drivers manage all the SCSI devices of a particular type, regardless of what HBA they're attached to. For example, there are SCSI class drivers for tapes, disks, and CD-ROM drives. Separating device control from HBA control makes it possible to mix and match SCSI devices and adapters from different vendors. If you have a device that attaches to a SCSI bus, this is the only kind of driver you'll need to write.

SCSI filter drivers   Filters are optional SCSI components that intercept and modify requests sent to a SCSI class driver. This allows you to take advantage of existing class driver capabilities without writing everything from scratch. Filters are useful if you're developing a class driver for hardware that's similar to some other device.

Network Drivers

In an effort to get better performance, many of the networking components in Windows NT are implemented as kernel-mode drivers. As you can see from Figure 1.6, Windows NT uses driver layering to disengage network protocol management from actual network data transfers. The result is much greater flexibility and support for a wider range of network protocols and hardware.

Network interface card (NIC) drivers   At the bottom of the stack are the NIC drivers that manage the actual networking hardware. NIC drivers present a standard interface at their top edge that allows higher-level drivers to send and receive packets, to reset or halt the NIC, and to query and set the characteristics of the NIC. The interface to a NIC driver is defined by the network driver interface specification (NDIS).

NDIS NIC drivers rely heavily on the services provided by the NDIS interface library. This library (sometimes referred to as the NDIS wrapper) handles many of the nasty details involved in managing asynchronous communications across a network. The NDIS library also exports a complete set of kernel-mode system functions so that a properly written NDIS driver doesn't need to deal with the operating system.

Based on the amount of help they get from the NDIS interface library, you can classify NIC drivers as either miniports or full drivers. NIC miniports perform

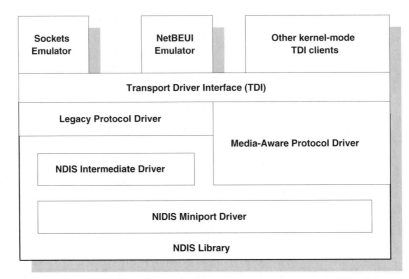

Copyright © 1996 by Cydonix Corporation. 940009a.vsd

Figure 1.6   Architecture of kernel-mode networking components in Windows NT

only those hardware-specific operations needed to manage a particular NIC. Code in the NDIS library takes care of issues common to all NIC miniports such as synchronization, notification of packet arrival, and queuing of outgoing packets. This is the preferred type of NIC driver for any new hardware.

By comparison, full NIC drivers do almost everything on their own. This makes them much harder to write and debug and often slower than NIC miniports. Originally introduced in the first release of Windows NT, full NIC drivers are supported only to maintain backward compatibility. No one in their right mind is developing full NIC drivers anymore.

NDIS intermediate drivers   Version 4.0 of NDIS (the one included with Windows NT 4.0) includes a new kind of component: the NDIS intermediate driver. NDIS intermediate drivers are sandwiched between transport drivers and NDIS NIC miniports. To the transport driver, they appear to be NDIS miniports while to the NIC driver, they look like transport drivers.

NDIS intermediate layers are useful if you have a legacy transport driver and you want to connect it to some new type of media unknown to the transport driver. In this situation, the intermediate driver performs any necessary translations between the transport driver and the NIC miniport managing the new media.

Transport drivers   A transport driver is responsible for implementing a specific network protocol such as TCP/IP or IPX/SPX. It is independent of the underlying network hardware and uses NDIS NIC or intermediate drivers to transfer packets over one or more physical network connections.

All Windows NT transport drivers offer their services to kernel-mode networking clients through the transport driver interface (TDI). The TDI specification defines a low-level interface that supports both connection-based and connectionless (i.e., datagram) protocols. Having all transport drivers expose a single, common interface simplifies the development of both the transport drivers and the clients they support.

Kernel-mode networking clients   Various kernel-mode components that access the network use the TDI interface to communicate with protocol drivers. These kernel-mode TDI clients fall into two broad categories: First, there are system components whose operation is transparent to user-mode applications. One example would be the Server and Redirector that handle requests for remote file access.

The other kind of TDI client is an emulator that exposes some well-known programming interface. User-mode applications access the network through one of these standard APIs rather than working directly with TDI. This approach makes it easier to port existing software to Windows NT and prevents the needless proliferation of networking APIs. Windows NT currently supports interfaces for sockets, NetBIOS calls, named pipes, and mailslots.

1.3   SPECIAL DRIVER ARCHITECTURES

Along with the relatively straightforward kernel-mode drivers described in section 1.2, Windows NT depends on a number of very specialized driver architectures. The following subsections describe each of them in detail.

Video Drivers

Video support in Windows NT is complicated by the fact that Win32 applications can use three different graphics APIs. First, there's the graphical device interface (GDI). This API provides a set of device-independent rendering functions for generating two-dimensional output on display or hardcopy devices. Most Win32 applications use this programming interface because it simplifies the task of producing identical display and printer output.

For programs that need to produce three-dimensional graphics, Win32 also supports the OpenGL API. These functions generate the kind of high-quality output needed by CAD software or scientific visualization tools. In return for the quality of the output, however, the OpenGL API demands a great deal of CPU horsepower or hardware rendering assistance.

Finally, for consumer applications (i.e., games), Windows NT supports a subset of the DirectDraw API included in Windows 95. DirectDraw is one piece of Microsoft's DirectX game-programming architecture. Its goal is to give user-mode applications more direct access to video and audio hardware without compromising the integrity of the system.

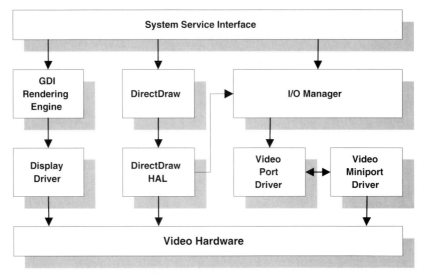

Figure 1.7   Architecture of NT kernel-mode video drivers

Supporting multiple APIs on video hardware from multiple vendors is a complex problem. Solving it in a flexible and portable manner requires the interaction of a number of software components. Figure 1.7 shows what they are.

GDI engine   The GDI engine is the key to Windows NT's device-independent output strategy. This Microsoft-supplied component provides full software rendering support for Win32 GDI calls. In response to a Win32 drawing request, the GDI engine uses the appropriate display or printer driver to generate commands for a specific piece of hardware.

Display drivers   Display drivers are vendor-supplied components that do the actual work of drawing on the display screen. By selectively overriding the rendering functions in the GDI engine, they also give Win32 access to any hardware acceleration features provided by the video card.[2] Along with a display driver for a specific piece of video hardware, vendors need to provide a corresponding video miniport (described below).

DirectDraw HAL   This vendor-supplied component exposes an abstract version of the video hardware. This includes the video frame buffer plus any hardware acceleration mechanisms supported by the DirectDraw API. Any features of

[2] In earlier versions of Windows NT, both the GDI engine and the display driver were user-mode components running in the context of the Win32 subsystem process. To improve graphics performance, this code runs in kernel mode in Windows NT 4.0.

the DirectDraw hardware model not supported by the video device are emulated by Microsoft's DirectDraw software.

Video port and miniport drivers   The main responsibility of these two drivers is to manage state changes in the system's video hardware. The video port and miniport do not take part in any drawing operations. The work of these drivers includes doing such things as:

- Finding and initializing the video controller.
- Managing any cursor or pointer hardware located on the video card.
- Handling mode-set and palette operations when a full-screen MS-DOS session is running. (This only applies to 80x86 platforms.)
- Making the video frame buffer available to user-mode processes.

The video port and miniport are actually a tightly-coupled pair of drivers. The port driver is a Microsoft-supplied framework that simplifies the task of writing video drivers. It contains only generic, hardware-independent code that is common to all video drivers.

The miniport is a vendor-supplied driver whose job is to manage a specific type of video card. In response to calls from the video port driver, it is the miniport that actually changes the state of the device. This division of labor between the port and miniport makes it easier to add support for new video cards to Windows NT.

Printer Drivers

In Windows NT, hardcopy devices are considered to be just another kind of graphical output hardware. Unlike display devices, however, there can be more than one printer on the system, and these printers may not all use the same kind of physical connection. Some of them may even be located somewhere else on the network. The Windows NT printing architecture (pictured in Figure 1.8) is an attempt to deal with all this variety.

Printer drivers   A printer driver is very much like a display driver in that it runs in kernel mode and helps the GDI engine convert Win32 API graphics calls into rendering commands. The difference is that a printer driver sends its output to the spooler (described below) rather than to a video device.

A printer driver is responsible for supporting a particular printer or family of printers. The Windows NT DDK contains sample drivers for raster-based printers, PostScript printers, and plotters. Most printers available today fall into one of these categories. Unless your printer uses some completely alien technology, it's unlikely that you'd need to write an entire driver from scratch.

For raster-based printers, most of the rendering operation is simply a matter of converting a specific drawing command into the proper set of printer escape

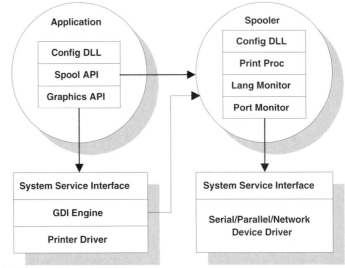

Figure 1.8   Architecture of the Windows NT printing components

codes. Because this is such a well-defined problem, you can use a Microsoft-supplied framework called the Unidriver to do most of the work. In this case, you
only need to write the device-specific pieces of code in the form of a miniprint
driver. Adding support for printers based on a page description language like
PostScript is a more complicated task.

Configuration DLL   To support a printer under Windows NT, it's not
enough to write a printer driver. You also have to supply a user-mode configuration DLL. The job of this DLL is to display the property-sheet dialog box that
changes the printer's settings. Application programs use the configuration DLL to
set up the printing environment for specific documents. It also appears when you
select one of the icons in the Windows NT shell's Printers folder.

Spooler   The spooler is the central component of Windows NT's printing
mechanism. It takes the output generated by a printer driver and either sends it to
the appropriate printer or stores it in a temporary file for later printing. The
spooler works either with local or networked printers.

The spooler is one of the integral subsystem processes that starts when the
operating system loads. Its architecture is very modular so that it can accommo-
date a wide variety of printing devices and environments. Printer vendors can
customize the spooler by supplying three different kinds of components: print
processors, language monitors, and port monitors.

Print processor DLL   A print processor is a DLL that reads the spooled data
produced by a specific printer driver and converts it into actual output. At its upper
edge, the print processor DLL exposes a standard set of functions to the spooler. It
generates output using the services provided by a language or port monitor.

The standard printer drivers can spool their output as text, as raw data (already rendered by the GDI engine), or as a series of enhanced metafile (EMF) commands to be rendered by the spooler.[3] Microsoft supplies a print processor that can interpret any of these three data formats. If you write a printer driver that uses a proprietary format for spooled data, you'll also have to write a print processor for it.

Language monitor DLL   In workgroup situations, it's very common for several users to be sharing a single printer or print server. Consequently, it's important to keep their jobs clearly separated and to be able to determine the status of a particular job at any point in time. It also may be necessary to set up a different printing environment for each job being output.

To meet these kinds of needs, many vendors offer smart, bidirectional printers that accept commands and report status over the same connection on which they receive output data. Normally, these command and status messages are in some kind of control language defined by the printer's manufacturer. For example, Hewlett Packard LaserJet printers use something called the Printer Job Language (PJL).

A language monitor is a DLL that allows the spooler to communicate with a bidirectional printer in a standardized way. It exposes a well-defined set of functions that the spooler can call to control and monitor a job on one of these printers. The language monitor then converts these requests into the proper stream of job-language commands and uses the port monitor (described below) to send them to the printer.

Windows NT comes with a language monitor for the Hewlett Packard PJL language. If your printer uses some home-brew set of commands, you'll need to write a language monitor for it.

Port monitor DLL   A port monitor is a DLL that manages a particular kind of output channel on behalf of the spooler subsystem. The monitor exposes a standard set of functions which the spooler invokes in order to generate output. The port monitor then converts these calls into the appropriate set of Win32 I/O requests.

Allowing the spooler to work with an abstraction of the output device makes it easier to add support for a variety of printer connections. Microsoft supplies the following port monitors with Windows NT:

- The local port monitor that communicates with the parallel and serial ports as well as printing data to a file.

- The LPR monitor that manages LPD printers and print-servers using a TCP/IP network connection.

---

[3] The use of EMF data for printing allows the program generating the output to finish its print request more quickly since the rendering operation takes place later in the context of the spooler process. Raw data slows the application because it's rendered before being sent to the spooler.

- Port monitors from Hewlett Packard, Apple, and Digital Equipment Corporation that control network-based printers and print-servers from these vendors.

Normally, you won't need to write a port monitor unless you've developed some new and strange way to link a printer to a computer. For example, an output device connected to a SCSI controller would need a new port monitor.

Multimedia Drivers

Multimedia is going to change our lives one day — if only someone can figure out how. For those who'd like to try, Windows NT supports a wide range of multimedia devices, including:

- Waveform audio hardware that samples and reconstructs analog audio signals
- MIDI ports that connect to external musical devices like keyboards, synthesizers, and drum machines
- Onboard MIDI synthesizers that are part of the computer itself
- Video capture devices that digitize either single frame or continuous video signals
- Related devices like CD players, video-disk players, and joysticks

Most application programs don't interact with multimedia hardware by calling such functions as CreateFile or DeviceIoControl. Instead they use some of the special-purpose multimedia functions provided by Win32. This indirect approach reduces their dependency on hardware from a specific vendor. Figure 1.9 shows the components involved in multimedia operations.

WINMM   To meet the requirements of different kinds of software, Win32 actually contains two separate multimedia APIs. The media control interface (MCI) functions provide high-level access to a wide variety of multimedia devices while hiding many of the details from the programmer. MCI is the interface used by most applications. For software needing more direct hardware control, Win32 also provides a group of low-level audio functions. Programs such as MIDI sequencers or waveform editors are more likely to use this low-level interface.

Support for both sets of multimedia functions comes from the WINMM system component. WINMM is a user-mode DLL that acts as a translation layer between the application and the vendor-supplied drivers that actually control the multimedia hardware. To do its job, WINMM relies on three kinds of drivers.

MCI drivers   An MCI driver is just a user-mode DLL that WINMM loads at runtime to process MCI commands for a specific device. In response to calls

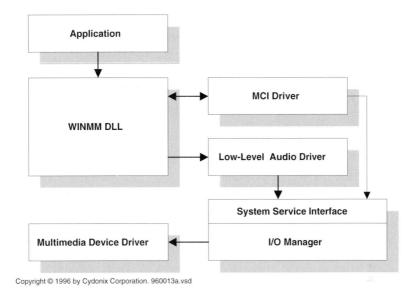

Figure 1.9   Multimedia driver architecture

from a multimedia application, WINMM sends various messages to the proper MCI driver. Depending on the device, the MCI driver then uses either the low-level audio interface (described below) or Win32 I/O functions to control the hardware.

Low-level audio drivers   When an application calls a low-level audio function, WINMM loads a vendor-supplied user-mode DLL (the low-level audio driver) and sends it various messages. The low-level audio driver then uses Win32 I/O functions to communicate with the audio hardware. This is very similar to the operation of the MCI drivers described previously.

Kernel-mode device drivers   Management of the multimedia hardware itself comes from a kernel-mode device driver. This includes data transfer operations, handling interrupts, processing errors, and so on.

Drivers for Legacy 16-bit Applications

When Microsoft first introduced Windows NT, a vast amount of software already existed for MS-DOS and 16-bit Windows. Any new operating system hoping to be a commercial success would have to be able to run the majority of this code without modification. At the same time, it would be necessary to protect system integrity by denying these 16-bit programs the kind of unlimited hardware access they enjoyed under MS-DOS and Windows. As you saw earlier in this chapter, Microsoft's solution was to run 16-bit code in the context of one or more virtual DOS machine (VDM) processes.

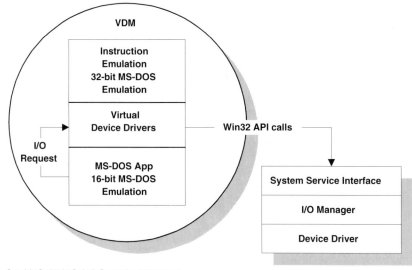

Copyright © 1996 by Cydonix Corporation. 960014a.vsd

Figure 1.10   Relationship of VDDs and kernel-mode drivers

To meet the challenge of allowing VDMs to perform I/O without giving them direct access to any hardware, Windows NT uses a piece of software called a virtual DOS driver (VDD). Figure 1.10 shows the relationship of such a VDD to the other parts of the operating system.

The VDD essentially acts as a translation layer between a 16-bit application and some custom piece of hardware. Whenever the application tries to touch the hardware directly, the VDD intercepts the request and turns it into a series of Win32 calls. These Win32 calls are then processed by a standard Windows NT kernel-mode driver.

A VDD can intercept a 16-bit program's attempts to access I/O ports and specific ranges of memory. It also has the ability to perform DMA transfers on behalf of the application, read and set the contents of CPU registers, and simulate the arrival of interrupts. All this makes it possible to fool the 16-bit application into thinking it's still running under MS-DOS or Windows.

The advantage of this approach is that the original 16-bit executable doesn't need to be modified to run under Windows NT. The disadvantage is that the extra layer of software can add significant amounts of processing overhead. Since you have to write a kernel-mode driver to support the underlying hardware, the real solution is to port the application to the Win32 environment.

One other point to make here: This technique supports the execution of MS-DOS programs that touch hardware directly. It also supports 16-bit DLLs that play with hardware (a common form of driver in the 16-bit Windows environment). It does not allow you to run Windows or Windows 95 VxDs under Windows NT.

1.4   SUMMARY

As you can see, Windows NT's rich architecture and multiple API environments add a certain amount of complexity to I/O processing. In particular, Windows NT uses a much broader definition of what constitutes a driver than many other operating systems. If you're in the process of adding support for a specific piece of hardware, you should have a good idea at this point of just what kind of driver(s) you'll need to write.

In the next chapter we'll start our descent into kernel-mode driver development by examining some of the hardware issues facing NT driver writers.

The Hardware Environment

*F*or some people (you know who you are), hot solder is the only true programming language. If you're not in that category, this chapter will give you a gentle introduction to those aspects of hardware that have an impact on writing drivers. You'll also find here a quick tour of the major bus architectures supported by Windows NT, and a few words to the wise about dealing with hardware in general.

2.1 HARDWARE BASICS

There are a number of things you need to know about a peripheral device before you can design a driver for it. At the very least, the following items are important:

- How to use the device's control and status registers
- What causes the device to generate an interrupt
- How the device transfers data
- Whether the device uses any dedicated memory
- Whether the device can be autoconfigured

The following subsections discuss each of these topics in a general way.

Device Registers

Drivers communicate with a peripheral by reading and writing various bits in a group of registers associated with the device. Each of these device registers will generally perform one of the following functions:

- **Command** — Setting and clearing bits in command registers causes the device to start an operation or change its behavior in some way.

- **Status** — The bits in a status register contain information about the current state of the device.

- **Data buffer** — Output devices accept data to be transmitted when it's written to their output buffer registers. Data coming from an input device will appear in the device's input buffer register.

Simple devices (like the parallel port interface in Table 2.1) have only a few registers, while complex hardware (like a graphics adapter or a network card) have a large set of registers. In the absence of any industry standard, the engineer designing the interface card is the one who decides how these registers are going to be used. So, if you expect to write a device driver, you'll need detailed information about all its control and data registers.

Table 2.1   These registers control a parallel port interface

Parallel port registers

Offset	Register	Access	Description
0	Data	R/W	Data byte transferred through parallel port
1	Status	R/O	Current parallel port status
	Bits 0 – 1		Reserved
	Bit 2		0 — interrupt has been requested by port
	Bit 3		0 — an error has occurred
	Bit 4		1 — printer is selected
	Bit 5		1 — printer is out of paper
	Bit 6		0 — acknowledge
	Bit 7		0 — printer is busy
2	Control	R/W	Commands sent to parallel port
	Bit 0		1 — strobe data to/from parallel port
	Bit 1		1 — automatic line feed
	Bit 2		0 — initialize printer
	Bit 3		1 — select printer
	Bit 4		1 — enable interrupts
	Bits 5 – 7		Reserved

Accessing Device Registers

Once you know what a set of device registers does, you still need two additional pieces of information before you can work with the device:

- The address of the device's first register
- The address space where these registers live

Since a given device's registers usually occupy consecutive locations, the address of the first register will get you to all the others. Unfortunately, finding the register base address is a rather involved process that will have to wait for Chapter 7.

That still doesn't answer the question of where these registers live. As you can see from Figure 2.1, device registers can occupy either of two different address spaces. The following subsections describe each of them.

I/O space registers   Some CPU architectures map device registers into a set of addresses known as *I/O space*. These I/O space addresses (often referred to as *ports*) are not part of the memory space seen by the CPU, and they can only be accessed with special machine instructions. For example, the 80x86 architecture has a 64-kilobyte I/O space, and **IN** and **OUT** instructions for reading and writing I/O ports.

One extra twist: To promote platform independence, an NT driver shouldn't actually use hardware instructions to touch I/O ports. Instead, it ought to use the HAL functions listed in Table 2.2.

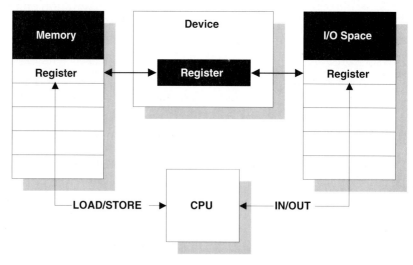

Figure 2.1   Memory-mapped device registers and I/O space ports

Table 2.2   Use these HAL functions to access ports in I/O space

HAL I/O space functions

Function	Description
READ_PORT_XXX	Read a single value from an I/O port
WRITE_PORT_XXX	Write a single value to an I/O port
READ_PORT_BUFFER_XXX	Read an array of values from consecutive I/O ports
WRITE_PORT_BUFFER_XXX	Write an array of values to consecutive I/O ports

Substitute one of the following for XXX: UCHAR, USHORT, or ULONG.

Memory-mapped registers   CPU architectures without a separate I/O space generally map device registers into some range of physical memory addresses. Access to these memory-mapped device registers is accomplished with the same load and store instructions used for normal memory operations (for example, **MOV** on the 80x86 platform).

Even on CPUs with a separate I/O space, some peripherals memory-map their control registers anyway. This improves the performance of high-speed devices with large register sets, since I/O instructions are typically much slower than memory-access instructions. For example, many SVGA video adapters for 80x86 machines can use memory addresses not only for their video buffers, but for their control registers as well.

Once again, the HAL provides a set of support functions (listed in Table 2.3) for accessing memory-mapped registers. Notice that these are not the same functions you use on a CPU with a separate I/O space. So, if you plan to support your driver on both kinds of architecture, you'll need to take this difference into account. Chapter 5 presents some coding techniques that make this easier to do.

Device Interrupts

Most reasonable pieces of hardware generate an interrupt request when they need some kind of attention from the CPU. This request takes the form of an

Table 2.3   Use these HAL functions to access memory-mapped device registers

HAL memory-mapped register functions

Function	Description
READ_REGISTER_XXX	Read a single value from an I/O register
WRITE_REGISTER_XXX	Write a single value to an I/O register
READ_REGISTER_BUFFER_XXX	Read of values from consecutive I/O registers
WRITE_REGISTER_BUFFER_XXX	Write values to consecutive I/O registers

Substitute one of the following for XXX: UCHAR, USHORT, or ULONG.

electrical signal on the interrupt lines in the bus. A device might yank on its interrupt line for any number of reasons, including:

- The device has completed a previously requested input or output operation and is now idle.
- A buffer or FIFO associated with the device is almost full (for input operations) or almost empty (for output operations). The device uses an interrupt to notify the driver that it must process the buffer if it wants the I/O
  to continue without a pause.
- The device encountered some kind of error during an I/O operation.

Some legacy devices don't use interrupts at all. Drivers for this kind of hardware usually have to poll their devices until some kind of interesting event
occurs. Under single-tasking operating systems like MS-DOS, this behavior
wasn't a problem, but in an environment like Windows NT, it would seriously
degrade system performance. Chapters 10 and 14 will present some techniques
you can use with non-interrupting hardware.

The various bus architectures supported by Windows NT take slightly different approaches to interrupts. Nonetheless, they all share several common features, which are described below.

Interrupt priorities   When several devices are connected to the same bus,
the CPU needs some way to rank the importance of their interrupt requests. This
allows devices that need immediate servicing to access the CPU ahead of devices
that can afford to wait. Although the exact mechanism depends on the bus, this
ranking generally works by assigning a priority value to each of the interrupt
request lines.

When the CPU accepts an interrupt request, it blocks out any further interrupts at or below the same priority and transfers control to an interrupt service
routine. Until the interrupt service routine handles and dismisses the interrupt,
only requests of a higher priority can take control of the CPU. Lower-priority
requests remain pending until the more important activity is finished.

Interrupt vectors   An *interrupt vector* is a unique, bus-relative number
which allows the CPU to identify the source of an interrupt and call the appropriate service routine. The interrupt controller usually passes this vector to the CPU
when it accepts an interrupt request. The CPU then uses the vector as an index
into a table containing the addresses of interrupt service routines.

Signaling mechanisms   Hardware designers have developed two basic
strategies that devices can use when they want to generate an interrupt. The older
mechanism defines an interrupt request as a transition from zero to one on the
interrupt signal line. These are called *edge-triggered* (or *latched*) interrupts because
they depend only on the leading edge of the pulse.

Unfortunately, this scheme has two problems. First, it's very sensitive to electrical noise — a random spike can easily be mistaken for an interrupt request. Second, if an interrupt arrives while another one is being serviced at the same priority, the second interrupt will be ignored. This limits sharing to situations where simultaneous interrupts will never occur on the same line.

These limitations led to the development of another signaling mechanism called a *level-sensitive* (or *level-triggered*) interrupt. This approach requires the device to send a continuous signal down the wire until the interrupt service routine explicitly dismisses the interrupt. In addition to greater noise immunity, this scheme makes it possible for multiple devices to share the same interrupt request line.

Processor affinity   To improve overall performance, multiprocessor platforms often contain special interrupt-routing hardware. The purpose of this hardware is to distribute interrupt requests from a given device to one or more specific CPUs. If a particular CPU can service interrupts from a device, those interrupts are said to have *affinity* for that CPU.

Data Transfer Mechanisms

Hardware designers have three basic options when it comes to moving data between a peripheral and memory.

- Programmed I/O
- Direct memory access
- Shared buffers

The transfer mechanism used by a given device usually depends on the device's speed, the amount of data it needs to transfer, and any applicable industry standards. In some cases, a complex piece of hardware may actually use more than one of these techniques.

The following subsections explain the differences between programmed I/O and direct memory access (illustrated in Figure 2.2). Shared memory buffers are covered later in the discussion of device-specific memory.

Programmed I/O (PIO)   PIO devices need the help of the CPU to perform data transfers. Their drivers are responsible for sending or receiving each byte of data, keeping track of the buffer in memory, and maintaining a running count of the number of bytes transferred.

PIO devices typically generate an interrupt after each byte or word of data is transferred. Some PIO devices have an internal buffer or a hardware FIFO that helps to reduce the interrupt count. Even so, lengthy transfers need a lot of attention from the CPU and produce a flood of interrupts. This can lead to very poor system performance.

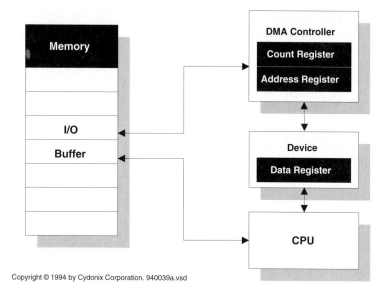

Figure 2.2   Paths followed by data in DMA and programmed I/O transfers

This style of I/O is best suited to slower devices that don't move large amounts of data in a single operation. Parallel ports, pointing devices, and the keyboard are all examples of PIO hardware. Chapter 9 will explain how to work with PIO devices.

Direct memory access (DMA)   DMA devices take advantage of special hardware called a *DMA controller (DMAC)*. A DMAC is actually a very simple auxiliary processor with just enough intelligence to transfer a specified number of bytes between a peripheral device and memory.

At the beginning of an I/O operation, the driver loads a transfer count and a memory address into the DMAC and then starts the device. All by itself, the DMAC moves data to or from successive memory locations, and when the transfer is complete, it generates an interrupt request. During the actual operation, the driver is suspended and the CPU can work on other tasks.

High-speed devices that perform large transfers generally use DMA because it significantly reduces driver overhead and system interrupt activity. Disks, sound samplers, and network cards are examples of DMA devices.

Direct Memory Access (DMA) Mechanisms

Chapter 12 will have a lot more to say about the mechanics of working with this kind of hardware. There are a number of twists and turns that aren't relevant here. At this point, it's only necessary to draw a distinction between two general kinds of DMA.

System DMA   Some devices are connected to the shared DMACs on the motherboard. These controllers each have a fixed number of data-transfer paths (called *channels*) that can all work simultaneously. More than one device can be attached to the same channel, but only one device at a time can transfer data over the channel. This is known as *system DMA* or *slave DMA*. By sharing hardware, slave DMA devices have a simpler architecture and lower chip count. On the downside, they may have to wait for a DMA channel to become available before they can start an operation. The floppy controller on most PCs is a slave DMA device.

Bus master DMA   Other devices (called *bus masters*) have their own DMAC hardware built into the peripheral card itself. This guarantees that high-speed devices won't have to wait for a system DMA channel to become free. The AHA-1742 SCSI controller from Adaptec is one example of a bus mastering device.

Device-Dedicated Memory

Some devices insist on having a private range of addresses in physical memory. There are several reasons why a peripheral card might need dedicated address space:

- Its control registers might be memory-mapped.
- It might have an internal ROM containing start-up code and data. For the CPU to execute this code, it has to appear somewhere in memory address space.
- It might use a block of memory as a temporary buffer for data that's being sent or received. High-speed devices like video capture boards and Ethernet adapters often use this technique.

Peripheral cards generally take one of two approaches to dedicated memory. Some insist on using a specific range of physical addresses. For example, VGA cards expect a 128-kilobyte block of addresses beginning at 0xA0000 to belong to them.

Alternatively, the card might have an address register that holds the base physical address of its dedicated memory. During initialization, the driver for the card will load this register with a pointer to some block of available memory. Figure 2.3 illustrates each of these two possible designs.

Regardless of which approach a card takes, it's important to remember that the card will be working with *physical* addresses. Since the only addresses available to a device driver are *virtual* addresses, drivers have to map any device memory somewhere into system virtual space before they can access it. Chapter 7 explains how all this works.

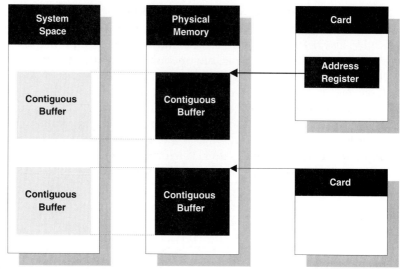

Figure 2.3   How drivers access device memory

Requirements for Autoconfiguration

Ever since the first add-on card hit the market, PC users have been struggling with ports, IRQs, and DMA channel assignments. In the beginning, things weren't too bad, and it usually didn't take too long to find an appropriate combination of DIP-switch and jumper settings. However, as people started attaching more and more optional equipment to their PCs, getting everything to work became a real nightmare.

To get around these problems, some bus architectures support various levels of automatic hardware recognition and configuration. The next section of this chapter will describe specific autoconfiguration capabilities of the major buses. Here, it's enough to introduce the kinds of features that make autoconfiguration possible.

Device resource lists   At the very least, a device must identify itself and provide the system with a description of the resources it needs. In the ideal case, this *resource list* contains the following information:

- Manufacturer ID
- Device type ID
- I/O space requirements
- Interrupt requirements
- DMA channels
- Device memory requirements

No jumpers or switches   Self-identification isn't enough, however. For true autoconfiguration, a device must be able to change its port, interrupt, and DMA channel assignments dynamically under software control. This allows a driver or some other part of the operating system to arbitrate resource conflicts among competing devices.

Change notification   Finally, the highest level of support also requires the bus to generate a notification signal whenever a card is plugged in or removed. Without this kind of mechanism, it's not possible to implement any of the Plug and Play hot-swapping features. Since the current release of Windows NT doesn't support Plug and Play, this isn't an issue right now. But it will be in the future.

2.2   BUSES AND WINDOWS NT

A *bus* is just a collection of data, address, and control lines that allows a peripheral device to communicate with memory and the CPU. The specification for a bus defines such things as the shape and size of physical connectors, the functions performed by each of the lines in the bus, and the timing and signaling protocols used by devices attached to the bus.

Over the last decade, hardware vendors have developed a wide variety of bus architectures with differing electrical and logical characteristics. As of version 4.0, Windows NT supports many of these buses. What follows are brief descriptions of the buses you're most likely to encounter. For more detailed information, see some of the books listed in the bibliography.

ISA — The Industry Standard Architecture

This is the old standby that made its first appearance on the IBM PC/AT. It was derived from the original IBM PC bus by adding extra data and address lines and increasing the number of IRQ levels and DMA channels. Both 16-bit ISA cards and the older IBM PC 8-bit cards fit into ISA sockets. Figure 2.4 shows the organization of an ISA-based machine.

The ISA bus isn't especially fast. To maintain backward compatibility with the IBM PC, the ISA bus clock rate is limited to 8.33 MHz. In the best case, a 16-bit transfer takes two clock cycles, so the maximum data rate is only about 8 MB/sec. This limit applies regardless of the clock rate of the CPU itself. That's why the CPU and memory communicate over a high-speed local bus (sometimes called the *X bus*).

Register access   There are very few rules when it comes to the layout of I/O space on ISA systems. Beyond some industry conventions, there aren't any real standards for the kinds of registers an ISA card should implement, nor what addresses they should use. Generally, I/O addresses between 0x0000 and 0x00FF belong only to devices on the system board, while the territory between 0x0100

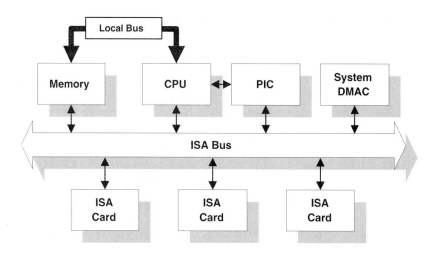

Figure 2.4   Layout of an ISA system

and 0x03FF is available for add-on cards. The space used by expansion cards is doled out in 32-byte chunks.

Unfortunately, many ISA add-on cards don't pay attention to all 16 I/O address bits. Instead, they look only at bits 5–9 to see if an I/O space reference belongs to them. If it does, they decode bits 0–4 to determine the exact register. Cards like this are a problem because they respond to multiple addresses in the 64-kilobyte I/O space, which can lead to some nasty behavior. The only way to prevent conflicts on a system with ISA boards is avoid these alias addresses altogether.[1]

Interrupt mechanisms   Interrupts on an ISA bus are normally handled by a pair of Intel 8259A programmable interrupt controller (PIC) chips, each of which provides eight levels of interrupt priority. These two chips are tied together in a master-slave configuration that leaves fifteen available priority levels. Table 2.4 lists the ISA priority levels and describes how they are normally used.

The 8259A chip can be programmed to respond to either edge-triggered or level-sensitive interrupts. This choice must be made for the entire chip; it can't be set on an IRQ-by-IRQ basis. The power-on self-test (POST) code in the ISA BIOS programs both chips to use edge-triggered interrupts. This means that multiple ISA cards cannot normally share the same IRQ levels.

DMA capabilities   The standard implementation of ISA DMA uses a pair of Intel 8237 DMAC chips (or their functional equivalent). Each of these chips

---

[1] In other words, the control registers of any cards using the range above 0x03FF have to use I/O space addresses with zeroes in bits 8 and 9.

Table 2.4   Interrupt priorities on ISA systems

ISA interrupt priority sequence

Priority	IRQ line	Controller	Used for...
Highest	0	Master	System timer
	1	Master	Keyboard
	2	Master	(Unavailable — pass-through from slave)
	8	Slave	Real-time clock alarm
	9	Slave	(Available)
	10	Slave	(Available)
	11	Slave	(Available)
	12	Slave	(Available — usually the mouse)
	13	Slave	Error output of numeric coprocessor
	14	Slave	(Available — usually the hard disk)
	15	Slave	(Available)
	3	Master	2nd serial port
	4	Master	1st serial port
	5	Master	2nd parallel port
	6	Master	Floppy disk controller
Lowest	7	Master	1st parallel port

provides four independent DMA channels. When they're ganged together in a master-slave configuration, the first slave channel (number 4) serves as a pass-through and becomes unavailable. Table 2.5 describes the capabilities of these DMA channels.

When several DMA channels request the bus simultaneously, the DMAC chips use a software-selected arbitration scheme to resolve the conflict. The ISA BIOS POST-code normally programs the DMACs for fixed-priority arbitration. This means that channel 0 always gets first crack at the bus, and channel 7 always goes last.

Also notice from Table 2.5 that the lower channels transfer individual bytes, while the upper ones move data only in words. Since the DMAC uses a 16-bit

Table 2.5   DMA architecture on the ISA bus

ISA DMA channels

Channel	Controller	Transfers...	Max transfer
0 — 3	Master	Bytes only	64 kilobytes
4	Slave	(Unavailable)	—
5 — 7	Slave	Words only	128 kilobytes

count register in both cases, the upper channels can transfer twice as much data in a single operation.

One other significant item about DMA operations: The ISA bus has only 24 address lines. This means that DMACs can access only the first 16 megabytes of system memory. Any DMA buffers outside this range are unavailable. In Chapter 12 you'll see how NT deals with this complication.

Device memory   The 24 address lines on the ISA bus have an impact on device memory as well as DMA buffers. Any device-dedicated memory must live in the first 16 megabytes of physical address space. This applies to any onboard ROM as well.

Autoconfiguration   Unfortunately, the ISA specification says nothing about autoconfiguration. ISA devices don't identify themselves (either by manufacturer or device type), nor do they provide a resource list. Since ISA cards aren't required to have any software configuration registers, users normally have to configure the card with DIP switches and jumpers.

Sometimes it's possible to make educated guesses about the presence of a particular device by tickling various addresses in I/O space and listening for an appropriate giggle from a device. This is generally not a very reliable way to do things. Even if you do manage to locate a piece of hardware using this technique, you still don't know anything about its DMA or interrupt settings.

The proposed Plug and Play extensions to ISA are intended to correct such problems. Until these extensions become available, you'll have to use some of the cruder methods described in Chapter 7.

MCA — The Micro Channel Architecture

IBM developed the Micro Channel architecture as a replacement for the aging ISA bus. In a bold move, they dumped ISA altogether and proposed a vastly improved architecture. Progress isn't cheap, however, and the cost of adopting this new design was that all legacy ISA or IBM PC adapter cards would have to be trashed. Most people were unconvinced, and the MCA bus hasn't achieved great popularity among hardware vendors.[2] Figure 2.5 shows the organization of a typical MCA system.

Since they weren't constrained by the 8.33-MHz clock rate of the ISA bus, IBM was able to design a pretty snappy architecture. Although the original MCA implementation[3] only supported data transfer rates of 10 megabytes/sec, later versions of the bus specification incorporated a streaming data protocol that raised this number by a factor of 16. Table 2.6 summarizes the data rates available from the MCA bus.

---

[2] Political problems also contributed to the failure of MCA. IBM patented the architecture and tried to impose licensing conditions that many hardware vendors found objectionable.

[3] This was the 16-bit version used for the original IBM PS/2.

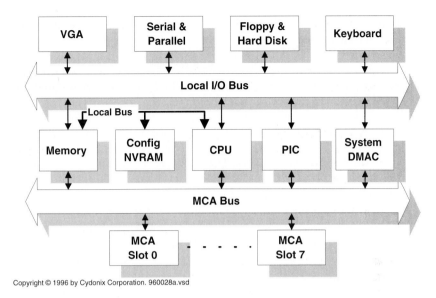

Figure 2.5   Layout of a Micro Channel system

Register access   An MCA bus can have at most eight card sockets, referred to as *slots*.[4] Each slot has an associated set of programmable option select (POS) registers that are used to configure the card. These POS registers replace the jumpers and DIP switches found on ISA devices. At the very least, an MCA card must implement a POS register that identifies the card.

Other than the POS registers (which are always at a fixed location), I/O space under MCA is just about as chaotic as it is on an ISA system. (The problem with ISA alias addresses doesn't occur, however.) At the option of the designer, MCA cards can have either fixed or programmable register addresses in I/O space. The only requirement is that if more than one of the same card will be

Table 2.6   MCA buses support a wide range of transfer speeds

MCA data transfer speed

Protocol	Data width	Transfer rate
Basic	16 bits	10 MB/sec
	32 bits	20 MB/sec
Streaming	16 bits	20 MB/sec
	32 bits	40 MB/sec
	64 bits	80 MB/sec
	64 bits	160 MB/sec

---

[4] Additional devices can live on the motherboard itself.

plugged into an MCA bus, the card must have a 3-bit POS field for setting the card's base register address.

Interrupt mechanisms   The Micro Channel architecture supports 15 interrupt request levels. Their functions and relative priorities follow the same pattern used by the ISA bus (refer back to Table 2.4). The only improvement is that MCA cards use level-sensitive interrupt signals, thus allowing more than one device to share a single IRQ line.

DMA capabilities   The MCA bus was designed to be shared. The system board can support up to eight system DMA channels, and there's room on the bus for an additional seven bus masters. Six of the system DMA channels follow a fixed priority arbitration scheme, while channels 0 and 4 have assignable priorities. The seven bus masters also have assignable priorities, although they will always defer to the system DMA hardware.

Older implementations of the system DMAC were limited to 16-bit transfers (even though the bus itself has a 32-bit data path), and buffers had to fall in the first 16 megabytes of physical memory. (Bus master cards didn't have this limitation.) Proposed improvements to the MCA specification allowed for 32- and even 64-bit data transfers.[5] These changes also gave the system DMAC access to a full 4-gigabyte address range.

Device memory   The MCA specification dictates that any device with onboard ROM must use 4 bits in one of its POS registers to select a starting address for the ROM. This gives card designers the option of mapping the ROM into any of 16 separate locations in physical memory.

Since the MCA bus has 32 address lines, device memory can exist anywhere in a 4-gigabyte address space.

Autoconfiguration   MCA autoconfiguration involves the POS registers and a card-specific script called an *adapter description file* (ADF). Whenever an MCA system bootstraps, it checks each slot to see what's there. If it finds a previously configured card, it downloads configuration data from nonvolatile RAM (NVRAM) into the card's POS registers.

If something appears in a slot that had previously been empty, the bootstrap configuration program uses the card's POS ID register to generate the name of the device's ADF file. After prompting the user for the floppy containing the ADF, the configuration program selects resource assignments for the new card that don't conflict with the resources used by any existing cards. These assignments are copied into NVRAM.

Windows NT can recognize many kinds of MCA devices all by itself. If you need to touch MCA slots directly, you can use **HalGetBusData** and **HalSetBusData** to access them.

---

[5] The extra 32 bits came from multiplexing the address lines on the MCA bus.

EISA — The Extended Industry Standard Architecture

The PC industry responded to IBM's Micro Channel architecture with the EISA bus. Most people simply weren't willing to throw away all their old hardware. The EISA bus reflects this sentiment by removing some of the ISA limitations while still allowing the use of legacy devices.

However, EISA's emphasis on compatibility limits the architecture in certain ways. For example, even though the bus supports 32-bit data transfers, the bus clock still runs at 8.33 MHz so the maximum transfer rate is only about 33 megabytes/sec. Also, since EISA sockets had to be able to accept ISA cards, it was impossible to fix some of the electrical noise problems caused by the layout of the ISA wiring. See Figure 2.6 for the layout of a typical EISA system.

Register access   Like MCA, the EISA bus contains a number of slots, each of which corresponds to one physical socket on the bus. As you can see from Table 2.7, each of the 15 EISA sockets has its own particular range of addresses in I/O space. Within the 4-kilobyte area assigned to a particular slot, four 256-byte ranges are guaranteed to be available to the card in that socket.[6]

Interrupt mechanisms   EISA's interrupt capabilities are a superset of the ISA mechanisms. Although EISA interrupt controllers provide the same 15 levels available on the ISA bus (see Table 2.4), each IRQ line can be individually programmed for edge-triggered or level-sensitive behavior. This allows both ISA cards and EISA cards to coexist on the same bus.

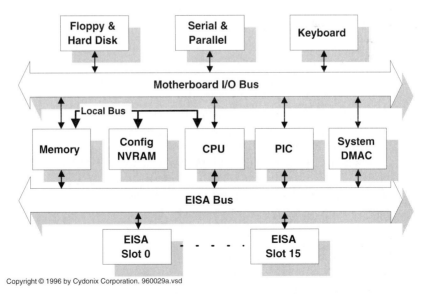

Copyright © 1996 by Cydonix Corporation. 960029a.vsd

Figure 2.6   Layout of an EISA system

---

[6] The other blocks of addresses have to be avoided because of the ISA aliasing problem.

Table 2.7   I/O space use by EISA systems

EISA I/O address ranges

Address range	Used by...
0x0400 — 0x04FF	EISA system board devices
0x0800 — 0x08FF	EISA system board devices
0x0C00 — 0x0CFF	EISA system board devices
0x1000 — 0x1FFF	EISA card slot 1
0x2000 — 0x2FFF	EISA card slot 2
:	:
0xF000 — 0xFFFF	EISA card slot 15

As you've already seen, edge-triggered interrupt lines can be used by only one device at a time. However, level-sensitive interrupt request lines (the norm for native EISA cards) are shareable. This makes it much easier to resolve conflicts between devices that want to use the same IRQ levels.

DMA capabilities   As with ISA systems, a pair of ganged DMACs provide seven independent system DMA channels, numbered 0 through 7. (Channel 4 is still unavailable.) The POST code programs these EISA DMA channels to use a fixed priority arbitration scheme.

The EISA architecture extends ISA DMA model in several ways. First, any of the seven channels can perform 8-, 16-, or 32-bit data transfers. This basically allows any device to be connected to any channel.

EISA DMA channels can also be individually programmed to use a variety of different bus cycle formats. This permits new devices to go faster while still maintaining compatibility with legacy ISA cards. Table 2.8 describes the EISA DMA bus cycles.

Another enhancement is the EISA DMAC's 24-bit count register. For 8-, 16-, and 32-bit devices, this register counts bytes — allowing a single transfer operation to move up to 16 megabytes. For compatibility, the DMAC can be programmed to use this as a word-count register for 16-bit transfers.

Finally, since EISA DMACs generate full 32-bit addresses, they can access a 4-gigabyte physical address space. As you'll see in Chapter 12, this can make it much easier for the I/O Manager to set up a data transfer operation.

Device memory   Again, the EISA bus has 32 address lines. Provided that an expansion card uses a 4-byte register as a pointer, its dedicated memory can live anywhere in a 4-gigabyte range. This also applies to any onboard ROM the device might have.

Autoconfiguration   Several components take part in the EISA configuration process. First, each card is required to implement a 4-byte ID register at location 0xnC80 (where n is an EISA slot number from 1 to 0xA). This register identifies the manufacturer, the device type, and the revision level of the card in that slot.

Table 2.8   The EISA architecture supports several DMA bus cycles

EISA DMA bus cycle formats

Bus cycle	Transfer size	Transfer rate	Compatible with...
ISA compatible	8-bit	1.0 MB/sec	Any ISA
	16-bit	2.0 MB/sec	Any ISA
Type A	8-bit	1.3 MB/sec	Most ISA
	16-bit	2.6 MB/sec	Most ISA
	32-bit	5.3 MB/sec	EISA only
Type B	8-bit	2.0 MB/sec	Some ISA
	16-bit	4.0 MB/sec	Some ISA
	32-bit	8.0 MB/sec	EISA only
Type C (burst)	8-bit	8.2 MB/sec	EISA only
	16-bit	16.5 MB/sec	EISA only
	32-bit	33.0 MB/sec	EISA only

Second, designers can use the remaining 124 bytes (from 0xnC84 to 0xnCFF) to implement other registers that configure the card. For example, there might be a configuration register for the DMA channel number the card should use, and another for setting its IRQ level. Storing values in these registers has the same effect as setting DIP switches and jumpers on an ISA device.

The third component is a script file that contains the card's resource list and defines the location and usage of any device-specific configuration registers on the card. This file is written in a standard EISA scripting language, and its name is based on the contents of the card's ID register. This script usually comes on a floppy disk supplied by the card's manufacturer.

The final piece of the puzzle is an EISA configuration program that runs when the system bootstraps. This program scans the EISA slots looking for cards in previously empty locations. If it finds one, it uses the contents of the slot's ID register to construct the name of a configuration script and then asks the user for the floppy containing that script. Once the disk is inserted, the configuration program assigns resources to the card. It also copies these assignments to nonvolatile CMOS memory associated with the slot, so that it won't be necessary to ask for the script file at the next bootstrap.

Again, Windows NT is able to auto-detect many kinds of native-mode EISA cards. If you need to access EISA slots directly, you can always use **HalGetBusData** and **HalSetBusData**.

PCI — The Peripheral Component Interconnect

Fast networks, full-motion video, and 24-bit-per-pixel displays all require extremely high data transfer rates. The PCI bus is an attempt to satisfy the needs of such demanding hardware. Although the initial design came from Intel, PCI is relatively processor-neutral, and it works as well with DEC Alphas and

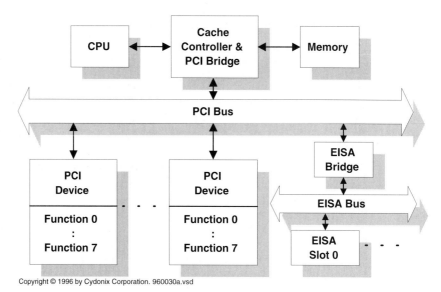

Figure 2.7 Layout of a PCI bus system

Motorola PowerPCs as it does with 80x86 CPUs. Figure 2.7 shows a typical PCI system.

By using a fast bus clock (33 MHz) and a number of clever tricks, the PCI architecture can hit 132 megabytes/sec for sustained 32-bit transfers and twice that rate for 64-bit operations. Some of the things that contribute to this zippy performance include

- The PCI protocol assumes that every transfer is going to be a burst operation. This results in higher throughput rates for fast devices trying to move large amounts of data.

- PCI supports multiple bus masters and permits direct device-to-device transfers (with no intermediate stops in memory). This can result in much more overlap between I/O and CPU operations.

- A central bus arbiter reduces latency by overlapping arbitration with data transfers. This allows the next owner to start an operation as soon as the current owner releases the bus.

- An intelligent bridge between the host CPU and the PCI bus performs various caching and read-ahead functions. This helps to reduce the amount of time the CPU spends waiting for data.

The PCI architecture allows 32 physical units (called *devices*) to be plugged into one bus.[7] Each of these physical units can contain up to eight separate func-

---

[7] The current version of the specification limits this to ten devices.

tional units (called *functions*). After taking away one function address that's used for generating broadcast messages, there can be up to 255 addressable functions on a single PCI bus. Furthermore, one system can have up to 256 separate PCI buses.

Register access   Although the PCI uses 32-bit addresses, I/O register space on 80x86 machines is still limited to 64 kilobytes. So any PCI registers have to be squeezed into I/O space along with everything else. Furthermore, on systems with an EISA/ISA bridge, designers still need to avoid any I/O addresses being used by legacy hardware.

Along with I/O space and memory addresses, PCI defines a range of addresses known as *configuration space*. The discussion of PCI autoconfiguration (below) will explain how configuration space works.

Interrupt mechanisms   The PCI bus has four equal-priority interrupt request lines (INTA–INTD) which are active-low, level-triggered, and shareable. A single-function PCI device has to use INTA, while a multi-function device can use any sequential combination of the four beginning with INTA. The only requirement is that each function can be connected to only one request line.

The PCI specification is relatively neutral when it comes to interrupt priorities. Instead, it depends on an external controller to redirect PCI interrupt requests to the proper system interrupt line. For example, on a PC the redirector converts a given PCI function's request on INTA–INTD into a request on one of the IRQ0–IRQ15 lines. To make this work, any PCI function that generates interrupts must implement the following two configuration registers:

- **Interrupt pin register** — This read-only register identifies the PCI signal line (INTA–INTD) used by this function.

- **Interrupt line register** — This read-write register specifies the priority and vector that the interrupt redirector should assign to this function. On a PC system the values 0x00–0x0F correspond to IRQ0–IRQ15.

This is a very flexible scheme because it doesn't impose any specific interrupt policies on the system designer. This makes it easier to support processor environments other than the 80x86.

DMA capabilities   The PCI specification doesn't include the notion of slave DMA. Instead, the native PCI functions are either bus masters doing their own DMA, or they use programmed I/O. The only devices that perform slave DMA on a PCI machine will be non-PCI boards plugged into the system's EISA or MCA bridge.

In a native PCI DMA operation, the participants are referred to as *agents*, and there are always two of them involved in any transaction:

- **Initiator** — This is a bus master that has won access to the bus and wants to set up a transfer operation.

- **Target** — This is the PCI function currently being addressed by the initiator with the goal of transferring data.

Because any PCI bus master can be an initiator, it's possible to transfer data directly between two PCI devices with no intermediate stops in memory. This powerful capability lends itself well to high-speed networking and video applications.

It's also worth mentioning that the PCI specification doesn't define the policy to be used for arbitrating access to the bus. It only defines the timing of the arbitration signals on the bus. The method used to determine who should go next is system-specific.

Device memory   Dedicated memory used by PCI functions can live anywhere in a 32-bit address space. The only kink is that you have to enable the function's ability to access memory. You do this by setting a bit in function's command register (located in the configuration space header).

An interesting feature of PCI is that a single function can have multiple onboard ROM images, each for a different CPU architecture. This gives vendors the ability to sell the same product in several different markets. The PCI specification defines a standard header format for ROM blocks, so that initialization software can locate the proper chunk of ROM and load it into memory for execution.

Autoconfiguration   The PCI specification dictates that each individual function on the bus must have its own 256-byte storage area for configuration data. This area is referred to as the PCI function's *configuration space*.

The first 64 bytes of any PCI function's configuration space (called the *header*) has a predetermined structure, while the remaining 192 bytes belong to the card designer. System software can use the header to identify a PCI function and assign resources to it. Some of the things in the header area include[8]

- Information about the vendor, the device type, and its revision level.

- A standard pair of command and status registers for enabling various features and reporting errors.

- A resource list that specifies the function's memory and I/O space requirements.

- The interrupt pin and line registers described above.

- Pointers to device-specific ROM

At 256 bytes per function, the configuration space for a PCI system could easily grow quite large — certainly much larger than the 64-kilobyte I/O space available on 80x86 processors. Mapping it into memory is always an option, but

---

[8]   See Shanley and Anderson's book on PCI architecture (listed in the bibilography) for a complete
      description of the configuration header.

that, too, would chew up a lot of address space. Instead, you access a PCI function's configuration data using the following two registers:

- **Configuration address register** — This identifies the bus number, the device, the function, and the address in configuration space that you want to access.

- **Configuration data register** — This acts as a data buffer between the CPU and configuration space. After you set the address register, writing or reading this register transfers information to or from configuration space.

Fortunately, Windows NT doesn't make you go through all this. The **Hal-GetBusData**, **HalSetBusData**, and **HalAssignSlotResources** HAL functions give you a simple way to access a PCI function's configuration data.

2.3   HINTS FOR WORKING WITH HARDWARE

If you haven't done much work with hardware, you're in for a shock when you write your first device driver. Hardware engineers have different priorities than software people do, and their idea of an optimal design may seem strange and quirky to a programmer. (If you doubt this, just think about the user interface on your VCR.) The following hints may help make it easier to work with a new piece of hardware.

Learn about the Hardware

Before you start writing the driver, learn as much as possible about the hardware itself. Most of the information you need should be in the hardware documentation. At the very least, you'll need to know:

Bus architecture   Your hardware's bus architecture will have a big impact on the design of your driver. In particular, ISA boards don't give the system a lot of autodetection information at power-up time, so you'll need to have some other way of determining the board's resource requirements. Chapter 7 explains how to do this.

Control registers   You need to know the size, relative positions, and contents of any control, status, and data registers belonging to the device. You should also find out about any odd behavior they exhibit. For example,

- Some device registers may be read-only or write-only.
- A single register address may perform different functions on a read than it does on a write.

- Data or status registers may not contain valid information until some fixed time interval after you issue a command.
- You may need to access registers in a specific order.

Error and status reporting   Determine any protocols used by the device for reporting hardware failures and device status.

Interrupt behavior   Find out exactly what device conditions cause the hardware to generate an interrupt, and whether the device uses more than one interrupt vector. If you're working with a multidevice controller, interrupts may come from the controller itself, and you'll need to know how to identify the actual device that wants attention.

Data transfer mechanisms   Drivers for programmed I/O devices are very different from DMA drivers, so this is one of the first things you need to know about a piece of hardware. Some devices are capable of doing both kinds of I/O. In the case of a DMA device, find out whether it's a bus master or slave, and whether there are any limitations on the range of physical buffer addresses it can use.

Device memory   If your device uses dedicated memory, find out how to access it. It could be mapped at a fixed physical location or there may be a register that your driver will need to set.

Make Use of Hardware Intelligence

Some peripherals contain their own microprocessors that perform both diagnostic and device control functions. The microprocessor may be running under the control of some firmware, or it may be possible for the driver itself to download code to onboard RAM at initialization time.

If you're working with a smart peripheral, it makes sense to take full advantage of the device's intelligence. Proper use of hardware features can result in significantly better driver performance and improved diagnostic capabilities.

Test the Hardware

It's a good idea to test your hardware very early in the development cycle. In addition to finding bugs, this will help you uncover any mistaken assumptions you may be making about the device's operation.

Basic tests   Make sure the device and any associated cables are all compatible with your development machine. Power up everything and try to boot the operating system. At a very gross level, this lets you know that the device isn't interfering with anything else on the box.

Standalone tests   If possible, write some stand-alone code that tests the board and any firmware it may contain. This will usually be a program that runs without the benefit of an operating system. If you're lucky, the hardware vendor will provide some sort of exerciser for this purpose.

Finally, remember to test any onboard diagnostics by putting the hardware in an illegal state and checking to see that the firmware detects the problem.

2.4   SUMMARY

This has been a very cursory look at hardware issues. The bottom line is your driver needs to find its devices and determine their various resource requirements. As you've seen, some bus architectures make this easier than others. When we start looking at actual driver code, you'll see how all this works under Windows NT.

Before we can tackle any code, however, it's a good idea to take a closer look at just what happens to an I/O request once it enters the gaping maw of the I/O Manager. That's the subject of the next chapter.

Kernel-Mode I/O Processing

Now that you're familiar with some of the major hardware issues, it's time to look at the NT Executive's role in processing I/O requests. This chapter covers three separate areas. First, in sections 3.1 through 3.4, it introduces some concepts and techniques that are important to I/O processing.

Next, we'll look at the various routines that make up a driver and give brief descriptions of the purpose of each routine. Later chapters will deal with actual coding details.

Finally, we'll tie everything together by examining the life of an I/O request in gory detail. A good understanding of the I/O flow of control is probably the most important piece of knowledge a driver writer can have.

3.1   HOW KERNEL-MODE CODE EXECUTES

The kernel-mode parts of Windows NT (including your driver) consist of a massive amount of code. But just what causes this code to execute? It turns out that there are three different contexts in which kernel-mode code might be running. As you develop your driver, it's very important for you to be clear about the context each routine will be running in.

Exceptions

First, a piece of kernel-mode code might be executing in response to a hardware or software exception generated by a user-mode thread. In this case, it's clear that the currently executing thread is the source of the exception, and there's no question about who occupies the user-portion of address space. This is the context in which NT system services (like I/O requests) are executing.

Interrupts

Kernel-mode code also executes in response to a hardware or software interrupt. There will be more to say about NT's use of interrupts in the next section, but for now it's enough to point out that they're not often the result of anything the current user-mode thread is doing. Rather, interrupts are asynchronous events that fall out of the sky and preempt whatever unsuspecting thread happens to be using the CPU at the time. This means that code running in interrupt context (which includes the bulk of your driver routines) can make very few assumptions about the identity of the current process or thread, or about what's currently located in the user portion of virtual address space.

Kernel-Mode Threads

The last possibility is that a piece of code is running in the context of a kernel-mode thread. With a few differences, these kernel threads behave very much like the user-mode threads you already know from Win32 programming. Some drivers use kernel-threads as a way of handling devices that need to be polled, or that have other characteristics which would interfere with the smooth operation of the I/O Manager. Chapter 14 discusses the use of kernel-mode threads.

3.2   USE OF INTERRUPTS BY NT

Chapter 2 introduced the idea of interrupts as a way of arbitrating among different I/O devices at the hardware level. It turns out that NT uses this hardware mechanism to prioritize not only I/O events, but also hardware events internal to the CPU, and even for scheduling various operating system tasks.

CPU Priority Levels

Different CPU architectures have different ways of handling hardware priorities. To avoid these architecture dependencies, Windows NT uses an idealized, abstract CPU priority scheme. The Kernel implements this model using whatever mechanisms are provided by a specific kind of CPU.

The operation of this abstract priority scheme depends on something called an *interrupt request level* (IRQL). The IRQL is a number that defines how important the CPU's current activity is. The higher the number, the greater the importance of continuing the current task. Table 3.1 shows the IRQL levels used in NT's priority scheme. Regardless of the underlying CPU or bus architecture, this is how IRQL levels will look to your driver.

Table 3.1   NT maps these IRQL levels onto platform-specific levels

IRQL Levels

Generated By	IRQL	Purpose
Hardware	HIGHEST_LEVEL	Machine checks and bus errors
	POWER_LEVEL	Power-fail interrupts
	IPI_LEVEL	Interprocessor doorbell for multiprocessor systems
	CLOCK2_LEVEL	Interval clock 2
	CLOCK1_LEVEL	Interval clock 1 (not used on 80x86 platforms)
	PROFILE_LEVEL	Profiling timer
	DIRQLs	Platform-dependent number of levels for I/O device interrupts
Software	DISPATCH_LEVEL	Thread scheduler and deferred procedure call execution
	APC_LEVEL	Asynchronous procedure call execution
	PASSIVE_LEVEL	Normal thread execution level

Interrupt Processing Sequence

When an interrupt reaches the CPU, the processor compares the IRQL value of the requested interrupt with the CPU's current IRQL value. If the IRQL of the request is equal to or less than the current IRQL, the request is ignored. In this case, the request remains pending until some later time when less important things are happening.

On the other hand, if the IRQL of the request is higher than the CPU's current IRQL, the processor does the following:

1. Suspends instruction execution.

2. Saves just enough state information on the stack to resume the interrupted code later on. At the very least, this will include the current PC address and the CPU status register.

3. Raises the IRQL value of the CPU to match the IRQL of the request, preventing interrupts of equal or lower priority from taking control until the current interrupt is satisfied.

4. Transfers control to an interrupt service routine associated with the request.

When it's finished, the service routine executes a special instruction that dismisses the interrupt. This instruction restores the CPU state information saved on the stack (including the previous IRQL value) and returns control to the interrupted code.

Notice that the hardware's priority rule allows higher-IRQL requests to interrupt the service routines of lower-IRQL interrupts. Because the whole mechanism is stack-based, this doesn't cause any confusion. However, it does raise some synchronization issues that we'll address in Chapter 5.

Software-Generated Interrupts

Some of the IRQLs listed in Table 3.1 are tagged as being software generated. This is because it's possible for kernel-mode code to start the interrupt processing sequence described above by executing a privileged instruction. NT uses these software interrupts to trigger activities like thread scheduling and to delay the execution of other operating system tasks until the CPU has finished processing hardware requests. The next section describes this use of software interrupts in greater detail.

3.3   DEFERRED PROCEDURE CALLS (DPCs)

While a piece of kernel-mode code is running at an elevated IRQL, nothing will execute on the same CPU at that or any lower IRQL. This can have the effect of making the system less responsive to time-critical events, and ultimately degrading overall performance. NT tries to avoid this situation by executing as much code as it can at the lowest possible IRQL. An important technique for doing this is the use of *deferred procedure calls* (DPCs).

Operation of a DPC

The DPC architecture uses software interrupts to defer the execution of less time-critical code until higher-IRQL activities have finished. Figure 3.1 illustrates the operation of a DPC.

Later chapters will present more specific information about using DPCs in a driver, but the following general description should give you a good idea of how they work:

1. When some piece of code running at a high IRQL wants to continue its work at a lower IRQL, it adds the DPC object to the end of the system's DPC dispatching queue and requests a DPC software interrupt. Since the current IRQL is above DISPATCH_LEVEL, the interrupt won't be taken right away, but it will remain pending.

2. Eventually, the processor's IRQL falls below DISPATCH_LEVEL and the interrupt is serviced by the DPC dispatcher.

3. One by one, the dispatcher removes each DPC object from its queue and calls the function whose pointer is stored in the object. Notice that this function is being called while the CPU is at DISPATCH_LEVEL.

4. When all the DPC objects have been removed from the queue, the DPC dispatcher dismisses the interrupt.

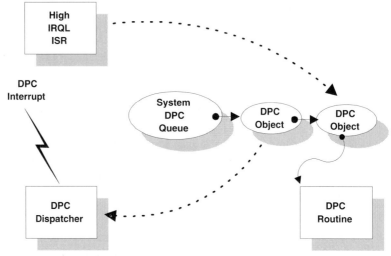

Figure 3.1   How deferred procedure calls work

Device drivers normally perform cleanup operations after an I/O request using a DPC routine. This has the effect of reducing the amount of time the driver spends at DIRQL and improves overall I/O system throughput.

Behavior of DPCs

For the most part, working with DPCs is fairly easy, because NT hides most of the nasty details from you. However, there are three aspects of DPC behavior that you need to be aware of.

First, if your driver tries to insert a DPC object into the dispatching queue, and that object is already in the dispatching queue waiting to execute, the Kernel will reject the queuing request. Consequently, there will be only one call to the DPC routine. In that single call, the DPC routine is expected to perform all the work that's been requested. This could happen if a piece of hardware generated multiple interrupts so rapidly that the DPC request from the one was still pending when another interrupt arrived.

It's up to your driver to handle this situation if it occurs. This could mean keeping an array of DPC objects that your interrupt service code could use, or setting up some kind of internal queue of work requests that the DPC routine would process. In any event, the responsibility is yours.

The second thing you have to watch out for has to do with SMP machines. On a multiprocessor, it's possible for the high-IRQL portion of a driver to submit a DPC request and have the DPC routine begin execution on another CPU even before the high-IRQL code finishes running. For this reason, your DPC routines must synchronize their access to any resources shared with the driver's interrupt service code.

Finally, on multiprocessor systems, the Kernel has a separate DPC dispatching queue for each individual CPU — thus allowing more than one DPC routine to execute *at the same time*. Consequently, each DPC routine must synchronize its access to any resources it might be sharing with another DPC routine. Normally, you use Executive spin locks for this purpose.

3.4   ACCESS TO USER BUFFERS

When a user-mode thread makes an I/O request, it usually passes the address of a data buffer located in user space. The problem this poses for any driver routines trying to access the buffer is that user-space addresses are paged. And as you've seen, any code executing at DISPATCH_LEVEL IRQL or higher must avoid page faults.

However, even if user space weren't in paged memory, there would be another problem. The process occupying user space at the time of the I/O request may not be the same process that's there when an interrupt or DPC routine executes. This means that any pointers to user space held by the driver probably won't refer to the correct physical memory when the driver tries to use them.

Buffer-Access Mechanisms

So just how do driver routines manage to access user-space buffers? Fortunately, the I/O Manager comes to the rescue by providing drivers with two different methods for accessing user buffers. When your driver initializes itself, it tells the I/O Manager which method it plans to use. The choice usually depends on the nature of the device. Figure 3.2 illustrates the difference between these two techniques.

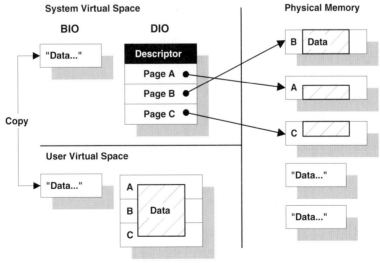

Copyright © 1994 by Cydonix Corporation. 940032a.vsd

Figure 3.2   Memory use in buffered and direct I/O

Buffered I/O (BIO)   Under this scheme, the I/O Manager allocates a buffer from nonpaged pool at the start of each I/O operation and passes the address of this buffer to the driver. The driver uses this buffer for any data transfer operations to or from the device.

For output requests, the I/O Manager copies the contents of the user's buffer into the system buffer before passing it to the driver. For input requests, the driver fills the system buffer with data from the device, and the I/O Manager copies it back into user space at the end of the operation.

There are two disadvantages to this technique. One is that all the memory-to-memory copying of data can slow things down, particularly for devices that transfer large amounts of data on a frequent basis. The other is that it can use up a lot of nonpaged pool. So, drivers should limit the use of buffered I/O to slow devices that don't transfer a lot of data at one time. For these reasons, you should never use Buffered I/O to perform transfers larger than one page of memory.

Direct I/O (DIO)   This scheme avoids the need for copying user data by giving the driver direct access to the physical pages of memory where the user buffer lives. At the beginning of an I/O operation, the I/O Manager locks the entire user buffer into memory to prevent deadly page faults. It then builds a list that identifies the physical pages making up the user buffer. The driver uses this list to perform an I/O operation using the actual pages of the user's buffer. When the I/O operation is complete, the I/O Manager will unlock the pages.

You should use Direct I/O for high-speed devices that need to transfer large amounts of data at once, particularly devices that perform DMA. The mechanics of Direct I/O are described in Chapter 12.

3.5   STRUCTURE OF A KERNEL-MODE DRIVER

One of the biggest differences between a driver and an application program is the driver's control structure. Application programs run from beginning to end under the control of a **main** or **WinMain** function that determines the sequence in which various subroutines are called.

A kernel-mode driver, on the other hand, has no main or WinMain function. Instead, it's just a collection of subroutines that are called as needed by the I/O Manager. Depending on the driver, the I/O Manager might call a driver routine in any of the following situations:

- When a driver is being loaded
- When the driver is being unloaded or the system is shutting down
- When a user-mode program issues an I/O system service call
- When a shared hardware resource becomes available to the driver
- At various points during an actual device operation

The remainder of this section briefly describes the major categories of routines making up a kernel-mode driver.

Driver Initialization and Cleanup Routines

Before any driver can begin processing I/O requests, there are a number of initialization tasks it must perform. Likewise, drivers need to clean things up when they leave the system. There are several routines a driver can use to perform these operations.

DriverEntry routine   The I/O Manager calls this routine when it loads the driver, either at system boot time if the driver is loaded automatically, or later if you load the driver manually from the Control Panel. The DriverEntry routine performs a wide range of initialization functions, including setting up pointers to other driver routines, finding and allocating any hardware resources used by the driver, and making the name of the device visible to the rest of the system.

Reinitialize routine   Some drivers may not be able to complete their initialization during the DriverEntry routine. This could happen if the driver depended on some other driver that wasn't yet loaded, or if the driver needed to initialize itself during different phases of the system boot. These kinds of drivers can use Reinitialize routines to spread out their initialization functions over time.

Unload routine   The I/O Manager calls a driver's Unload routine when a driver is unloaded manually using the Control Panel. The Unload routine is responsible for undoing everything that was done by the DriverEntry routine, including deallocating any hardware resources belonging to the driver and destroying any kernel objects that belong to the driver.

Shutdown routine   When the system goes through a user-initiated shutdown, the I/O Manager will call the Shutdown routines registered by any currently loaded drivers. The primary purpose of a Shutdown routine is to put the hardware into a known state. System resource cleanup is not as important here because the system is about to disappear anyway.

Bugcheck callback routine   If a driver needs to get control in the event of a system crash, it can register a Bugcheck callback routine with the Kernel. This mechanism gives the driver a chance to put its devices into a known state, and perhaps record some state information that will be helpful in debugging the crash.

I/O System Service Dispatch Routines

When the I/O Manager gets a request, it uses the function code of the request to call one of several Dispatch routines in the driver. The Dispatch routine verifies the request and may have the I/O Manager send it to the device for processing.

Open and close operations   All drivers must provide a Dispatch routine that handles Win32 **CreateFile** requests. Drivers that need to perform cleanup operations can supply a routine to handle **CloseHandle** calls, as well as separate Dispatch routines that perform special processing when the last handle on a shared device is closed.

Device operations   Depending on the device, a driver may have one or more Dispatch routines for handling actual data transfer and control operations. The I/O Manager calls these routines in response to Win32 **ReadFile**, **WriteFile**, and **DeviceIoControl** requests, or in response to an I/O request from a higher-level driver. These routines perform any final verification of the request and then pass it to the driver's device management routines for actual processing.

Data Transfer Routines

Device operations involve a number of different driver routines, depending on the nature and complexity of the device.

Start I/O routine   The I/O Manager calls the driver's Start I/O routine when it's time to begin a device operation. This routine allocates any resources needed to process the request and sets the device in motion. The I/O Manager provides simplified support for half-duplex drivers that only need a single Start I/O routine. Drivers of full-duplex devices that have to manage simultaneous input and output requests need a somewhat more complex architecture.

Interrupt Service routine (ISR)   The Kernel's interrupt dispatcher calls a driver's Interrupt Service routine whenever the driver's device generates an interrupt. The ISR is responsible for acknowledging the device, gathering any volatile state information needed by other parts of the driver, and asking the I/O Manager to execute a DPC routine.

DPC routine(s)   A driver can have one or more DPC routines that clean up after a device operation. Depending on the driver, this can involve releasing various system resources, reporting errors, handing completed I/O requests back to the I/O Manager, and starting the next device operation if one is waiting.

If you can do everything with a single DPC, the I/O Manager provides a simplified mechanism called a DpcForIsr routine. However, some drivers are easier to write and maintain if they have separate DPC routines for different kinds of processing. For example, drivers that perform full-duplex I/O might have one DPC routine that completed input operations, and another DPC routine for outputs. At your option, your driver can have any number of these CustomDpc routines.

Resource Synchronization Callbacks

As an extension of the I/O Manager, a driver must be ready to run as needed at the request of more than one user-mode process. For example, it could be asked to send data to one device while waiting for a previous operation to complete on the same or another device. Since there's only one copy of the driver in memory, it has to handle any contention issues that might result from processing overlapping requests.

The I/O Manager makes it easier for drivers to handle these kinds of problems through the use of various synchronization callback routines. When a driver needs to access some shared resource, it queues a request for that resource. When the resource becomes available, the I/O Manager invokes a driver callback routine associated with the request. This has the effect of serializing access to the resource and avoiding collisions. There are three types of synchronization callback routines a driver might use.

ControllerControl routine   If a peripheral card supports multiple physical devices, it's important that only one hardware operation is being performed at a time. Before doing anything to the controller's registers, the Start I/O routine requests exclusive ownership of the controller. If ownership is granted, the ControllerControl callback routine executes; otherwise the ownership request waits until the current owner releases the controller.

AdapterControl routine   DMA hardware is another shared resource that must be passed around from driver to driver. Before doing any DMA operations, the driver requests ownership of the proper DMA hardware. If ownership is granted, the AdapterControl callback routine executes; otherwise the ownership request waits until the current owner releases the DMA hardware.

SynchCritSection routines   The parts of your driver that service device interrupts run at DIRQL while other pieces of driver code execute at or below DISPATCH_LEVEL. If these low-IRQL sections of code need to touch any resources used by the Interrupt Service routine, they perform the operation inside a SynchCritSection routine. Resources in this category include all device control registers and any other context or state information shared with the Interrupt Service routine.

Other Driver Routines

In addition to the basic set of routines described above, your driver may contain some of the following additional functions.

Timer routines   Drivers that need to keep track of the passage of time during a device operation can do so using either an I/O Timer or a CustomTimerDpc routine. Chapter 10 describes both these mechanisms.

I/O completion routines   Drivers of higher-level routines may want to receive notification when a request they've sent to a lower-level driver has completed. This notification will come in the form of a call to the higher-level driver's I/O Completion routine. Chapter 15 discusses these routines in more detail.

Cancel I/O routines   Any driver that holds on to pending requests for a long time must attach a Cancel I/O routine to the request. If the request is canceled, the I/O Manager calls the Cancel I/O routine to perform any necessary cleanup operations. Chapter 11 describes the operation of these routines.

3.6   I/O PROCESSING SEQUENCE

When a user-mode thread requests an I/O operation, the request goes through several processing stages:

- Request preprocessing by NT and the I/O Manager
- Driver-specific preprocessing
- Device activation and interrupt servicing
- Driver-specific postprocessing
- Request postprocessing by the I/O Manage

The following sections describe these stages in more detail.

Request Preprocessing by NT

This phase takes care of all the device-independent setup and verification required by an I/O request.

1.   The Win32 subsystem converts the request into a native NT system service call. This triggers a change to kernel mode which is trapped by NT's system service dispatcher. Eventually, the call ends up inside the I/O Manager.

2.   The I/O Manager allocates a data structure called an *I/O Request Packet* (IRP). Subsequent chapters will have a lot to say about IRPs, but for now, just think of them as work orders that describe what the driver is supposed to do. The I/O Manager fills in the IRP with various pieces of information including a function code indicating what operation the user requested.

3.   The I/O Manager performs a number of validity checks on the arguments supplied by the caller. This involves verifying the file handle, checking access rights to the file object, making sure the device supports the requested function, and probing any input or output buffer addresses passed by the caller.

4.   If this is a Buffered I/O operation, the I/O Manager allocates a nonpaged pool buffer, and for outputs, copies data from user space into the system

buffer. If this is a Direct I/O operation, the user's buffer pages are faulted into memory and locked down, and the I/O Manager builds a list of the buffer's physical pages.

5.   The I/O Manager calls one of the driver's Dispatch routines.

Request Preprocessing by the Driver

Each driver provides a dispatch table that controls the device-dependent preprocessing of I/O requests. The I/O Manager uses the function code of the requested operation as an index into this table and calls the corresponding driver Dispatch routine. These routines might perform any of the following operations:

- Do any device-dependent parameter validation. An example would be testing whether the size of the request falls within the range of any limitations imposed by the device itself.

- If the request is such that it can be handled without any device activity, the Dispatch routine completes the request and sends it back to the I/O Manager.

- If device operation is required, the Dispatch routine marks the request as pending and tells the I/O Manager to send it to the driver's Start I/O routine.

Data Transfer

Data transfers and other device operations are managed by the driver's Start I/O and Interrupt Service routines.

Start I/O   When a Dispatch routine tells the I/O Manager to start a device operation, the I/O Manager checks to see if the target device is currently busy. If it is, the request is queued to the device for later processing. Otherwise, the I/O Manager calls the driver's Start I/O routine. Depending on the device, the driver's Start I/O routine performs some or all of the following steps:

1.   It checks the IRP function (read, write, device control, etc.) and performs any setup work specific to that type of operation.

2.   If the device is attached to a multiunit controller, the ControllerControl routine asks for exclusive ownership of the controller hardware.

3.   If the operation is a DMA transfer, the AdapterControl routine allocates DMA adapter resources.

4.   It uses a SynchCritSection routine to start the device.

5.   It returns control to the I/O Manager and waits for a device interrupt

ISR   When an interrupt occurs, the Kernel's interrupt dispatcher calls the driver's ISR. Depending on the device, the ISR performs some of the following steps:

1. It checks to see if the interrupt was expected.

2. It stops the device from interrupting.

3. If this is a programmed I/O operation and more data remains to be transferred, it moves the next chunk of data to or from the device and waits for the next interrupt.

4. If this is a DMA operation and more data remains to be transferred, it queues a DPC request to set up the DMA hardware for the next chunk of data.

5. If an error occurs or the data transfer is complete, it queues a DPC request to perform I/O postprocessing at a lower IRQL.

6. It dismisses the interrupt.

Postprocessing by the Driver

The Kernel's DPC dispatcher eventually calls the driver's DPC routine to perform device-specific postprocessing operations, including some or all of the following:

1. If this is a DMA operation and more data remains to be transferred, it sets up the DMA hardware for the next piece of data, starts the device, and waits for an interrupt. It then returns to the I/O Manager without performing any of the following steps.

2. If there was an error or timeout, the DPC routine might record it in the system event log and either retry or abort the I/O request.

3. It releases any DMA and controller resources being held by the driver.

4. Next, the DPC routine puts the size of the transfer and final status information into the IRP.

5. Finally, it tells the I/O Manager to complete the current request and start the next one, if one is waiting in the queue for this device.

Postprocessing by the I/O Manager

Once the driver's DPC routine releases an IRP, the I/O Manager performs various device-independent cleanup operations. These include the following.

1. If this was a Buffered I/O output operation, the I/O Manager releases the nonpaged pool buffer used during the transfer.

2. If this was a Direct I/O operation, it unlocks the user's buffer pages.

3. It queues a request to the original thread for a kernel-mode *asynchronous procedure call* (APC). This APC will execute a piece of I/O Manager code in the context of the thread that issued the original I/O request.

4. When the kernel-mode APC runs, it copies status and transfer-size information back into user space.

5. If this was a buffered input, the APC routine copies the contents of the non-paged pool buffer into the caller's user-space buffer. Then it frees the system buffer.

6. If the original request was for an overlapped operation, the APC routine sets the associated Event object into the signaled state.

7. If the original request included a completion routine (for example, from a **ReadFileEx** or **WriteFileEx** call), the kernel-mode APC requests a user-mode APC to execute the completion routine.

3.7   SUMMARY

That completes our quick tour of NT and the I/O subsystem. At this point, you should have a good sense of how various driver routines interact with the I/O Manager. Later chapters will explain how to apply this understanding.

Keeping track of all the details involved in I/O processing obviously requires a lot of bookkeeping. In the next chapter, we'll take a look at the data structures used by the I/O Manager and your driver.

CHAPTER 4

Drivers and Kernel-Mode Objects

*D*ata structures are the lifeblood of most operating systems, and Windows NT is no exception. What's interesting about NT is its use of object technology to manage all this data. After a quick look at NT's approach to objects, this chapter introduces the major structures involved in processing I/O requests. Later chapters will introduce additional data objects as they become necessary.

4.1 DATA OBJECTS AND WINDOWS NT

Just in case you've been living on Mars for the last decade, object-oriented programming (OOP) is one of the currently fashionable software design methodologies. In this scheme, data structures are viewed as black boxes (*objects*) whose contents are invisible, and any interaction with these data structures occurs through a limited set of access functions (*methods*). The goal is to improve the reliability and robustness of the resulting software by hiding implementation details from the users of an object, and by reducing unplanned dependencies between software modules.

Windows NT and OOP

Using a strict definition of OOP, the design of NT isn't truly object-oriented. Rather, you should think of it as being object-based, because it manages its internal data structures in an objectlike way. In particular, the Kernel and the various Executive modules each define their own sets of data structures, along with a corresponding group of access functions. All other modules are expected to use those access functions to manipulate the contents of the structure. The data structures themselves are supposed to be opaque outside the module that defines them.

That's the idea anyway. When it comes to drivers, things get a little fuzzy since a driver is essentially a trusted add-on component of the I/O Manager. Because of this special status, a driver is allowed to touch some object fields directly but must use access functions for other operations on the object. So, I/O Manager objects available to a driver are partially opaque. Objects defined by other NT components are entirely opaque.

NT Objects and Win32 Objects

If you compare internal NT objects with the Win32 user-mode objects, you'll see a couple of differences. First, with a couple of exceptions, most of these NT objects have no externally visible names. This is because these objects aren't being exported to user mode and don't need to be managed by the Object Manager.

Second, you don't use handles to access internal NT objects. Instead, you use a pointer to the object body itself. In some cases, NT will create the object for you and give you the pointer. In other cases, you'll need to allocate and initialize storage for the object.

4.2   I/O REQUEST PACKETS (IRPS)

Almost all I/O is packet-driven under Windows NT. Each separate I/O transaction is described by a work order that tells the driver what to do and tracks the progress of the request through the I/O subsystem. These work orders take the form of a data structure called an *I/O Request Packet* (IRP), and this is how they're used.

1.   The I/O Manager allocates an IRP from nonpaged system memory in response to an I/O request. Based on the I/O function specified by the user, it passes the IRP to the appropriate driver Dispatch routine.

2.   The Dispatch routine checks the parameters of the request, and if they're valid, passes the IRP to the driver's Start I/O routine.

3.   The Start I/O routine uses the contents of the IRP to set up a device operation.

4.   When the operation is complete, the driver's DpcForIsr routine stores a final status code in the IRP and sends it back to the I/O Manager.

5.   The I/O Manager uses the information in the IRP to complete the request and send the user the final status.

This describes what happens when requests are being sent to a lowest-level driver. If the initial request is sent to a higher-level driver, things get a little more complex, and a single IRP may travel through several layers of drivers before the request is finished. Higher-level drivers can also create additional IRPs and send them to other drivers.

Layout of an IRP

An IRP is a variable-sized structure allocated from nonpaged pool. As you can see from Figure 4.1, an IRP has two sections:

- A header area containing general bookkeeping information
- One or more parameter blocks called *I/O stack locations*

IRP header   This area of the IRP holds various pieces of information about the overall I/O request. Some parts of the header are directly accessible to your driver, while other pieces are the exclusive property of the I/O Manager. Table 4.1 list the fields in the header that your driver is allowed to touch.

The **IoStatus** member holds the final status of the I/O operation. When your driver is ready to complete the processing of an IRP, it sets the **Status** field of this block to a STATUS_XXX value. At the same time, your driver should set the **Information** field of the status block either to 0 (if there's an error) or to a function-code-specific value (for example, the number of bytes transferred).

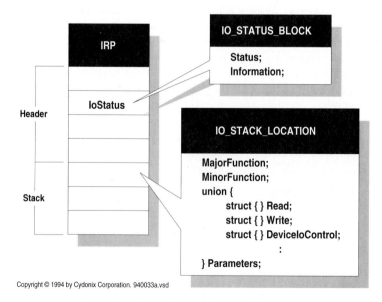

Copyright © 1994 by Cydonix Corporation. 940033a.vsd

Figure 4.1   The structure of an IRP

Table 4.1   Externally visible fields in an IRP header

IRP header fields

Field	Description
IO_STATUS_BLOCK IoStatus	Contains status of the I/O request
PVOID AssociatedIrp.SystemBuffer	Points to a system space buffer if device performs Buffered I/O
PMDL MdlAddress	Points to a Memory Descriptor List for a user-space buffer if device performs Direct I/O
PVOID UserBuffer	User-space address of I/O buffer
BOOLEAN Cancel	Indicates the IRP has been canceled

The **AssociatedIrp.SystemBuffer**, **MdlAddress**, and **UserBuffer** fields play various roles in managing the driver's access to data buffers. Later chapters will explain how to use these fields when your driver performs either Buffered or Direct I/O.

I/O stack locations   The main purpose of an I/O stack location is to hold the function code and parameters for an I/O request. By examining the **Major-Function** field of the stack location, a driver can decide what operation to perform and how to interpret the **Parameters** union. Table 4.2 describes some of the commonly used members of an I/O stack location.

For requests sent directly to a lowest-level driver, the corresponding IRP will have only one I/O stack location. For requests sent to a higher-level driver, the I/O Manager creates an IRP with separate I/O stack locations for each driver layer. Every driver in the hierarchy is allowed to touch only its own stack location, and if it's not at the bottom of the pile, to set up the stack location for the next driver beneath it.

When a driver passes an IRP to a lower-level driver, the I/O Manager automatically "pushes" the I/O stack-pointer so that it points at the I/O stack location belonging to the lower driver. When the lower driver releases the IRP, the I/O stack-pointer is "popped" so that it again points to the stack location of the higher driver. Chapter 15 will explain how to work with this mechanism.

Manipulating IRPs

IRP access functions fall into two general categories: Those that operate on the IRP as a whole, and those that deal specifically with the IRP's I/O stack locations. The following subsections describe each of groups.

IRPs as a whole   The I/O Manager exports a variety of functions that work with IRPs. Table 4.3 lists the most common ones. Later chapters will explain how to use them.

Table 4.2   Selected contents of an IRP stack location

IO_STACK_LOCATION, *PIO_STACK_LOCATION

Field	Contents
UCHAR MajorFunction	IRP_MJ_XXX function specifying the operation
UCHAR MinorFunction	Used by file system and SCSI drivers
union Parameters	Typed union keyed to MajorFunction code
struct Read	Parameters for IRP_MJ_READ
	• ULONG Length
	• ULONG Key
	• LARGE_INTEGER ByteOffset
struct Write	Parameters for IRP_MJ_WRITE
	• ULONG Length
	• ULONG Key
	• LARGE_INTEGER ByteOffset
struct DeviceIoControl	Parameters for IRP_MJ_DEVICE_CONTROL and IRP_MJ_INTERNAL_DEVICE_CONTROL
	• ULONG OutputBufferLength
	• ULONG InputBufferLength
	• ULONG IoControlCode
	• PVOID Type3InputBuffer
	:
struct Others	Available to driver
	• PVOID Argument1–Argument4
PDEVICE_OBJECT DeviceObject	Target device for this I/O request
PFILE_OBJECT FileObject	File object for this request, if any

Note: See NTDDK.H for additional members of the Parameters union.

Table 4.3   Functions that work with the whole IRP

IRP functions

Function	Description	Called by...
IoStartPacket	Sends IRP to Start I/O routine	Dispatch
IoCompleteRequest	Indicates that all processing is done	DpcForIsr
IoStartNextPacket	Sends next IRP to Start I/O	DpcForIsr
IoCallDriver*	Sends IRP to another driver	Dispatch
IoAllocateIrp*	Requests additional IRPs	Dispatch
IoFreeIrp*	Releases driver-allocated IRPs	I/O Completion

*These functions are used primarily by layered drivers.

Table 4.4   IO_STACK_LOCATION access-functions

IO_STACK_LOCATION access functions

Function	Description	Called by...
IoGetCurrentIrpStackLocation	Gets pointer to caller's stack slot	(Various)
IoMarkIrpPending	Marks caller's stack slot as needing further processing	Dispatch
IoGetNextIrpStackLocation*	Gets pointer to stack slot for next lower driver	Dispatch
IoSetNextIrpStackLocation*	Pushes the I/O stack pointer one location	Dispatch
IoSetCompletionRoutine*	Attaches I/O Completion routine to the next lower driver's I/O stack slot	Dispatch

*These functions are used primarily by layered drivers.

IRP stack locations   The I/O Manager also provides several functions that drivers can use to access an IRP's stack locations. These functions are listed in Table 4.4

4.3   DRIVER OBJECTS

DriverEntry is the only driver routine with an exported name. When the I/O Manager needs to locate other driver functions, it uses the Driver object associated with a specific device. This object is basically a catalog that contains pointers to various driver functions. Here's how it works.

1. The I/O Manager creates a Driver object whenever it loads a driver. If the driver fails during initialization, the I/O Manager deletes the object.

2. During initialization, the DriverEntry routine loads pointers to other driver functions into the Driver object.

3. When an IRP is sent to a specific device, the I/O Manager uses the associated Driver object to find the right Dispatch routine.

4. If a request involves an actual device operation, the I/O Manager uses the Driver object to locate the driver's Start I/O routine.

5. If the driver is unloaded, the I/O Manager uses the Driver object to find an Unload routine. When the Unload routine is done, the I/O Manager deletes the Driver object.

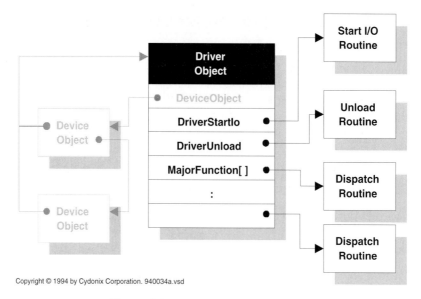

Copyright © 1994 by Cydonix Corporation. 940034a.vsd

Figure 4.2   Structure of a Driver object

Layout of a Driver Object

There is a unique Driver object for each driver currently loaded in the system. Figure 4.2 illustrates the structure of a Driver object. As you can see, the Driver object also contains a pointer to a linked list of devices serviced by this driver. A driver's Unload routine can use this list to locate any devices it needs to delete.

Unlike other objects, there are no access functions for modifying Driver objects. Instead, the DriverEntry routine sets various fields directly. Table 4.5 lists the fields you're allowed to touch.

Table 4.5   Externally visible fields of a Driver object

Driver object fields

Field	Description
PDRIVER_STARTIO DriverStartIo	Address of driver's Start I/O routine
PDRIVER_UNLOAD DriverUnload	Address of driver's Unload routine
PDRIVER_DISPATCH MajorFunction[ ]	Table of driver's Dispatch routines, indexed by I/O operation code
PDEVICE_OBJECT DeviceObject	Linked list of Device objects created by this driver

4.4   DEVICE OBJECTS AND DEVICE EXTENSIONS

Both the I/O Manager and the driver need to know what's going on with an I/O device at all times. Device objects make this possible by keeping information about a device's characteristics and state. There is one Device object for each virtual, logical, and physical device on the system. Here's how they're used.

1. The DriverEntry routine creates a Device object for each of its devices.

2. The I/O Manager uses a pointer in the Device object to locate the corresponding Driver object. There it can find driver routines to operate on I/O requests. It also maintains a queue of current and pending IRPs attached to the Device object.

3. Various driver routines use the Device object to locate the corresponding Device Extension. As an I/O request is processed, the driver uses the Extension to store any device-specific state information.

4. The driver's Unload routine deletes the Device object when the driver is unloaded.

Physical Device drivers aren't the only ones who use these objects. Chapter 15 describes the way higher-level drivers use Device objects.

Layout of a Device Object

Figure 4.3 illustrates the structure of a Device object and its relation to other structures.

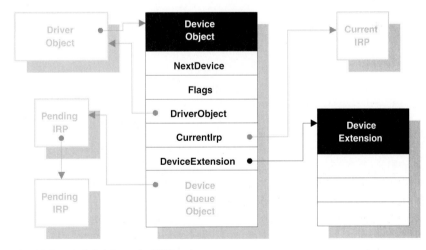

Copyright © 1994 by Cydonix Corporation. 940035a.vsd

Figure 4.3   Structure of a Device object

Table 4.6　Externally visible fields of a Device object

Device object fields

Field	Description
PVOID DeviceExtension	Points to Device Extension structure
PDRIVER_OBJECT DriverObject	Points to Driver object for this device
ULONG Flags	Specifies buffering strategy for device
	• DO_BUFFERED_IO
	• DO_DIRECT_IO
PDEVICE_OBJECT NextDevice	Points to next device belonging to this driver
CCHAR StackSize	Minimum number of I/O stack locations needed by IRPs sent to this device
ULONG AlignmentRequirement	Memory alignment required for buffers

Although the Device object contains a lot of data, much of it is the exclusive property of the I/O Manager. Your driver should limit its access to only those fields listed in Table 4.6.

Manipulating Device Objects

Table 4.7 lists many of the I/O Manager functions that operate on Device objects. The I/O Manager also passes a Device object pointer as an argument to most of the routines in your driver.

Table 4.7　Access functions for a Device object

Device object access functions

Function	Description	Called by...
IoCreateDevice	Creates a Device object	DriverEntry
IoCreateSymbolicLink	Makes Device object visible to Win32	DriverEntry
IoAttachDevice*	Attaches a filter to a Device object	DriverEntry
IoAttachDeviceByPointer*	Attaches a filter to a Device object	DriverEntry
IoGetDeviceObjectPointer*	Layers one driver on top of another	DriverEntry
IoCallDriver*	Sends request to another driver	Dispatch
IoDetachDevice*	Disconnects from a lower driver	Unload
IoDeleteSymbolicLink	Removes Device object from the Win32 namespace	Unload
IoDeleteDevice	Removes Device object from system	Unload

*These functions are used primarily by layered drivers.

Device Extensions

Connected to the Device object is another important data structure, the Device Extension. The Extension is simply a block of nonpaged pool that the I/O Manager automatically attaches to any Device object you create. You choose both the size and the contents of the Device Extension. Typically, you use it to hold any information associated with a particular device.

Drivers have to be fully reentrant, so global or static variables are a very bad idea. Any information that you might be tempted to keep in global or static storage probably belongs in the Device Extension. Other things you might want to store in the Extension include

- A back pointer to the Device object
- Any device state or driver context information
- A pointer to an Interrupt object and an interrupt-expected flag
- A pointer to a Controller object
- A pointer to an Adapter object and a count of mapping registers

Since the Device Extension is driver-specific, you'll need to define its structure in one of your driver's header files. Although the Extension's exact contents will depend on what your driver does, its general layout will look something like this:

```
typedef struct _DEVICE_EXTENSION {
    PDEVICE_OBJECT DeviceObject;
    :
    // Other driver-specific declarations
    :
} DEVICE_EXTENSION, *PDEVICE_EXTENSION;
```

In later chapters of this book, you'll see a great many uses for the Device Extension.

4.5   CONTROLLER OBJECTS AND CONTROLLER EXTENSIONS

Some peripheral adapters manage more than one physical device using the same set of control registers. The floppy disk controller is one example of this architecture. This kind of hardware causes the following synchronization problem: If the driver tries to perform simultaneous operations on more than one of the connected devices without first synchronizing its access to the shared register space, the control registers may get trashed. To help with this problem, the I/O Manager provides Controller objects.

The Controller object is a kind of token that can be owned by only one device at a time. Before accessing any device registers, the driver asks that ownership of the Controller object be given to a specific device. If the hardware is free, ownership is granted. If not, the device's request is put on hold until the current owner releases the hardware. By passing the Controller object around this way, the I/O Manager guarantees that multiple devices will access the hardware in an orderly manner. Here's a little more detail about how Controller objects are used.

1. The DriverEntry routine creates the Controller object and usually stores its address in a field of each device's Device Extension.

2. Before it starts a device operation, the Start I/O routine asks for exclusive ownership of the Controller object on behalf of a specific device.

3. When the Controller object becomes available, the I/O Manager grants ownership and calls the driver's ControllerControl routine. This routine sets up the device's registers and starts the I/O operation. As long as this device owns the Controller object, any further requests for ownership will block at step 2 until the object is released.

4. When the device operation is finished, the driver's DpcForIsr routine releases the Controller object, making it available for use by other pending requests.

5. The driver's Unload routine deletes the Controller object when the driver is unloaded.

Obviously, not all drivers need a Controller object. If your interface card supports only one physical or virtual device, or if multiple devices on the same card don't share any control registers then you can ignore Controller objects.

Layout of a Controller Object

Figure 4.4 shows the relationship of a Controller object to other system data structures.

The only externally visible field in a Controller object is the **PVOID ControllerExtension** field, which contains a pointer to the extension block.

Manipulating Controller Objects

The I/O Manager exports four functions that operate on Controller objects. These functions are listed in Table 4.8.

Controller Extensions

Like Device objects, Controller objects contain a pointer to an Extension structure that you can use to hold any controller-specific data. The Extension is also a place to store any information that's global to all the devices attached to a controller. Finally, if the controller (rather than individual devices) is the source of

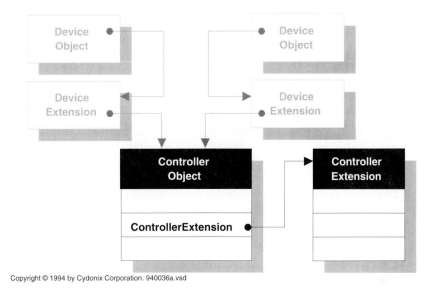

Copyright © 1994 by Cydonix Corporation. 940036a.vsd

Figure 4.4   Structure of a Controller object

interrupts, it makes sense to store pointers to Interrupt and Adapter objects in the Controller Extension.

Since the Controller Extension is driver-specific, you'll need to define its structure in one of your driver's header files. Although the Extension's exact contents will depend on what your driver does, its general layout will look something like this:

```
typedef struct _CONTROLLER_EXTENSION {
    PCONTROLLER_OBJECT ControllerObject;
    :
    // Other driver-specific declarations
    :
} CONTROLLER_EXTENSION, *PCONTROLLER_EXTENSION;
```

Table 4.8   Access functions for a Controller object

Controller object access functions

Function	Description	Called by...
IoCreateController	Creates a Controller object	DriverEntry
IoAllocateController	Requests exclusive ownership of controller	Start I/O
IoFreeController	Releases ownership of controller	DpcForIsr
IoDeleteController	Removes Controller object from the system	Unload

4.6 ADAPTER OBJECTS

Just as multiple devices on the same controller need to coordinate their hardware access, so devices that perform DMA need an orderly way to share system DMA resources. The I/O Manager uses Adapter objects to prevent arguments over DMA hardware. There is one Adapter object for each DMA data transfer channel on the system.

Like a Controller object, an Adapter object can be owned by only one device at a time. Before starting a DMA transfer, the Start I/O routine asks for ownership of the Adapter object. If the hardware is free, ownership is granted. If not, the device's request is put on hold until the current owner releases the hardware. Obviously, if your device supports only programmed I/O, you don't need to bother with Adapter objects. Here's how Adapter objects work.

1. The HAL creates Adapter objects for any DMA data channels detected at bootstrap time.

2. The DriverEntry routine locates the Adapter object for its device and stores a pointer in the Device or Controller Extension. Adapter objects for unrecognized DMA hardware may be created on the fly at this point.

3. The Start I/O routine requests ownership of the Adapter object on behalf of a specific device.

4. When ownership is granted, the I/O Manager calls the driver's Adapter Control routine. This routine then uses the Adapter object to set up a DMA transfer.

5. The driver's DpcForIsr routine may use the Adapter object to perform additional operations in the case of a split transfer. When a transfer is finished, DpcForIsr releases the Adapter object.

Another important function of the Adapter object is to manage some things called *mapping registers*. The HAL uses these registers to map the scattered physical pages of a user's buffer onto the contiguous range of addresses required by most DMA hardware. If that statement doesn't make any sense to you, don't worry. We'll be looking at the mechanics of DMA transfers in much greater detail in Chapter 12.

Layout of an Adapter Object

Figure 4.5 illustrates the relationship of Adapter objects to other structures. As you can see from the diagram, the Adapter object is completely opaque and has no externally visible fields. If you're working with DMA devices, you should

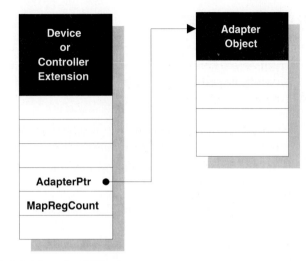

Figure 4.5   Structure of an Adapter object

store the pointer to your Adapter object, as well as the number of mapping registers it supports, either in a Device or Controller Extension

Manipulating Adapter Objects

Both the HAL and the I/O Manager export functions that you can use to manipulate Adapter objects. Table 4.9 lists the ones you're most likely to encounter.

Table 4.9   Access functions for an Adapter object

Adapter object access functions

Function	Description	Called by...
HalGetAdapter	Gets a pointer to an Adapter object	DriverEntry
IoAllocateAdapterChannel	Requests exclusive ownership of DMA hardware	StartIo (Controller Control)
IoMapTransfer	Sets up DMA hardware for a data transfer	Adapter Control / DpcForIsr
IoFlushAdapterBuffers	Flushes data after partial transfers	DpcForIsr
IoFreeMapRegisters	Releases map registers	DpcForIsr
IoFreeAdapterChannel	Releases Adapter object	DpcForIsr

4.7   INTERRUPT OBJECTS

That brings us to the last of the NT objects we'll be looking at in this chapter, the Interrupt object. Interrupt objects simply give the Kernel's interrupt dispatcher a way to find the right service routine when an interrupt occurs. Here's how Interrupt objects are used.

1.   The DriverEntry routine creates an Interrupt object for each interrupt vector supported by the device or the Controller

2.   When an interrupt occurs, the Kernel's interrupt dispatcher uses the Interrupt object to locate the Interrupt Service routine

3.   The Unload routine deletes the Interrupt object after disabling interrupts from the device.

Other than creating and deleting them, your driver has very little direct interaction with Interrupt objects. You will, however, need to store a pointer to the Interrupt object in a convenient place like the Device or Controller Extension.

Layout of an Interrupt Object

Figure 4.6 illustrates the structure of an Interrupt object. Like Adapter objects, they are completely opaque and have no externally visible fields.

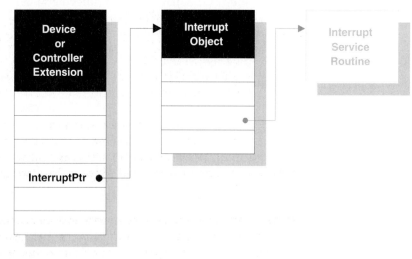

Copyright © 1994 by Cydonix Corporation. 940038a.vsd

Figure 4.6   Structure of an Interrupt object

Table 4.10   Access functions for an Interrupt object

Interrupt object access functions

Function	Description	Called by...
HalGetInterruptVector	Converts bus-relative interrupt vector to systemwide value	DriverEntry
IoConnectInterrupt	Associates Interrupt Service routine with a system interrupt vector	DriverEntry
KeSynchronizeExecution	Synchronizes driver routines that run at different IRQLs	(Various)
IoDisconnectInterrupt	Removes Interrupt object	Unload

Manipulating Interrupt Objects

Several system components export functions that work with Interrupt objects. Table 4.10 lists the most common ones.

4.8   SUMMARY

Although it may seem as if there are a lot of objects involved in I/O processing, they're all necessary and important. If you're feeling a little overwhelmed with all this background material, you can relax. The next chapter will show you how to put this information to work as we start writing some actual driver code.

CHAPTER 5

General Development Issues

Writing kernel-mode code is not the same as writing an application program. Because your driver is a trusted component of the system, you have to be much more careful about how you behave. This chapter is a short manual of good etiquette for driver writers.

5.1 DRIVER DESIGN STRATEGIES

Like most other kinds of software, drivers benefit from an organized approach to development. This section gives some guidelines that may help shorten development time.

Use Formal Design Methods

There's a certain cowboy mentality that pervades the driver-writing world. For some reason, it's easy to think that you can just sit down, scribble a flowchart on an old candy wrapper, and just start coding. Unfortunately, when you're dealing with a full-duplex driver for some asynchronous communication device, such ad hoc methods just don't work. So many things are going on that it becomes impossible to verify the flow of control.

A better approach is to use techniques that have proven helpful in other areas of real-time design. Some suggestions follow.

- Data flow diagrams can help you break your driver into discrete functional units. These diagrams make it easier to visualize how the functional units in your driver relate to each other, and how they transform input data into output data.

- State-machine models are another good way to describe the flow of control in a driver — especially one that manages an elaborate hardware or software protocol. In the process of verifying the state machine, you can also ferret out synchronization issues within the driver.

- An analysis of expected data repetition rates or mandatory input-to-output response will give you a set of quantitative timing requirements. These are important when it comes time to tune the driver.

- Another useful tool is an explicit list of external events and the driver actions these events should trigger. This list ought to include both hardware events from the device and I/O requests from users.

Using these techniques will help you to separate your driver into well-defined functional units, which makes the driver easier to develop. In some cases, this might even mean breaking a single driver into a pair of port and class drivers that handle hardware-dependent and hardware-independent functions. In any event, the time you spend analyzing and designing your driver at the start of the project will more than pay for itself in reduced debugging and maintenance.

Use Incremental Development

Once you've completed your initial analysis and design, it's time to start the actual development. Following the steps below can reduce your debugging time by helping you to detect problems while they're still easy to find.

1. Decide which kinds of kernel-mode objects your driver will need.

2. Decide on any additional context or state information your driver will need, and decide where you're going to store it.

3. Write the DriverEntry and Unload routines. To test the driver at this point, see if you can load and unload it using the Control Panel.

4. Add code that finds and allocates the driver's hardware, as well as code to deallocate the hardware when the driver unloads. Again, the test is just whether you can load and unload the driver using the Control Panel. You can also use the Registry editor (REGEDT32) to see whether your driver is allocating and deallocating its resources properly.

5. Add driver Dispatch routines that process IRP_MJ_CREATE, IRP_MJ_CLOSE, and any other operations that don't require device access.

You can test the driver with a simple Win32 program that calls **CreateFile** and **CloseHandle**.

6. Add Dispatch routines that process any other IRP_MJ_XXX function codes. Also, add the Start I/O logic but complete each I/O request without starting the device. Test these new code paths with a simple Win32 program that makes **ReadFile** and **WriteFile** calls, as appropriate.

7. Finally, implement the real Start I/O logic, the Interrupt Service routine, and the DPC routine. Now you can test the driver using live data.

Another tip: If you're unsure about the exact behavior of the hardware, add a **DeviceIoControl** function that gives you direct access to the device registers. This will allow you to find out how the device really works by writing a few simple Win32 programs. Just remember to disable this function when you ship the final version of the driver.

Use the Sample Drivers

The Windows NT device driver kit (DDK) contains a huge body of sample code in the **DDK****SRC** directory tree. There are many ways you can use all this code to make driver development easier. At the very least, you should read it for hints, clues, and comments. You might also want to be more direct about cutting and pasting helpful chunks of code (a procedure encouraged by Microsoft). The usual warning: If you do decide to cut and paste, make sure you thoroughly understand the code you're grabbing.

5.2   CODING CONVENTIONS AND TECHNIQUES

Writing a trusted kernel-mode component is not the same as writing an application program. This section presents some basic conventions and techniques that will make it easier to code in this environment.

General Recommendations

First of all, here are some general recommendations for things you should keep in mind when you're writing a driver:

*   Avoid the use of assembly language in your driver. It makes the code hard to read, nonportable, and difficult to maintain. In those rare situations where it's unavoidable, isolate the code in its own module. Whatever you do, don't go sprinkling inline assembly throughout your driver.

*   If you have any platform-specific code, either put it in its own module, or at the very least bracket it with **#ifdef/#endif** statements.

- Don't link your driver with the standard C runtime library. Some of those routines may hold state or context information in ways that are not driver safe. Instead use the **RtlXxx** support routines supplied for drivers.

- Commenting code is a religious issue. Some people swear by it; others think that out-of-date comments are worse than no comments at all.[1]

- Manage your driver project with some kind of source-code control program. This is especially important for larger drivers, or drivers being developed by several people.

Naming Conventions

It's a good idea to adopt some standard naming convention for the routines in your driver. This makes it easier to debug and test the driver during its initial development. It also simplifies maintenance of the driver should you have to reacquaint yourself with the code after being away from it for a year. Microsoft recommends the following:

- Add a driver-specific prefix to each of your routines. Choose one prefix for standard driver routines and another, shorter prefix for any internal functions.

- Give the routine itself a name that describes what it does.

For example, the mouse class driver supplied with the NT DDK adds the prefix MouseClass to all its standard routines which gives names like **MouseClassStartIo** and **MouseClassUnload**. The same class driver uses the prefix Mou for any internal routines like **MouConfiguration** and **MouConnectToPort**.

Regardless of whether you follow these conventions or come up with some of your own, it's important that you establish some consistent way of naming your driver routines. When you come back to a driver that you haven't looked at for six months, uniform naming will make it easier to figure out what you originally had in mind.

Header Files

NTDDK.H defines all the data types, structures, and constants used by base-level kernel-mode drivers. SCSI, network, and video drivers use other header files. Be sure you've included the appropriate headers in your driver.

You can use private header files to hide various hardware and platform dependencies. For example on 80x86 systems, you can address each byte in I/O space, but on other architectures, I/O registers may need to be aligned on 4-byte

---

[1] Personally, I attend services at the Church of the Detailed Comment.

or 8-byte boundaries. Hiding these differences in a header file means you can move your driver to a new platform just by redefining some symbols and rebuilding the driver.

Even if your driver doesn't face any of these issues, writing a few register access macros can make the driver itself easier to read. The following code fragment is an example of some hardware beautification macros for a parallel port device. This example assumes that some initialization code in the driver has put the address of the first device register in the **PortBase** field of the Device Extension.

```
//
// Define device registers as relative offsets
//
#define PAR_DATA     0
#define PAR_STATUS   1
#define PAR_CONTROL  2

//
// Define access macros for registers. Each macro takes
// a pointer to a Device Extension as an argument
//
#define ParWriteData( pDevExt, bData )      \
(WRITE_PORT_UCHAR(                           \
   pDevExt->PortBase + PAR_DATA, bData ))

#define ParReadStatus( pDevExt )            \
(READ_PORT_UCHAR(                            \
   pDevExt->PortBase + PAR_STATUS ))

#define ParWriteControl( pDevExt, bData )    \
(WRITE_PORT_UCHAR(                           \
   pDevExt->PortBase + PAR_CONTROL, bData ))
```

Status Return Values

The kernel-mode portions of NT operating system use 32-bit status values to describe the outcome of any particular operation. The data type of these codes is NTSTATUS. There are three situations in which you'll need to use these status codes:

- When you call one of the internal NT functions, it will communicate its displeasure at something you're trying to do by returning an NTSTATUS value

- When NT calls some driver-specific callback routines, the routines often have to return an NTSTATUS value to the system.

- When you complete the processing of an I/O request, you need to mark it with an NTSTATUS value. This value will ultimately be mapped onto a Win32 ERROR_XXX code.[2]

NTSTATUS.H defines symbolic names for a large number of NTSTATUS values. These names all have the form STATUS_XXX, where XXX describes the actual status message. STATUS_SUCCESS, STATUS_NAME_EXISTS, and STATUS_INSUFFICIENT_RESOURCES are all examples of these names.

When you call a system routine that returns an NTSTATUS value, you can either check for specific values, or you can use the NT_SUCCESS macro to test for general success or failure. The following code fragment illustrates this technique.

```
NTSTATUS status;
:
status = IoCreateDevice( ... );
if( !NT_SUCCESS( status )) {
// clean up and exit with failure
:
}
```

Always, always, always check the return values you get from any system routines you call. If you just assume that the call succeeded, your driver may damage the system somewhere down the line. If you're lucky, this kind of thing will crash the system and draw attention to itself; if not, it may just produce sporadic, hard-to-find errors.

NT Driver Support Routines

The I/O Manager and other kernel-mode components of NT export a large number of support functions that your driver can call. The reference section of the NT DDK documentation describes these functions, and you'll see plenty of examples of their use throughout this book. For the moment, it's enough to point out that these support routines fall into categories based on the NT module that exports them. Table 5.1 gives a brief overview of the kinds of support that each NT module provides.

The **ZwXxx** functions need a little explanation. These are actually an internal calling interface for all the **NtXxx** user-mode system services. The difference between the user- and kernel-mode interfaces is that the **ZwXxx** functions don't perform any argument checking. Although there are a large number of these

---

[2] NTSTATUS codes and Win32 error codes are not the same thing. The knowledge base that comes with the NT DDK has an article that shows the mapping between NTSTATUS values and their corresponding Win32 ERROR_XXX codes. It's worth taking a look at this article because the mappings from STATUS_XXX to ERROR_XXX codes don't always make a lot of sense.

Table 5.1   Categories of support routines available to drivers

NT driver support routines

Category	Supports...	Function names
Executive	Memory allocation	ExXxx()
	Interlocked queues	
	Zones	
	Lookaside lists	
	System worker threads	
HAL	Device register access	HalXxx()
	Bus access	
I/O Manager	General driver support	IoXxx()
Kernel	Synchronization	KeXxx()
	DPC	
Memory Manager	Virtual-to-physical mapping	MmXxx()
	Memory allocation	
Object Manager	Handle management	ObXxx()
Process Manager	System thread management	PsXxx()
Runtime library	String manipulation	RtlXxx() (mostly)
	Large integer arithmetic	
	Registry access	
	Security functions	
	Time and date functions	
	Queue and list support	
Security Monitor	Privilege checking	SeXxx()
	Security descriptor functions	
(All)	Internal system services	ZwXxx()

functions, the NT DDK reference material describes only a few of them. Microsoft may eventually tell us about the rest, but for now, limit yourself to using the ones that show up in the documentation.

One final point. To make life easier for driver writers, the I/O Manager provides several convenience functions that are really just wrappers around one or more lower-level calls to other NT modules. These wrappers usually offer a simpler interface than their low-level counterparts, and you should use them whenever you can.

Discarding Initialization Routines

Some compilers support the option of declaring certain functions as discardable. Functions in this category will disappear from memory after your driver has finished loading, making your driver smaller. If your development environment offers this feature, you should use it.

Good candidates for discardable functions are **DriverEntry** and any subroutines called only by **DriverEntry**. The following code fragment shows how to take advantage of discardable code.

```
#ifdef ALLOC_PRAGMA
#pragma alloc_text( init, DriverEntry )
#pragma alloc_text( init, XxStuffCalledByDriverEntry )
#pragma alloc_text( init, XxAlsoCalledByDriverEntry )
  :
#endif
```

The **alloc_text** pragma must appear after the function name is declared, but before the function itself is defined — so remember to prototype the function at the top of the code module (or in a suitable header file). Also, functions referenced in the pragma statement must be defined in the same compilation unit as the pragma. If you don't follow these rules, things break.

Controlling Driver Paging

Nonpaged system memory is a precious resource. You can further reduce the burden your driver puts on nonpaged memory by putting appropriate routines in paged memory. Any function that executes only at PASSIVE_LEVEL IRQL can be paged. This includes Reinitialize routines, Unload and Shutdown routines, Dispatch routines, thread functions, and any helper functions running exclusively at PASSIVE_LEVEL IRQL. Once again, it's the **alloc_text** pragma that performs this little miracle. Here's an example:

```
#ifdef ALLOC_PRAGMA
#pragma alloc_text( page, XxUnload )
#pragma alloc_text( page, XxShutdown )
#pragma alloc_text( page, XxDispatchRead )
#pragma alloc_text( page, XxDispatchHelper )
  :
#endif
```

Finally, there's another trick you can play if you have a seldom-used device driver and you want to get it out of the way. By calling the **MmPageEntireDriver** function, you can override a driver's declared memory management attributes and make the whole thing temporarily paged. Call this function at the end of the DriverEntry routine and from the Dispatch routine for IRP_MJ_CLOSE when there are no more open handles to any of your devices. Call **MmResetDriverPaging** from the IRP_MJ_CREATE Dispatch routine to make the driver's page attributes revert to normal.

If you use this technique, watch out for two things. First, make sure there aren't any IRPs being processed by high-IRQL portions of the driver when you make everything paged. Second, be certain that no device interrupts will arrive while the driver's ISR is paged. Handling these details is left as an exercise for the reader.

5.3   DRIVER MEMORY ALLOCATION

Just like application programs, drivers may need to allocate temporary storage from time to time. Unfortunately, drivers don't have the luxury of making simple calls to **malloc** and **free**. Instead, they have to be extremely careful about what kind of memory they allocate and how much of it they use. Drivers must also be sure to release any memory they may be holding, since there's no automatic cleanup mechanism for kernel-mode code. This section describes techniques your driver can use to work with temporary storage.

Memory Available to Drivers

You have three options when you need to allocate temporary storage in a driver. Which one you select will depend on how long you plan to keep the data around and what IRQL level your code is running at. You can choose from the following:

- **Kernel stack** — The *kernel stack* provides limited amounts of nonpaged storage for local variables during the execution of specific driver routines.

- **Paged pool** — Driver routines running below DISPATCH_LEVEL, IRQL can use a heap area called *paged pool*. As its name implies, memory in this area is pageable, and a page fault can occur when you touch it.

- **Nonpaged pool** — Driver routines running at elevated IRQLs need to allocate temporary storage from another heap area called *nonpaged pool*. The system guarantees that the virtual memory in nonpaged pool is always physically resident. The Device and Controller Extensions created by the I/O Manager come from this pool area.

Global variables are absent from this list because they introduce major synchronization problems. The problem is that everyone using a given driver is sharing the same copy of the driver's code and global data. Since a driver might be processing multiple requests at the same time, the contents of unprotected global variables can become unpredictable.

Local **static** variables in a driver subroutine are just as bad. Don't try using them to maintain state information between calls to a function. There's no guarantee that two successive calls to a driver routine will be made in the context of the same I/O request.

After saying that, it's worth pointing out that global variables can be helpful for storing read-only parameters that affect the overall behavior the driver. For example, your DriverEntry routine might pull a value from the Registry that controlled the amount of detail you report to the error-log. Storing this value in a global variable is acceptable since it will essentially be constant for the life of the driver. You could use a similar strategy for turning the collection of driver performance data on and off.

Working with the Kernel Stack

On 80x86 and MIPS platforms, the kernel stack is only 12 kilobytes long. On Alpha and PowerPC systems, the size is 16 kilobytes. This isn't a lot of space, so be careful how you use the kernel stack. Dreadful things will happen if you run out of space. You can avoid kernel stack overflow by following these guidelines.

- Don't design your driver in such a way that internal routines need to make deeply-nested calls to one another. Try to keep the calling tree as flat as possible.

- If any of your routines call themselves recursively, make sure you limit the depth of recursion. Drivers are not the place to be calculating Fibonacci numbers.

- Don't build large temporary data structures on the kernel stack. Use one of the pool areas instead.

Another characteristic of the kernel stack is that it lives in cached memory. This means you shouldn't use temporary buffers on the stack for DMA operations. Instead, your driver should allocate the buffer from nonpaged pool. Chapter 12 will describe DMA caching issues in more detail.

Working with the Pool Areas

Remember that kernel-mode drivers can't allocate memory by making calls to **malloc**. Instead, they have to use the **ExAllocatePool** and **ExFreePool** functions. These functions allocate the following kinds of memory:

- **NonPagedPool** — Memory available to driver routines running at or above DISPATCH_LEVEL IRQL.

- **NonPagedPoolMustSucceed** — Temporary memory that is crucial to the driver's continuing operation. If the allocation fails, the system will bugcheck. Use this memory for emergencies only and release it as quickly as possible.

- **NonPagedPoolCacheAligned** — Memory that's guaranteed to be aligned on the natural boundary of a CPU data-cache line. A driver might use this kind of memory for a permanent I/O buffer.

- **NonPagedPoolCacheAlignedMustS** — Storage for a temporary I/O buffer that is crucial to the operation of the driver.

- **PagedPool** — Memory available only to driver routines running below DISPATCH_LEVEL IRQL. Normally, this includes the driver's initialization, cleanup, and Dispatch routines and any system threads the driver is using.

- **PagedPoolCacheAligned** — I/O buffer memory used by file system drivers.

There are several things to keep in mind when you're working with the system memory areas. First and foremost, the pools are precious system resources, and you shouldn't be too extravagant in their use. This is especially true of the NonPaged and MustSucceed pool areas.

Second, your driver must be executing at or below DISPATCH_LEVEL IRQL when you allocate or free nonpaged memory, and at or below APC_LEVEL IRQL to allocate or free paged pool.

Finally, release any memory you've allocated as soon as have finished using it. Otherwise, the system may start to perform badly because of low memory conditions. In particular, be very sure to give back any pool memory when your driver is unloaded.

System Support for Memory Suballocation

Generally, you should avoid driver designs that constantly allocate and release blocks of pool memory smaller than PAGE_SIZE bytes. This kind of behavior causes fragmentation of the pool areas and can make it impossible for other parts of NT to allocate memory. Instead, if your driver needs to create and destroy lots of little dynamic data structures, you should allocate a single, large chunk of pool and write your own suballocation routines to carve it up.

Some kinds of drivers need to manage a collection of small, fixed-size memory blocks. For example, SCSI class drivers maintain a supply of SCSI Request Blocks (SRBs) which they use repeatedly to send commands to any devices under their control. If your driver needs to do something similar, the system provides two different mechanisms you can use to handle all the details of suballocation.

Zone buffers   A *zone buffer* is just a chunk of driver-allocated pool. By calling various Executive routines, your driver can use the zone buffer to manage collections of fixed-size blocks in paged or nonpaged memory.

If you plan to access a zone buffer at or above DISPATCH_LEVEL IRQL, you must also set up an Executive spin lock to guard it and use the interlocked versions of the zone management functions. Zone buffers used only below

DISPATCH_LEVEL IRQL can be guarded with a Fast Mutex.[3] In this case, use the noninterlocked set of functions.

To set up a zone buffer, you must declare a structure of type ZONE_HEADER. You may also need to declare and initialize a spin lock or Fast Mutex object. Then follow these steps to manage the zone buffer.

1. Call **ExAllocatePool** to claim space for the zone buffer itself. Then initialize the zone buffer with **ExInitializeZone**. Both these steps are normally performed in your DriverEntry routine.

2. To allocate a block from a zone, call either **ExAllocateFromZone** or **ExInterlockedAllocateFromZone**. The interlocked version of the function uses a spin lock to synchronize access to the zone buffer. The noninterlocked function leaves synchronization entirely up to your driver.

3. To release a block back to the zone, use either **ExFreeToZone** or **ExInterlockedFreeToZone**. Again, the interlocked version of the function synchronizes access to the zone, while the noninterlocked version does not.

4. In your driver Unload routine, use **ExFreePool** to release the memory used for the zone buffer. Your driver has to make sure that no blocks from the zone buffer are in use when you deallocate the zone buffer.

Zone buffers that are too large put a strain on the system's memory resources, so don't make a zone buffer any bigger than necessary. Try to pick a size that will allow your driver to handle the I/O demand level you expect on an average system. This is a more system-friendly approach than making the zone buffer big enough to handle the worst possible case.

If you're feeling really clever, you can try to base the size of your zone buffer on the characteristics of the local system. **MmQuerySystemSize** will give you a hint about the total amount of memory available. Systems with more memory can support larger zone buffers. **MmIsThisAnNtAsSystem** will tell you whether your driver is running under Windows NT Workstation or Server. Servers are likely to have more memory and higher I/O demand levels. Calling these functions in your DriverEntry routine may help you pick an appropriate zone buffer size.

If you try to allocate a block from a zone buffer and the allocation fails, your driver should use **ExAllocatePool** (or **ExAllocatePoolWithTag**) to get the block from one of the pool areas instead. To use this strategy, you'll need some kind of flag bit in the allocated structure to indicate whether it came from the zone buffer or from the general pool; otherwise you won't know what function to call when you want to release the block.

---

[3] Spin locks are described later in this chapter. Fast Mutexes show up in Chapter 14.

You can make an existing zone buffer larger by calling **ExExtendZone** or **ExInterlockedExtendZone**, but this is generally a bad thing to do. If you enlarge a zone buffer this way, the additional memory that the system gives to the zone will not be reclaimed until the next bootstrap. Don't do this unless the performance gains from using zone allocation (compared to repeated **ExAllocatePool** calls) significantly outweigh the damage it does to the system.

Lookaside lists   Windows NT 4.0 provides a more efficient mechanism called a *lookaside list* for managing driver-allocated memory. A lookaside list is a linked list of fixed size memory blocks. Unlike zone buffers, lookaside lists can grow and shrink dynamically in response to changing system conditions. Therefore, properly-sized lookaside lists are less likely to waste memory than zone buffers are.

Compared to zone buffers, the synchronization mechanism used with lookaside lists is also more efficient. If the CPU architecture has an 8-byte compare exchange instruction, the Executive uses it to guard access to the list. On platforms without such an instruction, it reverts to using a spin lock for lookaside lists in nonpaged pool and a Fast Mutex for lists in paged pool. Since most common platforms do have the necessary compare exchange instruction, lookaside lists have lower synchronization latency than zone buffers.

To use a lookaside list, you need to declare a header structure of type NPAGED_LOOKASIDE_LIST or PAGED_LOOKASIDE_LIST (depending on whether your list will be nonpaged or paged). Then follow these steps to manage the lookaside list.

1. Use one of the **ExInitializeXxxLookasideList** functions to initialize the list header structure.[4] Normally, this is done in you DriverEntry routine.

2. Call **ExAllocateFromXxxLookasideList** to allocate a block from a lookaside list.

3. Call **ExFreeToXxxLookasideList** when you want to release a block.

4. Use **ExDeleteXxxLookasideList** to release any resources associated with the lookaside list. Usually, this is something you do in the driver's Unload routine.

The operation of lookaside lists is rather interesting and deserves a little attention. For starters, the **ExInitializeXxxLookasideList** functions just set up the list header; they don't actually allocate any memory for the list. When you call one of these initialization functions, you can specify the maximum number of blocks that the list can hold. (This is referred to as the depth of the list.) You can

---

[4] In this series of instructions, replace the Xxx in the function name with either **NPaged** or **Paged**, depending on the location of the list.

also pass pointers to memory allocation and deallocation routines in your driver. The system will call these functions when it needs to add or remove memory from the list.[5]

Later, when you call one of the **ExAllocateFromXxxLookasideList** functions, the system allocates memory as needed. As you release blocks with **ExFreeToXxxLookasideList**, they are added to the lookaside list until it reaches its maximum allowable depth. At that point, any additional calls to **ExFreeToXxxLookasideList** result in memory being released back to the system. This behavior guarantees that, after awhile, the number of available blocks in the lookaside list will tend to remain near the depth of the list.

You should choose the depth value very carefully. If it's too shallow, the system will be performing expensive allocation and deallocation operations too often. If it's too deep, you'll be wasting memory by tying it up in the list and not using it. The statistics maintained in the list header structure can help you determine a proper value for the depth of the list.

5.4 UNICODE STRINGS

All character strings in the NT operating system are stored internally as Unicode. The Unicode scheme uses 16 bits to represent each character and makes it easier to move NT to language environments not based on the Latin alphabet. Unless otherwise noted, any character strings your driver sends to or receives from NT will be Unicode.[6]

Unicode String Datatypes

When you're working with Unicode, remember to do the following:

- Prefix Unicode string constants with the letter **L** to let the compiler know you want wide characters. For example, L"some text" generates Unicode text, whereas "some text" produces 8-bit ANSI.

- Use the WCHAR data type for Unicode characters and PWSTR to point to an array of Unicode characters.

- Use the constant UNICODE_NULL to terminate a Unicode string.

Many NT system routines work with counted Unicode strings described by a UNICODE_STRING structure (see Table 5.2 for the contents).

---

[5] If you don't pass the addresses of driver-defined memory management functions, the system uses **ExAllocatePoolWithTag** and **ExFreePool** by default.

[6] Note that this does *not* include data passed between a user's buffer and a device — unless the device specifically works with Unicode.

Table 5.2   This structure defines the basic string object used by drivers

UNICODE_STRING, *PUNICODE_STRING

Field	Contents
USHORT Length	Current string length, in bytes
USHORT MaximumLength	Maximum string length, in bytes
PWSTR Buffer	Address of driver-allocated buffer holding the string

It's up to you to allocate memory for the string buffer itself. If the **Buffer** field points to a NULL-terminated string, the **Length** field does *not* include the NULL character. Notice that the two length fields in the UNICODE_STRING structure specify a count in *bytes*, not *characters*.

Working with Unicode

The NT runtime library provides a number of functions for working with ANSI and Unicode strings. Table 5.3 presents a few of them. See the documentation for a complete list. Some of these functions have restrictions on the IRQL levels from which they can be called, so be careful when you're using them.

If you've never worked with Unicode before, you may have some programming habits that will cause you problems. Most of them result from

Table 5.3   The NT runtime library provides these Unicode manipulation functions

Unicode string manipulation functions

Function	Description
RtlInitUnicodeString	Initializes a UNICODE_STRING from a NULL-terminated Unicode string
RtlAnsiStringToUnicodeSize	Calculates number of bytes required to hold a converted ANSI string
RtlAnsiStringToUnicodeString	Converts ANSI string to Unicode
RtlIntegerToUnicodeString	Converts an integer to Unicode text
RtlAppendUnicodeStringToString	Concatenates two Unicode strings
RtlCopyUnicodeString	Copies a source string to a destination
RtlUpcaseUnicodeString	Converts Unicode string to uppercase
RtlCompareUnicodeString	Compares two Unicode strings
RtlEqualUnicodeString	Tests equality of two Unicode strings

making the assumption that a character and a byte are the same size. Watch out for the following when you start working with Unicode:

- Remember that the number of characters in a Unicode string is not the same as the number of bytes. Be very careful about any arithmetic you do that calculates the length of a Unicode string.

- Don't assume anything about the collating sequence of the characters or the relationship of upper- and lowercase characters.

- Don't assume that a table with 256 entries is large enough to hold the entire character set.

5.5   INTERRUPT SYNCHRONIZATION

Writing code that executes at multiple IRQL levels requires some attention to proper synchronization. This section examines the issues that arise in this kind of environment.

The Problem

If code executing at two different IRQLs attempts to access the same data structure simultaneously, the structure can be corrupted. Figure 5.1 illustrates the details of this synchronization problem.

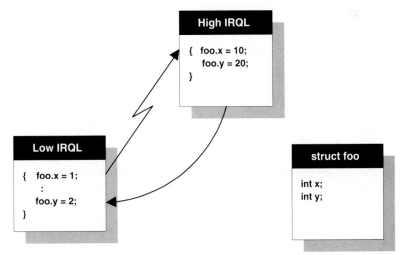

Figure 5.1   Data structures can be corrupted by unsynchronized access

To see the exact problem, consider this sequence of events:

1. Imagine that some piece of code executing at a low IRQL decides to modify several fields in the **foo** data structure. It gets as far as setting the field **foo.x** to 1.

2. Suddenly an interrupt occurs, and a higher-IRQL piece of code gets control of the CPU. This code also decides to modify **foo**, and it sets **foo.x** to 10 and **foo.y** to 20.

3. The higher-IRQL code dismisses its interrupt, and control returns to the lower IRQL routine which finishes its modifications to **foo** by setting **foo.y** to 2. The lower-IRQL code is completely unaware that it was interrupted.

4. The **foo** structure is now corrupted, with 10 in **x** and 2 in **y**.

In the following sections, you'll see some techniques your driver can use to avoid these kinds of collisions.

Interrupt Blocking

In the previous example, the lower-IRQL routine could have avoided these synchronization problems by preventing itself from being interrupted. It can do this by temporarily raising the IRQL of the CPU and then lowering it back to its initial level after completing the modification. This technique is called *interrupt blocking*. If you look at Table 5.4, you'll see the Kernel functions that your driver can use to manipulate a CPU's IRQL value.

Rules for Blocking Interrupts

If you plan to use any of these functions to block interrupts, there are certain rules you need to follow:

- Every piece of code touching a protected data structure has to agree on the IRQL to use for synchronization and must only touch the structure when it's running at the chosen IRQL.

Table 5.4   These Kernel functions control the CPU's IRQL level

Interrupt Blocking Functions

Function	Description
KeRaiseIrql	Changes the CPU IRQL to a specified value, blocking interrupts at or below that IRQL level
KeLowerIrql	Lowers the CPU IRQL value
KeGetCurrentIrql	Returns the IRQL value of the CPU on which this call is made

- Drivers using this technique shouldn't spend too much time at the elevated IRQL level. Depending on the blocking level, this can have a negative impact on NT's ability to service other interrupts quickly.

- Although your driver can raise the CPU's IRQL to a higher level and reduce it back to its previous value, you must never drop the CPU's IRQL below the level where you found it. Disobeying this rule will compromise the entire interrupt priority mechanism.

5.6   SYNCHRONIZING MULTIPLE CPUs

But everything is not yet safe. Modifying the IRQL of one CPU has no affect on other CPUs in a multiprocessor system. Consequently, IRQLs provide only local protection to shared data. To prevent corruption of data structures accessed by multiple CPUs, NT uses synchronization objects called *spin locks*.

How Spin Locks Work

A spin lock is simply a mutual-exclusion object that you associate with a specific group of data structures. When a piece of kernel-mode code wants to touch any of the guarded data structures, it must first request ownership of the associated spin lock. Since only one CPU at a time can own the spin lock, the data structure is safe from collisions. Any CPU requesting an already-owned spin lock will busy-wait until the spin lock becomes available. Look at Figure 5.2 to see how this works.

A given spin lock is always acquired and released at a specific IRQL level. This has the effect of blocking potentially dangerous interrupts on the local CPU and preventing the synchronization problems we saw in the last section. While a CPU is waiting for a spin lock, all activity at or below the IRQL of the spin lock is blocked on that CPU. Once the IRQL level has been raised, the CPU can request ownership of the spin lock, which will guarantee protection against other CPUs. Fortunately, all these details are hidden inside the Kernel's spin lock routines.

Using Spin Locks

There are two major kinds of spin locks provided by the Kernel. They are distinguished by the IRQL level at which you use them.

- **Interrupt spin locks** — These synchronize access to driver data structures shared by multiple driver routines. Interrupt spin locks are acquired at the DIRQL associated with the device.

- **Executive spin locks** — These guard various operating system data structures and their associated IRQL is DISPATCH_LEVEL.

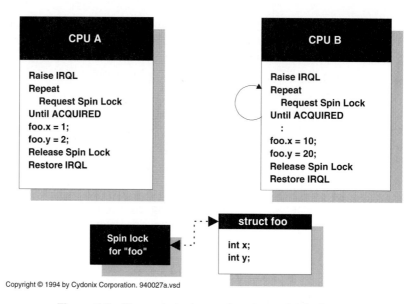

Figure 5.2 How spin locks synchronize multiple CPUs

When your driver uses Interrupt spin locks, most of the work happens behind the scenes. When we look at **KeSynchronizeExecution** in Chapter 9, you'll see the exact details.

Executive spin locks are another story. When you use them, you'll need to follow these steps:

1. Decide what data items you need to guard and how many spin locks to use. The tradeoff is that a larger number of spin locks may allow more of your driver to run in parallel, but it increases the chance of deadlocking if you need to acquire multiple locks at the same time.

2. Declare a data item of type KSPIN_LOCK for each lock. Storage for the spin lock must be permanently resident. Usually, you store spin locks in the Device or Controller Extension.

3. Initialize the spin lock once by calling **KeInitializeSpinLock**. You can call this function from any IRQL level, though most often you set up all your spin locks in the DriverEntry routine.

4. Call **KeAcquireSpinLock** before you touch any resource guarded by a spin lock. This function raises IRQL to DISPATCH_LEVEL, acquires the spin lock, and returns the previous IRQL value to you. To call this function, you must be at or below DISPATCH_LEVEL IRQL. If you're already running at DIS-PATCH_LEVEL, you can save some work by calling **KeAcquireSpinLockAt-DpcLevel** instead.

5.   When you've finished using the protected resource, call the **KeRelease-SpinLock** function to let go of the lock. You call this function from DIS-PATCH_LEVEL IRQL and it restores IRQL to its previous value. If you were already at DISPATCH_LEVEL when you acquired the lock, you can save some work by calling **KeReleaseSpinLockFromDpcLevel**, which releases the lock but doesn't change IRQL.

Some other driver support routines (like the interlocked lists and queues described in the next section) use Executive spin locks for protection. In these cases, your only responsibility is to initialize the spin lock object. The routines that manage the interlocked object will acquire and release the spin lock itself on your behalf.

Rules for Using Spin Locks

Spin locks aren't terribly difficult to use, but you do have to keep a few things in mind when you're working with them:

- Be sure to release a spin lock as quickly as possible, because while you're holding it, you may be blocking all activity on other CPUs. The official recommendation is not to hold a spin lock for more than about 25 microseconds.

- Don't cause any hardware or software exceptions while you're holding a spin lock. This is a sure way to crash the system.

- Don't try to access any paged code or data while you're holding a spin lock. This may result in a page fault exception, which is another quick way to crash the system.

- Don't try to acquire a spin lock that your CPU already owns. This will lead to a deadlock situation where the CPU freezes up waiting for itself to release the spin lock.

- Avoid driver designs that depend on holding multiple spin locks at the same time. Unless you're careful, this can also lead to deadlocks. If you must use multiple spin locks, be sure that everyone agrees to acquire them in a fixed order and release them in reverse order.

- Don't call any routines that violate the above rules.

5.7   LINKED LISTS

Drivers sometimes need to maintain various kinds of linked lists. You'll see examples of this in later chapters. The following subsections describe the support available from NT for managing singly- and doubly-linked lists.

Singly-Linked Lists

To use singly-linked lists, begin by declaring a list head of type **SINGLE_LIST_ENTRY**. This is also the data type of the link pointer itself. You need to initialize the list by setting the head to NULL, as demonstrated in the following code fragment.

```
typedef struct _DEVICE_EXTENSION {
    :
SINGLE_LIST_ENTRY listHead; // Declare head pointer
} DEVICE_EXTENSION, *PDEVICE_EXTENSION
    :
pDevExt->listHead.Next = NULL; // Initialize the list
```

To add or remove entries from the front of the list, call **PushEntryList** and **PopEntryList**. Depending on how you're using the list, the actual entries can be in either paged or nonpaged memory. Just remember that these functions don't perform any synchronization of their own.

NT also provides convenient support for singly-linked lists guarded by an Executive spin lock. This kind of protection is important if you're sharing a linked list among driver routines running at or below DISPATCH_LEVEL IRQL. To use one of these lists, set up the list head in the usual way, and then initialize an Executive spin lock that will guard the list.

```
typedef struct _DEVICE_EXTENSION {
    :
SINGLE_LIST_ENTRY listHead; // Declare head pointer
KSPIN_LOCK listLock;  // and the lock
} DEVICE_EXTENSION, *PDEVICE_EXTENSION
    :
KeInitializeSpinLock( &pDevExt->listLock );
pDevExt->listHead.Next = NULL;
```

You pass a pointer to this spin lock as an explicit argument to **ExInterlockedPushEntryList** and **ExInterlockedPopEntryList**. To make these interlocked calls, you must be running at or below DISPATCH_LEVEL IRQL. The list entries themselves must reside in nonpaged memory, since the system will be linking and unlinking them from DISPATCH_LEVEL IRQL.

Doubly-Linked Lists

To use doubly-linked lists, declare a list head of type LIST_ENTRY. This is also the data type of the link pointer itself. You need to initialize the list head, as demonstrated in the following code fragment.

```
typedef struct _DEVICE_EXTENSION {
      :
LIST_ENTRY listHead;   // Declare head pointer
} DEVICE_EXTENSION, *PDEVICE_EXTENSION
      :
InitializeListHead( &pDevExt->listHead );
```

To add entries to the list, call **InsertHeadList** or **InsertTailList**, and to pull entries out, call **RemoveHeadList** or **RemoveTailList**. You can determine if there's anything in a list by calling IsListEmpty. Again, the entries can be paged or nonpaged, but these functions don't perform any synchronization.

Not surprisingly, NT supports interlocked doubly-linked lists. To use these, set up the list head in the usual way, and then initialize an Executive spin lock that will guard the list.

```
typedef struct _DEVICE_EXTENSION {
      :
LIST_ENTRY listHead;   // Declare head pointer
KSPIN_LOCK listLock;   // and the lock
} DEVICE_EXTENSION, *PDEVICE_EXTENSION
      :
KeInitializeSpinLock( &pDevExt->listLock );
InitializeListHead( &pDevExt->listHead );
```

You pass this spin lock in calls to **ExInterlockedInsertTailList**, **ExInterlockedInsertHeadList**, and **ExInterlockedRemoveHeadList**. To make these interlocked calls, you must be running at or below DISPATCH_LEVEL IRQL. Just like their singly-linked cousins, entries for doubly-linked interlocked lists have to live in nonpaged memory.

Removing Blocks from a List

When you pull a block out of a list, what the system gives you is a pointer to the LIST_ENTRY or SINGLE_LIST_ENTRY structure within the block. What you probably want is the address of the block itself. If the XXX_LIST_ENTRY structure is at the top of the block, everything is easy. If it's buried in the block somewhere, you need to do a little arithmetic to get the address of the containing structure. Fortunately, NT provides a macro to make this easier. See Table 5.5 for the details.

The following code fragment shows how to use this macro. It assumes you're using the **Tail.Overlay.ListEntry** field of an IRP to maintain your own linked list of IRPs, and that the **listHead** field of your Device Extension points to the beginning of this list.

Table 5.5   CONTAINING_RECORD macro arguments

CONTAINING_RECORD

Parameter	Description
Address	Address of a field within a data structure
Type	The data type of the structure
Field	Field in structure pointed at by the Address argument
Return value	Base address of structure containing Field

```
PIRP pIrp;
PLIST_ENTRY pEntry;

pEntry = RemoveHeadList( &pDevExt->listHead );
pIrp = CONTAINING_RECORD( pEntry, IRP,
                    Tail.Overlay.ListEntry );
```

5.8   SUMMARY

In this chapter we've looked at some general guidelines for designing and coding your driver. We've also covered a number of basic techniques that will show up again and again throughout this book.

This is all just foundation material for the work ahead. In the next chapter, we'll start to implement some actual driver routines.

Initialization and Cleanup Routines

*E*verything has to start somewhere. In the case of an NT kernel-mode driver, the starting point is a function called DriverEntry. This chapter will show you how to write a DriverEntry routine along with various other pieces of initialization and cleanup code. By the time you finish this chapter, you'll be able to write a minimal driver that you can actually load into the system.

6.1 WRITING A DRIVERENTRY ROUTINE

Every NT kernel-mode driver, regardless of its purpose, has to expose a routine whose name is **DriverEntry**. This routine initializes various driver data structures and prepares the environment for all the other driver components.

Execution Context

The I/O Manager calls your DriverEntry routine once when it loads your driver. As you can see from Table 6.1, the DriverEntry routine runs at PASSIVE_LEVEL IRQL, which means it has access to paged system resources.

The DriverEntry routine receives a pointer to its own Driver object, which it must initialize. It also gets a UNICODE_STRING containing the path to the driver's service key in the Registry. This string takes the form, **HKEY_LOCAL_MA-**

Table 6.1   Function prototype for a DriverEntry routine

NTSTATUS DriverEntry	IRQL == PASSIVE_LEVEL
Parameter	**Description**
IN PDRIVER_OBJECT DriverObject	Driver object for this driver
IN PUNICODE_STRING RegistryPath	Registry path string for this driver's key
Return value	• STATUS_SUCCESS — success
	• STATUS_XXX — some error code

CHINE\System\CurrentControlSet\Services*DriverName*, and **DriverEntry** can use it to extract any driver-specific parameters stored in the Registry.[1]

What a DriverEntry Routine Does

Although the exact details will vary slightly from driver to driver, in general you should perform the following steps in your DriverEntry routine.

1. If you're writing a device driver, start by finding and allocating any hardware that the driver is supposed to manage.

2. Initialize the Driver object with pointers to other driver entry points.

3. If your driver manages a multiunit controller, call **IoCreateController** to create a Controller object and then initialize its Controller Extension.

4. Call **IoCreateDevice** to create a Device object and then initialize its Device Extension.

5. Make the device visible to the Win32 subsystem by calling **IoCreateSymbolic-Link**.

6. Connect the device to an Interrupt object and initialize any DPC objects needed by the driver.

7. Repeat steps 3–6 for all controllers and devices that belong to your driver.

8. Return STATUS_SUCCESS to the I/O Manager.

If you run into problems during initialization, your DriverEntry routine should release any system resources it may have allocated and return an appropriate NTSTATUS failure code to the I/O Manager.

The following sections describe some of these steps in greater detail. The process of finding and allocating hardware is complex enough that it needs to

---

[1] Chapter 7 explains how to extract these parameters from a driver's service key.

wait until the next chapter. We'll also have to postpone the discussion of interrupt processing and DPCs until we look at data transfer routines in Chapter 9.

Initializing DriverEntry Points

The I/O Manager is able to locate the DriverEntry routine because it has a well-known name. Other driver routines don't have fixed names, so the I/O Manager needs some other way to find them. It does this by looking in the Driver object for pointers to specific functions. Your DriverEntry routine is responsible for setting up these function pointers.

These function pointers fall into two categories:

- Functions with explicit slots in the Driver object.

- IRP Dispatch functions that are listed in the Driver object's **MajorFunction** array. These are discussed in more detail in Chapter 8.

The following code fragment shows how a DriverEntry routine initializes both kinds of function pointers.

```
pDO->DriverStartIo = XxStartIo;
pDO->DriverUnload = XxUnload;
//
// Initialize the function dispatch array
//
pDO->MajorFunction[ IRP_MJ_CREATE ] = XxDispatchCreate;
  :
pDO->MajorFunction[ IRP_MJ_CLOSE ] = XxDispatchClose;
  :
```

Creating Device Objects

Once you've found and allocated all your hardware, you need to create a Device object for each physical or virtual device you want to expose to the rest of the system. Most of the work is done by the **IoCreateDevice** function, which takes a description of your device and returns a Device object, complete with an attached Device Extension. **IoCreateDevice** also links the new Device object into the list of devices managed by this Driver object. Table 6.2 contains a description of this function.

Take a look at the **NTDDK.H** header file to see the standard definitions for the DeviceType argument. Try to choose a value that's as close as possible to your device.

If you truly believe your nuclear-powered laser retroscope is unlike any existing device, you can define a private device type value. Just remember that Microsoft reserves values in the range 0–32767 and leaves numbers between 32768 and 65535 for you. They also leave the bookkeeping up to you, so there's no

Table 6.2   Function prototype for IoCreateDevice

NTSTATUS IoCreateDevice	IRQL == PASSIVE_LEVEL
Parameter	**Description**
IN PDRIVER_OBJECT DriverObject	Pointer to Driver object
IN ULONG DeviceExtensionSize	Desired size of Device Extension in bytes
IN PUNICODE_STRING DeviceName	NT device name (see below)
IN DEVICE_TYPE DeviceType	FILE_DEVICE_XXX (see NTDDK.H)
IN ULONG DeviceCharacteristics	Characteristics for mass-storage device
	• FILE_REMOVABLE_MEDIA
	• FILE_READ_ONLY_DEVICE
	• FILE_FLOPPY_DISKETTE
	• FILE_WRITE_ONCE_MEDIA
	• FILE_REMOTE_DEVICE
IN BOOLEAN Exclusive	TRUE if device is nonshareable
OUT PDEVICE_OBJECT *DeviceObject	Variable that receives Device object
Return value	• STATUS_SUCCESS — success
	• STATUS_XXX — some failure code

guarantee that the number you choose for your retroscope won't be used by some other driver to refer to its microwave popcorn warmer.

One final point about creating Device objects. Although the vast majority of drivers call **IoCreateDevice** from their DriverEntry routines, it is possible to make this call from a Dispatch routine instead. For example, a driver that managed pseudo-devices could use this technique to dynamically create Device objects in response to a driver-defined **DeviceIoControl** request.

If you do create Device objects somewhere other than in your DriverEntry routine, you have to reset the DO_DEVICE_INITIALIZING bit in the **Flags** field of the object. In the normal course of events, the I/O Manager automatically resets this bit for a driver's Device objects when the DriverEntry routine is finished. Until this bit is cleared, the Device object can't be used, and **CreateFile** calls referencing it will fail. The following code fragment shows what you need to do.

```
pDevObj->Flags &= ~DO_DEVICE_INITIALIZING;
```

Don't clear this bit until the Device object is actually initialized and ready to process requests.

Choosing a Buffering Strategy

If the **IoCreateDevice** call succeeds, you need to let the I/O Manager know whether you want to do Buffered or Direct I/O with this device. You make this choice by ORing one of the following bits into the **Flags** field of the new Device object.[2]:

- **DO_BUFFERED_IO** — If you want the I/O Manager to copy data back and forth between user and system-space buffers.

- **DO_DIRECT_IO** — If you want the I/O Manager to lock user buffers into physical memory for the duration of an I/O, and build a descriptor list of the pages in the buffer.

Chapter 8 will explain how to work with user buffers in both of these cases. If you don't set either of these bits, the I/O Manager will assume that you're handling everything yourself. Making user data available to a driver is a nasty process, so it's best to let the I/O Manager do the work for you.

NT and Win32 Device Names

Just like T.S. Elliot's cats, NT devices have more than one name. The one you specify to **IoCreateDevice** is the name by which the device is known to the NT Executive itself. If you want to make the device available to the Win32 subsystem, the Win16 subsystem, and virtual DOS machines, you have to give the device a DOS name as well.

These two types of names live in different parts of the Object Manager's namespace. You'll find NT device names dangling beneath the **\Device** section of the tree, while the Win32 name appears beneath the **\DosDevices** area. Notice that the DOS name is actually a symbolic link that connects it to the NT device. Figure 6.1 illustrates this relationship.

Also notice that NT and DOS follow different device naming conventions. NT device names tend to be longer, and they always end in a zero-based number (FloppyDisk0, FloppyDisk1, etc). DOS devices follow the usual pattern of A through Z for file-system devices, and names ending in a one-based number for any other devices (LPT1, LPT2, etc).

6.2   CODE EXAMPLE: DRIVER INITIALIZATION

This example shows how a basic device driver initializes itself. You can find the code for this example in the **CH06** directory on the disk that accompanies this book.

---

[2] Make sure you use a logical OR to set the **Flags** field of the Device object. The I/O Manager uses other bits in this field to synchronize its own operation, and if you accidentally clear some of them, bad things will happen.

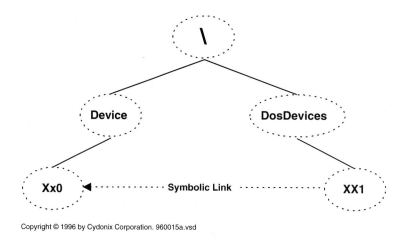

Copyright © 1996 by Cydonix Corporation. 960015a.vsd

Figure 6.1   NT and Win32 device names in the Object Manager's namespace

INIT.C

The functions in this module perform all the essential setup tasks needed to manage one or more physical devices. Although the code supports multiple devices, it assumes they are all on separate controllers, so it doesn't create any Controller objects.

DriverEntry   This particular implementation isn't very forgiving of initialization errors. If anything fails along the way, the whole driver refuses to load. A real driver might take a more flexible approach.

```
//
// Header files...
//
#include "xxdriver.h"❶

//
// Forward declarations of local functions
//
static NTSTATUS
XxCreateDevice (
        IN PDRIVER_OBJECT DriverObject,
        IN INTERFACE_TYPE BusType,
        IN ULONG BusNumber,
        IN PDEVICE_BLOCK DeviceBlock,
        IN ULONG NtDeviceNumber
        );

//
// If the platform can handle it, make the DriverEntry
```

```
// routine discardable, so that it doesn't waste space
//
#ifdef ALLOC_PRAGMA
#pragma alloc_text( init, DriverEntry )❷
#pragma alloc_text( init, XxCreateDevice )
#endif

//++
// Function:
//          DriverEntry
//
// Description:
//          This function initializes the driver, locates
//          and claims hardware resources, and creates
//          various NT objects needed to process I/O
//          requests.
//
// Arguments:
//          Pointer to the Driver object
//          Registry path string for driver service key
//
// Return Value:
//          NTSTATUS signaling success or failure
//--
NTSTATUS
DriverEntry(
        IN PDRIVER_OBJECT DriverObject,
        IN PUNICODE_STRING RegistryPath
        )
{
        PCONFIG_ARRAY ConfigList; ❸
        PCONFIG_ARRAY ConfigArray;
        ULONG NtDeviceNumber;
        NTSTATUS status;
        ULONG i;

        //
        // Load up the Config list...
        //
        status = XxGetHardwareInfo( ❹
                    RegistryPath,
                    &ConfigList );
        if( !NT_SUCCESS( status ))
        {
                return status;
        }
```

```
//
// Allocate the hardware...
//
status = XxReportHardwareUsage(
            DriverObject,
            ConfigList );
if( !NT_SUCCESS( status ))
{
      XxReleaseHardwareInfo( ConfigList );
      return status;
}

//
// Export other driver entry points...
//
DriverObject->DriverUnload = XxDriverUnload;

DriverObject->MajorFunction[ IRP_MJ_CREATE ] =
      XxDispatchOpen;
DriverObject->MajorFunction[ IRP_MJ_CLOSE ] =
      XxDispatchClose;
DriverObject->MajorFunction[ IRP_MJ_WRITE ] =
      XxDispatchWrite;
DriverObject->MajorFunction[ IRP_MJ_READ ] =
      XxDispatchRead;

//
// Initialize a Device object for each piece
// of hardware we've found
//
ConfigArray = ConfigList;
NtDeviceNumber = 0;

while( ConfigArray != NULL )
{
      for( i = 0;
          i < ConfigArray->Count;
          i++ )

      {

      status = XxCreateDevice(
                  DriverObject,
                  ConfigArray->BusType,
                  ConfigArray->BusNumber,
                  &ConfigArray->Device[i],
                  NtDeviceNumber );
          if( !NT_SUCCESS( status )) break;
```

```
                        NtDeviceNumber++;
                        }
                    if( !NT_SUCCESS( status )) break;
                    //
                    // Get next array in the chain
                    //
                    ConfigArray = ConfigArray->NextConfigArray;
            }
            if( !NT_SUCCESS( status ))
            {
                    XxReleaseHardware( DriverObject );
            }

            XxReleaseHardwareInfo( ConfigList );

            return status;
    }
```

❶ This header includes both the system-supplied **NTDDK.H** and our private **HARDWARE.H** file. It also contains definitions of any driver-defined structures.

❷ NT will discard these routines after DriverEntry executes. You should also include any functions called only by the DriverEntry routine. Do *not* discard any code needed after driver initialization.

❸ The Config list is a driver-defined data structure that will follow us through the DriverEntry routine. It holds information about any hardware that this driver manages. Chapter 7 will show you how to use this structure.

❹ We'll see this routine in the next chapter. It uses one of two techniques to locate any hardware this driver is responsible for and put a description of that hardware into the Config list.

XxCreateDevice   This is a helper function that does all the grunt work. It creates and initializes a single Device object using one of the hardware descriptions in the Config list.

```
static NTSTATUS
XxCreateDevice (
        IN PDRIVER_OBJECT DriverObject,
        IN INTERFACE_TYPE BusType,
        IN ULONG BusNumber,
        IN PDEVICE_BLOCK DeviceBlock,
        IN ULONG NtDeviceNumber
        )
{
```

```
NTSTATUS status;

PDEVICE_OBJECT pDevObj;
PDEVICE_EXTENSION pDevExt;

UNICODE_STRING deviceName;
WCHAR deviceNameBuffer[ XX_MAX_NAME_LENGTH ];

UNICODE_STRING linkName;
WCHAR linkNameBuffer[ XX_MAX_NAME_LENGTH ];

UNICODE_STRING number;
WCHAR numberBuffer[10];

number.Buffer = numberBuffer;
number.MaximumLength = 10;

//
// Form the base NT device name...
//
deviceName.Buffer = deviceNameBuffer;
deviceName.MaximumLength = XX_MAX_NAME_LENGTH;
deviceName.Length = 0;
RtlAppendUnicodeToString(
      &deviceName,
      XX_NT_DEVICE_NAME );

//
// Convert the device number into a string and
// attach it to the end of the device name.
//
number.Length = 0;
RtlIntegerToUnicodeString(
      NtDeviceNumber,
      10,
      &number );
RtlAppendUnicodeStringToString(
      &deviceName,
      &number );

//
// Create a Device object for this device...
//
status = IoCreateDevice(
            DriverObject,
            sizeof( DEVICE_EXTENSION ),
            &deviceName,
            FILE_DEVICE_UNKNOWN,  ❶
            0,
```

```
                    TRUE,
                    &pDevObj );
        if( !NT_SUCCESS( status ))
        {
             return status;
        }
        pDevObj->Flags |= DO_BUFFERED_IO; ❷
        //
        // Initialize the Device Extension
        //
        pDevExt = pDevObj->DeviceExtension;
        pDevExt->DeviceObject = pDevObj;
        pDevExt->NtDeviceNumber = NtDeviceNumber;

        //
        // Copy things from Device Block ❸
        //
        pDevExt->PortBase = DeviceBlock->PortBase;

        //
        // Prepare a DPC object for later use
        //
        IoInitializeDpcRequest(
             pDevObj,
             XxDpcForIsr );

        //
        // Form the Win32 symbolic link name.
        //
        linkName.Buffer = linkNameBuffer;
        linkName.MaximumLength = XX_MAX_NAME_LENGTH;
        linkName.Length = 0;
        RtlAppendUnicodeToString(
             &linkName,
             XX_WIN32_DEVICE_NAME );
        //
        // Reset the number string and do another
        // conversion. Win32 device numbers are
        // one greater than the NT equivalent.
        //
        number.Length = 0;
        RtlIntegerToUnicodeString(
             NtDeviceNumber + 1,
             10,
             &number );
```

```
RtlAppendUnicodeStringToString(
    &linkName,
    &number );
//
// Create a symbolic link so our device is
// visible to Win32...
//
status = IoCreateSymbolicLink(
        &linkName,
        &deviceName );
//
// See if the symbolic link was created...
//
if( !NT_SUCCESS( status ))
{
    IoDeleteDevice( pDevObj );
    return status;
}
//
// Make sure device interrupts are OFF
//
XxDisableInterrupts( pDevExt );
//
// Connect to an Interrupt object... ❹
//
status =
    IoConnectInterrupt(
        &pDevExt->pInterrupt,
        XxIsr,
        pDevExt,
        NULL,
        DeviceBlock->SystemVector,
        DeviceBlock->Dirql,
        DeviceBlock->Dirql,
        DeviceBlock->InterruptMode,
        DeviceBlock->ShareVector,
        DeviceBlock->Affinity,
        DeviceBlock->FloatingSave );
if( !NT_SUCCESS( status ))
{
    IoDeleteSymbolicLink( &linkName );
    IoDeleteDevice( pDevObj );
    return status;
}
```

```
        //
        // Initialize the hardware and enable interrupts
        //
        KeSynchronizeExecution(
                pDevExt->pInterrupt,
                XxInitDevice,
                pDevExt );

        return status;
    }
```

❶ Choose a FILE_DEVICE_XXX value that's as close as possible to the type of device your driver manages.

❷ Select an I/O method for data transfer operations. In this case, we'll let the I/O Manager copy things to and from user space for us.

❸ The Config list will be going away soon, so we need to move anything important into the Device Extension. At the least, this includes the control register base address; for DMA devices it would also include the Adapter object pointer and count of mapping registers. More on this in Chapter 12.

❹ Chapters 7 and 9 will explain more about interrupt processing.

6.3   WRITING REINITIALIZE ROUTINES

Intermediate-level drivers loading at system boot time may need to delay their initialization until one or more lower-level drivers have finished loading. If all the drivers belong to you, you can determine their load sequence by setting various Registry entries at installation. But if you don't own all the underlying drivers, your intermediate driver will need a Reinitialize routine.

Execution Context

If your DriverEntry routine discovers that it can't finish its initialization because system bootstrapping hasn't yet gone far enough, it can register a Reinitialize routine by calling **IoRegisterDriverReinitialization**. The I/O Manager will call the Reinitialize routine at some later point during the bootstrap.

As you can see from Table 6.3, the Reinitalize routine runs at PASSIVE_LEVEL IRQL, which means it has access to paged system resources. Reinitialize routines are useful only for drivers that load automatically at system boot.

What a Reinitialize Routine Does

The Reinitialize routine can perform any driver initialization that the Driver-Entry routine was unable to complete. If the Reinitialize routine discovers that the environment still isn't suitable, it can call **IoRegisterDriverReinitialization** to register itself again.

Table 6.3   Function prototype for a Reinitialize routine

VOID XxReinitialize	IRQL == PASSIVE_LEVEL
Parameter	**Description**
IN PDRIVER_OBJECT DriverObject	Pointer to Driver object
IN PVOID Context	Context block specified at registration
IN ULONG Count	Zero-based count of reinitialization calls
Return value	—

6.4   WRITING AN UNLOAD ROUTINE

By default, once a driver is loaded, it remains in the system until a reboot occurs. To make a driver unloadable, you need to write an Unload routine and store a pointer to the routine in your Driver object's **DriverUnload** field. The I/O Manager will then call this routine in response to an unload request from the Control Panel's Devices applet. If your driver will never be unloaded, then you can forget about this routine.

Execution Context

The I/O Manager calls your Unload routine once when it unloads the driver, usually because someone is playing with the Control Panel Devices applet. As you can see from Table 6.4, the Unload routine runs at PASSIVE_LEVEL IRQL, which means it has access to paged system resources.

What an Unload Routine Does

Although the exact details will vary slightly from driver to driver, in general you should perform the following steps in your Unload routine:

1. For some kinds of hardware, you may need to save the state of the device in the Registry. That way, you'll be able to put the device back in the same state the next time your DriverEntry routine executes. For example, an audio card driver might save the current volume setting of the card.

Table 6.4   Function prototype for an Unload routine

VOID XxUnload	IRQL == PASSIVE_LEVEL
Parameter	**Description**
IN PDRIVER_OBJECT DriverObject	Pointer to Driver object for this driver
Return value	—

2. Disable interrupts from the device and disconnect the device from its Interrupt object. It's crucial that the device not generate any interrupt requests once the Interrupt object is gone.

3. Deallocate any hardware belonging to your driver.

4. Use **IoDeleteSymbolicLink** to remove the device from the Win32 namespace.

5. Remove the Device object itself using **IoDeleteDevice**.

6. If you're managing multiunit controllers, repeat steps 4 and 5 for each device attached to the controller. Then remove the Controller object itself using **IoDeleteController**.

7. Repeat steps 4–6 for all controllers and devices that belong to your driver.

8. Deallocate any pool memory held by the driver

Keep in mind that your Unload routine will *not* be called at system shutdown time. If you need to do any special work at system shutdown, you'll need to write a shutdown routine.

6.5   CODE EXAMPLE: DRIVER CLEANUP

This example shows how a simple driver removes itself from the system. You can find the complete code for this example in the **CH06** directory on the disk that accompanies this book.

UNLOAD.C

The functions in this module basically just undo the work that was performed in the DriverEntry code. Again, it assumes there aren't any Controller objects to deal with.

XxUnload   In this case, the Unload routine is just a wrapper for calling XxReleaseHardware.

```
VOID
XxDriverUnload( IN PDRIVER_OBJECT DriverObject ) {
    //
    // Stop interrupt processing and release hardware
    //
    XxReleaseHardware( DriverObject );
}
```

XxReleaseHardware   The real cleanup work done by the driver happens in this routine. It's been separated out as a helper routine because parts of the driver initialization code needs to perform the same kinds of cleanup.

```
VOID
XxReleaseHardware( IN PDRIVER_OBJECT DriverObject )
{
        PDEVICE_OBJECT pDevObj;
        PDEVICE_EXTENSION pDevExt;

        UNICODE_STRING linkName;
        WCHAR linkNameBuffer[ XX_MAX_NAME_LENGTH ];

        UNICODE_STRINGnumber;
        WCHAR numberBuffer[10];

        CM_RESOURCE_LIST ResList;
        BOOLEAN bConflict;

        linkName.Buffer = linkNameBuffer;
        linkName.MaximumLength = XX_MAX_NAME_LENGTH;

        number.Buffer = numberBuffer;
        number.MaximumLength = 10;

        pDevObj = DriverObject->DeviceObject;❶

        //
        // Traverse the list of Device objects
        // and clean up each one in turn...
        //
        while( pDevObj != NULL ) {

                pDevExt = pDevObj->DeviceExtension;

        //
        // Add code here to save the state of
        // the hardware in the Registry and/or
        // to set the hardware into a known condition.
        //

        //
        // Stop handling interrupts from device
        //
        XxDisableInterrupts( pDevExt );

        IoDisconnectInterrupt( pDevExt->pInterrupt );

        //
        // Deallocate hardware resources belonging ❷
        // only to this Device object...
        //
        ResList.Count = 0;      // Build an empty list
```

```
        IoReportResourceUsage(
            NULL,                   // Default class name
            DriverObject,           // Ptr to Driver object
            NULL,                   // No driver resources
            0,
            pDevObj,                // Ptr to Device object
            &ResList,               // Device resources
            sizeof( ResList ),
            FALSE,
            &bConflict );           // Junk, but required
    //
    // Form the Win32 symbolic link name.
    //
    linkName.Length = 0;
    RtlAppendUnicodeToString(
            &linkName,
            XX_WIN32_DEVICE_NAME );

    //
    // Attach Win32 device number to the
    // end of the name; DOS device numbers
    // are one greater than NT numbers...
    //
    number.Length = 0;
    RtlIntegerToUnicodeString(
            pDevExt->NtDeviceNumber + 1,
            10,
            &number );
    RtlAppendUnicodeStringToString(
            &linkName,
            &number );

    //
    // Remove symbolic link from Object
    // namespace...
    //
    IoDeleteSymbolicLink( &linkName );

    //
    // Get address of next Device object
    // and get rid of the current one...
    //
    pDevObj = pDevObj->NextDevice;
    IoDeleteDevice( pDevExt->DeviceObject );
    }
```

```
        //
        // Deallocate hardware resources owned ❷
        // by the Driver object...
        //
        ResList.Count = 0;        // Build an empty list

        IoReportResourceUsage(
                NULL,             // Default class name
                DriverObject,     // Pointer to Driver object
                &ResList,         // Driver resources
                sizeof( ResList ),
                pDevObj,          // Pointer to Device object
                NULL,             // Device resources
                0,
                FALSE,            // Don't override conflicts
                &bConflict );     // Junk, but required
    }
```

❶ We're going to run the linked list of Device objects in order to do our cleanup. Get the first Device object from the Driver object.

❷ The mechanics of actually releasing allocated hardware will be the subject of Chapter 7. For the moment, just treat these two calls to IoReportResourceUsage as a piece of necessary magic.

6.6   WRITING SHUTDOWN ROUTINES

If your driver has any special processing to do before the operating system disappears, you'll need to write a Shutdown routine.

Execution Context

The I/O Manager calls your Shutdown routine once during system shutdown. As you can see from Table 6.5, the Shutdown routine runs at PASSIVE_LEVEL IRQL, which means it has access to paged system resources.

Table 6.5   Function prototype for a Shutdown routine

NTSTATUS XxShutdown	IRQL == PASSIVE_LEVEL
Parameter	**Description**
IN PDRIVER_OBJECT DriverObject	Pointer to Driver object for this driver
IN PIRP Irp	Pointer to shutdown IRP
Return value	• STATUS_SUCCESS — success
	• STATUS_XXX — appropriate error code

What a Shutdown Routine Does

The main purpose of a Shutdown routine is to put the device into a known state and perhaps store some device information in the Registry. Again, saving the current volume settings from a sound card is a good example of something a Shutdown routine would do.

Unlike the driver's Unload routine, Shutdown routines don't have to worry about releasing driver resources because the operating system is about to disappear anyway.

Enabling Shutdown Notification

If you examine the fields in the Driver object, it won't be obvious where the address of your Shutdown routine should go. That's because shutdown notifications are delivered to your driver in the form of an I/O request whose function code is IRP_MJ_SHUTDOWN. This means that your Shutdown routine is really a Dispatch routine which needs to be added to the Driver object's **MajorFunction** array.

But wait, it doesn't stop there. You also need to tell the I/O Manager that you're interested in receiving shutdown notifications. You do this by making a call to **IoRegisterShutdownNotification**.

The following code fragment, taken from a DriverEntry routine, shows how to enable shutdown notifications in your driver.

```
NTSTATUS DriverEntry(
  IN PDRIVER_OBJECT pDO,
  IN PUNICODE_STRING RegistryPath )
{
  :
  pDO->MajorFunction[ IRP_MJ_SHUTDOWN ] = XxShutdown;
  IoRegisterShutdownNotification( pDO );
  :
}
```

6.7   TESTING THE DRIVER

Even though your driver is far from being complete, there are still a few things you can do at this point to verify its operation. In particular, you can test the driver to be sure that it

- Compiles and links successfully
- Loads and unloads without crashing the system
- Creates Device objects and Win32 symbolic links
- Releases any resources when it unloads

These goals may not seem very ambitious, but once you've reached them, you know you have a solid base on which to build the rest of your driver.

Testing Procedure

You can use the following procedure to test your driver. If any of the steps fail, or if you crash the system, find and correct the problem before going on to the next phase of the test.

1. Write a SOURCES file for your driver.

2. Use the BUILD utility to create the driver file.

3. Move the driver to its target destination.

4. Install the driver using REGEDT32. Specify manual loading.

5. Reboot the system.

6. Use the Control Panel Devices applet to load and start the driver.

7. Use WINOBJ to see if your driver has created a Device object and its Win32 symbolic link.

8. Stop the driver using the Control Panel Devices applet.

9. Examine the Object Manager's namespace with WINOBJ to be certain the driver has removed any objects it created.

The WINOBJ Utility

WINOBJ is a tool that comes with the Win32 SDK (*not* the DDK). This little gem lets you view the NT Object Manager's namespace and determine whether your driver has created its Device object and symbolic link. Microsoft supplies executable versions of WINOBJ for the Alpha, Intel, and MIPS architectures. Unfortunately, you won't find any source code for WINOBJ since it makes direct calls to some native NT system services.

To use WINOBJ, just run the executable. The program will display the window pictured in Figure 6.2. The left pane shows the NT object directory in the form of file folders. Double-clicking on a particular folder will show its contents in the right window pane. Double-clicking on *some* objects in the right-hand pane will display additional information about the object.[3] As a driver writer, you'll be mainly interested in the **driver, DosDevices**, and **device** directories.

---

[3] WINOBJ is a little "throw-away" application that someone at Microsoft wrote. It doesn't know how to display information about all object types, nor do all of its informational displays make sense. Unfortunately, because it uses some of the "secret" **NtXxx** system calls, its source code isn't included with the SDK.

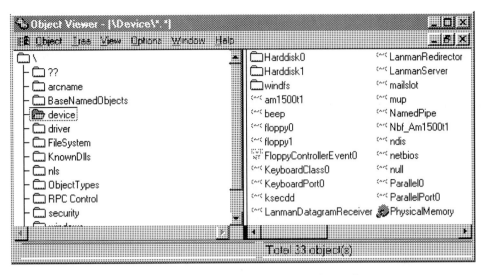

Figure 6.2   Main window of the WINOBJ utility

6.8   SUMMARY

At this point, your driver is on its way. It can initialize itself and present both NT and Win32 devices to the system. Depending on your specific needs, it may also be able to perform various cleanup operations, either when it's unloaded manually or when the system shuts down.

Unfortunately, your driver still can't locate the hardware it's supposed to be managing. This is a serious deficiency for a device driver, and it's one we'll see how to remedy in the next chapter.

Hardware Initialization

*O*ne of the first things a device driver does is to locate any devices it has to manage. This means finding their control registers, determining their DMA capabilities and the IRQ levels at which they interrupt, and locating any device-specific memory. In other words, the driver has to come up with a list of the hardware resources used by its devices. This turns out to be a much easier task if the hardware is auto-detectable. This chapter explains how to determine the resources needed by a device regardless of whether it auto-detects or not.

However, it's not enough to know what resources a device uses. Device drivers also have to claim ownership of any hardware resources they plan to use, in order to avoid collisions with other drivers. At the end of this chapter, you'll learn how to allocate and deallocate system hardware.

7.1 FINDING AUTO-DETECTED HARDWARE

During system bootstrap, NT goes to a lot of trouble to figure out what kinds of peripherals are attached to the system. This section explains how the process works and how your driver can access auto-detected hardware information.

How Auto-Detection Works

The exact mechanism used for detecting hardware depends on the platform architecture. On 80x86 systems, a bootstrap component called NTDETECT gathers information about the hardware environment, while on RISC-based machines, the ARC firmware performs a similar function. In either case, the detection component makes this hardware data available to the operating system loader, which in turn writes it into the **...\HARDWARE\DESCRIPTION** area of the Registry. Later, device drivers can use this information to control their initialization.

The detection components use whatever methods they can to determine the identity and characteristics of a given system. This includes both interrogating the hardware directly, as well as using information in the ROM BIOS to draw conclusions about devices attached to the system. Among other things, auto-detection tries to determine

- The number and type of any I/O buses on the system
- Extended information about the bootstrap device itself
- Information about the monitor and video adapter used to display bootstrap messages
- The presence and location of keyboard and mouse hardware
- Number and location of serial and parallel controllers and any recognizable printers or terminals attached to them
- The presence and identity of any network cards
- Information about any other devices on each I/O bus

The specific kinds of data that auto-detection searches for include the address and number of a device's control registers, hardware interrupt levels used by the device, information about a device's DMA capabilities, and any ranges of physical memory used by the device. If the hardware offers any device-specific data, auto-detection will collect that as well.

This is a wonderful scheme, and it promises to make the lives of driver writers much easier in the long run. Later releases of Windows NT will use this strategy as a basis for supporting Plug and Play capabilities. At the moment, however, most ISA devices don't have a lot to say for themselves and therefore don't show up during auto-detection. This means that drivers of ISA devices have to use other means for locating their hardware. Fortunately, PCI, native EISA, and MCA devices are much more talkative.

Auto-Detected Hardware and the Registry

Regardless of how NT auto-detects a given piece of hardware, Registry information about the hardware always has a standard format. This isolates drivers from any bus or platform peculiarities and generally makes life easier for driver writers. Figure 7.1 shows a portion of the Registry's hardware description area.

The keys and subkeys below **...\System** form a tree-structured model of any auto-detectable hardware. Keys with alphanumeric names correspond to

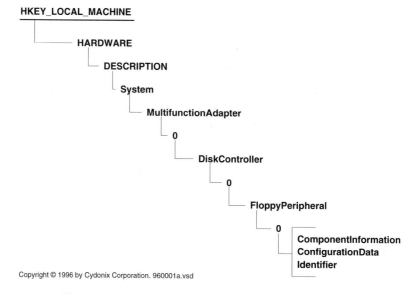

Figure 7.1   Auto-detected hardware data in the Registry

general classes of hardware. Hanging from each of these keys will be one or more subkeys whose names are integers. These numeric subkeys identify specific instances of a CPU, a floating-point unit, a bus, a controller, or a device. In the figure, the **MultifunctionAdapter** key represents a category of buses (in this case ISA), and the subkey 0 below it represents the first actual instance of such a bus. **DiskController\0** is connected to this bus, and **FloppyPeripheral\0** is attached to this controller.

Tucked away in the numeric subkeys, you'll find value items containing any information that NT was able to auto-detect. Three value items can show up in one of these numeric subkeys:

- **ComponentInformation** — This is binary data that (hopefully) the driver will know how to interpret.

- **ConfigurationData** — This names the resources needed by the hardware in the form of a REG_FULL_RESOURCE_DESCRIPTOR item.

- **Identifier** — This is an identifier string generated by the hardware or the system BIOS. It's converted to Unicode when it goes into the Registry.

You can use the Registry editor, REGEDT32, to browse through this auto-detected hardware data. This is very helpful if you're trying to resolve conflicts or make sure that something is auto-detecting properly. Once you've selected a controller or peripheral's numeric subkey, double-clicking on the **ComponentInfor-**

mation value will bring up a display of the resources needed by that piece of hardware.

Querying the Hardware Database

Although you're free to wander through the hardware description area using **RtlXxx** and **ZwXxx** routines, **IoQueryDeviceDescription** (shown in Table 7.1) makes the process a little less painful. You give this function a pattern describing the kind of hardware information you want, and a callback routine. **IoQueryDeviceDescription** will then rummage around in the Registry and invoke your callback routine each time it finds something that matches the pattern.

You tell **IoQueryDeviceDescription** what level of detail you want by using the XxxType arguments listed in Table 7.2. Only the following combinations will work:

- **BusType** alone gets just bus-level information.[1]
- **BusType** and **ControllerType** gets bus and controller information
- **BusType**, **ControllerType**, and **PeripheralType** together will give you device-level information.

Table 7.1   Prototype for IoQueryDeviceDescription

NTSTATUS IoQueryDeviceDescription	IRQL == PASSIVE_LEVEL
Parameter	**Description**
IN PINTERFACE_TYPE BusType	Desired bus architecture (see below)
IN PULONG BusNumber	Zero-based bus number
IN PCONFIGURATION_TYPE ControllerType	Desired controller type (see below)
IN PULONG ControllerNumber	Zero-based controller number
IN PCONFIGURATION_TYPE PeripheralType	Desired device type (see below)
IN PULONG PeripheralNumber	Zero-based device number
IN PIO_QUERY_DEVICE_ROUTINE Callback	Address of ConfigCallback routine
IN PVOID Context	Address of driver's configuration buffer
Return value	• STATUS_OBJECT_NAME_NOT_FOUND • STATUS_XXX from ConfigCallback

---

[1] To get information about all the buses on a machine, call **IoQueryDeviceDescription** in a loop and iterate the **BusType** from zero to MaximumInterfaceType. Alternatively, you can use the **HalQuerySystemInformation** function to get an explicit list of the buses on the machine.

Table 7.2   Bus, controller, and peripheral types for IoQueryDeviceDescription

XxxType arguments for IoQueryDeviceDescription

BusType	ControllerType	PeripheralType
CBus	AudioController	DiskPeripheral
Eisa	CdromController	FloppyDiskPeripheral
Internal	DiskController	KeyboardPeripheral
Isa	DisplayController	LinePeripheral
MicroChannel	KeyboardController	ModemPeripheral
MPIBus	NetworkController	MonitorPeripheral
MPSABus	ParallelController	NetworkPeripheral
NuBus	PointerController	PointerPeripheral
PCIBus	SerialController	PrinterPeripheral
PCMCIABus	TapeController	TapePeripheral
TurboChannel	WormController	TerminalPeripheral
VMEBus	OtherController	OtherPeripheral

Notice that the XxxType arguments are pointers to variables and *not* the values themselves. You pass a NULL pointer to indicate that you don't want a particular kind of information.

You can get data about specific buses, controllers, or devices using one or more of the XxxNumber parameters. These arguments are pointers to variables containing the number of the bus, controller, or device that you're asking about. Passing a NULL pointer causes the I/O Manager to enumerate all items of a particular type.

To see how this works, suppose you call **IoQueryDeviceDescription** and specify BusType as **Eisa**, BusNumber as 0, ControllerType as **DiskController**, and NULL for the ControllerNumber. The I/O Manager will call your ConfigCallback routine once for each disk controller on EISA bus 0. With each invocation, the callback will receive data about EISA bus 0 and one particular controller, but nothing about any devices connected to that controller. Since multiple disk controllers can be attached to a single bus, the ConfigCallback might get the same bus information more than once, even though the controller information will be different each time.

Now, suppose you make the same call to **IoQueryDeviceDescription**, but this time you further restrict the search by specifying PeripheralType as **FloppyDiskPeripheral** and NULL for the PeripheralNumber. In this case, your ConfigCallback will be called for each floppy drive on EISA bus 0. Along with bus and controller data, each call will receive information about a different floppy disk device. In this case, both the bus and controller information may be repeated for multiple calls (because several floppies can share the same controller).

If **IoQueryDeviceDescription** can't find anything in the Registry that matches your request, it returns STATUS_OBJECT_NAME_NOT_FOUND without invoking the ConfigCallback routine. Otherwise, it continues to execute your callback until it runs out of matching items, or until your callback returns a value other than STATUS_SUCCESS. In this case, it's supposed to return the last NTSTATUS value sent back by your callback routine.

That's the theory. In practice, if you pass a NULL BusNumber parameter, you *always* get STATUS_OBJECT_NAME_NOT_FOUND from **IoQueryDevice-Description**. This value comes back regardless of whether your callback was invoked, and it supersedes whatever status value your callback might have returned. This problem doesn't occur with the other two XxxNumber arguments. For this reason, the code example in the next section manually iterates both BusType and BusNumber.

What a ConfigCallback Routine Does

Each time **IoQueryDeviceDescription** invokes your ConfigCallback routine, it passes the arguments listed in Table 7.3. These arguments are valid only within the ConfigCallback routine itself, so you have to store any configuration

Table 7.3   Function prototype for a configuration callback

NTSTATUS XxConfigCallback	IRQL == PASSIVE_LEVEL
Parameter	**Description**
IN PVOID Context	Address of configuration buffer
IN PUNICODE_STRING PathName	Registry path for bus, controller, or device information
IN INTERFACE_TYPE BusType	Bus architecture
IN ULONG BusNumber	Zero-based bus number
IN PKEY_VALUE_FULL_INFORMATION *BusInformation	Pointer to Registry information
IN CONFIGURATION_TYPE ControllerType	Controller type
IN ULONG ControllerNumber	Zero-based controller number
IN PKEY_VALUE_FULL_INFORMATION *ControllerInformation	Pointer to Registry information
IN CONFIGURATION_TYPE PeripheralType	Device type
IN ULONG PeripheralNumber	Zero-based device number
IN PKEY_VALUE_FULL_INFORMATION *PeripheralInformation	Pointer to Registry information
Return value	• STATUS_SUCCESS • STATUS_XXX — error code

data that you'll need later in a temporary buffer. Usually, you allocate this buffer somewhere in your DriverEntry routine and pass its address as the Context argument to **IoQueryDeviceDescription**.

Although the specific steps will depend on the hardware you're working with, a ConfigCallback routine generally does the following:

1. It scans the Registry information for base-register address, count of registers, interrupt level and vector information, and DMA channel requirements.

2. The ConfigCallback then stores the Registry values in the Config block allocated by DriverEntry.

3. It translates the Registry's bus-specific values into systemwide values that your driver can use and stores these values in the Config block as well.

Each time **IoQueryDeviceDescription** calls your ConfigCallback routine, you repeat this procedure for a new controller or device that matches your query.

Using Configuration Data

Your main sources of information in a ConfigCallback routine come from the various XxxType, XxxNumber, and XxxInformation arguments. The meaning of the XxxType and XxxNumber items should be pretty obvious, but the XxxInformation arguments need some explanation.

Each XxxInformation argument is actually a pointer which may or may not be NULL, depending on what you've asked for. If you follow this pointer, you come to an array of three items. Use one of these predefined constants to index into this array:

*   **IoQueryDeviceIdentifier** — Points to any auto-detected hardware name information stored in the Registry as a Unicode string.

*   **IoQueryDeviceConfigurationData** — Points to any bus-relative Registry information about the bus, controller, or device that was discovered during auto-detection.

*   **IoQueryDeviceComponentInformation** — Points to information about a device's subcomponents.

Of these, IoQueryDeviceConfigurationData is probably the most helpful. Using this constant as an index into one of the XxxInformation arrays gets you a pointer to a KEY_VALUE_FULL_INFORMATION structure which, in turn, contains the actual Registry data about a bus, controller, or device. Figure 7.2 shows how this works for the ControllerInformation argument to a ConfigCallback routine.

The group of CM_PARTIAL_RESOURCE_DESCRIPTOR items hanging from the bottom of this whole mess contains the actual hardware information you're looking for. As you can see from Table 7.4, each descriptor identifies one

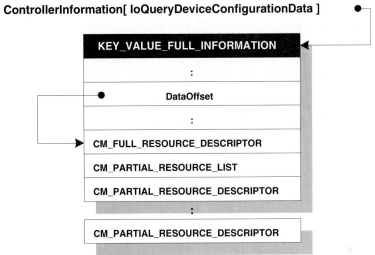

ControllerInformation[IoQueryDeviceConfigurationData]

KEY_VALUE_FULL_INFORMATION

⋮

DataOffset

⋮

CM_FULL_RESOURCE_DESCRIPTOR

CM_PARTIAL_RESOURCE_LIST

CM_PARTIAL_RESOURCE_DESCRIPTOR

⋮

CM_PARTIAL_RESOURCE_DESCRIPTOR

Copyright © 1994 by Cydonix Corporation. 960003a.vsd

Figure 7.2   Hardware information given to a configuration callback

Table 7.4   Contents of a partial resource descriptor

CM_PARTIAL_RESOURCE_DESCRIPTOR

Field	Description
UCHAR Type	Identifies resource being described: • CmResourceTypePort • CmResourceTypeInterrupt • CmResourceTypeDma • CmResourceTypeMemory • CmResourceTypeDeviceSpecificData
UCHAR ShareDisposition	Level of sharing for this resource: • CmResourceShareDeviceExclusive • CmResourceShareDriverExclusive • CmResourceShareShared

USHORT Flags
 union u
     struct Port
     struct Interrupt
     struct Dma
     struct Memory
     struct DeviceSpecificData
	Type-specific values
	 Union based on **Type** field
	 • Control register address and span
	 • Interrupt level and vector
	 • DMA channel and port
	 • Device memory address and span
	 • Device-specific information

kind of hardware resource used by the device. To extract this data, you need to do a little pointer arithmetic and then examine each of the partial resource descriptors.

There's something you need to be aware of when you start pulling information from Partial Resource Descriptors: The partial descriptors are in no particular order, so you need to walk through all of them to find the information you want. The only exception to this is device-specific data, which if present, will always be the last partial descriptor.[2]

Translating Configuration Data

After you've pulled all this data from the Registry, there's still one more step. The information in the partial descriptors is all bus-relative, just the way the auto-detection component found it. To use these values in your driver, you need to translate them into their systemwide equivalents. Specifically, you need to call some of the following functions:

- **HalTranslateBusAddress** — Converts device memory and register addresses from bus-relative to system-wide values.

- **HalGetInterruptVector** — Converts bus-specific interrupt information into system-assigned values for the vector, DIRQL, and affinity mask. Chapter 9 explains how to use these values to connect to an Interrupt object.

- **HalGetAdapter** — locates an Adapter object your driver can use to perform DMA operations with a specific device. Chapter 12 explains how to use this function.

It's worth mentioning that, in some environments, some of these translations may not do very much, but for portability, you need to perform them anyway.

7.2   CODE EXAMPLE: LOCATING AUTO-DETECTED HARDWARE

This rather long example shows how to pull auto-detected hardware information from the Registry. Specifically, it looks for all the hardware of type ParallelController. You can find these files in the **CH07** directory on the disk that accompanies this book.

---

[2] This is because device-specific data is variable in length. Another implication is that there can be only one device-specific data item in a group of partial resource descriptors.

XXDRIVER.H

The following excerpts from the driver's header file show the driver-defined data structures involved in hardware configuration.[3]

DEVICE_BLOCK   This temporary structure is carved out of paged pool and is used only during driver initialization. It holds information about one specific piece of hardware. Some of the items in this block will later be copied into the Device Extension block for safekeeping.

```
typedef struct _DEVICE_BLOCK {
  //
  // Original values pulled from the Registry
  //
  PHYSICAL_ADDRESS OriginalPortBase;
  ULONG PortSpan;
  ULONG OriginalIrql;
  ULONG OriginalVector;
  KINTERRUPT_MODE InterruptMode;
  BOOLEAN ShareVector;
  BOOLEAN FloatingSave;
  ULONG OriginalDmaChannel;
  //
  // Converted values that will be used by
  // the driver
  PUCHAR PortBase; // First control register
  ULONG SystemVector;
  KIRQL Dirql;
  KAFFINITY Affinity;

} DEVICE_BLOCK, *PDEVICE_BLOCK;
```

CONFIG_ARRAY   This structure is an array of DEVICE_BLOCKs that hold temporary information about all the hardware belonging to the driver on one particular bus. In theory, multiple devices might show up on different buses, in which case there would be a linked list of CONFIG_ARRAYs. The **Count** field keeps track of how many DEVICE_BLOCKs actually contain valid data.

```
typedef struct _CONFIG_ARRAY {
  //
  // We keep a list of these arrays, one
  // for each bus-type/bus-number combination
```

---

[3] You'll notice some DMA-related fields in the following structures. Since the parallel port doesn't perform any DMA, these won't be used. Chapter 12 will show you how to fill them in.

```
// where we find our hardware.
//
struct _CONFIG_ARRAY *NextConfigArray;
//
// The bus to which all the devices in this
// array are attached.
//
INTERFACE_TYPE BusType;
ULONG BusNumber;
//
// Number of devices in this array
//
ULONG Count;

//
// One array-element for each device
//
DEVICE_BLOCK Device[ XX_MAXIMUM_DEVICES ];

} CONFIG_ARRAY, *PCONFIG_ARRAY;
```

DEVICE_EXTENSION   This driver-defined structure is created from non-paged pool by **IoCreateDevice** and automatically attached to our Device object. It holds information that will be needed throughout the life of the driver.

```
typedef struct _DEVICE_EXTENSION {
  PDEVICE_OBJECT DeviceObject;   // Back pointer

  ULONG NtDeviceNumber;          // Zero-based device num
  PUCHAR PortBase;               // First control register

  PKINTERRUPT pInterrupt;        // Interrupt object

  PADAPTER_OBJECT pAdapter;      // DMA Adapter object
  ULONG cMapRegs;                // Count of mapping regs
  UCHAR DeviceStatus;            // Most recent status

} DEVICE_EXTENSION, *PDEVICE_EXTENSION;
```

AUTOCON.C

This group of functions scans the Registry's hardware description map for all the parallel controllers. It fills in a separate DEVICE_BLOCK for each piece of hardware it finds. The result is a linked list of CONFIG_ARRAYs describing all the parallel controllers on all buses in this machine.

XxGetHardwareInfo   This routine just loops through all the known bus types and checks to see if one or more of our devices live on each bus. This is mainly a harness for the call to **IoQueryDeviceDescription**.

```
NTSTATUS
XxGetHardwareInfo(
  IN PUNICODE_STRING RegistryPath, // (unused)
  OUT PCONFIG_ARRAY *ConfigList
  )
{
  INTERFACE_TYPE InterfaceType;
  ULONG InterfaceNumber;
  CONFIGURATION_TYPE CtrlrType = ParallelController; ❶
  PCONFIG_ARRAY ConfigArray;
  NTSTATUS status;

  *ConfigList = NULL; // No devices located yet
  //
  // Run through all the various bus types and
  // see if our device is on any of them...
  //
  for(  InterfaceType = 0;
        InterfaceType < MaximumInterfaceType;
        InterfaceType++ )
  {
        InterfaceNumber = 0;
        do {
              status = IoQueryDeviceDescription( ❷
                          &InterfaceType,
                          &InterfaceNumber,
                          &CtrlrType,
                          NULL,
                          NULL,
                          NULL,
                          XxConfigCallback,
                          ConfigList );
              //
              // Return to caller if a real
              // error occurs
              //
              if( !NT_SUCCESS( status ) ❸
                    && status !=
                          STATUS_OBJECT_NAME_NOT_FOUND )
              {
                    XxReleaseHardwareInfo(
                          *ConfigList );
                    *ConfigList = NULL;
                    return status;
              }
```

```
                InterfaceNumber++;
        } while( status !=
                    STATUS_OBJECT_NAME_NOT_FOUND );
    } // end of for-loop
    if( *ConfigList == NULL )
        return STATUS_NO_SUCH_DEVICE;
    else
        return STATUS_SUCCESS;
}
```

❶ This is the hardware category. Notice that the parallel port is considered to be a controller rather than a device.

❷ Since we're specifying a controller type, our callback will be invoked once for each piece of hardware on the current bus that matches the Parallel-Controller type.

❸ STATUS_OBJECT_NAME_NOT_FOUND simply means there is no such item on the current bus — so we keep looking. Other kinds of errors cause us to abort.

XxConfigCallback   This routine gets called by the I/O Manager once for each device that matches the category ParallelController. We have to scan through the Registry data for information about I/O port addresses and interrupt behavior.

```
static NTSTATUS
XxConfigCallback(
        IN PVOID Context,
        IN PUNICODE_STRING PathName,
        IN INTERFACE_TYPE BusType,
        IN ULONG BusNumber,
        IN PKEY_VALUE_FULL_INFORMATION *BusInfo,
        IN CONFIGURATION_TYPE CtrlrType,
        IN ULONG CtrlrNumber,
        IN PKEY_VALUE_FULL_INFORMATION *CtrlrInfo,
        IN CONFIGURATION_TYPE DeviceType,
        IN ULONG DeviceNumber,
        IN PKEY_VALUE_FULL_INFORMATION *DeviceInfo
        )
{
        //
        // So we don't have to typecast the context.
        //
        PCONFIG_ARRAY *ConfigList = Context;

        //
        // Short-hand pointers to resource data
        //
```

```
PCM_FULL_RESOURCE_DESCRIPTOR pFrd;
PCM_PARTIAL_RESOURCE_DESCRIPTOR pPrd;
PCONFIG_ARRAY ConfigArray;
PDEVICE_BLOCK DeviceBlock;

//
// These booleans will tell us whether we got
// all the information that we needed.
//
BOOLEAN bFoundPort = FALSE;
BOOLEAN bFoundInterrupt = FALSE;
NTSTATUS status;

ULONG i;                        // Generic loop control

//
// Locate the Config Array for this bus
//
status = XxFindMatchingConfigArray(❶
            BusType,
            BusNumber,
            ConfigList,
            &ConfigArray );
if( !NT_SUCCESS( status ))
{
    return status;
}
//
// See if there's any room left in the Config
// Array; if not, just drop this device on the
// floor
//
if( ConfigArray->Count >= XX_MAXIMUM_DEVICES )
{
    return STATUS_SUCCESS;
}
//
// Make it easier to refer to the slot in the
// Config Array belonging to this device
//
DeviceBlock =
    &ConfigArray->Device[ConfigArray->Count];

//
// Get pointer to beginning of configuration
// data for this device in the Registry
//
```

```
pFrd = (PCM_FULL_RESOURCE_DESCRIPTOR) ❷
     (((PUCHAR)CtrlrInfo
          [IoQueryDeviceConfigurationData])
     + CtrlrInfo
          [IoQueryDeviceConfigurationData]
               ->DataOffset);
//
// Loop through all Partial Resource Descriptors
// looking for Port and Interrupt information
//
for ( i = 0; ❸
     i < pFrd->PartialResourceList.Count;
     i++ )
{
     pPrd = &pFrd->PartialResourceList
                    .PartialDescriptors[i];

     //
     // Switch on the various partial resource
     // types. Pull out the pieces we need...
     //
     switch( pPrd->Type ) ❹
     {
          case CmResourceTypePort:

               bFoundPort =
                    XxGetPortInfo(
                         pPrd,
                         BusType,
                         BusNumber,
                         DeviceBlock );
               break;
          case CmResourceTypeInterrupt:

               bFoundInterrupt =
                    XxGetInterruptInfo(
                         pPrd,
                         BusType,
                         BusNumber,
                         DeviceBlock );
               break;

          default:
               break;

     } // end of switch
} // end of for-loop
```

```
            if( !( bFoundPort && bFoundInterrupt )) ❺
            {
                    return STATUS_NO_SUCH_DEVICE;
            }

            //
            // Account for the slot that we've just
            // filled up...
            //
            ConfigArray->Count++; ❻
            return STATUS_SUCCESS;
}
```

❶ XxFindMatchingBus is a helper function that locates the Config Array for a specific bus type and number combination. If this is the first time a particular bus has been encountered, it creates an empty Config Array and links it into the caller-supplied Config List.

❷ Create a pointer to the Full Resource Descriptor for this device. To do this, we need to skip over the header information by adding the **DataOffset** field to the starting address of the block.

❸ The Partial Resource Descriptors are in no particular order, so we have to loop through all of them looking for information about ports and interrupts. Anything we don't recognize, we ignore.

❹ Switch on the Partial Resource type and call a helper function to extract the useful information from it. The parallel controller needs only port and interrupt data; for other devices you might need to add cases for CmResourceTypeDma, CmResourceTypeMemory, or CmResourceTypeDeviceSpecificData.

❺ When the entire scan is complete, check to be sure that all the components have been found. If anything is missing, signal an error.

❻ Each time we successfully locate a device, we use up one more slot in the Config Array. The Count field keeps track of this.

XxGetPortInfo and XxGetInterruptInfo   Here are the two helper functions. Each one simply pulls information out of a specific kind of Partial Resource Descriptor and stores it in the appropriate fields of a DEVICE_BLOCK. They also translate bus-specific values into their systemwide equivalents.

```
//++
// Function:
//      XxGetPortInfo
//
// Description:
//      This function pulls I/O Port infomation
```

```
//      from a Partial Resource Descriptor
//
// Arguments:
//      Pointer to a Partial Resource Descriptor
//      Bus type for this device
//      Bus number for this device
//      Pointer to this device's slot in Config Array
//
// Return Value:
//      This function returns TRUE if we found the
 //     data we wanted, FALSE otherwise.
//--
static BOOLEAN
XxGetPortInfo(
      IN PCM_PARTIAL_RESOURCE_DESCRIPTOR pPrd,
      IN INTERFACE_TYPE BusType,
      IN ULONG BusNumber,
      IN PDEVICE_BLOCK DeviceBlock
      )
{
      PHYSICAL_ADDRESS TranslatedPortBase;
      ULONG uAddressSpace = 1;

      DeviceBlock->OriginalPortBase =
          pPrd->u.Port.Start;

      DeviceBlock->PortSpan = pPrd->u.Port.Length;
      if( !HalTranslateBusAddress(
          BusType,
          BusNumber,
          DeviceBlock->OriginalPortBase,
          &uAddressSpace,
          &TranslatedPortBase ))
      {
          return FALSE;
      }
      DeviceBlock->PortBase =
          (PUCHAR)TranslatedPortBase.LowPart;
      return TRUE;
}
//++
// Function:
//      XxGetInterruptInfo
//
// Description:
//      This function pulls Interrupt infomation
//      from a Partial Resource Descriptor
```

```
//
// Arguments:
//     Pointer to a Partial Resource Descriptor
//     Bus type for this device
//     Bus number for this device
//     Pointer to this device's slot in Config Array
 //
// Return Value:
//     This function returns TRUE if we found the
//     data we wanted, FALSE otherwise.
//--
static BOOLEAN
XxGetInterruptInfo(
    IN PCM_PARTIAL_RESOURCE_DESCRIPTOR pPrd,
    IN INTERFACE_TYPE BusType,
    IN ULONG BusNumber,
    IN PDEVICE_BLOCK DeviceBlock
    )
{
    if( pPrd->Flags == CM_RESOURCE_INTERRUPT_LATCHED )
       DeviceBlock->InterruptMode = Latched;
    else
       DeviceBlock->InterruptMode = LevelSensitive;
    DeviceBlock->OriginalIrql =
       pPrd->u.Interrupt.Level;
    DeviceBlock->OriginalVector =
       pPrd->u.Interrupt.Vector;
    DeviceBlock->ShareVector = FALSE;
    DeviceBlock->FloatingSave = FALSE;
    DeviceBlock->SystemVector =
       HalGetInterruptVector(
         BusType,
         BusNumber,
         pPrd->u.Interrupt.Level,
         pPrd->u.Interrupt.Vector,
         &DeviceBlock->Dirql,
         &DeviceBlock->Affinity );
    return TRUE;
}
```

7.3 FINDING UNRECOGNIZED HARDWARE

If your device doesn't show up under auto-detection, or if you just need to supplement the auto-detected information, you can hard-code additional information into the Registry. This section explains how.

Adding Driver Parameters to the Registry

One way to tell your driver about hardware is to hard-code the information in a nonvolatile area of the Registry. Although this doesn't seem like a very elegant solution, in the absence of any auto-detection capabilities, it may be your only option. Many ISA devices will require the use of this technique.

The standard convention is to store device information in one or more value entries beneath a subkey called **Parameters**, which dangles off the driver's service key in the Registry. Figure 7.3 shows how this works. It's usually up to the driver's installation procedure to set up the **Parameters** area. For example, suppose your driver works with a device that the user has to configure manually with DIP switches. When the driver's installation program runs it displays a dialog box asking the user for the port address, IRQ, and DMA settings selected on the device. It then stores this information in the Parameters area where the driver can find it.

There are no particular standards for the format of driver-specific parameter data. You simply need to store the same kinds of information that your device would generate if it auto-detected. As we've already seen, this can include the addresses of any control registers, the IRQ level used by the device, information about its DMA capabilities, and the address and span of any device memory. If your driver supports multiple devices, it's probably a good idea to create separate subkeys underneath **Parameters** for each individual device. In Figure 7.3, these are the **Device0** and **Device1** subkeys.

Retrieving Parameters from the Registry

You use **RtlQueryRegistryValues** (described in Table 7.5) to retrieve values from the **Parameters** subkey of your driver's Registry key. This is a very powerful

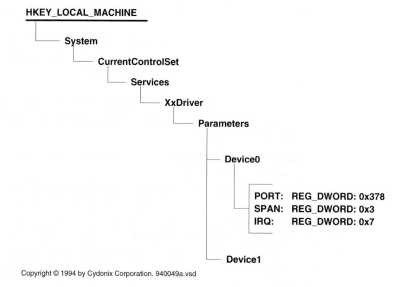

Figure 7.3   Registry path for driver-specific parameters

Table 7.5   Prototype for RtlQueryRegistryValues function

NTSTATUS RtlQueryRegistryValues	IRQL == PASSIVE_LEVEL
Parameter	**Description**
IN ULONG RelativeTo	Specifies beginning of Registry path • RTL_REGISTRY_ABSOLUTE • RTL_REGISTRY_SERVICES • RTL_REGISTRY_CONTROL • RTL_REGISTRY_WINDOWS_NT • RTL_REGISTRY_DEVICE_MAP • RTL_REGISTRY_USER • RTL_REGISTRY_OPTIONAL • RTL_REGISTRY_HANDLE
IN PWSTR Path	Identifies an absolute or relative path
IN PRTL_QUERY_REGISTRY_ TABLE QueryTable	Address of a table describing the query
IN PVOID Context	Context passed to a QueryRoutine
IN PVOID Environment	Environment block used to expand any REG_EXPAND_SZ registry entries
Return value	• STATUS_SUCCESS • STATUS_INVALID_PARAMETER • STATUS_OBJECT_NAME_NOT_FOUND

function, and if you're going to be doing anything fancy with the Registry, you should become familiar with all its capabilities. For our purposes, we won't need to do much with it except translate a few value names.

To work with **RtlQueryRegistryValues**, you need to construct a query table describing the values you want to translate. The query table is an array of RTL_QUERY_REGISTRY_TABLE items terminated with an entry containing NULL **QueryRoutine** and **Name** fields. Table 7.6 shows the format of the individual items.

As with auto-detected hardware information, it's a good idea to store the Registry data in a configuration buffer that other parts of your DriverEntry routine can use. That way, you can move the driver to an auto-detecting environment without having to rewrite too much code. Also remember that values from the Registry still must be translated into systemwide values.

Other Sources of Device Information

Before we look at an example of using the Registry, it's worth mentioning some other sources of hardware information. The first is the **HalGetBusData** function which allows you to interrogate a specific slot on a specific bus. This

Table 7.6   Query table entries

RTL_QUERY_REGISTRY_TABLE	
Field	**Description**
PRTL_REGISTRY_QUERY_ ROUTINE QueryRoutine	Optional query routine to be called for each item found in the Registry
ULONG Flags	Control interpretation of other fields • RTL_QUERY_REGISTRY_SUBKEY • RTL_QUERY_REGISTRY_TOPKEY • RTL_QUERY_REGISTRY_REQUIRED • RTL_QUERY_REGISTRY_NOVALUE • RTL_QUERY_REGISTRY_NOEXPAND • RTL_QUERY_REGISTRY_DIRECT
PWSTR Name	Name of the value caller wants to query
PVOID EntryContext	32-bit value to be passed to QueryRoutine
ULONG DefaultType	Type of data
PVOID DefaultData	Data item to be used if queried item not present
ULONG DefaultLength	Default length of data item

function returns a buffer containing any device-specific data available from a device. **HalGetBusData** is only useful if you're working with buses like PCI or EISA that generate a lot of information.

Also, the I/O Manager keeps a data structure that tracks the number of disk, tape, floppy, SCSI-HBA, serial, and parallel Device objects that have been created by various drivers. Calling **IoGetConfigurationInformation** returns a pointer to this structure, which you can use to pick an appropriate number for a new device name. It's also your responsibility to increment the counts in this structure if you create any of the device types listed above.

Finally, if none of the techniques we've looked at will work, you may have no alternative but to locate your hardware by poking various control register addresses. This a potentially dangerous and error-prone way to do things. If you take this approach, make sure you temporarily allocate the hardware before you fiddle with it. If the allocation fails, don't touch the hardware. Otherwise, you may be doing something that confuses an already-loaded driver that owns the hardware and has put it into a specific state.

7.4   CODE EXAMPLE: QUERYING THE REGISTRY

Here is another hardware locator. This one pulls information about ISA cards from the Parameters subkey of the driver's service key. You can find this code in the **CH07** directory on the disk that accompanies this book.

REGCON.C

This group of functions scans the driver's **Parameters** key looking for sub-keys with names like **Device0**, **Device1**, and so on. Each time it finds one, it fills out another DEVICE_BLOCK using values from the Registry.

XxGetHardwareInfo   This routine checks for the existence of an ISA bus on the machine; if no ISA bus shows up, it checks for an EISA bus where the ISA card might live. If neither type of bus exists on this machine, the routine fails. This indirect approach is necessary because ISA cards don't give any feedback about their presence.

```
NTSTATUS
XxGetHardwareInfo(
        IN PUNICODE_STRING RegistryPath,
        IN PCONFIG_BLOCK pConfig
        )
{
        NTSTATUS status;
        PCONFIG_ARRAY ConfigArray;
        INTERFACE_TYPE BusType;
        ULONG BusNumber;
        UNICODE_STRING TempString;

        //
        // Check for a bus we can use. Look for an ISA bus
        // first, then look for an EISA bus. If neither one
        // shows up, quit.
        //
        BusType = Isa;
        BusNumber = 0;

        status = XxCheckForBus( Isa, BusNumber );

        if( !NT_SUCCESS( status ))
        {
                BusType = Eisa;
                status = XxCheckForBus( Eisa, BusNumber );
        }

        if( !NT_SUCCESS( status ))
        {
                *ConfigList = NULL;
                return STATUS_NO_SUCH_DEVICE;
        }
        //
        // We found a compatible bus. Allocate
        // space for the (single) Config array
```

```
// that we'll be passing back to the
// caller.
//
if(( ConfigArray = ExAllocatePool(
                        PagedPool,
                        sizeof( CONFIG_ARRAY )))
        == NULL )
{
    *ConfigList = NULL;
    return STATUS_INSUFFICIENT_RESOURCES;
}

RtlZeroMemory(
    ConfigArray,
    sizeof( CONFIG_ARRAY ));
*ConfigList = ConfigArray;
ConfigArray->BusType = BusType;
ConfigArray->BusNumber = BusNumber;

//
// Make a copy of the Registry path name
// and be sure it has a terminator at the
// end...
//
TempString.Length = 0; ❶
TempString.MaximumLength =
            RegistryPath->Length +
                sizeof( UNICODE_NULL );

if(( TempString.Buffer =
            ExAllocatePool(
            PagedPool,
            TempString.MaximumLength ))
== NULL )
{
    *ConfigList = NULL;
    ExFreePool( ConfigArray );
    return STATUS_INSUFFICIENT_RESOURCES;
}
RtlCopyUnicodeString( &TempString, RegistryPath );

TempString.Buffer[ TempString.Length ] =
    UNICODE_NULL;

//
// Keep looping until we run out of device
// slots or Registry entries, or until an
// error occurs.
```

```
    //
    ConfigArray->Count = 0;

    while( ConfigArray->Count < XX_MAXIMUM_DEVICES )  ❷
    {
        status = XxFindNextDevice(
                    BusType,
                    BusNumber,
                    &TempString,
                    ConfigArray );

        if( !NT_SUCCESS( status )) break;

        ConfigArray->Count++;

    } // end while-loop

    ExFreePool( TempString.Buffer );

    if( !NT_SUCCESS( status ) &&
        status != STATUS_OBJECT_NAME_NOT_FOUND )  ❸
    {
        *ConfigList = NULL;
        ExFreePool( ConfigArray );
        return status;
    }

    //
    // See if we found anything after all
    // that work
    //
    if( ConfigArray->Count == 0 )  ❹
    {
        *ConfigList = NULL;
        ExFreePool( ConfigArray );
        return STATUS_NO_SUCH_DEVICE;
    }
    //
    // Everything worked...
    //
    return STATUS_SUCCESS;
}
```

❶ We need to go through all these shenanigans because the RegistryPath argument is a counted UNICODE_STRING object, but the Registry query function wants a NULL-terminated array of Unicode characters.

❷ This loop keeps going until we run out of slots in the Configuration block, or until we don't find a matching entry in the Registry. The organization of this routine means that all the DeviceN subkeys must be consecutive.

❸ STATUS_OBJECT_NAME_NOT_FOUND means we ran out of DeviceN subkeys, but it's not really an error.

❹ There must have been at least one valid set of parameter information, or there's a problem somewhere.

XxFindNextDevice   This function extracts information about one device from the driver's service key and stores it in a slot in the Configuration block.

```
static NTSTATUS
XxFindNextDevice(
        IN INTERFACE_TYPE BusType,
        IN ULONG BusNumber,
        IN PUNICODE_STRING RegistryPath,
        IN PCONFIG_ARRAY ConfigArray
        )
{

        UNICODE_STRING SubPath;
        WCHAR PathNameBuffer[ 30 ];

        UNICODE_STRING  Number;
        WCHAR NumberBuffer[10];

        RTL_QUERY_REGISTRY_TABLE Table[5]; ❶
        NTSTATUS status;

        PDEVICE_BLOCK pDevice =
                &ConfigArray->Device[ ConfigArray->Count ];

        //
        // Prepare to interrogate the Registry by
        // setting up the query-table
        //
        RtlZeroMemory( Table, sizeof(Table));
        //
        // Create a name string for the
        // query table. Start by forming
        // the base path name
        //
        SubPath.Buffer = PathNameBuffer; ❷
        SubPath.MaximumLength = sizeof( PathNameBuffer );
        SubPath.Length = 0;

        RtlAppendUnicodeToString(
                &SubPath,
                L"Parameters\\Device" );

        //
        // Convert the device number into a string and
```

```
// attach it to the end of the path name.
//
Number.Buffer = NumberBuffer;
Number.MaximumLength = sizeof( NumberBuffer );
Number.Length = 0;

RtlIntegerToUnicodeString(
     ConfigArray->Count,
     10,                        // base-10 conversion
     &Number );

RtlAppendUnicodeStringToString(
     &SubPath,
     &Number );
//
// Fabricate the query
//
Table[0].Name     = SubPath.Buffer;
Table[0].Flags    = RTL_QUERY_REGISTRY_SUBKEY;  ❸
Table[1].Name     = L"PORT"; // I/O port addr
Table[1].Flags    = RTL_QUERY_REGISTRY_DIRECT;
Table[1].EntryContext =
            &pDevice->OriginalPortBase;
Table[2].Name     = L"SPAN"; // Number of ports
Table[2].Flags    = RTL_QUERY_REGISTRY_DIRECT;
Table[2].EntryContext =
            &pDevice->PortSpan;

Table[3].Name = L"IRQ"; // IRQ level
Table[3].Flags = RTL_QUERY_REGISTRY_DIRECT;
Table[3].EntryContext =
            &pDevice->OriginalIrql;
//
// Query the Registry...
//
status = RtlQueryRegistryValues( ❹
            RTL_REGISTRY_ABSOLUTE,
            RegistryPath->Buffer,
            Table,
            NULL, NULL );

if( !NT_SUCCESS( status )) return status;

//
// Fix up and translate the information
// from the Registry
//
```

```
        status = XxGetPortInfo(  ❺
                    BusType,
                    BusNumber,
                    pDevice );

    if( !NT_SUCCESS( status )) return status;

    status = XxGetInterruptInfo(
                    BusType,
                    BusNumber,
                    pDevice );
    return status;
}
```

❶ We need four entries in the query table for our own use, plus one extra to terminate the query request.

❷ We need to create a string that looks like "Parameters\DeviceN" to represent the subkey under the driver's service entry.

❸ This query just moves us down a level in the Registry so that all future queries will be taken from the **Parameters\DeviceN** subkey.

❹ One call to **RtlQueryRegistryValues** does it all. It adds the subkey to the end of the driver's service key name, looks for all four value items, and dumps their contents back into the Configuration block.

❺ From here on, we use some helper functions to make the data from the Registry usable.

XxGetPortInfo and XxGetInterruptInfo   Here are the helper functions again. You'll notice that **XxGetInterruptInfo** has to do some fix-up work on the data it gets from the Registry.

```
//++
// Function:
//          XxGetPortInfo
//
// Description:
//          This function fixes up I/O port infomation
//          pulled from the driver's Registry service key
//
// Arguments:
//          Bus type
//          Bus number
//          Pointer to this device's slot in Config Array
//
// Return Value:
//          STATUS_SUCCESS
//          STATUS_XXX if error
```

```
//--
static NTSTATUS
XxGetPortInfo(
        IN  INTERFACE_TYPE BusType,
        IN  ULONG BusNumber,
        IN  PDEVICE_BLOCK pDevice
        )
{
        ULONG AddressSpace;
        PHYSICAL_ADDRESS TranslatedPortBase;
        //
        // Convert bus-relative port-information into NT
        // system-mapped values, and save the results...
        //
        AddressSpace = 1; // Ports should be in I/O space.

        if( !HalTranslateBusAddress(
                    BusType,
                    BusNumber,
                    pDevice->OriginalPortBase,
                    &AddressSpace,
                    &TranslatedPortBase ))
        {
                return STATUS_INSUFFICIENT_RESOURCES;
        }
        pDevice->PortBase =
                    (PUCHAR)TranslatedPortBase.LowPart;
        return STATUS_SUCCESS;
}

//++
// Function:
//          XxGetInterruptInfo
//
// Description:
//          This function fixes up IRQ infomation
//          pulled from the driver's Registry service key
//
// Arguments:
//          Bus type
//          Bus number
//          Pointer to this device's slot in Config array
//
// Return Value:
//          STATUS_SUCCESS
//          STATUS_XXX if error
```

```
//--
static NTSTATUS
XxGetInterruptInfo(
        IN INTERFACE_TYPE BusType,
        IN ULONG BusNumber,
        IN PDEVICE_BLOCK pDevice
        )
{
        //
        // Fill in the gaps by providing values for things
        // that aren't in the Registry...
        //
        pDevice->InterruptMode = Latched;
        pDevice->OriginalVector = pDevice->OriginalIrql;
        pDevice->ShareVector = FALSE;
        pDevice->FloatingSave = FALSE;

        //
        // Convert bus-relative interrupt information into
        // NT system-mapped values, and save the results...
        //
        pDevice->SystemVector =
            HalGetInterruptVector(
                BusType,
                BusNumber,
                pDevice->OriginalIrql,
                pDevice->OriginalVector,
                &pDevice->Dirql,
                &pDevice->Affinity );
        return STATUS_SUCCESS;
}
```

XxCheckForBus and XxBusCallback   These little functions allow you to check for the existence of a particular bus on the system. They make use of **IoQueryDeviceDescription** to test for the presence of the bus.

```
//++
// Function:
//            XxCheckForBus
//
// Description:
//            This function verifies the existence of a
//            particular bus-type and number.
//
// Arguments:
//            BusType -- Isa, Eisa, etc
```

```
//              BusNumber -- 0, 1, etc
//
// Return Value:
//              STATUS_SUCCESS or some error condition.
//--
static NTSTATUS
XxCheckForBus(
        IN INTERFACE_TYPE BusType,
        IN ULONG BusNumber )
{

        return( IoQueryDeviceDescription(
                        &BusType, &BusNumber,
                        NULL, NULL,
                        NULL, NULL,
                        XxBusCallback,
                        NULL ));
}

//++
// Function:
//              XxBusCallback
//
// Description:
//              This is a dummy function. The fact that the
//              system calls it means that the bus type and
//              number both exist, so all that's necessary
//              is to return STATUS_SUCCESS.
//
// Arguments:
//              (Unused)
//
// Return Value:
//              This function always returns STATUS_SUCCESS
//--
static NTSTATUS
XxBusCallback(
        IN PVOID Context,
        IN PUNICODE_STRING PathName,
        IN INTERFACE_TYPE BusType,
        IN ULONG BusNumber,
        IN PKEY_VALUE_FULL_INFORMATION *BusInfo,
        IN CONFIGURATION_TYPE CtrlrType,
        IN ULONG CtrlrNumber,
        IN PKEY_VALUE_FULL_INFORMATION *CtrlrInfo,
        IN CONFIGURATION_TYPE DeviceType,
```

```
        IN ULONG DeviceNumber,
        IN PKEY_VALUE_FULL_INFORMATION *DeviceInfo )
{

        return STATUS_SUCCESS;
}
```

7.5 ALLOCATING AND RELEASING HARDWARE

At this point, your driver has gone to a lot of trouble to locate some hardware. Before you can use any of it, though, you have to make sure the hardware doesn't belong to any other driver. This section explains how to allocate hardware for your driver's exclusive use.

How Resource Allocation Works

NT maintains a central database of all currently owned hardware in the ...\HARDWARE\RESOURCEMAP section of the Registry. Before touching any hardware resources, a driver checks this map to be sure someone else isn't using them. If everything is free, the driver claims the hardware by adding a description of its resource requirements to the resource map. If the resources aren't free, the driver must leave them alone.[4]

Resources owned by a particular driver are recorded in a key with the same name as the driver. In the resource map, these resource keys are organized in arbitrary classes. Your driver has the option of declaring its own class, using an existing class declared by another driver, or using the default resource class called **OtherDrivers**. Resource classes are purely decorative and have no effect on resource allocation or conflict detection.

Within a driver's resource key, there are two values called **.Raw** and **.Translated**. Each of these items is a list describing the resources owned by the driver. The raw list contains bus-specific information returned by routines like **IoQueryDeviceDescription**, while the translated list holds the systemwide numbers returned by the **HalTranslateXxx** functions.

Drivers can also declare some resources as the property of the whole driver, and others as belonging to individual devices. In this case, resources shared by multiple devices go into the driver's **.Raw** and **.Translated** values, while device-specific resources have their own value items in the resource key. These device-specific values are called **\Device**_DeviceName_**.Raw** and **\Device**_Device-Name_**.Translated**. Figure 7.4 shows how all this works.

---

[4] For the stability of the operating system, it's vital that all device drivers abide by this arbitration scheme. As a trusted kernel-mode component, no one can stop a driver from touching hardware without allocating it. However, this can lead to confusing, unpredictable interactions between multiple drivers that think they each have exclusive access to a piece of hardware.

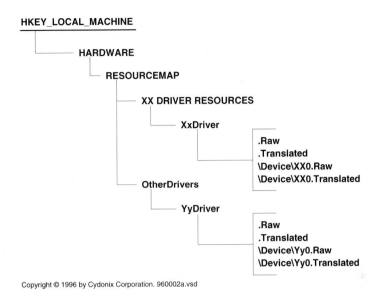

Figure 7.4   Format of hardware-allocation data in the Registry

In the figure, XXDRIVER has declared a private class (called **XX DRIVER RESOURCES**) for its resource list. Some resources are allocated to the driver itself, while others belong only to the device Xx0. YYDRIVER, being somewhat more shy, doesn't use a private class for its resources, so its resource key ends up in the **OtherDrivers** class. Again, some resources belong to the entire driver while others have been claimed only for one device.

Again, the Registry editor, REGEDT32, gives you an easy way to poke around in the system resource map. In the initial phases of driver development, you can use this tool to make sure your driver is allocating all the right resources. REGEDT32 also lets you verify that an unloadable driver has released whatever hardware it may have claimed.

How to Claim Hardware Resources

To claim hardware, your driver needs to build a list of the resources it wants to allocate. Figure 7.5 shows one of these lists. At the very top is a structure called a CM_RESOURCE_LIST. As you can see, a Resource List is basically an array of the CM_FULL_RESOURCE_DESCRIPTOR structures that you saw back in Figure 7.2. Each Full Resource Descriptor in this array identifies all the resources used by the driver on a single bus type and bus number. Collectively, all the Full Resource Descriptors in a single Resource List describe the resources used on multiple buses.

As with the data passed to a ConfigCallback routine, individual resources are identified by Partial Resource Descriptors. The only difference is that the information given to a ConfigCallback routine is about one specific device or controller. When you fabricate a Full Resource Descriptor to allocate hardware, you

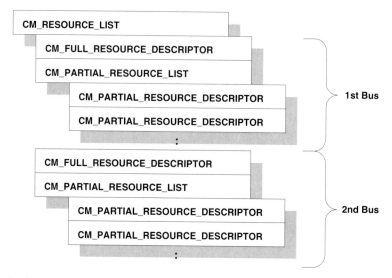

Copyright © 1994 by Cydonix Corporation. 940047a.vsd

Figure 7.5   Structures passed to IoReportResourceUsage

have to group together the Partial Descriptors for all resources on one bus in the same Full Resource Descriptor.[5]

You request ownership of the items in a CM_RESOURCE_LIST by passing the list to **IoReportResourceUsage** (described in Table 7.7). This function checks for any conflicts with previously allocated hardware and adds your claims to the Registry's resource map. When you call this function, it completely replaces any existing resource list associated with the specified Driver or Device object.

If you include a class-name string, the I/O Manager will create a private class key for your driver's resources. Passing NULL puts your driver's resource key in the **OtherDrivers** class. If you allocate resources using a private class, you'll also need to specify the class name when you release these resources.

Remember that you can associate a resource list either with the Driver object itself or with a particular Device object. Any resources being used by multiple devices should be in the **DriverList**, while device-dedicated resources should go in the **DeviceList**. If you break your resources up this way, you'll need to call **IoReportResourceUsage** several times: once for the **DriverList** and once for each **DeviceList**.

If **IoReportResourceUsage** returns STATUS_SUCCESS, you have to check the value returned in the **ConflictDetected** boolean. If this variable is TRUE, it

---

[5] It's also worth emphasizing that these Partial Resource Descriptors contain the original bus-relative values for such things as the I/O port base and the IRQ level — not the translated values returned by functions like HalTranslateBusAdress.

Table 7.7   Prototype for IoReportResourceUsage

NTSTATUS IoReportResourceUsage	IRQL == PASSIVE_LEVEL
Parameter	**Description**
IN PUNICODE_STRING ClassName	Optional class name for driver
IN PDRIVER_OBJECT DriverObject	Driver object associated with this driver
IN PCM_RESOURCE_LIST DriverList	Resources used by all driver's devices
IN ULONG DriverListSize	Size of list in bytes
IN PDEVICE_OBJECT DeviceObject	Device that will own the resources
IN PCM_RESOURCE_LIST DeviceList	Resources used by a single device
IN ULONG DeviceListSize	Size of list in bytes
IN BOOLEAN OverrideConflict	• TRUE — ignore resource conflicts • FALSE — return error if conflict
OUT PBOOLEAN ConflictDetected	• TRUE — resources already claimed • FALSE — no conflict
Return value	• STATUS_SUCCESS • STATUS_INSUFFICIENT_RESOURCES

means that one or more items in your resource list already belong to someone else. In this case, your driver mustn't use any of the hardware in the list.

The **OverrideConflict** parameter determines the behavior of **IoReportResourceUsage** when it detects a conflict. If you pass FALSE, the function makes no changes to the Registry's resource map. Instead, it puts a message in the event log identifying the conflicting resources and their current owner.[6] If **OverrideConflict** is TRUE, **IoReportResourceUsage** *does* add your resource list to the resource map but doesn't send a message to the system event log. However, even though your resource list is in the Registry, your driver mustn't touch any hardware in the list; someone else thinks they own it.

One odd bit of behavior is worth mentioning: Sometimes when there's a resource conflict, **IoReportResourceUsage** returns an unsuccessful status code that has no corresponding Win32 error number. The sample code in the next section shows how to handle this situation properly.

How to Release Hardware

When you want to free up resources held by your driver, you build an empty resource list and call **IoReportResourceUsage**. Since the new list completely replaces the previous one, this has the effect of releasing any resources described in the old list. If you allocated hardware on a device-specific or driver-wide basis, you

---

[6] Your driver has to be identified in the Registry as a system event logging component in order for the Event Viewer to display these messages. Chapter 13 explains how to set this up. These messages can be very helpful for debugging resource conflicts.

need to release it the same way. Also, if you used a private class name to allocate the hardware, you'll need to use the same class name to free it.

The following code fragment shows how a driver's Unload routine might release hardware resources associated with a specific Device object.

```
CM_RESOURCE_LIST ResList;
BOOL bConflict;

ResList.Count = 0;

IoReportResourceUsage(
  NULL,               // Default class name
  pDriverObject,      // Pointer to Driver object
  NULL,               // No driver-wide resources
    0,
  pDeviceObject,      // Pointer to Device object
  &ResList,           // Device-specific resources
  sizeof( ResList ),
  FALSE,              // Don't override conflict
  &bConflict );       // Junk, but required
```

Mapping Device Memory

If your device uses a range of dedicated memory addresses, your driver will need to make that memory available during initialization. Depending on the architecture of the device, your driver will need to perform one of the following two procedures.

Driver-chosen addresses   Some devices (like Ethernet adapters) have a control register that specifies the starting address of a device specific memory area. In this case, your driver needs to allocate memory for the device and let the device know where the memory is located.[7] Follow these steps to set up this memory area:

1.   Call **IoReportResourceUsage** to allocate the device's control registers.

2.   Call **HalGetAdapter** to find the Adapter object associated with your device.

3.   Call **HalAllocateCommonBuffer** to allocate buffer space for your device's memory. This function returns both a system virtual address and a physical address.

4.   Save the system virtual address of this buffer somewhere in your Device Extension. Use this virtual address from within your driver whenever you need to reference the device's memory area.

---

[7] This is actually just a special case of something called common buffer bus master DMA which is described in Chapter 12.

5. Write the buffer's physical address into whatever device registers control access to the device memory.

6. When your driver unloads, call **HalFreeCommonBuffer** to release the buffer.

Hard-wired addresses   Some pieces of hardware (like VGA controllers) have very specific ideas about where their shared buffers should be located. If your device needs to use a particular range of physical addresses for device memory, follow these steps to make the memory available to your driver:

1. Call **IoReportResourceUsage** to request exclusive ownership of the range of physical addresses belonging to the device.

2. Call **HalTranslateBusAddress** to convert the device's bus-relative physical addresses into systemwide values.

3. Call **MmMapIoSpace** to map the device's memory into system virtual space. Save the address returned by this function and use it to access device memory from within your driver.

4. When your driver unloads, call **MmUnmapIoSpace** to break the connection between the device's memory and system virtual space.

Loading Device Microcode

As part of their initialization, some complex devices need to have microcode loaded into them from a disk file. If the quantity of microcode is small, you can store it as a REG_BINARY value in the driver's **Parameters** subkey. For a device that needs large amounts of microcode, this may not be feasible.

Fortunately, NT provides several functions that give drivers handle-based access to files and directories. As you can see from Table 7.8, these routines bear a strong resemblance to the Win32 user-mode file API. Using these functions, a driver could load vast quantities of microcode into a device without overburdening the Configuration Manager. In this case, only the path-name for the microcode file would need to be stored in the driver's **Parameters** subkey.

There are three important things to keep in mind if you decide to use these functions. First, you can only call them from parts of your code running at PASSIVE_LEVEL IRQL. This effectively limits their use to **DriverEntry**, the Unload routine, Dispatch routines, and any thread-based parts of your driver.

Second, you can't access any files with these calls until the file-system driver for the target volume has finished initializing itself. If your driver loads during system bootstrap, you can guarantee that it loads after any file systems by setting up proper group dependencies in the Registry. Chapter 16 explains how to do this.

Finally, avoid the temptation to store driver initialization parameters in disk files. That kind of thing belongs only in the Registry. The proliferation of .INI files in earlier versions of Windows was a bad thing; don't litter NT with them.

Table 7.8   Kernel-mode code can access files using these functions

ZwXxx file functions	IRQL == PASSIVE_LEVEL
IF you want to...	**THEN call...**
Create or open a file, device, or directory	ZwCreateFile
Read data into memory from a file	ZwReadFile
Write data from memory to a file	ZwWriteFile
Get file size, position, attribute information	ZwQueryInformationFile
Set file size, position, attribute information	ZwSetInformationFile
Close an open file handle	ZwClose

For more information about the functions listed in Table 7.8, take a look at the online documentation in the NT DDK. The DDK also contains some sample code that shows how to use these routines.

7.6   CODE EXAMPLE: ALLOCATING HARDWARE

This example illustrates the hardware allocation techniques we've just been looking at. It assumes that the device uses a DMA channel, but no device-specific memory or other device-specific data. You can find this code in the **CH07** directory on the disk that accompanies this book.

RESALLOC.C

The functions in this file allocate a group of resources for exclusive use by a specific Driver object.

XxReportHardwareUsage   Given a linked list of CONFIG_ARRAYs, this routine buids a Resource List and marks the resources as belonging to the entire Driver object. No resources are tagged as belonging to specific Device objects.

```
NTSTATUS
XxReportHardwareUsage(
        IN PDRIVER_OBJECT DriverObject,
        IN PCONFIG_ARRAY ConfigList
        )
{
        ULONG ListSize;
        PCM_RESOURCE_LIST ResourceList;
        PCM_FULL_RESOURCE_DESCRIPTOR Frd;
        PCM_PARTIAL_RESOURCE_DESCRIPTOR Prd;
        PCONFIG_ARRAY CurrentArray;
```

```
        BOOLEAN bConflictDetected;
        NTSTATUS status;
        ULONG i;

        //
        // Calculate size of resource list ❶
        //
        ListSize =
              FIELD_OFFSET( CM_RESOURCE_LIST, List[0] );

        CurrentArray = ConfigList;

        while( CurrentArray != NULL )
        {
              ListSize +=
                    sizeof( CM_FULL_RESOURCE_DESCRIPTOR ) +
                    ((( CurrentArray->Count *
                        XX_RESOURCE_ITEMS_PER_DEVICE ) - 1) *
                        sizeof(
                          CM_PARTIAL_RESOURCE_DESCRIPTOR ));

              CurrentArray = CurrentArray->NextConfigArray;
}

//
// Try and allocate paged memory for the resource
// list. If it works, zero out the list.
//
ResourceList =
      ExAllocatePool( PagedPool, ListSize ); ❷
      if( ResourceList == NULL )
      {
            return STATUS_INSUFFICIENT_RESOURCES;
      }

RtlZeroMemory( ResourceList, ListSize );

CurrentArray = ConfigList; ❸
Frd = &ResourceList->List[0];

while( CurrentArray != NULL )
{
      ResourceList->Count++;
      Frd->InterfaceType = CurrentArray->BusType;
      Frd->BusNumber = CurrentArray->BusNumber;

      //
      // Set the number of Partial Resource
      // Descriptors in this FRD.
```

```
      //
      Frd->PartialResourceList.Count =
              CurrentArray->Count *
              XX_RESOURCE_ITEMS_PER_DEVICE;

      //
      // Get pointer to first Partial Resource
      // Descriptor in this FRD.
      //
      Prd = &Frd->PartialResourceList.
                    PartialDescriptors[0];

      for( i=0; i < CurrentArray->Count; i++ )  ❹
      {
          Prd = XxBuildPartialDescriptors(
                  &CurrentArray->Device[i],
                  Prd );
      }

      //
      // Point to beginning of next Full Resource
      // Descriptor.
      //
      (PUCHAR)Frd +=
          ((( Frd->PartialResourceList.Count - 1 ) *
          sizeof( CM_PARTIAL_RESOURCE_DESCRIPTOR ))
          + sizeof( CM_FULL_RESOURCE_DESCRIPTOR ));
      //
      // Get next Config array from linked-list
      //
      CurrentArray = CurrentArray->NextConfigArray;
}

status = IoReportResourceUsage(  ❺
          NULL,
          DriverObject,
          ResourceList,
          ListSize,
          NULL,
          NULL,
          0,
          FALSE,        // Don't override
          &bConflictDetected );

ExFreePool( ResourceList );

if( !NT_SUCCESS( status ) || bConflictDetected )
      return STATUS_INSUFFICIENT_RESOURCES;
else
```

```
        return STATUS_SUCCESS;
}
```

❶ Start by accounting for header space between the beginning of the Resource List and first Full Resource Descriptor (FRD). For the whole Resource List, we need one FRD per bus type and bus number. We have to run the Config List to find them all. Each FRD contains a separate group of Partial Resource Descriptors (PRDs) for each device we're allocating. Since an FRD has one PRD already embedded in it, we subtract one from the total PRD count for each FRD.

❷ Once the hideous calculations are complete, we allocate a chunk of paged pool that's large enough to hold the whole thing. As always, it's important to zero out any memory allocated from the system pool areas. You don't know where they've been.

❸ Run the Config List again. This time, build a separate FRD for each Config Array in the list.

❹ Loop through all the Device Blocks in the current Config Array. For each Device Block, call a helper function to create PRDs for any resources used by that device.

❺ Once the Resource List is complete, call **IoReportResourceUsage** to request ownership of the hardware. Afterwards, release the pool memory used for the Resource List.

XxBuildPartialDescriptors   Give a Device Block and a pointer to the first available Partial Resource Descriptor in an FRD, this function adds all the PRDs for one device to the current FRD.

```
static PCM_PARTIAL_RESOURCE_DESCRIPTOR
XxBuildPartialDescriptors(
        IN PDEVICE_BLOCK Device,
        IN PCM_PARTIAL_RESOURCE_DESCRIPTOR Prd
        )
{
        //
        // Set up PRD for control registers
        //
        Prd->Type = CmResourceTypePort;

        Prd->ShareDisposition =
                CmResourceShareDriverExclusive;

        Prd->Flags = CM_RESOURCE_PORT_IO;  ❶

        Prd->u.Port.Start =
                    Device->OriginalPortBase;
        Prd->u.Port.Length = Device->PortSpan;
        Prd++;  ❷
```

```
                      //
                      // Set up PRD for Interrupt resource
                      //
                      Prd->Type = CmResourceTypeInterrupt;

                      Prd->ShareDisposition =
                              CmResourceShareDriverExclusive;

                      if( Device->InterruptMode == Latched )
                              Prd->Flags =
                                    CM_RESOURCE_INTERRUPT_LATCHED;  /
                      else
                              Prd->Flags =
CM_RESOURCE_INTERRUPT_LEVEL_SENSITIVE;

                      Prd->u.Interrupt.Level =
                                  Device->OriginalIrql;  ❸

                      Prd->u.Interrupt.Vector =
                                  Device->OriginalVector;
                      Prd++;
                      return Prd;
              }
```

❶ This example assumes that device control registers are always in I/O space. A truly general driver would need to take a more flexible approach.

❷ Point to the beginning of the next PRD. (C is a wonderful language.)

❸ The setup operations for all the PRDs are very similar; just fill in the necessary fields of the PRD. Remember to use the original values, and not the ones returned by translation functions such as HalGetInterruptVector or HalTranslateBusAddress.

7.7 SUMMARY

In this chapter, we've looked at various techniques your driver can use to locate the hardware it has to manage. For some kinds of devices, the hardware will identify itself and provide the system with a lot of information. Other devices (including most ISA cards) are very shy, so you'll need to supplement any auto-detected information with other data sources, including hard-wired Registry values. Whatever method you use to find your hardware, you absolutely must claim it for your driver's exclusive use.

Now that we have a driver that loads and unloads without crashing the system, the next step is to make a connection with the NT system service dispatcher. That's the subject of Chapter 8.

Driver Dispatch Routines

When an I/O request begins its arduous journey through the NT I/O subsystem, the first challenge it faces is to get by one of your driver's Dispatch routines. The Dispatch routine decides whether the request should go any further, or whether it should be sent back to the original caller in disgrace. This chapter will help you set up your Dispatch routines and explain how these routines should behave in various situations. It also fills in some of the details involved in processing buffered and direct I/O requests.

8.1 ENABLING DRIVER DISPATCH ROUTINES

Before your driver can receive I/O requests, you need to tell the I/O Manager what kinds of operations the driver supports. This section describes the I/O Manager's dispatching mechanism and explains how to enable receipt of specific I/O function codes. It also presents some guidelines for deciding which function codes your driver needs to support.

I/O Request Dispatching Mechanism

Recall from earlier chapters that most I/O operations under NT are packet-driven. When a user-mode application issues an I/O request, the I/O Manager first builds an IRP to keep track of the request. Among other things, it stores an IRP_MJ_XXX code in the **MajorFunction** field of the IRP's I/O stack location to identify the exact operation being performed.

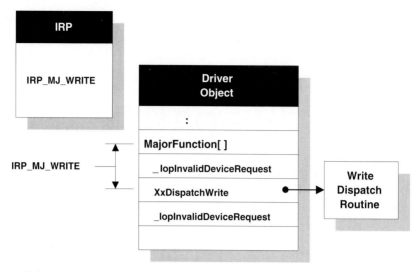

Copyright © 1994 by Cydonix Corporation. 940030a.vsd

Figure 8.1   How the I/O Manager selects Dispatch routines

When it's time to process the IRP, the I/O Manager uses the IRP_MJ_XXX value as an index into the Driver object's **MajorFunction** table. From the table, it gets a pointer to a routine that handles this specific IRP_MJ_XXX code, which it then calls. If the driver doesn't support the requested operation, the table entry points to the I/O Manager's internal **_IopInvalidDeviceRequest** function — which returns an error to the original caller. If the driver does support the operation, the table entry points to one of the driver's own Dispatch routines. Figure 8.1 illustrates this process.

Enabling Specific Function Codes

To enable dispatching for a specific IRP_MJ_XXX function code, your DriverEntry routine must put the address of a Dispatch routine into the **MajorFunction** table of the Driver object. You use the I/O function code itself as an index into the dispatching table. The following code fragment illustrates how to do this.

```
NTSTATUS
DriverEntry(
  IN PDRIVER_OBJECT pDO,
  IN PUNICODE_STRING RegistryPath )
{
  :
  pDO->MajorFunction[ IRP_MJ_CREATE ] = XxDispCreate;
  pDO->MajorFunction[ IRP_MJ_CLOSE ] = XxDispClose;
  pDO->MajorFunction[ IRP_MJ_CLEANUP ] = XxDispCleanup;
```

```
pDO->MajorFunction[ IRP_MJ_READ ] = XxDispRead;
pDO->MajorFunction[ IRP_MJ_WRITE ] = XxDispWrite;
:
return STATUS_SUCCESS;
}
```

Note that you can use the same Dispatch routine to service more than one I/O function code. The choice of how many Dispatch routines to implement is entirely up to you.

Also, you can ignore **MajorFunction** table entries corresponding to function codes your driver doesn't support. By the time the I/O Manager calls your DriverEntry routine, it has already filled every entry in the table with pointers to **_IopInvalidDeviceRequest**, so any slots you don't explicitly fill will appear as unsupported device operations.

Deciding Which Function Codes to Support

All drivers must support the IRP_MJ_CREATE function code, since this is the one generated by a Win32 **CreateFile** call. If you don't process this function code, Win32 programs will have no way to get a handle to your device.

The choice of other function codes will depend on the nature of your device and the kinds of operations it can perform. Use Table 8.1 to decide which IRP function codes might be appropriate. If you're writing an intermediate driver, you must provide Dispatch entry points for all the I/O function codes supported by any drivers below yours in the chain.

If you're writing a driver for one of the standard system devices, or if you're writing a layered driver that sits on top of such a device, it's important that you support a specific set of required IRP function codes. Part II of the *Windows NT DDK Kernel-mode Driver Reference* contains extensive descriptions of the IRP_MJ_XXX function codes your driver must process if it supports one of the standard devices.

8.2   EXTENDING THE DISPATCH INTERFACE

What do you do if you need to perform a device operation other than the ones listed in Table 8.1? The I/O Manager doesn't permit you to add any new IRP function codes, so that's not an option. Fortunately, two of the standard IRP_MJ_XXX values are escape codes that allow you to define any number of driver-specific operations:

- **IRP_MJ_DEVICE_CONTROL** — Lets you define functions that are available to user-mode clients through the Win32 DeviceIoControl function. Other drivers can also issue these control requests by building appropriate IRPs.

- **IRP_MJ_INTERNAL_DEVICE_CONTROL** — Lets you define functions that are only available to kernel-mode clients (usually other drivers). There is no user-mode API function that can generate one of these requests.

Both these functions pass a driver-defined 32-bit value as a parameter in the IRP. This value is referred to as an I/O control code (IOCTL), and your driver uses it to determine just what operation it should perform. The rest of this section

Table 8.1   Commonly used IRP function codes and their Win32 functions

IRP_MJ_XXX function codes

Function code	Description
IRP_MJ_CREATE	Request for a handle. • **CreateFile**
IRP_MJ_CLEANUP	Cancel pending IRPs when handle closes • **CloseHandle**
IRP_MJ_CLOSE	Close the handle. • **CloseHandle**
IRP_MJ_READ	Get data from device. • **ReadFile**
IRP_MJ_WRITE	Send data to device. • **WriteFile**
IRP_MJ_DEVICE_CONTROL	Control operation available to user- or kernel-mode clients. • **DeviceIoControl**
IRP_MJ_INTERNAL_DEVICE_CONTROL	Control operation only available to kernel-mode clients. (No Win32 call)
IRP_MJ_QUERY_INFORMATION	Get length of file. • **GetFileSize**
IRP_MJ_SET_INFORMATION	Set length of file. • **SetEndOfFile**
IRP_MJ_FLUSH_BUFFERS	Write output buffers or discard input buffers. • **FlushFileBuffers** • **FlushConsoleInputBuffer** • **PurgeComm**
IRP_MJ_SHUTDOWN	System shutting down. • **InitateSystemShutdown**

Note: See NTDDK.H or the online documentation for a complete list of IRP_MJ_XX codes.

explains how this interface works. Later in the chapter, you'll see how to process these functions when they appear in an IRP.

Defining Private IOCTL Values

The IOCTL values passed to your driver have a very specific structure. Figure 8.2 illustrates the fields that make up one of these codes.

Although you can fabricate these control codes by hand, it's much easier to generate them using the CTL_CODE macro that comes with the DDK. As you can see from Table 8.2, the arguments to this macro parallel the fields of an IOCTL code.

IOCTL Argument-Passing Methods

In many situations, you'll want to define IOCTL codes that either need additional arguments from the caller, or that need to pass information back to the caller. For example, an IOCTL that queried a driver for performance data would need some way to return the data. The Win32 **DeviceIoControl** function solves this problem by letting the user specify a pair of input and ouput buffer addresses along with the IOCTL code. The question then becomes: Does the I/O Manager pass these buffers to your driver using Buffered or Direct I/O?

You may be tempted to think that the buffering method used for IOCTLs will be the same one you specified with the DO_BUFFERED_IO or DO_DIRECT_IO flags in the Device object. However, the method used for a device's IOCTLs is not necessarily the same as the method used for data transfers. For greater flexibility, the I/O Manager uses a field in the IOCTL code itself to determine the buffering method. This allows you to choose different buffering methods for each individual IOCTL.

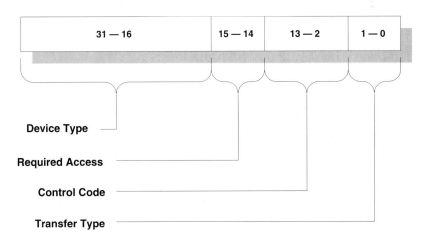

Copyright © 1996 by Cydonix Corporation. 960016a.vsd

Figure 8.2   Layout of an IOCTL code

Table 8.2   Use the CTL_CODE macro to define IOCTL codes

CTL_CODE macro

Parameter	Description
DeviceType	FILE_DEVICE_XXX value given to IoCreateDevice • 0x0000 to 0x7FFF — reserved for Microsoft • 0x8000 to 0xFFFF — available for customer device types
ControlCode	Driver-defined IOCTL code • 0x000 to 0x7FF — reserved for Microsoft • 0x800 to 0xFFF — available for customer IOCTLs
TransferType	Buffer-passing mechanism for this control code (see below) • METHOD_BUFFERED • METHOD_IN_DIRECT • METHOD_OUT_DIRECT • METHOD_NEITHER
RequiredAccess	Access that must be requested when user calls Win32 CreateFile • FILE_ANY_ACCESS • FILE_READ_DATA • FILE_WRITE_DATA • FILE_READ_DATA | FILE_WRITE_DATA

As you can see from Figure 8.2, the **TransferType** field is located in the lowest two bits of the IOCTL code. It can take on one of the following values:

- **METHOD_BUFFERED** — The I/O Manager moves IOCTL data to and from the driver using an intermediate nonpaged pool buffer.

- **METHOD_IN_DIRECT** — IOCTL data coming from the caller is passed using Direct I/O; data going from the driver back to the caller is passed through an intermediate system-space buffer.

- **METHOD_OUT_DIRECT** — Data coming from the caller passes through a system-space buffer; data going back to the caller is passed using Direct I/O.

- **METHOD_NEITHER** — The I/O Manager simply gives the driver raw user-space addresses for the caller's incoming and outgoing IOCTL buffers.

If your driver supports a public IOCTL defined by Windows NT, it has to use the method embedded in the IOCTL.[1] For private IOCTLs, you can choose the I/O method that makes the most sense for the operation. The guidelines for choosing an IOCTL buffering method are the same as those for choosing a data

---

[1] For a complete list of public IOCTLs, see the header file **MSTOOLS\H\WINIOCTL.H**.

transfer buffering method. Buffered I/O is suitable for small amounts of data (less than PAGE_SIZE bytes), while Direct I/O is a better approach for large buffers or DMA operations.

Writing IOCTL Header Files

It's a good idea to write a separate header file for your control-code definitions. This header file should also contain any structures that describe the contents of the IOCTL's input or output buffers. You'll need to include this header file in both the driver and any user-mode programs that issue Win32 DeviceIoControl calls to the driver.[2] The following is an example of an IOCTL header file:

```
#define IOCTL_XXDEVICE_AIM³ CTL_CODE(         \
            FILE_DEVICE_UNKNOWN,              \
            0x801,                            \
            METHOD_BUFFERED,                  \
            FILE_ACCESS_ANY )
// Structures used by IOCTL_XXDEVICE_AIM
//
typedef struct _XX_AIM_IN_BUFF {
  ULONG Longitude;
  ULONG Latitude;
} XX_AIM_IN_BUFF, *PXX_AIM_IN_BUFF;

typedef struct _XX_AIM_OUT_BUFF {
  ULONG ExtendedStatus;
} XX_AIM_OUT_BUFF, *PXX_AIM_OUT_BUFF;

#define IOCTL_XXDEVICE_LAUNCH   CTL_CODE(\
            FILE_DEVICE_UNKNOWN,              \
            0x802,                            \
            METHOD_NEITHER,                   \
            FILE_ACCESS_ANY )
```

8.3 WRITING DRIVER DISPATCH ROUTINES

Once you've chosen an appropriate set of I/O function codes, you need to write the Dispatch routines themselves. This section explains how to code these routines.

---

[2] Additionally, the Win32 program will need to include **WINIOCTL.H** and the driver will need to include **DEVIOCTL.H** to get the definition of the CTL_CODE macro. These header files need to be included before you include the file with your IOCTL defintions.

[3] Microsoft recommends that the names you give to private IOCTLs look like IOCTL_*Device_Function*, where *Device* identifies the device that supports the IOCTL, and Function describes the effect of the IOCTL.

Execution Context

By the time it calls your Dispatch routine, the I/O Manager has already checked the accessibility of the caller's buffer. If this is a Buffered I/O operation, it has also allocated a system buffer from nonpaged pool, and for output requests, copied the caller's data into the system buffer. For Direct I/O operations, the caller's buffer has been faulted into physical memory and locked down.

Like your driver's initialization and cleanup routines, Dispatch routines run at PASSIVE_LEVEL IRQL, which means they can access paged system resources. Table 8.3 shows the prototype for a Dispatch routine.

Normally, a Dispatch routine works only with the contents of the IRP. If a Dispatch routine touches any data structures shared with other parts of the driver, it has to synchronize itself properly. This means using a spin lock to coordinate with driver routines running at DISPATCH_LEVEL IRQL and **KeSynchronizeExecution** to synchronize with the Interrupt Service code.

Never forget that you're sharing the IRP with the I/O Manager. In particular, the system uses various fields in the **Parameters** union to clean up after I/O operations. For example, after a Buffered I/O, it eventually needs to deallocate its nonpaged pool buffer. A field in the IRP gives it the location of this buffer. Changing the contents of the IRP can lead to unspecified (but dreadful) results when the I/O Manager tries to finish processing the request.

If you need to modify any IRP fields, make working copies in local variables or in the Device Extension. Modify these working copies and not the data in the IRP. The only exceptions to this rule are the I/O status block and the **Others** structure in the **Parameters** union. Chapter 15 will discuss the use of this structure by higher-level drivers.

What Dispatch Routines Do

Keep in mind that the exact behavior of a Dispatch routine will depend on the function code it supports. However, the general responsibilities of these routines include the following:

1. Call **IoGetCurrentIrpStackLocation** to get a pointer to the IRP stack location belonging to this driver.

Table 8.3   Function prototype for a Dispatch routine

NTSTATUS XxDispatch	IRQL == PASSIVE_LEVEL
Parameter	**Description**
IN PDEVICE_OBJECT DeviceObject	Pointer to target device for this request
IN PIRP Irp	Pointer to IRP describing this request
Return value	• STATUS_SUCCESS — request complete
	• STATUS_PENDING — request pending
	• STATUS_XXX — appropriate error code

2. Perform any additional sanity checking or parameter validation specific to this function code and device.

3. If this is an intermediate-level driver, and there are limitations on the underlying physical device (for example, its maximum transfer size), the Dispatch routine may need to split the caller's request into multiple requests to the device driver. Chapter 15 explains how to do this.

4. Continue processing the IRP until one of three exit conditions occur.

The following subsections describe some of these steps in greater detail.

Exiting the Dispatch Routine

When a Dispatch routine processes an IRP, there are only three possible outcomes:

- The IRP's request parameters don't pass whatever validation tests you're applying and you need to reject the request.
- You can complete the request entirely in the Dispatch routine without performing any device operations.
- You need to start a device operation in order to complete the request.

Signaling an error   If your Dispatch routine uncovers a problem with the IRP parameters, you need to send the request back to the caller with a nasty message. Follow these steps to reject an IRP:

1. Put an appropriate error code in the **Status** field of the IRP's I/O status block and clear the **Information** field.

2. Call **IoCompleteRequest** to release the IRP with no priority increment.

3. When you exit the Dispatch routine, return the same error code you put in the IRP.

The code fragment below shows how a Dispatch routine rejects an I/O request.

```
NTSTATUS
XxDispWhatever(
   IN PDEVICE_OBJECT pDO,
   IN PIRP Irp )
   {
   :
   Irp->IoStatus.Status = STATUS_BADVIBES;[4]
```

---

[4] No, STATUS_BADVIBES isn't a real NTSTATUS code.

```
   Irp->IoStatus.Information = 0;
   IoCompleteRequest( Irp, IO_NO_INCREMENT );
   return STATUS_BADVIBES;
}
```

Completing a request   You can process some kinds of IRP function codes without actually performing any device operations. Opening a handle to a device, or returning information stored in the Device object are examples of these kinds of requests. To complete a request in the Dispatch routine, do the following:

1. Put a successful completion code in the **Status** field of the IRP's I/O status block, and set the **Information** to some appropriate value.

2. Call **IoCompleteRequest** to release the IRP with no priority increment.

3. Exit the Dispatch routine with a value of STATUS_SUCCESS.

The code fragment below shows how a Dispatch routine completes a request.

```
NTSTATUS
XxDispClose(
   IN PDEVICE_OBJECT pDO,
   IN PIRP Irp )
{
   :
   Irp->IoStatus.Status = STATUS_SUCCESS;
   Irp->IoStatus.Information = 0;
   IoCompleteRequest( Irp, IO_NO_INCREMENT );
   return STATUS_SUCCESS;
}
```

Starting a device operation   The last possibility is that the IRP is requesting an actual device operation. This could be either a data transfer, a control function, or an informational query. In this case, the Dispatch routine has to pass the IRP to the driver's Start I/O routine. To start a device operation, do the following:

1. Call **IoMarkIrpPending** so that the I/O Manager won't try to complete the request.

2. Call **IoStartPacket** to send the request to your driver's Start I/O routine. If you manage your own IRP queues, call your driver's internal routine to start the I/O.

3. Exit the Dispatch routine with a value of STATUS_PENDING.

The following code fragment shows how a Dispatch routine starts a device operation.

```
NTSTATUS
XxDispWrite(
  IN PDEVICE_OBJECT pDO,
  IN PIRP Irp )
{
  :
  IoMarkIrpPending( Irp );
  IoStartPacket( pDO, Irp, 0, NULL );
  return STATUS_PENDING;
}
```

It's a little-known fact that the I/O Manager automatically completes any IRP that isn't marked pending as soon as the Dispatch function returns. Unfortunately, this automatic mechanism doesn't work the same way as an explicit call to **IoCompleteRequest**. In particular, it doesn't include calling any I/O Completion routines attached to the IRP by higher-level drivers. Consequently, it's important that your driver either marks an IRP as pending or completes it explicitly with **IoCompleteRequest**.

8.4   PROCESSING SPECIFIC KINDS OF REQUESTS

The previous section described the general kinds of processing done by a driver's Dispatch routines. These routines may also need to perform various operations that depend on the IRP's function code and the buffering strategy used with the device. This section discusses some of these request-specific issues. This material is also relevant to the Start I/O routine and other parts of a driver, but it appears here because this is the first place where you might run into it.

Processing Read and Write Requests

Chapter 6 explained how to create Device objects, which included setting the DO_BUFFERED_IO or DO_DIRECT_IO bits in the Device object's **Flags** field. These bits control the I/O Manager's behavior for all IRP_MJ_READ and IRP_MJ_WRITE requests sent to the device. Here's what happens once you've set these flags.

Buffered I/O   At the start of both read and write requests, the I/O Manager checks the accessibility of the user buffer. It then allocates a piece of nonpaged pool as big as the caller's buffer and puts its address in the **AssociatedIrp.System-Buffer** field of the IRP. This is the buffer your driver should use for the actual data transfer.

For IRP_MJ_READ operations, the I/O Manager also sets the IRP's **User-Buffer** field to the user-space address of the caller's buffer. Later, when the request is completed, it will use this address to copy data from the driver's system-space buffer back to the caller's buffer. For an IRP_MJ_WRITE request, the I/O Manager sets the IRP's **UserBuffer** field to NULL and copies the contents of the user buffer into the system buffer.

Direct I/O   The I/O Manager checks the accesibility of the user buffer and locks it in physical memory. It then builds a Memory Descriptor List (MDL) for the buffer and stores the address of the MDL in the IRP's **MdlAddress** field. Both the **AssociatedIrp.SystemBuffer** and **UserBuffer** fields are set to NULL.

Normally, you use the MDL to set up a DMA operation, as you'll see in Chapter 12. If you're performing Direct I/O with a programmed I/O device, you can use the **MmGetSystemAddressForMdl** function to get a system-space address for the user buffer. This function doubly maps the caller's buffer into a range of nonpaged system space. (In effect, the buffer lives at two virtual addresses at one time.) When your driver completes the I/O request, the system automatically unmaps the buffer from system space.[5]

Neither method   If you specify neither Buffered nor Direct I/O when you create a Device object, it's up to your driver to decide how to handle buffering issues. The I/O Manager simply puts the user-space address of the caller's buffer into the IRP's **UserBuffer** field. In this case, the IRP's **AssociatedIrp.SystemBuffer** and **MdlAddress** fields have no meaning and are set to NULL.

Be very careful about accessing the caller's buffer in user space with the **UserBuffer** field of the IRP — even if the buffer is locked down. Since IRPs are processed asynchronously, there's no guarantee that the calling process will still be mapped into user space by the time your driver executes. The only exception to this rule is that the Dispatch routines (and only the Dispatch routines) of a highest-level driver can use **UserBuffer** to access the caller's buffer. This is because these routines always run in the context of the thread issuing the I/O request. Other routines in a highest-level driver (and any routine in a lower driver) don't have this guarantee.

Processing IOCTL Requests

Once your driver has filled in either the IRP_MJ_DEVICE_CONTROL or the IRP_MJ_INTERNAL_DEVICE_CONTROL slots in the Driver object's **MajorFunction** table, the I/O Manager starts passing these requests to the associated Dispatch routines. At this point, your driver has to decide what to do with the request.

Other than buffer access checking (described later), the I/O Manager does no validation of either the IOCTL control code itself or the contents of the caller's buffers. (For example, the FILE_DEVICE_XXX field of the IOCTL does not have to

---

[5] Drivers ought to avoid this technique, because releasing the doubly-mapped pages causes every CPU in the system to flush its data cache. This is terrible for system performance.

match that of the target Device object.) The caller could pass any random number as an IOCTL code, and it would find its way to your IOCTL Dispatch routine. So, it's up to you to do any necessary sanity checking.

IOCTL dispatchers usually turn into one of those horrendous switch statements that Microsoft finds so intriguing. The following skeleton of code shows the general layout of a Dispatch routine that processes IOCTL requests.

```
NTSTATUS
XxDispIoControl(❶
        IN PDEVICE_OBJECT pDO,
        IN PIRP Irp )
{

        PIO_STACK_LOCATION IrpStack;
        ULONG ControlCode;
        ULONG InputLength, OutputLength;
        NTSTATUS Status;

        IrpStack = IoGetCurrentIrpStackLocation( Irp );

        // Extract useful information from the I/O stack
        //
        ControlCode = IrpStack->
            Parameters.DeviceIoControl.IoControlCode;
        InputLength = IrpStack->
            Parameters.DeviceIoControl.InputBufferLength;
        OutputLength = IrpStack->
            Parameters.DeviceIoControl.OutputBufferLength;

        switch( ControlCode ) {
        case IOCTL_XXDEVICE_AIM:❷
            // Check buffer sizes and fail if
            // not enough space...
            //
            if(( InputLength < ❸
                    sizeof( XX_AIM_IN_BUFF ))
            || ( OutputLength <
                    sizeof( XX_AIM_OUT_BUFF )))
            {
                Status = STATUS_INVALID_BUFFER_SIZE;
                break;
            }
            // Everything's OK; pass IRP to Start I/O
            //
            IoMarkIrpPending( Irp );❹
            IoStartPacket( pDO, Irp, 0, NULL );
            return STATUS_PENDING;
```

```
      case IOCTL_XXDEVICE_LAUNCH:
            if( InputLength > 0 ❺
            || OutputLength > 0 )
            {
                  Status = STATUS_INVALID_PARAMETER;
                  break;
            }
            // Same kind of processing as the case
            // above;
            :
      // It's not a recognized control code...
      //
      default:
            Status = STATUS_INVALID_DEVICE_REQUEST;
            break;
  }
  // We only wind up here if there's an error
  //
  Irp->IoStatus.Status = Status;❻
  Irp->IoStatus.Information = 0;
  IoCompleteRequest( Irp, IO_NO_INCREMENT );
  return Status;
}
```

❶ If you support both external IRP_MJ_DEVICE_CONTROL and internal
   IRP_MJ_INTERNAL_DEVICE_CONTROL (kernel-mode only) interfaces,
   you'll probably want individual IOCTL Dispatch routines for each major
   function code.

❷ Include a separate case for each IOCTL code that might appear. Any code
   that isn't supported will end up in the default case and fail.

❸ You have to make sure that any buffers associated with the IOCTL are big
   enough. This has to be checked individually for each IOCTL code, since
   different control codes may have different input and output structures.

❹ If the IOCTL makes it through all the validation checks, it gets sent to the
   driver's Start I/O routine. This assumes that the IOCTL causes some kind
   of device operation. For IOCTLs that don't require device activity, you
   can perform the operation and complete the IRP successfully from the
   XxDispIoControl routine.

❺ If you're not expecting any buffers for a particular IOCTL code, you might
   want to return STATUS_INVALID_PARAMETER and fail. This isn't really
   an error, but it makes you wonder if the caller is missing a clue or two.

❻ If something is wrong with this IOCTL request, fail the IRP using whatever status value was generated by the switch statement.

Managing IOCTL Buffers

IOCTL requests can involve both an input buffer coming from the caller and an output buffer being returned to the caller. As a result, they act like a combination of a write operation followed by a read. From previous sections of this chapter, you know that the buffering strategy used for an IOCTL request is determined by the low-order 2 bits of the IOCTL code itself. The following paragraphs describe how the various buffering methods work.

METHOD_BUFFERED   The I/O Manager starts by allocating a single chunk of nonpaged pool that's big enough to hold either the caller's input or output buffer (whichever is larger). It puts the address of the nonpaged pool buffer in the IRP's **AssociatedIrp.SystemBuffer** field. It then copies the IOCTL's input data into the system buffer and sets the **UserBuffer** field of the IRP to the user-space output buffer address. When your driver completes the IOCTL IRP, the I/O Manager copies the contents of the system buffer back into the caller's output buffer.

Since the same piece of nonpaged pool is being used for both the input and output buffers, your driver should read all incoming data before it writes any output data to the buffer.

METHOD_IN_DIRECT   The I/O Manager checks the accessibility of the caller's input buffer and locks it into physical memory. It then builds an MDL for the input buffer and stores a pointer to the MDL in the **MdlAddress** field of the IRP.

It also allocates an output buffer from nonpaged pool and stores the address of this buffer in the IRP's **AssociatedIrp.SystemBuffer** field. The IRP's **UserBuffer** field is set to the original caller's output buffer address. When the IOCTL IRP is completed, the contents of the system buffer will be copied back into the caller's original output buffer.

METHOD_OUT_DIRECT   The I/O Manager checks the accessibility of the caller's output buffer and locks it into physical memory. It then builds an MDL for the output buffer and stores a pointer to the MDL in the **MdlAddress** field of the IRP.

The I/O Manager also allocates an input buffer from nonpaged pool and stores its address in the IRP's **AssociatedIrp.SystemBuffer** field. It copies the contents of the caller's original input buffer into the system buffer and sets the IRP's **UserBuffer** field to NULL.

METHOD_NEITHER   The I/O Manager puts the address of the caller's input buffer in the **Parameters.DeviceIoControl.Type3InputBuffer** field of the IRP's current I/O stack location. It stores the address of the output buffer in the IRP's **UserBuffer** field. Both of these are user-space addresses.

8.5   TESTING DRIVER DISPATCH ROUTINES

Your driver still has a long way to go, but once again, you can verify some aspects of its operation. In particular, you can test the driver to be sure that it

- Opens and closes a handle to the device
- Supports Win32 I/O function calls that return successfully
- Manages requests from multiple callers

Still not very ambitious goals, but if you complete these tests successfully, your driver will be one step closer to full operation.

Testing Procedure

The following procedure will let you check all the code paths through your driver's Dispatch routines.

1. Write IRP_MJ_CREATE and IRP_MJ_CLOSE Dispatch routines for your driver.

2. Test the driver with a simple Win32 console program that gets a handle to your device and then closes the handle.

3. Write other Dispatch routines but modify them so that they always call **IoCompleteRequest** rather than starting any device operations.

4. Modify your Win32 test program to make **ReadFile**, **WriteFile**, and **DeviceIo-Control** calls that exercise each driver Dispatch routine.

5. If your device is shareable, run several copies of the test program at once to be sure the driver works with multiple open handles.

6. If your driver supports multiple physical devices, repeat the tests with each device unit.

Sample Test Program

This is an example of the kind of test program you can use to verify the code paths through a driver's Dispatch routines.

```
#include <windows.h>
#include <stdio.h>

VOID main( VOID )
{
  HANDLE hDevice;
  BOOL status;
```

```
    hDevice = CreateFile( "\\\\.\\XX1"... );
    :
    status = ReadFile( hDevice... );
    :
    status = WriteFile( hDevice... );
    :
    status = DeviceIoControl( hDevice... );
    :
    status = CloseHandle( hDevice );
}
```

8.6   SUMMARY

In this chapter, you've seen the beginning of the I/O processing cycle. By now, you should have a good idea of what IRP function codes your driver will need to support. If some of these functions include IOCTLs, the information in this chapter will help you implement them correctly. If you're writing a higher-level driver, that may be the end of the story.

For device drivers, however, there's still more to do. In the next chapter, you'll see how to perform actual data transfer operations.

Programmed I/O Data Transfers

*D*evices that do programmed I/O need a great deal of attention from the CPU while they transfer data. Usually, these are slow devices (like the mouse or keyboard) that don't move large amounts of data in a single operation. This chapter explains how to write the data transfer sections of drivers for this kind of hardware.

9.1   HOW PROGRAMMED I/O WORKS

This section describes the events that occur during a programmed I/O operation, as well as describing some of the other issues a driver will have to face.

What Happens during Programmed I/O

In a programmed I/O operation, the CPU transfers each unit of data to or from the device in response to an interrupt. Referring to Figure 9.1, the following sequence of events takes place:

1.   The Start I/O routine performs any necessary preprocessing and setup based on the IRP_MJ_XXX function code in the IRP. It then starts the device.

2.   Eventually, the device generates an interrupt which the Kernel passes to the driver's Interrupt Service routine.

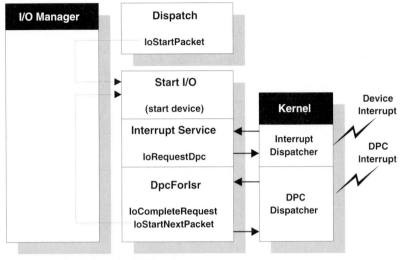

Copyright © 1994 by Cydonix Corporation. 940052a.vsd

Figure 9.1   Sequence of events in a programmed I/O

3. If there is any more data, the Interrupt Service routine starts the next transfer. Steps 2 and 3 may repeat any number of times until the operation is complete.

4. When the operation completes, either because there's no more data or because an error occurs, the Interrupt Service routine queues a request to fire off the driver's DpcForIsr routine.

5. The DPC dispatcher eventually runs the DpcForIsr which releases the current IRP back to the I/O Manager. If there are any more IRPs waiting, the Dpc-ForIsr sends the next packet to the driver's Start I/O routine, and the whole cycle repeats.

Synchronizing Various Driver Routines

Driver routines running at an IRQL below DIRQL must synchronize their access to any device registers or memory areas shared with the driver's Interrupt Service routine. Without this protection, an interrupt might arrive while a low-IRQL routine was using the shared resource, and the outcome would be unpredictable (but probably nothing good). You solve this synchronization problem by putting code that touches these shared resources in a SynchCritSection routine. Table 9.1 shows you the prototype for one of these routines.

When you need to execute a SynchCritSection routine, you pass its address as an argument to **KeSynchronizeExecution** (see Table 9.2). This function raises IRQL to the DIRQL level of the Interrupt object, acquires the object's Interrupt spin lock and then calls your SynchCritSection routine. While it's running, your

Table 9.1   Function prototype for a SynchCritSection routine

BOOLEAN XxSynchCritSection	IRQL == DIRQL
Parameter	**Description**
IN PVOID Context	Pointer to context passed to **KeSynchronizeExecution**
Return value	• TRUE — success
	• FALSE — something failed

Table 9.2   Function prototype for KeSynchronizeExecution

BOOLEAN KeSynchronizeExecution	IRQL < DIRQL
Parameter	**Description**
IN PKINTERRUPT Interrupt	Address of an Interrupt object
IN PKSYNCHRONIZE_ROUTINE Routine	SynchCritSection callback routine
IN PVOID Context	Argument for SynchCritSection routine
Return value	Value returned by SynchCritSection routine

SynchCritSection code is guaranteed not to be interrupted by the device associated with the Interrupt object. When your routine finishes, **KeSynchronizeExecution** releases the spin lock, drops IRQL back to its original level, and returns to the caller.

Notice that you're allowed to pass some context information to the SynchCritSection routine. Typically, this will be a pointer to the Device or Controller Extension structure.

9.2   DRIVER INITIALIZATION AND CLEANUP

Along with the general initialization and cleanup issues we've seen in previous chapters, there are some specific things that a programmed I/O device driver needs to take care of. The following subsections describe them in detail.

Initializing the Start I/O Entry Point

If your driver has a Start I/O routine, you need to let the I/O Manager know where to find it. You do this by putting the address of the Start I/O routine into the **DriverStartIo** field of the Driver object, as in the following code fragment:

```
NTSTATUS
DriverEntry(
  IN PDRIVER_OBJECT DriverObject,
  IN PUNICODE_STRING RegistryPath
  )
{
  :
  //
  // Export other driver entry points...
  //
  DriverObject->DriverStartIo = XxStartIo;
  DriverObject->DriverUnload = XxDriverUnload;

  DriverObject->MajorFunction[ IRP_MJ_CREATE ] =
  XxDispatchOpenClose;
  :
}
```

If you forget to initialize this entry point, you'll get an access violation (and a bright blue screen) when your Dispatch routines call **IoStartPacket**.

Initializing a DpcForIsr Routine

The I/O Manager provides you with a simplified version of the DPC mechanism. Tucked away inside each Device object is a single DPC object. To use it, your DriverEntry routine just calls **IoInitializeDpcRequest** and associates a DpcForIsr callback with the Device object. Later, your driver's Interrupt Service routine can trigger this DPC by calling **IoRequestDpc**.

For some kinds of drivers, this simplified mechanism is too limited. In Chapter 11, you'll see how to set up your own DPC objects if you need the flexibility of multiple DPCs.

Connecting to an Interrupt Source

Before you can process interrupts, you have to establish a connection between your device's interrupt vector and an Interrupt Service routine in your driver. You do this by calling the **IoConnectInterrupt**[1] function described in Table 9.3. Given an Interrupt Service routine and some of the translated information generated by your hardware location code, this function adds your ISR to the Kernel's list of interrupt handlers.

---

[1] If you recall, we first bumped into this function in the driver initialization code in Chapter 6, where we treated it as a necessary bit of magic.

Table 9.3 Function prototype for IoConnectInterrupt

NTSTATUS IoConnectInterrupt	IRQL == PASSIVE_LEVEL
Parameter	**Description**
OUT PKINTERRUPT *InterruptObject	Address of variable that receives pointer to Interrupt object
IN PKSERVICE_ROUTINE SeviceRoutine	ISR that handles this interrupt
IN PVOID ServiceContext	Context argument passed to ISR; usually the Device Extension
IN PKSPIN_LOCK SpinLock	Initialized spin lock (see below)
IN ULONG Vector	Translated interrupt vector value
IN KIRQL Irql	DIRQL value for device
IN KIRQL SynchronizeIrql	Usually same as DIRQL (see below)
IN KINTERRUPT_MODE InterruptMode	• LevelSensitive • Latched
IN BOOLEAN ShareVector	If TRUE, identifies this vector as shareable
IN KAFFINITY ProcessorEnableMask	Set of CPUs on which device interrupt can occur
IN BOOLEAN FloatingSave	If TRUE, save the state of the FPU during an interrupt
Return value	• STATUS_SUCCESS • STATUS_INVALID_PARAMETER • STATUS_INSUFFICIENT_RESOURCES

If it works, **IoConnectInterrupt** returns a pointer to an Interrupt object. You should store this pointer in your Device or Controller Extension because you'll need it in order to disconnect from the interrupt source or to execute any Synch-CritSection routines.

Three things are worth mentioning about **IoConnectInterrupt**. First, if your ISR handles more than one interrupt vector, or if your driver has more than one ISR, you need to supply the system with a spin lock to prevent collisions over the ISR's ServiceContext. If you're not doing either of those things, then this spin lock is unnecessary.[2]

Second, if the ISR manages more than one interrupt vector, or your driver has more than one ISR, make sure that the value you specify for **SynchronizeIrql** is the highest DIRQL value of any of the vectors you're using.

---

[2] Normally, you declare storage space for this spin lock in the Device or Controller Extension. Remember to call **KeInitializeSpinLock** before you connect to an interrupt source.

Finally, your driver's Interrupt Service routine must be ready to run as soon as you call this function. Interrupts from your device (or from other devices at the same IRQL) may preempt any additional initialization done by your driver, and the ISR has to handle these interrupts correctly. So, make sure all the necessary driver setup work is done before you connect to an interrupt. In general, you should follow this kind of sequence:

1. Call **IoInitializeDpcRequest** to initialize the Device object's DPC and perform any initialization needed to make the DpcForIsr routine execute properly.

2. Disable interrupts from the device by setting appropriate bits in the device's control registers.

3. Perform any driver initialization required by the ISR in order for it to run properly.

4. Call **IoConnectInterrupt** to attach your ISR to an interrupt source and store the address of the Interrupt object in the Device Extension.

5. Use a SynchCritSection routine to put the device into a known initial state and enable device interrupts.

Disconnecting from an Interrupt Source

If your driver is unloadable, you need to detach its Interrupt Service routine from the Kernel's list of interrupt handlers before the driver is removed from memory. If you forget to do this and your device generates an interrupt after the driver is unloaded, the Kernel will try to call the address in nonpaged pool where your ISR used to lived. Nothing good will happen.

Disconnecting from an interrupt is a two-step procedure. First, use **KeSynchronizeExecution** and a SynchCritSection routine to disable the device and prevent it from generating any further interrupts. Second, remove your ISR from the Kernel's list of handlers by passing the device's Interrupt object to **IoDisconnectInterrupt**.

9.3   WRITING A START I/O ROUTINE

In the rest of this chapter, we'll be developing a programmed I/O driver for a parallel port. To keep things simple, this driver ignores many of the details you'd have to consider if you were writing a commercial driver. Take a look at the sample driver that comes with the NT DDK to see what's involved in managing these devices.

Execution Context

The I/O Manager calls your Start I/O routine (described in Table 9.4) either when a Dispatch routine calls **IoStartPacket** (if the device was idle), or when

Table 9.4   Function prototype for a Start I/O routine

VOID XxStartlo	IRQL == DISPATCH_LEVEL
Parameter	**Description**
IN PDEVICE_OBJECT DeviceObject	Target device for this request
IN PIRP Irp	IRP describing the request
Return value	—

some other part of the driver calls **IoStartNextPacket**. In either case, Start I/O runs at DISPATCH_LEVEL IRQL, so it mustn't do anything that causes a page fault.

What the Start I/O Routine Does

Your driver's Start I/O routine is responsible for doing any function-code-specific processing needed by the current IRP and then starting the actual device operation. In general terms a Start I/O routine will do the following:

1. Call **IoGetCurrentStackLocation** to get a pointer to the IRP's stack location.

2. If your device supports more than one IRP_MJ_XXX function code, examine the I/O stack location's **MajorFunction** field to determine the operation.

3. Make working copies of the system buffer pointer and byte count stored in the IRP. The Device Extension is the best place to keep these items.

4. Set a flag in the Device Extension indicating that you expect an interrupt.

5. Begin the actual device operation.

To guarantee proper synchronization, any of these steps that access data shared with the ISR should be performed inside a SynchCritSection routine rather than in Start I/O itself.

9.4   WRITING AN INTERRUPT SERVICE ROUTINE (ISR)

Once a device operation begins, the actual data transfer is driven by the arrival of hardware interrupts. When an interrupt arrives, the driver's Interrupt Service routine acknowledges the request and either transfers the next piece of data or invokes a DPC routine.

Execution Context

When the Kernel gets a device interrupt, it uses its collection of Interrupt objects to locate an ISR willing to service the event. It does this by running through all the Interrupt objects attached to the DIRQL of the interrupt and calling ISRs until one of them claims the interrupt.

The Kernel interrupt dispatcher calls your ISR at the synchronization IRQL you specified in the call to **IoConnectInterrupt**. Usually this will be the DIRQL level of the device. The Kernel dispatcher also acquires and releases the device spin lock for you.

Running at such a high IRQL, there are lots of things your ISR isn't allowed to do. In addition to the usual warning about page faults, your ISR shouldn't try to allocate or free various system resources (like memory). If you plan to call any system support routines from your ISR, check for restrictions on the level at which they can run. You may need to perform those kinds of operations in a DPC routine rather than in the ISR itself.

As you can see from Table 9.5, the Kernel passes you a pointer to whatever context information you identified in **IoConnectInterrupt**. Most often, this will be a pointer to the Device or Controller Extension.

What the Interrupt Service Routine Does

The Interrupt Service routine is the real workhorse in a programmed I/O driver. In general, one of these routines will do the following:

1. Determine if the interrupt belongs to this driver. If not, immediately return a value of FALSE.

2. Perform any operations needed by the device to acknowledge the interrupt.

3. Determine if any more data remains to be transferred. If there is, start the next device operation. This will eventually result in another interrupt.

4. If all the data has been transferred (or if a device error occurred), queue up a DPC request by calling **IoRequestDpc**.

5. Return a value of TRUE.

Always code an ISR for speed. Any work that isn't absolutely essential should go in a DPC routine. It's especially important that your ISR doesn't drag its

Table 9.5 Function prototype for an Interrupt Service routine

BOOLEAN XxISR	IRQL == DIRQL
Parameter	**Description**
IN PKINTERRUPT Interrupt	Interrupt object generating the interrupt
IN PVOID ServiceContext	Context area passed to **IoConnectInterrupt**
Return value	• TRUE — interrupt was serviced by XxISR
	• FALSE — interrupt not serviced

feet while determining whether or not to service an interrupt. There may be any number of other ISRs waiting in line behind yours for a given interrupt, and if you do a lot of processing before you decide not to handle the event, you can slow them down.

9.5   WRITING A DpcForIsr ROUTINE

Your driver's DpcForIsr routine is responsible for determining a final status for the current request, completing the IRP, and starting the next one.

Execution Context

In response to the ISR's call to **IoRequestDpc**, your driver's DpcForIsr routine (described in Table 9.6) is added to the DPC dispatch queue. When the CPU's IRQL value drops below DISPATCH_LEVEL, the DPC dispatcher calls the DpcForIsr routine. Your DpcForIsr routine runs at DISPATCH_LEVEL IRQL, which means it has no access to pageable addresses.

Once you call **IoRequestDpc** for a given device, the I/O Manager ignores any further **IoRequestDpc** calls for that device until the DpcForIsr routine executes. This is standard behavior for DPC objects. If your driver design is such that you might issue overlapping DPC requests for the same device, then it's up to you to handle this situation properly. You'll need to keep track of the pending requests and have the DPC routine perform the work for all of them each time it executes.

What the DpcForIsr Routine Does

Since most of the work happens during interrupt processing, the DpcForIsr routine in a programmed I/O driver doesn't have a lot do. In particular, this routine should

1. Set IRP's I/O status block. Put an appropriate STATUS_XXX code in the **Status** field and the actual number of bytes transferred in the **Information** field.

Table 9.6   Function prototype for a DpcForIsr routine

VOID XxDpcForIsr	IRQL == DISPATCH_LEVEL
Parameter	**Description**
IN PKDPC Dpc	DPC object responsible for this call
IN PDEVICE_OBJECT DeviceObject	Target device for I/O request
IN PIRP Irp	IRP describing the current request
IN PVOID Context	Context passed to **IoRequestDpc**
Return value	—

2. Call **IoCompleteRequest** to complete the IRP with an appropriate priority boost. Once you've made this call, don't touch the IRP again.

3. Call **IoStartNextPacket** to send the next IRP to Start I/O.

Priority Increments

The NT thread-scheduler uses a priority-boosting strategy to keep the CPU and I/O devices as busy as possible. As you can see from the boost values listed in Table 9.7, priority increments are weighted so as to favor threads working with interactive devices like the mouse and keyboard.

As part of this strategy, your driver should compensate any thread that waits for an actual device operation by giving it a priority boost. Choose an appropriate increment from the table and specify it as an argument to **IoCompleteRequest**.

9.6   SOME HARDWARE: THE PARALLEL PORT

Before we walk through an example of a programmed I/O driver, it will be helpful to look at some actual hardware. This serves the dual purpose of showing you what kinds of devices tend to perform programmed I/O and of giving us something to control with our driver.

How the Parallel Port Works

The parallel interface found on most PCs is based on an ancient standard from the Centronics Company. Although its original purpose was to communicate

Table 9.7   Specify one of these values when you complete an I/O request

Priority increment values

Symbol	Boost	Use when completing...
IO_NO_INCREMENT	0	Requests involving no device I/O
IO_CD_ROM_INCREMENT	1	CD-ROM input
IO_DISK_INCREMENT	1	Disk I/O
IO_PARALLEL_INCREMENT	1	Parallel-port I/O
IO_VIDEO_INCREMENT	1	Video output
IO_MAILSLOT_INCREMENT	2	Mailslot I/O
IO_NAMED_PIPE_INCREMENT	2	Named pipe I/O
IO_NETWORK_INCREMENT	2	Network I/O
IO_SERIAL_INCREMENT	2	Serial-port I/O
IO_MOUSE_INCREMENT	6	Pointing-device input
IO_KEYBOARD_INCREMENT	6	Keyboard input
IO_SOUND_INCREMENT	6	Sound board I/O

with printers, clever people have found ways of attaching everything from disks to optical scanners to the parallel port. The DB-25 connector on this port carries a number of signals, the most important ones being:

- **Initialize**—The CPU sends a pulse down this line when it wants to initialize the printer.

- **Data**—The CPU uses these eight lines to send one byte of data to the printer. On systems with extended parallel interfaces, these lines can also be used for input.

- **Strobe#**—The CPU pulses this line once to let the printer know that valid information is available on the data lines.[3]

- **Busy**—The printer uses this line to let the CPU know that it can't accept any data.

- **Ack#**—The printer sends a single pulse down this line when it is no longer busy.

- **Errors**—The printer can use several lines to indicate a variety of not-ready and error conditions to the CPU.

The following sequence of events occurs during a data transfer from the CPU to a printer attached to the parallel port:

1. The CPU places a byte on the eight data lines and lets the data settle for at least half a microsecond.

2. The CPU grounds the STROBE# line for at least half a microsecond and then raises it again. This is the signal to the printer that it should latch the byte on the data lines.

3. In response to the new data, the printer raises the BUSY line and starts to process the byte. This usually means moving the byte to an internal buffer.

4. After it processes the character (which may take microseconds or seconds, depending on how full the printer's buffer is), the printer lowers the BUSY line and pulses the ACK# wire by grounding it briefly.[4]

You can see from this description that the parallel port offers a very low-level interface to the outside world. Most of the signaling protocol involved in a data transfer has to be implemented by the CPU itself. This is going to have a major impact on the design of our driver.

---

[3] Following the standard convention, a line with # in its name means that ground indicates a logic-1, while presence of a signal on the line indicates a logic-0.

[4] Yes, using two lines to indicate a ready status is redundant.

Device Registers

The software interface to the parallel port is through a set of three registers, described in Table 9.8. Since the parallel port is one of the things detected by auto-configuration (even on an ISA system), our driver will be able to use the Configuration Manager to find the base address of the data register.

If you look at the bit settings in Table 9.8, you'll notice that some of the bits have the opposite polarity from the signals they represent. For example, you need to set the STROBE bit to 1 if you want to ground the STROBE# wire and get the printer to accept your data. Also, the BUSY wire going to ground causes the BUSY bit in the status register to set itself — so it's really a NOT-BUSY bit. The "solder people" may have a good explanation for all this, but it's usually best to hide these oddities in a hardware header file.[5]

Table 9.8   These registers control a parallel port interface

Parallel port registers

Offset	Register	Access	Description
0	Data	R/W	Data byte transferred through parallel port
1	Status	R/O	Current parallel port status
	Bits 0 – 1		Reserved; normally contain a 1
	Bit 2		0 — interrupt has been requested by port
	Bit 3		0 — an error occurred
	Bit 4		1 — printer is selected
	Bit 5		1 — printer is out of paper
	Bit 6		0 — acknowledge
	Bit 7		0 — printer is busy
2	Control	R/W	Commands sent to parallel port
	Bit 0		1 — strobe data to/from parallel port
	Bit 1		1 — automatic line feed
	Bit 2		0 — initialize printer
	Bit 3		1 — select printer
	Bit 4		1 — enable interrupts
	Bit 5		1 — read data from parallel port*
	Bits 6 – 7		Reserved; must be 1

*Only valid for extended parallel ports; otherwise this must be 0.

---

[5] See the HARDWARE.H header file included in the on-disk version of the sample source code that accompanies this chapter.

Interrupt Behavior

On ISA machines, the parallel port designated as LPT1 normally uses IRQ 7 and LPT2 uses IRQ 5. A device connected to a parallel port generates an interrupt by grounding the ACK# line momentarily. Most printers yank on this line for any of the following reasons:

- The printer has finished initializing itself.
- The printer has processed one character and is now ready for another.
- Power to the printer has been switched off.
- The printer has gone offline or has run out of paper.

There's some variability in the way different printers implement these features. For example, not all of them generate an interrupt when they've completed their initialization, nor do all printers interrupt when they go offline or run out of paper. The driver developed later in this chapter assumes that all these conditions produce interrupts.

A Driver for the Parallel Port

So, just what is it about the parallel port that makes it a good candidate for programmed I/O? Looking at the device's behavior, one clue is that each byte sent to the device has to be transferred through the CPU. DMA devices work independently of the CPU and don't demand this much attention.

Another hint is that it generates an interrupt after each byte is accepted by the device. This means a large number of interrupts will probably occur before an operation is complete. DMA devices typically generate only a single interrupt when a transfer is complete.

9.7 CODE EXAMPLE: PARALLEL PORT DRIVER

This example shows how to write a basic programmed I/O driver for the parallel port. You can find the code for this example in the **CH09\DRIVER** directory on the disk that accompanies this book.

XXDRIVER.H

This version of the main header file builds on the ones seen in previous chapters. Only one structure from this file is of much interest.

DEVICE_EXTENSION   The following excerpt shows the changes in the Device Extension needed to support the parallel port.

```
typedef struct _DEVICE_EXTENSION {

  :

  ULONG FifoSize;        // Bytes to send at once
  ULONG BytesRequested;  // Requested transfer size
  ULONG BytesRemaining;  // Chars left to transfer❶
  PUCHAR pBuffer;        // Next char to send
  BOOLEAN TransferInProgress; ❷

  UCHAR DeviceStatus;    // Most recent status❸

} DEVICE_EXTENSION, *PDEVICE_EXTENSION;
```

❶ These two fields are working copies of the requested transfer size and the system buffer pointer taken from the IRP. They are used to keep track of where we are in the transfer. Modifying the IRP itself would be a disaster because the I/O Manager uses it to clean up after the request.

❷ This flag is used to detect spurious interrupts. It's set at the beginning of a transfer and cleared when the request is completed.

❸ This field keeps track of the most recent status of the parallel port. The DpcForIsr routine uses it to figure out what kind of status to give back to the caller.

INIT.C

Most of the code in this module is the same as it was in Chapter 6. The changes have to do with some hardware-specific initialization.

XxCreateDevice   This excerpt shows the proper sequence of operations for enabling interrupts and initializing a piece of hardware.

```
static NTSTATUS
XxCreateDevice (
  IN PDRIVER_OBJECT DriverObject,
  IN PCONFIG_BLOCK pConfig, // Config block
  IN ULONG uNum // Device number
  )
{
  :
  status = IoCreateSymbolicLink(
  &linkName, &deviceName );
  //
  // See if the symbolic link was created...
  //
  if( !NT_SUCCESS( status )) {
        IoDeleteDevice( pDevObj );
        return status;
  }
```

```
    //
    // Make sure device interrupts are OFF
    //
    XxWriteControl(❶
          pDevExt,
          XX_CTL_DEFAULT | XX_CTL_NOT_INI );

    //
    // Connect to an Interrupt object...
    //
    status = IoConnectInterrupt(❷
                &pDevExt->pInterrupt,
                XxIsr,
                pDevExt,
                NULL,
                pConfig->Device[uNum].SystemVector,
                pConfig->Device[uNum].Dirql,
                pConfig->Device[uNum].Dirql,
                pConfig->Device[uNum].InterruptMode,
                pConfig->Device[uNum].ShareVector,
                pConfig->Device[uNum].Affinity,
                pConfig->Device[uNum].FloatingSave );

    if( !NT_SUCCESS( status )) {
         IoDeleteSymbolicLink( &linkName );
         IoDeleteDevice( pDevObj );
         return status;
    }

    //
    // Initialize the hardware and enable interrupts
    //
    KeSynchronizeExecution(❸
          pDevExt->pInterrupt,
          XxInitDevice,
          pDevExt );

    return status;
}
```

❶ It's important to put the device into a known state. This includes disabling interrupts from the port.

❷ The driver uses values recovered by XxGetHardwareInfo to attach its Interrupt Service Routine to the device's interrupt vector.

❸ Finally, the driver uses a Synch Critical Section routine to initialize the device, including turning on its interrupts. Keep in mind that the Interrupt Service Routine may actually get called as soon as the **KeSynchro-nizeExecution** function returns.

XxInitHardware   This function cycles the INIT line, causing the printer to start initializing itself. This will eventually produce an interrupt. The function then sets the SELECT line and enables interrupts from the port. This might result in an immediate interrupt. However, since this function is being called by **KeSynchronizeExecution**, it's not in any danger of being disturbed by parallel port interrupts.

```
static BOOLEAN
XxInitDevice(
  IN PVOID SynchContext
  )
{
  PDEVICE_EXTENSION pDE =
        (PDEVICE_EXTENSION) SynchContext;

  XxWriteControl( pDE, XX_CTL_DEFAULT ); ❶
  KeStallExecutionProcessor( 60 );

  XxWriteControl(❷
        pDE,
        XX_CTL_DEFAULT
        | XX_CTL_NOT_INI
        | XX_CTL_SELECT
        | XX_CTL_INTENB );
  KeStallExecutionProcessor( 60 );
  return TRUE;
}
```

❶ Clear the NOT_INIT bit. This begins the printer's initialization cycle. The driver waits 60 microseconds to be sure the signal has stabilized.

❷ To complete the cycle, the driver sets the NOT_INIT bit. It also enables interrupts and tells the printer to select itself. Again, it's necessary to wait a little while the signals stabilize.

TRANSFER.C

The routines in this file do the actual work of transferring data out to the parallel port. This includes starting each operation, handling interrupts, and cleaning up with a DPC.

XxStartlo   This function does any preprocessing needed by the current IRP and then starts the actual device operation.

```
VOID
XxStartIo(
  IN PDEVICE_OBJECT DeviceObject,
  IN PIRP Irp
  )
{
  PIO_STACK_LOCATION IrpStack =
        IoGetCurrentIrpStackLocation( Irp );

  PDEVICE_EXTENSION pDE =
        DeviceObject->DeviceExtension;

  switch( IrpStack->MajorFunction ) {❶
        //
        // Use a SynchCritSection routine to
        // start the write operation...
        //
        case IRP_MJ_WRITE:
            //
            // Set up counts and byte pointer❷
            //
            pDE->BytesRequested =
                IrpStack->Parameters.Write.Length;

            pDE->BytesRemaininng =
                pDE->BytesRequested;

            pDE->pBuffer =
                Irp->AssociatedIrp.SystemBuffer;

            if( !KeSynchronizeExecution(❸
                    pDE->pInterrupt,
                    XxTransmitBytes,
                    pDE ))
            {
                XxDpcForIsr(
                    NULL,
                    DeviceObject,
                    Irp,
                    pDE );
            }
            break;

  default: ❹
            Irp->IoStatus.Status =
                        STATUS_NOT_SUPPORTED;
```

```
                        Irp->IoStatus.Information = 0;
                        IoCompleteRequest(
                                Irp,
                                IO_NO_INCREMENT );
                        IoStartNextPacket( DeviceObject, FALSE );
                        break;
        }
    }
```

❶ Since all requests get funneled through a single Start I/O routine, it's necessary to switch on the major-function code if you have to do any function-specific preprocessing.

❷ These are the private copies of the pointer and byte counts that the driver uses to keep track of its place in the system buffer.

❸ The driver tries to send some number of bytes out to the device. If anything goes wrong, it calls XxDpcForIsr as a regular subroutine to complete the request.

❹ The driver should never get to the default case, because unsupported functions have been filtered out by the I/O Manager during the dispatching process. But it's better to be safe than sorry.

XxTransmitBytes   This function sends as many bytes as possible to the parallel port. This will be either one FIFO's worth, or as many as are left in the system buffer. Both XxStartIo and XxIsr call this function. In either case, it expects to be running at DIRQL, synchronized with the driver's ISR

```
static BOOLEAN
XxTransmitBytes(
  IN PVOID Context // Pointer to the Device Extension
  )
{
  PDEVICE_EXTENSION pDE =
          (PDEVICE_EXTENSION)Context;
  ULONG XferSize;

  UCHAR Control = XxReadControl( pDE );
  pDE->DeviceStatus = XxReadStatus( pDE ); ❶

  if( (pDE->BytesRemaining == 0) ❷
          || !XX_OK( pDE->DeviceStatus ))
  {
        pDE->TransferInProgress = FALSE;
        return FALSE;
  }
```

```
//
// A transfer is happening. Calculate the number
// of bytes to send in one bunch.
//
pDE->TransferInProgress = TRUE;  ❸

if( pDE->BytesRemaining < pDE->FifoSize )
     XferSize = pDE->BytesRemaining;
else
     XferSize = pDE->FifoSize;
//
// Send as many bytes to the device as it
// can handle. Each byte must be strobed
// out.
//
while( XferSize > 0 ) {❹

     //
     // Make sure the STROBE bit is off
     //
     XxWriteControl(
          pDE,
          Control & ~XX_CTL_STROBE );

     //
     // Send a byte and hold it for at least
     // 500 nano-seconds
     //
     XxWriteData( pDE, *pDE->pBuffer );
     KeStallExecutionProcessor( 1 );

     //
     // Turn on the STROBE bit and hold it
     // for at least 500 nano-seconds
     //
     XxWriteControl(
          pDE,
          Control | XX_CTL_STROBE );
     KeStallExecutionProcessor( 1 );

     //
     // Turn off the STROBE line
     //
     XxWriteControl(
          pDE,
          Control & ~XX_CTL_STROBE );
     KeStallExecutionProcessor( 1 );
```

```
        //
        // Update pointer and counters
        //
        pDE->pBuffer++;
        XferSize--;
        pDE->BytesRemaining--;
    }

    return TRUE;
}
```

❶ The XxDpcForIsr routine will use this status field to figure out what happened during the I/O processing cycle.

❷ If all the bytes have been sent, or there was a problem with the printer, just return a FALSE and quit.

❸ Send either one FIFO's worth of data, or as many bytes as are left in the buffer — whichever is less.

❹ This loop sends out one bucketful of data to the port. The body of the loop incorporates the strobing protocol required for sending data to the parallel port.

XxIsr   The Kernel calls this function in response to a device interrupt. If XxIsr processes the interrupt, it returns TRUE; otherwise, FALSE. It runs at DIRQL level, holding the Interrupt spin lock for this device.

```
BOOLEAN
XxIsr(
  IN PKINTERRUPT Interrupt,
  IN PVOID ServiceContext  // Ptr to Device Extension
  )
{
  PDEVICE_EXTENSION pDE = ServiceContext;
  PDEVICE_OBJECT pDevice = pDE->DeviceObject;
  PIRP Irp = pDevice->CurrentIrp;
  UCHAR Status = XxReadStatus( pDE );

  if(( Status & XX_STS_NOT_IRQ ) != 0 ) ❶
      return FALSE;

  if( pDE->TransferInProgress ) ❷
      if( !XxTransmitBytes( pDE ))
            IoRequestDpc( pDevice, Irp, (PVOID)pDE );
  return TRUE;
}
```

❶ Check the parallel port to see if it generated an interrupt. Not all parallel
devices support this bit, but the ones that don't hold it at 0. If the device
didn't request an interrupt, leave the ISR as soon as possible.

❷ The port interrupted. If there's no transfer in progress, just ignore the interrupt; otherwise try to send the next chunk of data. If XxTransmitBytes fails,
it means either an error occurred, or there are no more bytes to send.

XxDpcForIsr   Once the data transfer finishes, this function performs any
required cleanup operations. The XxStartIo also calls this function if it needs to fail
an IRP before starting a transfer. XxDpcForIsr runs at DISPATCH_LEVEL IRQL.

```
VOID
XxDpcForIsr(
  IN PKDPC Dpc,
  IN PDEVICE_OBJECT DeviceObject,
  IN PIRP Irp,
  IN PVOID Context // Pointer to Device Extension
  )
{
  PDEVICE_EXTENSION pDE = Context;

  Irp->IoStatus.Information =
            pDE->BytesRequested -
            pDE->cBytesRemaining; ❶
  //
  // Figure out what the final status
  // should be
  //
  if( XX_OK( pDE->DeviceStatus )) ❷
        Irp->IoStatus.Status = STATUS_SUCCESS;

  else if( XX_POWERED_OFF( pDE->DeviceStatus ))
        Irp->IoStatus.Status =
            STATUS_DEVICE_POWERED_OFF;

  else if( XX_NOT_CONNECTED( pDE->DeviceStatus ))
        Irp->IoStatus.Status =
            STATUS_DEVICE_NOT_CONNECTED;

  else if( XX_OFF_LINE( pDE->DeviceStatus ))
        Irp->IoStatus.Status =
            STATUS_DEVICE_OFF_LINE;

  else if( XX_PAPER_EMPTY( pDE->DeviceStatus ))
        Irp->IoStatus.Status =
            STATUS_DEVICE_PAPER_EMPTY;
```

```
    else Irp->IoStatus.Status =
            STATUS_DEVICE_DATA_ERROR;
    //
    // If we're being called directly from Start I/O,
    // don't give the user any priority boost.
    //
    if( Dpc == NULL ) ❸
        IoCompleteRequest( Irp, IO_NO_INCREMENT );
    else
        IoCompleteRequest( Irp, IO_PARALLEL_INCREMENT );
    IoStartNextPacket( DeviceObject, FALSE ); ❹
}
```

❶ The **Information** field should contain the number of bytes actually transferred when the IRP goes back to the I/O Manager.

❷ This section of code uses several macros defined in **HARDWARE.H** to figure out what the final status should be.

❸ It's necessary to know whether this function is being called directly from **XxStartIo** or by the system DPC dispatcher. In the former case, the original thread gets no priority boost. The NULL DPC argument means **XxDpcForIsr** is being called from **XxStartIo**.

❹ Once the current IRP is completed, it's necessary to tell the I/O Manager to start the next one.

9.8   TESTING THE DATA TRANSFER ROUTINES

At this point, you've got a real driver to work with and you can do serious testing. Among other things, you can verify that the driver

- Sends IRPs from its Dispatch routines to its Start I/O routine
- Responds to device interrupts
- Transfers data successfully
- Completes requests
- Manages requests from multiple callers

Testing Procedure

The following procedure will let you check all the code paths through your driver's data transfer routines.

1. Write a minimal Start I/O routine that simply completes each IRP as soon as it arrives. This will allow you to test the linkage between the driver's Dispatch and Start I/O routines.

2. Write the real Start I/O routine, the ISR, and the DpcForIsr routine. If the driver supports both read and write operations, implement and test each path separately.

3. Exercise all the data transfer paths through the driver with a simple Win32 program that makes **ReadFile**, **WriteFile**, and **DeviceIoControl** calls.

4. Stress test the driver with a program that generates large numbers of I/O requests as quickly as possible. Run this test on a busy system.

5. If your device is shareable, run several copies of the test program at once to be sure the driver works with multiple open handles.

6. If your driver supports multiple physical devices, repeat the tests with each device unit.

7. If possible repeat steps 4–6 on a multiprocessor system to verify SMP synchronization.

9.9   SUMMARY

At this point, it looks as if you have all the components of a working driver. Its Start I/O routine is setting up each request, its ISR is servicing interrupts, and its DpcForIsr is handling all the details of I/O postprocessing. What more could you want?

Unfortunately, the little parallel port driver we built in this chapter isn't ready for prime time distribution. In particular, it doesn't handle device timeouts, so if an interrupt never arrives, the request will simply lock up. In the next chapter, you'll see how to remedy this situation.

Timers

*I*t's a sad fact, but true: Hardware is perverse stuff that doesn't necessarily behave the way it should. For example, error conditions may prevent a device from generating an interrupt when you're expecting one. Even worse, some devices don't even use interrupts to signal interesting state changes. Handling these situations often requires some kind of timer or polling mechanism, and that's just what we're going to look at in this chapter.

10.1 HANDLING DEVICE TIMEOUTS

Your driver should never assume that an expected device interrupt will arrive. The device might be offline, it might be waiting for some kind of operator intervention, or perhaps it's just broken. This section explains how to use I/O Timer routines to detect unresponsive devices.

How I/O Timer Routines Work

An I/O Timer routine is an optional piece of driver code that your Driver-Entry routine attaches to a specific Device object. After you start the Device object's timer, the I/O Manager begins calling the I/O Timer routine once every second. These calls continue until you stop the timer. Table 10.1 lists the functions available for working with I/O timers.

Table 10.2 shows the prototype for the I/O Timer routine itself. When it executes, it receives a pointer to the associated Device object and whatever context

Table 10.1   Using I/O timers

How to use an I/O Timer routine		
IF you want to...	**THEN call...**	**IRQL**
Attach a timer routine to a device	IoInitialzeTimer	PASSIVE_LEVEL
Start a device's timer	IoStartTimer	≤ DISPATCH_LEVEL
Stop a device's timer	IoStopTimer	≤ DISPATCH_LEVEL

Table 10.2   Function prototype of an I/O Timer routine

VOID XxIoTimer	IRQL == DISPATCH_LEVEL
Parameter	**Description**
IN PDEVICE_OBJECT DeviceObject	Device object whose timer just fired
IN PVOID Context	Context passed to **IoInitializeTimer**
Return value	—

information you passed to **IoInitializeTimer**. As always, the address of the Device Extension is a good choice for context.

How to Catch Device Timeout Conditions

In general terms, a driver that wants to catch device timeouts should do the following:

1. Its DriverEntry routine calls **IoInitializeTimer** to associate an I/OTimer routine with a specific device.

2. When a user-mode program attaches a handle to the device by calling **CreateFile**, the Dispatch routine for IRP_MJ_CREATE calls **IoStartTimer**. As long as this handle is open, the device will receive I/O Timer calls. This same Dispatch routine also sets a timeout counter in the Device Extension to –1 — a "do nothing" value.

3. When the Start I/O routine starts the device, it also sets the timeout counter to the maximum number of seconds the driver is willing to wait for an interrupt.

4. The ISR will do one of two things when an interrupt arrives. If there's more data, it resets the timeout counter to its maximum value and transfers the next piece of data. Otherwise, it sets the timeout counter to –1 and issues a DPC request to complete the IRP.

5. Meanwhile the system is calling the driver's I/O Timer routine once every second. When it executes, the I/O Timer routine checks the timeout counter.

A value of –1 means "ignore the I/O Timer call." A positive value causes the I/O Timer routine to decrement the device's timeout counter. If the counter reaches zero before an interrupt arrives, the I/O Timer routine stops the device, sets the timeout counter to –1, and processes the request as a timed out operation.

6. When the user-mode program calls **CloseHandle**, the Dispatch routine for IRP_MJ_CLOSE calls **IoStopTimer** and disables I/O Timer callbacks for the device.

Notice that the Start I/O and I/O Timer routines (running at DISPATCH_LEVEL IRQL), and the ISR (running at DIRQL) all have access to the timeout counter in the Device Extension. This can lead to problems unless these driver routines synchronize themselves. The code example that appears later in this chapter shows how to do this properly.

It's also worth pointing out that not all drivers use their Dispatch routines to start and stop the I/O Timer calls. Some drivers just start a device's I/O Timer in DriverEntry and stop it in the Unload routine. While the driver is loaded, it simply ignores I/O Timer callbacks whenever the timeout counter is set to –1. The only disadvantage of this scheme is that it incurs some system overhead even when the device isn't being used.

Your driver has a number of options for processing a request that has timed out. Some of the common things drivers do include:

- Retrying the device operation some fixed number of times before failing the IRP that generated it.

- Failing the IRP by calling **IoCompleteRequest** with an appropriate final status value.[1]

- Logging a timeout error for the device in the system event log. This can help system administrators to track down flaky hardware.

10.2 CODE EXAMPLE: CATCHING DEVICE TIMEOUTS

This example does show how to add timeout support to the simple parallel port driver developed in the previous chapter. You can find the code for this example in the **CH10\TIME–OUT\DRIVER** directory on the disk that accompanies this book.

---

[1] Watch out if you're tempted to use STATUS_IO_TIMEOUT as the final status for a timedout IRP. Unfortunately, this status code maps onto the ERROR_SEM_TIMEOUT in Win32. The message for this code ("The semaphore timeout period has expired.") may be a little confusing to users of your driver, so it's usually best to find some other NT status code.

XXDRIVER.H

This version of the main header file builds on the ones seen in previous chapters. Only one structure from this file is of much interest.

DEVICE_EXTENSION   The following excerpt shows the changes in the Device Extension needed to catch parallel port timeout errors.

```
typedef struct _DEVICE_EXTENSION {
  :
  PUCHAR    pBuffer;     // Working buffer pointer
  LONG  TimeRemaining;  // Seconds until timeout❶
  UCHAR DeviceStatus;   // Most recent status byte
} DEVICE_EXTENSION, *PDEVICE_EXTENSION;
```

❶ This counter keeps track of the number of seconds remaining until the driver declares a timeout condition. If it's set to –1, I/O Timer callbacks are ignored. Anyone accessing this variable needs to be synchronized with the ISR.

INIT.C

Here's an excerpt from the driver initialization code. Only a few changes are necessary to prepare for I/O Timer support.

XxCreateDevice   In this modified version of the function that creates Device objects, notice the addition of code to set up the I/O timer.

```
static NTSTATUS
XxCreateDevice (
  IN PDRIVER_OBJECT DriverObject,
  IN PCONFIG_BLOCK pConfig,     // Config block
  IN ULONG uNum                 // Device number
  )
{
  :
  //
  // Initialize the device extension structure
  //
  pDevExt = pDevObj->DeviceExtension;
  pDevExt->DeviceObject = pDevObj;
  pDevExt->NtDeviceNumber = uNum;
  pDevExt->FifoSize = XX_FIFO_SIZE;
  pDevExt->TimeRemaining = -1;❶
  :
  //
  // Prepare the device's DPC object for later use
  //
```

```
IoInitializeDpcRequest(
        pDevObj,
        XxDpcForIsr );
//
// Initialize the device's timeout clock
//
IoInitializeTimer( pDevObj, XxIoTimer, pDevExt );❷
    :
}
```

❶ Set the initial value of the timeout counter to its "do nothing" state. There's no need to synchronize here because the driver's ISR hasn't been activated yet with a call to **IoConnectInterrupt**.

❷ Associate the Device object with the driver's I/O Timer routine. Each time XxIoTimer is called, pass it a pointer to the Device Extension.

TRANSFER.C

Most of the changes in these versions of the data transfer routines involve checking and setting the state of the timeout counter.

XxTransmitBytes For proper synchronization, this function expects to be holding the Interrupt spin lock when it runs. This means it either must be called from **XxIsr** or as a Synch Critical Section routine.

```
static BOOLEAN
XxTransmitBytes(
  IN PVOID Context
  )
{
  PDEVICE_EXTENSION pDE =
        (PDEVICE_EXTENSION)Context;

  UCHAR Control;
  ULONG i;

  pDE->DeviceStatus = XxReadStatus( pDE );

  //
  // If all the bytes have been sent or the
  // device is unhappy, inhibit any further
  // processing of this request and just quit.
  //
  if( (pDE->BytesRemaining == 0)
        || !XX_OK( pDE->DeviceStatus ))
  {
        pDE->TimeRemaining = -1; ❶
```

```
            return FALSE;
    }
    :
    //
    // Send as many bytes to the device as it
    // can handle. Each byte must be strobed
    // out.
    //
    Control = XxReadControl( pDE );

    for( i=0; i < pDE->XferSize; i++ ) {❷

            //
            // Make sure the STROBE line is off
            //
            XxWriteControl(
                    pDE,
                    Control & ~XX_CTL_STROBE );
            :
            //
            // Update pointer and counters
            //
            pDE->pBuffer++;
    }

    //
    // Start the timeout clock and wait
    // for an interrupt
    //
    pDE->TimeRemaining = XX_TIMEOUT_VALUE; ❸

    return TRUE;
}
```

❶ If the device is unhappy or there are no more bytes to transfer, this is the end of the request. Disable the timeout counter.

❷ There's no danger of the timeout routine failing the IRP during the data transfer loop. This is because I/O Timer routine won't access the timeout counter variable until it acquires the Interrupt spin lock.

❸ Now that more data has been sent, reset the timeout counter and wait for the next interrupt to arrive.

XxIsr   This function responds to interrupts from the parallel port. It differs from the previous version in that it uses the timeout counter variable to determine if a transfer is currently in progress.

```
BOOLEAN
XxIsr(
  IN PKINTERRUPT Interrupt,
  IN PVOID ServiceContext
  )
{
  PDEVICE_EXTENSION pDE = ServiceContext;
  PDEVICE_OBJECT pDevice = pDE->DeviceObject;
  UCHAR Status = XxReadStatus( pDE );

  //
  // See if this device requested an interrupt
  //
  if(( Status & XX_STS_NOT_IRQ ) != 0 )
       return FALSE;

  if( pDE->TimeRemaining == -1 ) return TRUE; ❶

  //
  // Otherwise, try to send the next bunch of
  // bytes. If XxTransmitBytes fails, it means
  // either an error occurred or there's no more
  // data to send.
  //
  pDE->BytesRemaining -= pDE->XferSize;

  if( !XxTransmitBytes( pDE )) ❷
  {
       IoRequestDpc(
             pDevice,
             pDevice->CurrentIrp,
             (PVOID)pDE );
  }

  return TRUE;
}
```

❶ If the timeout clock is –1, either there's no transfer in progress, or the device has already timedout. In either case, there's nothing to be done here.

❷ After the return from **XxTransmitBytes**, the timeout counter has either been set to its maximum value (if the next piece of data has been sent), or –1 (if there was no more data to send or the device had an error).

TIMER.C

Here are the routines that actually process the timer events. In this particular driver, the Dispatch routine for IRP_MJ_CREATE starts the device's timer, and the

Dispatch routine for IRP_MJ_CLOSE stops it. While the timer is running, the contents of the timeout counter variable determine the behavior of the I/O Timer routines.

XxIoTimer   As long as the I/O Timer for a device is running, the system will call this routine once every second.

```
VOID
XxIoTimer(
  IN PDEVICE_OBJECT DeviceObject,
  IN PVOID Context
  )
{
  PDEVICE_EXTENSION pDE = Context;

  if( pDE->TimeRemaining == -1 ) return; ❶

  else if( !KeSynchronizeExecution(❷
                    pDE->pInterrupt,
                    XxProcessTimerEvent,
                    pDE ))
  {
      //
      // Call the DPC routine to figure out a
      // final status and complete the IRP.
      //
      XxDpcForIsr(❸
            NULL,
            DeviceObject,
            DeviceObject->CurrentIrp,
            pDE );
  }
}
```

❶ Do a quick check of the timeout counter. Either there's no data transfer in progress, or an expected interrupt has arrived. Making this quick check at DISPATCH_LEVEL avoids needless trips up to DIRQL.

❷ The timeout counter appears to contain some value other than –1. To process the timer event safely, synchronize with **XxIsr** using a Synch Critical Section routine.

❸ The Sync Critical Section routine returns FALSE if the current IRP has timed out. In this case, we just fail the IRP. Other options might include retrying the operation a fixed number of times, logging an error, and so forth.

XxProcessTimerEvent   This function does the real work of processing timer events. It runs as a Synch Critical Section routine because it has to synchronize its access to the timeout counter with **XxIsr**.

```
static BOOLEAN
XxProcessTimerEvent(
  IN PDEVICE_EXTENSION pDE
  )
{
  if( pDE->TimeRemaining == -1 ) return TRUE; ❶

  //
  // Decrement and test the timer.
  //
  if( --pDE->TimeRemaining > 0 ) return TRUE; ❷

  //
  // A timeout has occurred. Prevent further
  // processing of this request
  //
  pDE->TimeRemaining = -1; ❸
  pDE->DeviceStatus = XxReadStatus( pDE );
  return FALSE;
}
```

❶ It's necessary to test the timeout counter again because the ISR may have changed it while we were waiting for the Interrupt spin lock. If that's the case, do nothing.

❷ The timeout counter contains something other than –1. In this case, decrement the count. If it's still above 0, the IRP hasn't timedout yet.

❸ The counter hit 0 so the IRP has timedout. Setting the timeout counter to –1 blocks further processing of this request by the ISR (should an interrupt just happen to arrive). Returning FALSE will cause the IRP to be completed by **XxIoTimer**.

10.3 MANAGING DEVICES WITHOUT INTERRUPTS

Some devices don't generate interrupts every time they make a significant state change. Legacy ISA devices can be especially bad about this kind of thing. This section presents alternative ways of working with noninterrupting devices.

Working with Noninterrupting Devices

Under operating systems like MS-DOS, a driver managing a noninterrupting device could simply poll the device or busy-wait until it has changed state.

However, this kind of behavior would cause serious performance problems for NT. Instead, NT drivers can use one of the following techniques for suspending their execution during a repeated polling operation:

- Driver routines running at PASSIVE_LEVEL IRQL can call **KeDelayExecutionThread** to introduce a time delay. This method can only be used by the driver's initialization and cleanup code, or any Kernel-mode threads the driver has created.

- If you occasionally have to delay execution for intervals less than about 50 microseconds, you can call **KeStallExecutionProcessor**. This is better than busy-waiting because the delay interval doesn't depend on a specific CPU architecture.[2]

- If parts of your driver running at DISPATCH_LEVEL IRQL need to introduce a time delay, you can use a CustomTimerDpc routine.

If your device needs to be polled repeatedly and the delay interval between each polling operation is over 50 microseconds, base your driver design on the use of system threads (discussed in Chapter 14).

How CustomTimerDpc Routines Work

A CustomTimerDpc routine is just a DPC routine that you associate with a Kernel Timer object. You get the CustomTimerDpc routine to run by setting the Timer's timeout value. When it expires, the Kernel automatically queues your DPC routine for execution. Eventually, the Kernel's DPC dispatcher pulls your request from the queue and executes the CustomTimerDpc routine. Keep in mind that, depending on system activity, there could be some delay between the moment the Timer object expires and the actual execution of the DPC routine.

In earlier versions of Windows NT, a CustomTimerDpc routine would fire only once. If you wanted one of these routines to execute repeatedly, you had to manually reset the Timer object each time it fired. With NT 4.0, you have the option of specifying a repetition interval when you set the Timer object's initial timeout value. Each time it fires, the Timer object will automatically reset itself to fire again when the repetition interval has elapsed.[3]

Like all other DPC routines, a CustomTimerDpc runs at DISPATCH_LEVEL IRQL. Table 10.3 shows the prototype for one of these routines. Notice that a Cus-

---

[2] Don't use this function too often. It essentially freezes the CPU on which it's called at whatever IRQL level it's called from.

[3] If you need to implement a repeating CustomTimerDpc routine, it's generally a good idea to use the Timer object's automatic repetition feature rather than resetting the Timer yourself each time it fires. It's more efficient because your driver won't be making so many calls to Kernel support routines. It also guarantees that there won't be any skewing of the timeout interval.

Table 10.3 Function prototype of a CustomTimerDpc routine

VOID XxCustomTimerDpc	IRQL == DISPATCH_LEVEL
Parameter	**Description**
IN PKDPC Dpc	DPC object generating the request
IN PVOID Context	Context passed to **KeInitializeDpc**
IN PVOID SystemArg1	(Not used — contents unspecified)
IN PVOID SystemArg2	(Not used — contents unspecified)
Return value	—

tomTimerDpc routine always receives two junk arguments from the system. The contents of these two system arguments are undefined, so don't use them.[4] With CustomTimerDpc routines, you're limited to just a single context argument that is permanently associated with the DPC object.

It's worth comparing CustomTimerDpc routines with the I/O Timers you saw in the first part of this chapter. Although both mechanisms operate with time, they differ in several significant ways. In particular:

- Unlike I/O Timer routines, a CustomTimerDpc is not associated with any particular Device object. You can have as many or as few of them as you like.

- The minimum resolution of an I/O Timer is one second; you specify the expiration time of a CustomTimerDpc in units of 100 nanoseconds.

- The I/O Timer always uses a one-second interval. You can specify different expiration intervals each time you start a CustomTimerDpc.

- The storage for an I/O Timer object is automatically part of the Device object. You need to declare nonpaged storage for both a KDPC and a KTIMER object if you want to use a CustomTimerDpc.

How to Set Up a CustomTimerDpc Routine

Working with CustomTimerDpc routines is very straightforward. Your driver simply needs to follow these steps:

1. Allocate nonpaged storage (usually in a Device or Controller Extension) for both a KDPC and a KTIMER object.

2. DriverEntry calls **KeInitializeDpc** to associate a DPC routine and a context item with the DPC object. This context item will be passed to your CustomTimerDpc

---

[4] Regular CustomDpc routines (not associated with a Timer object) can make use of these arguments. The discussion of CustomDpc routines in the next chapter shows how to use them.

routine when it fires. The address of the Device or Controller Extension is a good choice for the context item.

3. DriverEntry also calls **KeInitializeTimer** just once to set up the Timer object.

4. To start a one-shot Timer, call **KeSetTimer**; to set up a repeating Timer, use **KeSetTimerEx** instead. If you call these functions using a Timer object that is currently active, the previous request is canceled and the new expiration time replaces the old one.

If you want to keep a Timer from firing, call **KeCancelTimer** before the Timer object expires. This also cancels a repeating Timer. If you need to find out whether a Timer has already expired, call **KeReadStateTimer**.

You must be executing at PASSIVE_LEVEL IRQL when you initialize the DPC and Timer object. To set, cancel, or read the state of a Timer, you must be running at or below DISPATCH_LEVEL IRQL. In general, you should avoid calling **KeInsertQueueDpc** with a DPC object being used for a CustomTimerDpc routine. This can lead to race conditions in your driver.

How to Specify Expiration Times

Internally, NT maintains the current system time by counting the number of 100-nanosecond intervals since January 1, 1601. This is a very big number, so NT defines a 64-bit data type called a LARGE_INTEGER to hold it. Table 10.4 lists the functions drivers can use to work with time values.

Table 10.4   Functions that operate on system time values

Time functions

Function	Description
KeQuerySystemTime	Return 64-bit absolute system time
RtlTimeToTimeFields	Break 64-bit time into date and time fields
RtlTimeFieldsToTime	Convert date and time into 64-bit system time
KeQueryTickCount	Return number of clock interrupts since boot
KeQueryTimeIncrement	Return number of 100-nanosecond units added to system time for each clock interrupt
RtlConvertLongToLargeInteger	Create a signed LARGE_INTEGER
RtlConvertUlongToLargeInteger	Create a positive LARGE_INTEGER
RtlLargeIntegerXxx	Perform various arithmetic and logical operations on LARGE_INTEGERs

Note: Callers of these functions can be running at any IRQL level.

When you call **KeSetTimer** to start the clock ticking on a Timer object, you can specify the expiration time in one of two ways:

- A positive LARGE_INTEGER value represents an absolute system time at which you want the Timer to expire. Absolute times correspond to some exact moment in the future, like "February 23, 2051 at 6:45 PM."
- A negative LARGE_INTEGER value represents the length of an interval measured from the current moment, like "10 seconds from now." This is the form you're most likely to use.

This fragment of code shows how to set a Timer object to expire after an interval of 75 microseconds. It assumes that **pDE** holds a pointer to a Device Extension, and that the Extension contains initialized Timer and DPC objects.

```
LARGE_INTEGER DueTime;

DueTime = RtlConvertLongToLargeInteger( -75 * 10 );
KeSetTimer( &pDE->Timer, DueTime, &pDE->DPC );
    :
```

Since the number is negative, the system will interpret it as a relative time value. Scaling the number by ten is necessary because the basic unit of system time is 100 nanoseconds (or 0.1 microseconds).

Other Uses for CustomTimerDpc Routines

In the next section, you'll see an example of a driver that performs data transfers using a CustomTimerDpc instead of device interrupts. It's worth pointing out that, in some situations, you might want to use this kind of technique even with devices that do generate interrupts. This could be helpful if your device generates so many interrupts that it overwhelms the Kernel's interrupt dispatcher and degrades system performance.

The sample parallel port driver that comes with the NT DDK is one example of a driver that uses this technique. This driver monitors the arrival rate of interrupts for its device. When a flood of interrupts threatens to drown the system, the driver intentionally disables parallel port interrupts and uses a CustomTimerDpc to send data to the device. Depending on the device you're working with, this kind of adaptive behavior might be something you want to consider.

10.4 CODE EXAMPLE: A TIMER-BASED DRIVER

This modified version of the parallel port driver disables interrupts and uses a CustomTimerDpc routine to transfer data at fixed intervals. You can find the code for this example in the **CH10\POLLING\DRIVER** directory on the disk that accompanies this book.

XXDRIVER.H

This version of the main header file builds on the ones seen in previous chapters. Only one structure from this file is of much interest.

DEVICE_EXTENSION   The following excerpt shows the changes in the Device Extension needed to support polling.

```
typedef struct _DEVICE_EXTENSION {
    PDEVICE_OBJECT DeviceObject; // Back pointer

    ULONG NtDeviceNumber;          // Zero-based device num

    PUCHAR PortBase;               // First control register❶

    KDPC PollingDpc;               // Components of the ❷
    KTIMER PollingTimer;           // polling mechanism
    LARGE_INTEGER PollingInterval; // ❸

    ULONG FifoSize;                // Bytes to send at once ❹
    ULONG BytesRequested;          // Requested transfer size
    ULONG BytesRemaining;          // Chars left to transfer
    PUCHAR pBuffer;                // Next char to send

    UCHAR DeviceStatus;            // Most recent status

} DEVICE_EXTENSION, *PDEVICE_EXTENSION;
```

❶ While we need to have access to the device's control registers, we're not keeping a pointer to an Interrupt object in this driver. All interrupts from this device will be turned off.

❷ The Dpc and Timer objects together will activate the CustomTimerDpc routine.

❸ The **PollingInterval** field holds the expiration interval for the polling timer. For convenience in this driver, we'll keep the value in microseconds rather than tenths of microseconds.

❹ The rest of the structure is the same as the interrupt-driven version.

INIT.C

Here is a tiny excerpt from the driver's initialization code. The rest of it is the same boilerplate we've been looking at for several chapters. Not shown (but equally important) is the hardware initialization code that disables interrupts from the parallel port.

XxCreateDevice   This function sets up the Device object. It differs from the interrupt-driven version in that it never calls **IoConnectInterrupt**, and it has to initialize the polling timer.

```
static NTSTATUS
XxCreateDevice (
   IN PDRIVER_OBJECT DriverObject,
   IN PCONFIG_BLOCK pConfig, // Config block
   IN ULONG uNum    // Device number
   )
{
   :
   //
   // Copy things from Config block
   //
   pDevExt->PortBase = pConfig->Device[uNum].PortBase;

   //
   // Calculate the polling interval
   //
   pDevExt->PollingInterval =
         RtlConvertLongToLargeInteger(
               XX_POLLING_INTERVAL * -10 ); ❶

   //
   // Prepare the polling timer and its DPC object
   //
   KeInitializeTimer( &pDevExt->PollingTimer ); ❷

   KeInitializeDpc( ❸
         &pDevExt->PollingDpc,
         XxPollingTimerDpc,
         (PVOID)pDevObj );

   //
   // Form the Win32 symbolic link name.
   //
   :
}
```

❶ We use an RtlXxx convenience function to create the polling interval. Since the number is negative, the timeout will be measured relative to the moment the Timer object is started. Multiplying the value by ten allows us to specify XX_POLLING_INTERVAL in microseconds.

❷ Get the Kernel to turn the blob of memory into a Timer object.

❸ Attach the CustomTimerDpc routine to the DPC object. Pass a pointer to the Device object each time the CustomTimerDpc is called.

TRANSFER.C

Since this driver uses polling rather than interrupts to send data, you won't find any Interrupt Service routine here.

XxStartIo   This function is called to begin the processing of each IRP. It
looks very much like the interrupt-driven version.

```
VOID
XxStartIo(
  IN PDEVICE_OBJECT DeviceObject,
  IN PIRP Irp
  )
{
  PIO_STACK_LOCATION IrpStack =
        IoGetCurrentIrpStackLocation( Irp );

  PDEVICE_EXTENSION pDE =
        DeviceObject->DeviceExtension;

  switch( IrpStack->MajorFunction ) {

        case IRP_MJ_WRITE:  ❶

                pDE->BytesRequested =
                        IrpStack->Parameters.Write.Length;

                pDE->BytesRemaining =
                        pDE->BytesRequested;

                pDE->pBuffer =
                        Irp->AssociatedIrp.SystemBuffer;

                if( !XxTransmitBytes( pDE ))  ❷
                {
                        XxFinishCurrentRequest(
                                DeviceObject,
                                pDE,
                                Irp,
                                IO_NO_INCREMENT );
                }
                break;
        //
        // Should never get here -- just get rid
        // of the packet...
        //
        default:
                Irp->IoStatus.Status =
                                        STATUS_NOT_SUPPORTED;
                Irp->IoStatus.Information = 0;
                IoCompleteRequest(
                        Irp,
                        IO_NO_INCREMENT );
```

```
                    IoStartNextPacket( DeviceObject, FALSE );
                    break;
        }
    }
```

❶ If this turns out to be an IRP_MJ_WRITE request, just set up the necessary counters and pointers, and try to send the first bunch of bytes to the device.

❷ Notice that **XxTransmitBytes** is being called directly from DISPATCH_LEVEL IRQL. There's no need to synchronize it using a Synch Critical Section routine because there is no interrupt activity from the device.

XxTransmitBytes   This routine sends a fixed number of bytes out to the parallel port. If the device has a personal problem or there are no more bytes left in the buffer, it returns a FALSE. This data

```
static BOOLEAN
XxTransmitBytes(
  IN PDEVICE_EXTENSION pDE
  )
{
  ULONG XferSize;

  UCHAR Control = XxReadControl( pDE );
  pDE->DeviceStatus = XxReadStatus( pDE );

  //
  // If all the bytes have been sent or the
  // device is unhappy, just quit
  //
  if( (pDE->BytesRemaining == 0)
        || !XX_OK( pDE->DeviceStatus ))
  {
        return FALSE;
  }

  //
  // Calculate the number of bytes to
  // send in one bunch.
  //
  if( pDE->BytesRemaining < pDE->FifoSize )
        XferSize = pDE->BytesRemaining;
  else
        XferSize = pDE->FifoSize;

  while( XferSize > 0 ) {❶
```

```
            //
            // Make sure the STROBE line is off
            //
            XxWriteControl(
                    pDE,
                    Control & ~XX_CTL_STROBE );
                    :
                    //
                    // Update pointer and counters
                    //
                    pDE->pBuffer++;
                    XferSize--;
                    pDE->BytesRemaining--;
            }

            //
            // Start the polling timer
            //
            KeSetTimer(❷
                    &pDE->PollingTimer,
                    pDE->PollingInterval,
                    &pDE->PollingDpc );

            return TRUE;
}
```

❶ Send as many bytes to the device as it can handle. Since this is a parallel port device, each byte has to be strobed out.

❷ Start the polling Timer object. When the Timer expires, the associated DPC routine will be queued automatically.

XxPollingTimerDpc   This function runs each time the polling timer expires. It replaces both the ISR and the DpcForIsr routines in the interrupt-driven version of this driver.

```
VOID
XxPollingTimerDpc(
  IN PKDPC Dpc,
  IN PVOID Context,
  IN PVOID SystemArgument1, ❶
  IN PVOID SystemArgument2
  )
{
  PDEVICE_OBJECT DeviceObject = Context;

  if( !XxTransmitBytes(❷
            DeviceObject->DeviceExtension ))
```

```
        {
                XxFinishCurrentRequest(❸
                        DeviceObject,
                        DeviceObject->DeviceExtension,
                        DeviceObject->CurrentIrp,
                        IO_PARALLEL_INCREMENT );
        }
}
```

❶ Remember that the contents of the two system arguments are undefined in a CustomTimerDpc routine.

❷ Try to send the next bunch of bytes. If **XxTransmitBytes** fails, it means either an error occurred, or there is no more data to send. If it succeeds, it restarts the polling timer, which will eventually result in another call to **XxPollingTimerDpc**.

❸ Call **XxFinishCurrentRequest** to come up with an appropriate status code and complete the IRP. Again, notice that everything is happening at DISPATCH_LEVEL IRQL. **XxFinishCurrentIrp** runs in response to a regular function-call, *not* a DPC request.

10.5 SUMMARY

This chapter has presented two different aspects of using time in your driver. Handling device timeouts is something that will always be important, while the use of CustomTimerDpc routines may only be useful for certain kinds of devices. One important use of CustomTimerDpc routines is to implement various polling strategies.

You now have enough tools to write reasonable drivers for many simple pieces of hardware. In the next chapter, we'll look at some additional techniques for managing full-duplex devices and devices that generate asynchronous events.

Full-Duplex Drivers

*T*he driver model described in the last few chapters has one significant limitation: It allows you to process only a single IRP at a time per Device object. While this is fine for many situations, it doesn't cut it if your driver has to perform both input and output operations simultaneously.

This chapter presents a modified driver architecture that lifts the single-IRP restriction. To implement this architecture, it uses several new techniques (like CustomDpc and Cancel routines) that can be helpful in any kind of driver. At the end of the chapter, sample code for a tiny serial port driver will tie all the loose ends together.

11.1 DOING TWO THINGS AT ONCE

Just what is it about the standard driver architecture that prevents a single Device object from processing two IRPs at once? The problem becomes clear if you consider what happens when a Dispatch routine sends an IRP to **IoStartPacket**.

Calling **IoStartPacket** with a pointer to an idle Device object makes the object busy and invokes the driver's Start I/O routine. From then on, any calls to **IoStartPacket** targeting the same Device object result in IRPs being added to the object's queue of pending requests. This continues until the Start I/O or DpcForIsr routines call **IoStartNextPacket** to mark the Device object as being idle. This kind of behavior makes it very difficult to start another IRP before the current one is completed.

Do You Need to Process Concurrent IRPs?

The first thing to ask yourself is whether your driver really needs to process multiple IRPs concurrently. This is actually a question about the kind of software interface your driver is going to expose. For purposes of this discussion, you can divide driver interfaces into the following categories:

- **Simplex interface** — These drivers can transfer data only in one direction.

- **Half-duplex interface** — These drivers manage hardware that transfers data in both directions, but (for whatever reason) the drivers only process one request at a time.

- **Full-duplex interface** — Here, the driver can perform both inputs and outputs simultaneously.

The standard driver model easily supports both the simplex and half-duplex cases. Unfortunately, since it can't handle two requests at the same time, you can't use this model to provide a full-duplex driver interface.

An important factor in choosing a software interface is the behavior of the underlying hardware. Usually, this will tell you what kind of driver is most appropriate. Broadly speaking, you can divide hardware into three families.

Simplex devices   These devices can transfer data in only one direction. The standard parallel port and the mouse are both examples of simplex hardware. It's very unlikely that you'd need a full-duplex driver for a simplex device.

Half-duplex devices   This type of device can transfer data in both directions, but only one transfer can take place at a time. Disk controllers and Ethernet cards are both examples of half-duplex hardware. The choice of driver interface will depend on how the device is used. It's natural for disk controllers to process only one request at a time. Network cards need to give the appearance of performing simultaneous input and output operations, even though the device itself can only send or receive one packet at a time.

Full-duplex devices   These devices can perform simultaneous input and output operations. The standard serial port exhibits this kind of behavior. A full-duplex driver is almost always a necessity for this type of device.

How the Modified Driver Architecture Works

In a nutshell, if you want a single Device object to process two concurrent IRPs, you need to establish a complete secondary path through your driver. IRPs taking this alternate route will be processed in parallel with those following the standard path. To do this, you must:

1. Divide the IRP_MJ_XXX functions supported by your driver into two categories: Those to be processed by the standard Start I/O routine (the *primary* IRPs) and those that will travel the alternate path (the *alternate* IRPs).

2. Set up various bookkeeping structures to handle IRPs with alternate function codes. This involves maintaining a queue of alternate IRPs, as well as keeping track of the current alternate IRP. In this chapter, we'll be using Device Queue objects to hold the alternate IRPs.

3. Duplicate some of the logic in the I/O Manager's **IoStartPacket** and **IoStart-NextPacket** functions. Your versions of these routines will be responsible for controlling the flow of IRPs along the alternate path.

4. Write additional Start I/O and DPC routines to handle alternate IRPs.

5. Modify the Interrupt Service routine so that it can process both primary and alternate DPC functions.

Data Structures for a Full-Duplex Driver

In Chapter 4 you saw that a standard Device object contains a **CurrentIrp** field that keeps track of the primary IRP being processed. Although it wasn't discussed in any detail, you also saw that the Device object contains an embedded Device Queue object for holding primary IRPs that arrive after the Device object has become busy. In a full-duplex driver, you need to set up parallel structures to manage the alternate IRPs. Normally, this bookkeeping happens in the Device Extension, as shown in Figure 11.1.

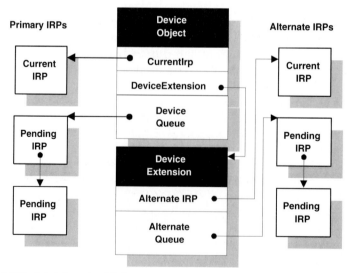

Figure 11.1 A full-duplex driver uses these data structures

Along with the alternate IRP pointer and the Device Queue object, there are some other changes to the Device Extension. If you're doing Buffered I/O, you'll need two sets of buffer pointers and counters to keep track of your progress through an I/O request. In addition, the strategy adopted in this chapter uses separate DPC routines for completing primary and alternate IRPs, so you'll need to leave room in the Device Extension for a KDPC object.

Implementing the Alternate Path

Setting up the alternate path requires changes to several parts of your driver's code. The following subsections describe the modifications you'll need to make.

Dispatch routines   In a full-duplex driver, Dispatch routines for the alternate IRP_MJ_XXX function codes don't use the **IoStartPacket** function. Instead, they call the driver-defined start-packet routine to send IRPs down the alternate processing path.

Start I/O routines   The modified driver architecture is going to use two Start I/O routines: One for IRPs with primary IRP_MJ_XXX function codes and another for the IRPs with alternate codes. Implementing these functions as separate pieces of code usually makes them easier to manage.

Interrupt Service routine   When an interrupt arrives, the Interrupt Service routine has to perform different kinds of processing for primary and alternate operations. It needs to send primary and alternate IRPs to different DPC routines for postprocessing.

DPC routines   Although you could write a full-duplex driver with only a single DpcForIsr routine, it's usually easier to have a separate CustomDpc routine for the alternate IRPs. When this CustomDpc routine completes an IRP, it calls the driver-defined version of **IoStartNextPacket** to begin processing the next alternate IRP.

11.2 USING DEVICE QUEUE OBJECTS

A full-duplex driver needs some way to keep track of pending IRPs that arrive while the driver is already processing an alternate IRP. Although there are several ways to handle this situation, the driver model developed in this chapter is going to use a Device Queue object to hold on to pending alternate IRPs. This is the same strategy that the I/O Manager uses for the driver's primary IRPs.

How Device Queue Objects Work

A Device Queue is a Kernel object that contains a linked list guarded by an embedded Executive spin lock. Although a Device Queue object can hold any structure with a KDEVICE_QUEUE_ENTRY in it, they are most commonly used to store a Device object's pending IRPs.

A Device Queue object is always in one of two states: *Busy* if there's been at least one attempt to insert an entry into the queue and *Not Busy* if there's been an attempt to remove an entry from an empty queue. Table 11.1 shows how Device Queue state transitions work.

The basic pattern is fairly simple: If you try to insert an entry into a Device Queue that isn't Busy, the insertion fails but the queue becomes Busy. Once it has become Busy, insertion operations succeed. Removing entries from a Busy Device Queue causes no change in the object's state. Once the Device Queue has no more entries, the next attempt to remove one causes the object to return to the Not-Busy state.

The **IoStartPacket** and **IoStartNextPacket** functions use the state of the Device object's built-in Device Queue to guarantee that a driver's Start I/O routine receives only one IRP at a time per Device object. The Device Queue is Not Busy if the associated Device object is ready to process another IRP, and Busy if the Device object is currently working on an IRP.

How to Use Device Queue Objects

It's fairly easy to work with Device Queue objects. The code example appearing later in this chapter will show you the specific details. In general, what you do is:

1. Declare a KDEVICE_QUEUE item in your Device Extension structure.

2. In your DriverEntry routine, call **KeInitializeDeviceQueue**. This sets up both the Device Queue object and its associated Executive spin lock.

3. Use the functions in Table 11.2 to insert or remove IRPs. These routines automatically acquire and release the Executive spin lock hidden in the Device Queue object.

There are two things to notice about Device Queue objects. First, you must be at DISPATCH_LEVEL IRQL in order to call the functions that insert and

Table 11.1   State transitions in Device Queue objects

Device Queue state transitions

Initial state	Action	Final state	Entry is...
Not Busy	Insert into empty	Busy	Not inserted
Busy	Insert into empty	Busy	Inserted
Busy	Insert into non-empty	Busy	Inserted
Busy	Remove from non-empty	Busy	Removed
Busy	Remove from empty	Not Busy	—

Table 11.2 Use these functions to work with Device Queue objects

How to use Device Queue objects

IF you want to...	THEN call...	IRQL
Create a Device Queue	KeInitializeDeviceQueue	PASSIVE_LEVEL
Insert an IRP at the end	KeInsertDeviceQueue	DISPATCH_LEVEL
Insert IRP in sort-order	KeInsertByKeyDeviceQueue	DISPATCH_LEVEL
Remove first IRP	KeRemoveDeviceQueue	DISPATCH_LEVEL
Remove specific IRP	KeRemoveEntryDeviceQueue	DISPATCH_LEVEL

remove Device Queue entries. To call these functions from some part of your driver running at PASSIVE_LEVEL IRQL, you have to change levels by calling **KeRaiseIrql** and **KeLowerIrql**.

Second, Device Queue objects must live in nonpaged storage. Since you normally declare them as part of your Device Extension structure, this poses no particular problem.

To link an IRP into a Device Queue, you use a predefined Device Queue entry that's a standard part of the IRP. The code looks like this:

```
KeInsertDeviceQueue(
        &pDevExt->AlternateIrpQueue,
        &Irp->Tail.Overlay.DeviceQueueEntry );
```

Here, **AlternateIrpQueue** is a KDEVICE_QUEUE structure that's part of the Device Extension.

When you remove an item from a Device Queue, you get a pointer to the queue entry. As this fragment of code illustrates, you still need to use the CONTAINING_RECORD macro to convert this entry back into the address of an IRP:

```
PIRP Irp;
PKDEVICE_QUEUE_ENTRY QueueEntry;
        :
QueueEntry = KeRemoveDeviceQueue(
            &pDevExt->AlternateIrpQueue );
if( QueueEntry != NULL )
{
  Irp = CONTAINING_RECORD(
            QueueEntry,
            IRP,
            Tail.Overlay.DeviceQueueEntry );
        :
  // Do something with the IRP
        :
}
```

Also remember to check for a NULL return value. There's always the possibility that the queue might be empty.

11.3 WRITING CUSTOMDPC ROUTINES

Chapter 3 briefly introduced DPC objects as a general-purpose way for high-IRQL code to perform less-important processing at a lower IRQL level. All the drivers you've seen since then have taken advantage of the I/O Manager's Dpc-ForIsr mechanism to simplify the use of DPCs. For many situations, this may provide all the functionality you'll need. In the case of full-duplex drivers, however, funneling everything through a single DpcForIsr routine adds unnecessary complications to the design of the software.

This section explains how to work directly with Kernel DPC objects using CustomDpc routines. Although the main focus will be on their use in full-duplex drivers, CustomDpc routines can be valuable in any situation where a driver's Interrupt Service routine needs to perform some action that isn't allowed at DIRQL.

How to Use a CustomDpc Routine

Working directly with Kernel DPC objects isn't terribly difficult. This is what you need to do:

1. When you define your Device or Controller Extension, declare a separate KDPC item for each CustomDpc routine you plan to use.

2. In your DriverEntry routine, initialize each KDPC object by calling **KeInitializeDpc**. This sets up a correspondence between the KDPC object and a specific CustomDpc routine in your driver.

3. When you want to fire off the CustomDpc routine (usually from the driver's ISR), call **KeInsertQueueDpc** (see Table 11.3). To cancel a pending DPC request, you can call **KeRemoveQueueDpc**.

Table 11.3   Function prototype for KeInsertQueueDpc

BOOLEAN KeInsertQueueDpc	IRQL ‡ DISPATCH_LEVEL
Parameter	**Description**
IN PKDPC Dpc	Address of initialized DPC object to be queued
IN PVOID SystemArg1	First call-specific DPC parameter
IN PVOID SystemArg2	Second call-specific DPC parameter
Return value	• TRUE — the DPC was successfully queued
	• FALSE — the DPC is already in the queue

Table 11.4 Prototype for a CustomDpc routine

VOID XxCustomDpc	IRQL == DISPATCH_LEVEL
Parameter	**Description**
IN PKDPC Dpc	DPC object that generated the call
IN PVOID Context	Context parameter passed to **KeInitializeDpc**
IN PVOID SystemArg1	1st DPC parameter passed to **KeInsertQueueDpc**
IN PVOID SystemArg2	2nd DPC parameter passed to **KeInsertQueueDpc**
Return value	—

Remember that you can't queue a DPC object that's already in the queue. If you try, **KeInsertQueueDpc** will return FALSE. This kind of thing might happen if your device has such a high interrupt rate that the DPC routine doesn't get a chance to run before the next interrupt arrives. In this case, it's up to your driver to decide what to do. Depending on the design of your driver, one solution might be to initialize a pool of DPCs for the ISR to use. In any event, remember that it's your responsibility to take care of this situation.

Execution Context

The Kernel's DPC dispatcher eventually removes your DPC routine from the queue and calls the associated CustomDpc routine. Table 11.4 shows the prototype for the DPC routine itself.

Notice that you can pass three driver-specific parameters to a CustomDpc routine. Along with the Context item that **KeInitializeDpc** associates with the DPC object, you can pass two additional parameters each time you call **KeInsertQueueDpc**. This is a little more flexible than the I/O Manager's DpcForIsr mechanism, which always passes the Device object, the IRP, and one call-specific argument. Depending on what you're trying to do, this can be useful.

11.4 CANCELING I/O REQUESTS

One issue we haven't addressed yet is how to deal with I/O requests that get abandoned. Although there's nothing about full-duplex drivers that makes them more prone to canceled requests, this is as good a place as any to bring up the subject. Specifically, a driver has to be prepared for any of the following situations:

- A thread issues one or more overlapped I/O requests to a Device object. Before the driver processes these IRPs, the thread either terminates or closes its handle to the Device object.

- A thread issues one or more overlapped I/O requests and then calls some other Win32 function that cancels any previous requests. For example, one side-effect of calling **SetupComm** is that it automatically cancels all pending IRPs.

- A higher-level driver allocates an IRP and sends it to another driver using **IoCallDriver**. Before the IRP completes, the higher-level driver calls the **IoCancelIrp** function to cancel the request.[1]

In all three of these cases, the I/O Manager will notify the driver that the IRPs involved in the I/O need to be cancelled. Once it's been notified, the driver's job is to complete the affected IRPs with an **IoStatus.Status** value of STATUS_CANCELLED and an **IoStatus.Information** value of zero.

This section explains the mechanics of canceling I/O requests. You'll see examples of how to implement cancellation routines in the sample UART driver at the end of the chapter.

How IRP Cancellation Works

In general, any driver that's going to hold IRPs in a pending state for a long time needs to support cancellation. This really includes most device drivers, since any Device object can have multiple overlapped requests waiting in its Device Queue for the Start I/O routine. Cancellation support is also necessary in any driver that stores IRPs temporarily in a driver-defined queue during the course of processing.

Some of the issues will become a little more clear if you think about just what might be going on when a cancel notification arrives. An IRP can be in one of the following states at the time it gets cancelled:

- It might be in a queue waiting for the driver to get to it. This could be the Device object's Device Queue of pending requests (waiting for the Start I/O routine), or some private, internal queue managed by the driver.

- The IRP might have been removed from a queue, but the driver *hasn't* started to work on it yet. For example, an IRP might have become the Device object's current IRP but the Start I/O routine hasn't quite begun processing it.

- It might have been removed from a queue, and the next driver routine *has* begun processing it.

The I/O Manager's philosophy is that if an IRP is waiting in a queue when a cancellation request occurs, then the driver should dequeue the IRP and cancel it. Similarly, if the IRP has just been removed from a queue but processing hasn't begun, the driver should cancel it. On the other hand, if the IRP has already been

---

[1] Incidentally, a driver is only allowed to cancel IRPs that it has allocated and sent to a lower-level driver. It must *not* try to cancel any IRPs sent to it by the I/O Manager or by a higher-level driver.

started (and if it won't take too long to complete), then the driver should finish processing the request the normal way.

The I/O Manager provides two independent mechanisms for cancelling IRPs. First of all, a driver can attach a Cancel routine to an IRP before it puts the IRP into any queue. If the IRP is cancelled while it's still in the queue, the Cancel routine dequeues the IRP and performs the cancellation. If there's no cancellation request, some other part of the driver eventually dequeues the IRP, removes its Cancel routine, and continues processing it. This allows individual IRPs to be cancelled selectively.

Second, a driver can have a Cleanup Dispatch routine that processes the IRP_MJ_CLEANUP major function code. The I/O Manager automatically sends an IRP with this function code whenever a thread terminates or closes a handle. The job of the Cleanup Dispatch is to cancel any queued IRPs belonging to the thread. This is a more general mechanism that all drivers ought to support.

Synchronization Issues

Keep in mind that a driver's I/O processing, Cleanup Dispatch, and Cancel routines all execute asynchronously. On a multi-processor system, they could literally be running at the same time. As a result, various driver routines have to coordinate their activities with care. Otherwise, there's always the chance one part of a driver might keep working on an IRP that another part of the driver has already cancelled.

For example, imagine that an IRP with an attached Cancel routine is sitting in the Device Queue of some Device object. The I/O Manager dequeues the IRP, makes it the Device object's current IRP, and then calls the driver's Start I/O routine. Start I/O gets control, but before it can remove the IRP's Cancel routine, the IRP is cancelled (perhaps on another CPU) and the Cancel routine executes. Now, the Start I/O routine will begin processing the IRP and the Cancel routine will cancel it.[2]

Or consider the case where a driver's Cleanup Dispatch routine is in the process of cancelling an IRP with an attached Cancel routine. If the Cancel routine starts running before the Cleanup Dispatch function can disable it, again there will be a very nasty collision.

The I/O Manager uses two mechanisms to prevent these kinds of synchronization problems. The following subsections describe how they work.

The Cancel spin lock   The I/O Manager's Cancel spin lock is the primary safeguard against collisions during IRP cancellation. Ownership of this spin lock guarantees exclusive access to any IRP fields involved in cancelling a request. It

---

[2] This race condition is not limited to the Start I/O routine. Any time a queued IRP has an attached Cancel routine, there's the chance that the Cancel routine may execute between the moment when the IRP is dequeued and the moment when its Cancel routine is disabled.

also protects the IRP from the time it leaves a Device object's Device Queue until it becomes the current IRP.

Any driver-defined data structures that are shared among the Cleanup Dispatch routine, a Cancel routine, and some other driver routine should also be guarded by this spin lock. This includes any internal queues where the driver might be holding IRPs.

To use this lock, you need to call **IoAcquireCancelSpinLock** before you touch any of the various **CancelXxx** fields of the IRP and **IoReleaseCancelSpinLock** when you're finished. This is an Executive spin lock, so you have to be at or below DISPATCH_LEVEL IRQL when you acquire it. During the time you actually hold the Cancel spin lock, you'll be running at DISPATCH_LEVEL IRQL, so it's important not to cause any page faults.

Two important points about working with the Cancel spin lock: First, make sure you release it *before* you call **IoCompleteRequest**. If you break this rule, you can cause a system deadlock.

Second, remember that there's only one of these locks for the whole system, so don't hold on to it for too long. Doing so can prevent other drivers from running, which can degrade system performance.

The IRP Cancel flag   Any time a driver removes an IRP with a Cancel routine from a queue, there's always the danger that the Cancel routine will execute in the brief interval before it can be disabled. This would lead to a situation where the driver continued processing an IRP that had already been completed by the Cancel function.

To avoid this problem, each IRP contains a Boolean **Cancel** flag. By setting this flag to TRUE before it calls the IRP's Cancel routine, the I/O Manager lets other parts of the driver know that the IRP has already been completed. Like other cancellation fields in the IRP, the **Cancel** flag is guarded by the Cancel spin lock.

A driver's processing routines check the **Cancel** flag after they remove an IRP from a queue. If the flag is TRUE, it means the Cancel routine has already grabbed the IRP and nothing more should be done with it. If the flag is FALSE, the processing routine sets the **CancelRoutine** field of the IRP to NULL using **IoSetCancelRoutine** and starts to work on it.[3] From this point on, the Cancel routine can't run anymore, so there's no more danger.

What a Cancel Routine Does

Whenever a driver puts an IRP into a queue where it might remain for an indefinite time, the driver should give the I/O Manager the option of canceling the IRP. To do this, the driver attaches a queue-specific Cancel routine to the IRP

---

[3] Calling **IoSetCancelRoutine** requires that you first become the owner of the Cancel spin lock.

by calling **IoSetCancelRoutine**. The Cancel routine is responsible for doing whatever is necessary to cancel the IRP. The exact actions it takes will depend on where the IRP is in its processing cycle. If the driver has multiple internal queues, it can attach different Cancel routines to an IRP at different stages of processing.

A driver can have a Cancel routine attached to an IRP only while the driver actually owns the IRP. In other words, the IRP is only cancelable between the time the driver receives the IRP and when it either completes the IRP or sends it to another driver with **IoCallDriver**. Before releasing an IRP, the driver must set its **CancelRoutine** field to NULL using **IoSetCancelRoutine**.

As described at the beginning of this section, the I/O Manager will call an IRP's Cancel routine if the thread issuing the request terminates or closes its handle before the request completes. The Cancel routine will also execute if a higher-level driver explicitly cancels the request with **IoCancelIrp**.

An IRP's Cancel routine runs at DISPATCH_LEVEL IRQL. As input, it receives a pointer to the Device object and a pointer to the IRP being cancelled. Before calling a **Cancel** routine, the I/O Manager acquires the Cancel spin lock, sets the IRP's Cancel flag to TRUE and its **CancelRoutine** field to NULL. The Cancel routine has to release the Cancel lock before it returns.

The specific actions taken by a Cancel routine will depend on the state of the IRP at the time it gets cancelled. The following subsections describe each of the possibilities.

IRP is in the Device Queue   If the IRP has not become current yet, then it must still be in the Device object's Device queue. In this case, the Cancel routine takes the following actions:

1.   It calls **KeRemoveEntryDeviceQueue** to pull the IRP from the Device Queue.

2.   The Cancel routine then calls **IoReleaseCancelSpinLock** to let go of the Cancel lock.

3.   Next, it puts STATUS_CANCELLED in the IRP's **IoStatus.Status** field and 0 in its **IoStatus.Information** field.

4.   The Cancel routine calls **IoCompleteRequest** to give the IRP back to the I/O Manager. The priority boost is set to IO_NO_INCREMENT.

There's no need to call **IoStartNextPacket** since the IRP was canceled while it was still in the Device Queue and hadn't yet entered the Start I/O routine.

IRP is current   A Cancel routine might run in the brief interval *after* the I/O Manager has put an IRP's address into a Device object's **CurrentIrp** field but *before* the Start I/O routine has set the IRP's **CancelRoutine** field to NULL. The Cancel routine normally checks to see if the IRP being cancelled is the Device object's current IRP, and if it is, it does the following:

1. It calls **IoReleaseCancelSpinLock** to let go of the Cancel lock.

2. The Cancel routine next sets the IRP's **IoStatus.Status** field to STATUS_CANCELLED and its **IoStatus.Information** field to 0.

3. Next, it calls **IoCompleteRequest** to give the IRP back to the I/O Manager. The priority boost is set to IO_NO_INCREMENT.

4. Finally, the Cancel routine calls **IoStartNextPacket** to make the driver start the next IRP.

IRP is in some other queue   A driver can always maintain its own private queue of IRPs. If an IRP is in such a queue at the time it gets cancelled, its queue-specific Cancel routine does the following:

1. It calls **RemoveEntryList** to dequeue it.[4]

2. The Cancel routine then calls **IoReleaseCancelSpinLock** to let go of the Cancel lock.

3. Next, it puts STATUS_CANCELLED in the IRP's **IoStatus.Status** field, and zero in its **IoStatus.Information** field.

4. The Cancel routine calls **IoCompleteRequest** to give the IRP back to the I/O Manager. The priority boost is set to IO_NO_INCREMENT.

5.   Depending on the design of the driver, it may be necessary to call **IoStartNextPacket** to get the driver working on the next request.

What a Dispatch Cleanup Routine Does

At the time a user-mode thread terminates (either normally or abnormally), it may still have incomplete I/O requests associated with one or more Device objects. Similarly, it's possible for a thread to close a Device object handle with requests pending. In both these cases, the I/O Manager will try to clean up the outstanding I/O requests by doing two things: It sends the Device object an IRP with the major function code IRP_MJ_CLEANUP and it calls the Cancel routine of any IRPs associated with the thread.

After this, the I/O Manager delays execution of the thread, giving the driver time to process the IRPs. If the driver completes the IRPs, the I/O Manager responds by sending an IRP_MJ_CLOSE IRP to the Device object.

If the IRPs aren't completed during the timeout interval (which can last more than five minutes), things get ugly. In this case, the I/O Manager displays a message box for each IRP (naming the offending driver) and detaches the IRP

---

[4] This assumes the driver-defined queue is protected by the Cancel spin lock. The **RemoveEntryList** function is not interlocked.

from the thread. These zombie IRPs are lost to the system, as is any system buffer space associated with them. Another side-effect is that the driver can't be unloaded since it still has outstanding IRPs. No IRP_MJ_CLOSE ever gets sent.

From this description, you can see how important it is for a driver to clean up pending I/O requests. As you already know, one way to do this is to attach Cancel routines to every IRP. For some drivers, this may be overkill, and a simpler method is just to ask for cleanup notifications. To receive these notifications, the Driver object has to have a Dispatch routine registered for IRP_MJ_CLEANUP in its **MajorFunction** table.

The job of the Cleanup Dispatch routine is to cancel any queued requests associated with a specific Device object. For nonshareable Device objects, this means flushing all IRPs out of the Device Queue and any other driver-defined queues where they may be hiding. Depending on the nature of the device, the driver might also abort a request in progress, or let it complete normally.

If a Device object is shareable, cleanup involves a little more work. In this case, the Cleanup Dispatch routine must cancel only those IRPs associated with the specific user-mode handle being closed. To do this, it uses the File object pointer stored in the I/O stack location of each IRP. This pointer uniquely identifies the user-mode handle that issued the request. The Cleanup Dispatch routine simply has to compare the File object pointer in each queued IRP with the pointer in the IRP_MJ_CLEANUP IRP. If they match, the queued IRP needs to be cancelled.

Like any Dispatch routine, the Cleanup Dispatch executes at PASSIVE_LEVEL IRQL. Although the specific steps will depend on the driver, a Cleanup Dispatch routine generally has to do the following:

1. It calls **IoAcquireCancelSpinLock** to acquire the Cancel spin lock. Unlike a Cancel routine, the Cleanup Dispatch routine doesn't automatically hold this spin lock when it's called.

2. Next, it scans the Device Queue of the target Device object looking for IRPs whose File object pointer matches the File object pointer of the IRP_MJ_CLEANUP IRP itself.

3. The Dispatch Cleanup routine removes each matching IRP from the Device Queue and sets the IRP's **CancelRoutine** field to NULL. It also sets the IRP's **Cancel** flag to TRUE and its **CancelIrql** field to DISPATCH_LEVEL. The IRP is then added to a list of requests to be cancelled.

4. If the driver maintains any private queues where IRPs might be held, the Dispatch Cleanup routine performs a similar scan. Any IRPs with matching File object pointers are removed from these queues, their various **CancelXxx** fields are modified and they are also put in the list of requests to be cancelled.

5. After releasing the Cancel spin lock, the Dispatch Cleanup routine completes all the IRPs in its cancellation list with a status of STATUS_ CANCELLED and a boost of IO_NO_INCREMENT.

6. Finally, it completes the IRP_MJ_CLEANUP request itself with a status of STATUS_SUCCESS and a priority boost value of IO_NO_INCREMENT.

11.5 Some More Hardware: The 16550 UART

This section describes the operation of the 16550 UART (*Universal Asynchronous Receiver/Transmitter*), a typical full-duplex device. Knowing how this hardware works will make it easier to understand the sample driver in the next section.

What the 16550 UART Does

The 16550 UART is an integrated circuit that performs serial input and output. Normally the UART is coupled to some kind of line-driver chip that interfaces with the outside world. For example, this is how the RS-232 serial ports on most computers are implemented.

The beauty of the UART is that it hides all the unpleasant details of framing the data with START and STOP bits, as well as generating parity and making sure all the bits are shifted out at the proper rate. To perform serial data transfers, you just move individual bytes to or from the UART's buffer registers.

On output, you send a data byte to the UART's Transmit Data register from which it is moved into a 16-byte FIFO on the chip. When the data byte makes it to the other end of the FIFO, it goes into a shift register that sends it out over the serial line one bit at a time. When the FIFO empties out, the UART sets its TBE (*transmit buffer empty*) flag.

Meanwhile, the UART's receiver section is constantly monitoring the serial line for input. As bits appear, they are added to a shift register that assembles them into a single byte of data. When the byte is complete, it goes into the input FIFO and the UART sets its RxRDY (*receive data ready*) flag to indicate that data is available. This flag stays up as long as any data remains in the FIFO. You pull data bytes one by one from the UART's Receive Data register.

Device Registers

You interact with the 16550 UART by reading and writing a set of one-byte registers, which are described briefly in Table 11.5. Although this chapter gives you enough information to talk intelligently about the 16550 at a dinner party, you should read the data sheets from National Semiconductor if you want the whole story.[5]

If you count carefully, you'll notice that there are twelve registers sandwiched into an eight-byte span. How can this be? Actually, it's the hardware

---

[5] Joe Campbell's definitive book on serial communications (listed in the bibliography) is another excellent source of information.

Table 11.5   Control and status registers for a 16550 UART

UART register definitions

Offset	Register	Access	Description
0	Receive Data	R/O	Fetches first byte from input FIFO
	Transmit Data	W/O	Sends byte to output FIFO
	Baud rate LSB	R/W	Low byte of baud rate divisor*
1	Interrupt Enable	R/W	Enables various interrupts
	Bit 0		Received data ready
	Bit 1		Transmit buffer empty
	Bit 2		Error or BREAK
	Bit 3		RS-232 input has changed state
	Bits 4–7		Always zero
	Baud rate MSB	R/W	High byte of baud rate divisor*
2	Interrupt ID	R/O	Identifies source of an interrupt
	Bit 0		If set, no interrupts pending
	Bits 1–2		Source of interrupt (see below)
	Bit 3		FIFO timeout interrupt
	Bits 4–5		Reserved
	Bits 6–7		Set if FIFOs are enabled
	FIFO Control	W/O	Controls FIFO behavior
	Bit 0		Enable both FIFOs
	Bit 1		Clear all bytes from Receive FIFO
	Bit 2		Clear all bytes from Transmit FIFO
	Bit 3		Enable DMA support
	Bits 4–5		Reserved
	Bits 6–7		Trigger-level of Receive FIFO
3	Line Control	R/W	Controls data bits, stop bits, parity
	Bits 0–1		Number of data bits
	Bit 2		Number of STOP bits
	Bits 3–5		Parity control
	Bit 6		BREAK control
	Bit 7		Divisor latch access bit (DLAB)
4	Modem Control	R/W	Controls state of DTR and RTS lines
5	Line Status	R/W	Reports status of I/O operation
6	Modem Status	R/W	Reports state changes in DTR, RTS
7	Scratch-pad	R/W	Unused, possibly not implemented

*Accessible only when DLAB in the Line Control register is 1.

people playing those little tricks they like so much. The first trick is that some addresses go to different registers on the UART depending on whether you're reading or writing them. For example, if you read from offset 0, you get the contents of the Receive Data register, but if you write to 0, your byte goes to the Transmit Data register instead.

That accounts for ten registers, but what about the remaining two? The other trick is that when you set the DLAB bit of register 3, the low and high bytes of the baud-rate control mysteriously appear at offsets 0 and 1. You restore things to normal by clearing the bit. Since you're not likely to change baud rates frequently, this doesn't cause much of a problem.

One other thing to watch out for is register 7. Although the official data sheets say you should be able to use it as a one-byte store for anything you like, the truth is that it may not work. National Semiconductor licenses this UART design to a number of other manufacturers, and they don't all implement the scratch-pad.

Interrupt Behavior

The 16550 UART uses interrupts to let the CPU know about a number of interesting conditions. Specifically, it generates an interrupt whenever:

- A framing error or a BREAK occurs.
- The Receive FIFO reaches the trigger level set by the FIFO Control register.
- There is at least one character in the Receive FIFO, no other characters have arrived recently, and the CPU hasn't read the Receive Data register for awhile. This FIFO timeout interrupt prevents data from wasting away in the FIFO.
- The transmit FIFO is empty. Usually, this is the signal to send more data. A single, spurious FIFO empty interrupt can occur when you first enable transmitter interrupts.
- Any of the RS-232 input lines changes state.

Your interrupt service routine determines the cause of the interrupt by examining the UART's Interrupt ID register. Notice the use of negative logic in this register: The UART *clears* the low-order bit when an interrupt occurs and *sets* it when all pending interrupts have been serviced. The remaining bits in this register describe the exact source of the interrupt. See Table 11.6 for more information about UART interrupts.

Since several of these conditions might occur simultaneously, the UART imposes a priority arbitration scheme on interrupt events. When an interrupt occurs, the 16550 locks out UART events of equal or lower priority until the current interrupt has been dismissed.

Table 11.6 Determining the cause of a 16550 interrupt

UART interrupts

Cause	Priority	ID register
(No interrupt)	—	1
Error or BREAK	0	6
FIFO receiver trigger level	1	4
Receive-FIFO timeout	1	12
Transmitter buffer empty	2	2
RS-232 input	3	0

Priority 0 is the most important, priority 3 the least.

The Interrupt ID register only shows you the highest-priority UART event. After you service this event, any other pending interrupts appear in the ID register in order of priority. This means that when you service a single UART interrupt, you need to check for any other events that might be pending before you dismiss the interrupt. Your service routine isn't really finished until the UART sets the low bit of the ID register.

The action your service routine takes to clear an interrupt depends on the cause of the interrupt. Table 11.7 shows how to clear various UART interrupts. Notice that you can clear Transmit interrupts either by sending more data, or (if this is the end of the I/O operation) simply by reading the ID register again.

Table 11.7 Clearing interrupts on the 16550 UART

Clearing UART interrupts

Interrupt source	To clear it...
Receiver error or BREAK	Read the Line Status register
Received data	Read data from the Receiver register
Transmit buffer empty	• Write to the Transmit buffer • Read the Interrupt ID register
RS-232 input	Read the RS-232 Status register

11.6 CODE EXAMPLE: FULL-DUPLEX UART DRIVER

This is an example of a simple driver that performs simultaneous input and output operations using a 16550 UART. Because the driver is rather large, only selected pieces will appear here. You can find the complete code for this example in the **CH11\DRIVER** directory on the disk accompanying this book.

What to Expect

As you're poking around in the code, keep in mind that this is a toy driver whose real purpose is to illustrate the techniques presented earlier in this chapter. As a result, it ignores a number of issues that a real serial port driver needs to worry about.[6] Before examining the driver itself, it's a good idea to describe some of the things it *doesn't* do.

Perhaps this driver's biggest limitation is that it doesn't handle unsolicited input. In other words, it only accepts data from the device when an IRP_MJ_READ IRP is pending. Data arriving at any other time is simply dropped on the floor. In a real serial port driver, the Interrupt Service routine would probably dump unsolicited input into a type-ahead buffer, where it could be used to satisfy IRP_MJ_READ requests as they arrived.

Secondly, this driver uses a very simple signaling protocol between the sender and the receiver: It relies on the timeout interrupt from the UART's input-FIFO to terminate a read request. If the sender slows down enough to trigger this interrupt, the receiver will essentially ignore the rest of the transmission. Conversely, if the sender doesn't leave enough of a gap between successive transmissions, the receiver will run them together. This is the only kind of flow-control supported by the driver.

Finally, as a concession to simplicity, this driver doesn't worry about device operations that time out. Since this can lead to situations where an IRP never gets completed, it's definitely something you'd want to handle in a real driver. The first code example in Chapter 10 shows how to deal with device time-outs.

DEVICE_EXTENSION in XXDRIVER.H

The following excerpt from the driver-specific header file shows the layout of the Device Extension.

```
typedef struct _DEVICE_EXTENSION {
  PDEVICE_OBJECT DeviceObject; // Back pointer

  ULONG NtDeviceNumber;    // Zero-based device number

  PUCHAR PortBase;         // First control register
  PKINTERRUPT pInterrupt;  // Interrupt object

  //
  // Current UART settings
  //
```

---

[6] If you want to see what really goes into managing a standard COM port, take a look at the serial port driver source code included in the NT DDK.

```
            ULONG InputFifoTriggerLevel;
            ULONG DataBits;
            ULONG StopBits;
            ULONG Parity;

            KDEVICE_QUEUE AlternateIrpQueue; ❶
            KDPC AlternateDpc;
            PIRP CurrentAlternateIrp;

            ULONG OutputFifoSize;        // Bytes to send at once ❷
            ULONG OutputBytesRequested; // Output buffer size
            ULONG OutputBytesRemaining; // Chars left to send
            PUCHAR pOutputBuffer;        // Next char to send

            BOOLEAN OutputInterruptsValid;

            ULONG InputFifoSize;         // Count of bytes ❸
            ULONG InputBytesRequested;   // Input buffer size
            ULONG InputBytesRemaining;   // Space left in buffer
            PUCHAR pInputBuffer;         // Next available slot

            BOOLEAN InputInterruptsValid;

            UCHAR DeviceStatus;          // Most recent status
        } DEVICE_EXTENSION, *PDEVICE_EXTENSION;
```

❶ The Device Queue object and **AlternateCurrentIrp** pointer keep track of input requests. In this driver, all input operations will follow the alternate processing path. The DPC object is used to request I/O postprocessing of alternate IRPs.

❷ Here are the bookkeeping items used for output requests. Since the driver is using Buffered I/O, it has to keep a count of the bytes left to be transferred and a pointer to the location of the next output byte in the system buffer. The **OutputInterruptsValid** flag is set to TRUE whenever an output operation is in progress.

❸ These items do the bookkeeping for input requests. Notice how they parallel the output items.

DISPATCH.C

This portion of the example shows the Dispatch routines for writing, reading, and performing IRP cleanup operations.

XxDispatchWrite   This function processes Win32 **WriteFile** calls by sending the IRP along the standard driver processing path.

```
NTSTATUS
XxDispatchWrite(
  IN PDEVICE_OBJECT DeviceObject,
  IN PIRP Irp
  )
{
  PIO_STACK_LOCATION IrpStack =
            IoGetCurrentIrpStackLocation( Irp );

  if( IrpStack->Parameters.Write.Length == 0 )  ❶
  {
        Irp->IoStatus.Status = STATUS_SUCCESS;
        Irp->IoStatus.Information = 0;
        IoCompleteRequest( Irp, IO_NO_INCREMENT );
        return STATUS_SUCCESS;
  }

  //
  // Start device operation
  //
  IoMarkIrpPending( Irp );

  IoStartPacket(  ❷
        DeviceObject,
        Irp,
        0,
        XxCancelPrimaryIrp );  ❸

  return STATUS_PENDING;
}
```

❶ This driver doesn't consider zero-length transfers to be an error, so the IRP is just completed immediately.

❷ To send an IRP along the standard processing path, the driver calls **IoStartPacket**.

❸ While the IRP is waiting in the Device object's pending queue, this Cancel routine will be responsible for canceling it.

XxDispatchRead   This function processes Win32 ReadFile calls by sending the IRP along the alternate driver processing path.

```
NTSTATUS
XxDispatchRead(
  IN PDEVICE_OBJECT DeviceObject,
  IN PIRP Irp
  )
{
```

```
PIO_STACK_LOCATION IrpStack =
              IoGetCurrentIrpStackLocation( Irp );
//
// Check for zero-length transfers
//
if( IrpStack->Parameters.Read.Length == 0 )
{
      Irp->IoStatus.Status = STATUS_SUCCESS;
      Irp->IoStatus.Information = 0;
      IoCompleteRequest( Irp, IO_NO_INCREMENT );
      return STATUS_SUCCESS;
}

IoMarkIrpPending( Irp ); ❶

XxAlternateStartPacket( ❷
              DeviceObject,
              Irp,
              XxCancelAlternateIrp ); ❸

return STATUS_PENDING;
}
```

❶ Begin the device operation. As always, the IRP must be marked pending.

❷ Unlike the previous Dispatch routine, this one uses a driver-defined function to send the IRP along the alternate processing path.

❸ Once again, there's a Cancel routine to process the IRP if it should be canceled before the driver actually starts working on it.

XxDispatchCleanup   This Dispatch routine gets called when a thread that opened a handle either calls CloseHandle or terminates. Its job is to pull any IRPs associated with the handle from the two Device Queues and cancel them.

```
NTSTATUS
XxDispatchCleanup(
  IN PDEVICE_OBJECT DeviceObject,
  IN PIRP Irp
  )
{
  PIO_STACK_LOCATION CleanupIrpStack =
              IoGetCurrentIrpStackLocation( Irp );

  PDEVICE_EXTENSION DeviceExtension =
              DeviceObject->DeviceExtension;

  XxCleanupDeviceQueue( ❶
        &DeviceObject->DeviceQueue,
        CleanupIrpStack->FileObject );
```

```
XxCleanupDeviceQueue( ❷
      &DeviceExtension->AlternateIrpQueue,
      CleanupIrpStack->FileObject );

Irp->IoStatus.Status = STATUS_SUCCESS; ❸
Irp->IoStatus.Information = 0;
IoCompleteRequest( Irp, IO_NO_INCREMENT );
return STATUS_SUCCESS;
}
```

❶ **XxCleanupDeviceQueue**, a helper function that appears later in this example, does the actual work. Here, it's being called to cancel IRP_MJ_WRITE IRPs waiting in the Device object's primary queue. The File object pointer identifies the handle to look for when canceling IRPs.

❷ Here, **XxCleanupDeviceQueue** will cancel IRP_MJ_READ IRPs associated with the handle.

❸ Finally, the IRP_MJ_CLEANUP IRP itself is completed. Once this IRP is passed back to the I/O Manager, it will be followed by an IRP_MJ_CLOSE request for the same handle.

DEVQUEUE.C

The routines in this file manage the Device Queue object used for processing alternate IRPs.

XxAlternateStartPacket   Given an IRP, this function either sends it to the alternate Start I/O routine or queues it for later processing if the alternate path is busy. In many ways, this function resembles the I/O Manager's **IoStartPacket** routine.

```
VOID
XxAlternateStartPacket(
  IN PDEVICE_OBJECT DeviceObject,
  IN PIRP Irp,
  IN PDRIVER_CANCEL CancelFunction
  )
{
  KIRQL OldIrql;

  PDEVICE_EXTENSION DeviceExtension =
            DeviceObject->DeviceExtension;

  IoAcquireCancelSpinLock( &OldIrql ); ❶
  IoSetCancelRoutine( Irp, CancelFunction );

  if( KeInsertDeviceQueue( ❷
        &DeviceExtension->AlternateIrpQueue,
```

```
                &Irp->Tail.Overlay.DeviceQueueEntry ))
    {

            IoReleaseCancelSpinLock( OldIrql );

    }
    else ❸
    {
            DeviceExtension->CurrentAlternateIrp = Irp; ❹
            IoReleaseCancelSpinLock( OldIrql );

            KeRaiseIrql( DISPATCH_LEVEL, &OldIrql ); ❺
            XxAlternateStartIo( DeviceObject, Irp );
            KeLowerIrql( OldIrql );

    }
}
```

❶ It's necessary to be holding the Cancel spin lock in order to modify the IRP's **CancelRoutine** field. This driver also uses the Cancel spin lock to guard the alternate IRP queue and the pointer to the alternate IRP currently being processed.

❷ Try to put the IRP into the alternate queue. If the Device Queue object was already busy, the IRP will be inserted and the driver will simply release the Cancel spin lock.

❸ If the Device Queue was not-busy, **KeInsertDeviceQueue** will fail, and the Device Queue will flip into the busy state. In that case, it's necessary to start processing the IRP.

❹ The first step is to record the IRP as the current alternate IRP. Once this is done, it's safe to release the Cancel spin lock.

❺ The next step is to call the alternate Start I/O routine. Since **XxAlternate-StartPacket** runs at PASSIVE_LEVEL IRQL, and the alternate Start I/O routine runs at DISPATCH_LEVEL, it's necessary for requests to raise and lower the CPU's IRQL value.

XxAlternateStartNextPacket   This routine does the same job as the I/O Manager's **IoStartNextPacket** function. If there is an available IRP in the queue of pending alternate IRPs, this function sends it to the alternate Start I/O entry point. This piece of code expects to run at DISPATCH_LEVEL IRQL only.

```
VOID
XxAlternateStartNextPacket(
  IN PDEVICE_OBJECT DeviceObject,
  IN BOOLEAN Cancelable
  )
{
  PDEVICE_EXTENSION DeviceExtension =
            DeviceObject->DeviceExtension;
```

```
PKDEVICE_QUEUE_ENTRY QueueEntry;
PIRP Irp;
KIRQL OldIrql;

if( Cancelable )
     IoAcquireCancelSpinLock( &OldIrql ); ❶

QueueEntry =
     KeRemoveDeviceQueue(
          &DeviceExtension->AlternateIrpQueue ); ❷

if( QueueEntry != NULL )
{
     Irp = CONTAINING_RECORD( ❸
               QueueEntry,
               IRP,
               Tail.Overlay.DeviceQueueEntry );

     DeviceExtension->CurrentAlternateIrp = Irp;

     if( Cancelable )
          IoReleaseCancelSpinLock( OldIrql ); ❹

          XxAlternateStartIo( DeviceObject, Irp );
}
else
{
     DeviceExtension->CurrentAlternateIrp = NULL; ❺

     if( Cancelable )
          IoReleaseCancelSpinLock( OldIrql );
}
}
```

❶ In imitation of the I/O Manager's routine, this function uses an explicit argument to decide whether the whole operation should be protected by the Cancel spin lock. Since this driver always attaches a Cancel routine to an alternate IRP, this argument will always be TRUE.

❷ Try to get the next pending IRP from the alternate Device Queue. If the queue was empty, **KeRemoveDeviceQueue** sets the Device Queue's state to not-busy and returns NULL.

❸ There was something in the queue. Reconstitute the address of the IRP itself and make it the new current IRP for the alternate path.

❹ If necessary, let go of the Cancel spin lock, then call the driver's alternate Start I/O entry point.

❺ If the queue was empty, the only work to do is to clear out the current-IRP slot for the alternate path and drop the Cancel spin lock.

INPUT.C

In this driver, IRP_MJ_READ requests are sent down the alternate path. This file contains routines that process these alternate IRPs. You'll find similar code for handling IRP_MJ_WRITE requests in OUTPUT.C.

XxAlternateStartIo   Like any Start I/O routine, this one is responsible for setting up various bookkeeping values and then starting the actual device operation.

```
VOID
XxAlternateStartIo(
  IN PDEVICE_OBJECT DeviceObject,
  IN PIRP Irp
  )
{
  KIRQL OldIrql;

  PIO_STACK_LOCATION IrpStack =
        IoGetCurrentIrpStackLocation( Irp );

  PDEVICE_EXTENSION DeviceExtension =
              DeviceObject->DeviceExtension;

  IoAcquireCancelSpinLock( &OldIrql ); ❶

  if( Irp->Cancel )
  {
        IoReleaseCancelSpinLock( OldIrql ); ❷
        return;
  }
  else ❸
  {
        IoSetCancelRoutine( Irp, NULL );
        IoReleaseCancelSpinLock( OldIrql );
  }

  switch( IrpStack->MajorFunction ) {

        case IRP_MJ_READ: ❹

              DeviceExtension->InputBytesRequested =
                  IrpStack->Parameters.Read.Length;

              DeviceExtension->InputBytesRemaining =
                  DeviceExtension->InputBytesRequested;

              DeviceExtension->pInputBuffer =
                  Irp->AssociatedIrp.SystemBuffer;

              if( !KeSynchronizeExecution( ❺
```

```
                            DeviceExtension->pInterrupt,
                            XxReceiveBytes,
                            DeviceExtension ))
                {
                        XxDpcForInputs(
                                NULL,
                                DeviceObject,
                                Irp,
                                DeviceExtension );
                }
                break;
        //
        // Should never get here -- just get rid
        // of the packet...
        //
        default:
                //
                // Fail the IRP and start the next one.
                //
                Irp->IoStatus.Status =
                                STATUS_NOT_SUPPORTED;
                Irp->IoStatus.Information = 0;
                IoCompleteRequest(
                        Irp,
                        IO_NO_INCREMENT );

                XxAlternateStartNextPacket(
                                        DeviceObject,
                                        TRUE );
                break;
        }
}
```

❶ Before starting the operation, see if the Cancel routine has run between the time the IRP was removed from the Device Queue and now. This requires ownership of the Cancel spin lock.

❷ If the Cancel flag is set, it means the IRP has already been processed by the Cancel routine. In this case, the only thing to do is to release the spin and return immediately.

❸ The Cancel flag is clear. Remove the IRP from the cancelable state by setting its Cancel routine to NULL, then start to process it. From this point on, only normal completion or an error can stop this request.

❹ Set up various pointers and counters in preparation for the data transfer operation.

❺ Next, start the device. If something goes wrong, use the DPC routine to fail the IRP. Pass NULL for the DPC object argument to let the DPC routine know that it's been called early and not as part of a normal I/O completion.

XxDpcForInputs   Here's the CustomDpc routine used for inputs. It does the usual work of putting a final status in the IRP, completing the current request, and trying to start another.

```
VOID
XxDpcForInputs(
   IN PKDPC Dpc,
   IN PDEVICE_OBJECT DeviceObject,
   IN PIRP Irp,
   IN PVOID Context
   )
{
   PDEVICE_EXTENSION DeviceExtension = Context;

   Irp->IoStatus.Information = ❶
         DeviceExtension->InputBytesRequested -
         DeviceExtension->InputBytesRemaining;

   Irp->IoStatus.Status = STATUS_SUCCESS; ❷

   if( Dpc == NULL ) ❸
         IoCompleteRequest( Irp, IO_NO_INCREMENT );
   else
         IoCompleteRequest( Irp, IO_SERIAL_INCREMENT );

   XxAlternateStartNextPacket( DeviceObject, TRUE ); ❹
}
```

❶ Calculate the number of bytes actually transferred.

❷ Come up with a final status code for the IRP. A real driver would probably use the last recorded contents of the device's status register (stored in the Device Extension) to produce a real status value.

❸ If this routine is being called directly from the alternate Start I/O routine, the DPC argument will be NULL. This means the IRP is being failed before it got started. In that case, don't give the calling thread a priority boost.

❹ This request is done. Use a driver-defined routine to start the next alternate IRP (if there is one).

ISR.C

This file contains the interrupt service code for the UART driver. To make things a little more readable, processing for input events happens in some auxiliary subroutines.

Xxlsr   The Kernel's interrupt dispatcher calls this function at DIRQL, holding the Interrupt spin lock for the device. Since the UART can request multiple kinds of interrupts at the same time, **XxIsr** has to keep checking for possible interrupts until nothing more shows up.

```
BOOLEAN
XxIsr(
  IN PKINTERRUPT Interrupt,
  IN PVOID ServiceContext
  )
{
  PDEVICE_EXTENSION pDE = ServiceContext;
  PDEVICE_OBJECT pDevice = pDE->DeviceObject;

  UCHAR InterruptId = XxReadIntId( pDE );

  if(( InterruptId & XX_IIR_NO_INTERRUPT ) != 0 ) ❶
      return FALSE;

  do
  {
      InterruptId &= XX_IIR_INTERRUPT_ID_MASK; ❷

      switch( InterruptId )
      {
          case XX_IIR_ERR:
              XxReadLineStatus( pDE ); ❸
              break;

          case XX_IIR_RDA:
              XxHandleInputFifoTrigger( pDE ); ❹
              break;

          case XX_IIR_FIFO_TMO:
              XxHandleInputFifoTimeOut( pDE ); ❺
              break;

          case XX_IIR_TBE:
              if( pDE->OutputInterruptsValid ) ❻
                  if( !XxTransmitBytes( pDE ))
                      IoRequestDpc(
                          pDevice,
                          pDevice->CurrentIrp,
                          (PVOID)pDE );
              break;

          case XX_IIR_RS232:
              XxReadModemStatus( pDE ); ❼
              break;
      }
```

```
            InterruptId = XxReadIntId( pDE ); ❽
    } while(( InterruptId &
            XX_IIR_NO_INTERRUPT ) == 0 );

    return TRUE;
}
```

❶ If the low-order bit of the Interrupt ID register is set, then this device didn't generate an interrupt. Return control to the Kernel's interrupt dispatcher.

❷ The UART interrupted. Enter a loop that will keep processing interrupt until there's nothing left to do. Begin by masking out any irrelevant bits, then switch on the interrupt-type.

❸ This driver doesn't process any device errors. Just read the status register to clear the pending interrupt.

❹ This interrupt means that the input FIFO hit its trigger level. Call a helper routine to get the input characters from the FIFO.

❺ This interrupt means there's been a little data (less than the trigger level) sitting and aging in the input FIFO. For this driver, that's a signal to end an input operation. Call a helper function to empty the FIFO and complete the IRP.

❻ During an output operation, this interrupt means that it's time to refill the output FIFO and send more data. The interrupt-valid flag in the Device Extension prevents the driver from responding to spurious Transmit Buffer Empty interrupts when no output request is being processed.

❼ This driver ignores modem events, but it's still necessary to read the Modem Status register in order to clear the interrupt.

❽ That ends the processing for the first UART interrupt. There might be more waiting in line behind it. Read the Interrupt ID register to get the next one and do the whole thing over again. If there is no other interrupt pending in the UART, drop out of the loop and return.

XxHandleInputFifoTrigger   This function is called by **XxIsr** during an input operation to get the next bunch of characters from the UART.

```
static VOID
XxHandleInputFifoTrigger(
  IN PDEVICE_EXTENSION pDE
  )
{
  ULONG i;

  //
  // Read one less than the number of bytes in
```

```
// the FIFO; this guarantees a FIFO time-out
// which will end the read request.
//
for( i=0; i < pDE->InputFifoSize - 1; i++ ) ❶
{
        if( pDE->InputInterruptsValid &&
            pDE->InputBytesRemaining > 0 ) ❷
        {
                *pDE->pInputBuffer++ =
                    XxReadDataBuffer( pDE );
                pDE->InputBytesRemaining--;
        }
        else XxReadDataBuffer( pDE );
}
}
```

❶ This loop reads one less than the number of bytes in the FIFO. This last lonely byte, pining away in the FIFO, will eventually generate a FIFO timeout interrupt and terminate the input operation.

❷ If an input operation is in progress, and if there's room left in the buffer, move a byte from the FIFO to the input buffer. Otherwise, drop the byte on the floor. This behavior throws away both excess characters and unsolicited input.

XxHandleInputFifoTimeOut   This function is called from **XxIsr** when some bytes have been languishing in the input FIFO for more than four character periods. In this driver, the FIFO timeout interrupt signals the end of an input operation.

```
static VOID
XxHandleInputFifoTimeOut(
  IN PDEVICE_EXTENSION pDE
  )
{
  while( XxReadLineStatus( pDE ) & XX_LSR_DATA_RDY ) ❶
  {
        if( pDE->InputInterruptsValid &&
            pDE->InputBytesRemaining > 0 )
        {
                *pDE->pInputBuffer++ =
                    XxReadDataBuffer( pDE );
                pDE->InputBytesRemaining--;
        }
        else XxReadDataBuffer( pDE );
  }
```

```
        if( pDE->InputInterruptsValid ) ❷
        {
                pDE->InputInterruptsValid = FALSE;

                KeInsertQueueDpc( ❸
                        &pDE->AlternateDpc,
                        (PVOID)pDE->CurrentAlternateIrp,
                        (PVOID)pDE );
        }
}
```

❶ Read bytes from the FIFO until it's empty. If this is a genuine input operation and there's still some room left in the buffer, store the bytes. Otherwise, drop them on the floor.

❷ If this was a spurious interrupt, there's nothing more to do. If an input
operation really was in progress, clear the interrupt-valid flag (so additional interrupts will be ignored). Then complete the current input IRP.

❸ Input operations use a CustomDpc routine to complete the IRP.

CANCEL.C

This file contains routines that support IRP cancellation.

XxCleanupDeviceQueue   This function is called by the driver's Cleanup
Dispatch routine. Its job is to cancel any IRPs in a Device Queue whose File object
pointer matches the one passed as an argument.

```
VOID
XxCleanupDeviceQueue(
  IN PKDEVICE_QUEUE DeviceQueue,
  IN PFILE_OBJECT FileObject
  )
{
  KIRQL OldIrql;
  PIRP CancelIrp;
  PIRP RequeueIrp;

  PIO_STACK_LOCATION CancelIrpStack;

  LIST_ENTRY CancelList;
  LIST_ENTRY RequeueList;
  PLIST_ENTRY ListHead;
  PKDEVICE_QUEUE_ENTRY QueueEntry;

  InitializeListHead( &CancelList ); ❶
  InitializeListHead( &RequeueList );
```

```
IoAcquireCancelSpinLock( &OldIrql );

if( IsListEmpty( &DeviceQueue->DeviceListHead )) ❷
{
     IoReleaseCancelSpinLock( OldIrql );
     return;
}

while(( QueueEntry =
            KeRemoveDeviceQueue(
                              DeviceQueue )) != NULL )❸
{
     CancelIrp =
          CONTAINING_RECORD(
               QueueEntry,
               IRP,
               Tail.Overlay.DeviceQueueEntry );

     CancelIrpStack =
        IoGetCurrentIrpStackLocation( CancelIrp );

     if( CancelIrpStack->FileObject == FileObject )❹
     {
          CancelIrp->Cancel = TRUE;
          CancelIrp->CancelIrql = OldIrql;
          CancelIrp->CancelRoutine = NULL;

          InsertTailList(
             &CancelList,
             &CancelIrp->Tail.Overlay.ListEntry );
     }
     else ❺
     {
          InsertTailList(
             &RequeueList,
             &CancelIrp->Tail.Overlay.ListEntry );
     }
}

while( !IsListEmpty( &RequeueList )) ❻
{
     ListHead = RemoveHeadList( &RequeueList );
     RequeueIrp =
          CONTAINING_RECORD(
               ListHead,
               IRP,
               Tail.Overlay.ListEntry );

     if( !KeInsertDeviceQueue( ❼
```

```
                           DeviceQueue,
                           &RequeueIrp->
                               Tail.Overlay.DeviceQueueEntry ))
          {
                    KeInsertDeviceQueue(
                           DeviceQueue,
                           &RequeueIrp->
                               Tail.Overlay.DeviceQueueEntry );
          }
    }

    //
    // Then release the Cancel spin lock
    //
    IoReleaseCancelSpinLock( OldIrql );

    //
    // Run the length of the holding queue and
    // complete every IRP that we found in it.
    //
    while( !IsListEmpty( &CancelList ))  ❽
    {
          ListHead = RemoveHeadList( &CancelList );
          CancelIrp =
                 CONTAINING_RECORD(
                      ListHead,
                      IRP,
                      Tail.Overlay.ListEntry );

          CancelIrp->IoStatus.Status = STATUS_CANCELLED;
          CancelIrp->IoStatus.Information = 0;

          IoCompleteRequest(
                      CancelIrp,
                      IO_NO_INCREMENT );
    }
}
```

❶ These temporary work-lists will hold IRPs that are chosen for cancellation and for requeuing. The list-heads need to initialized. It's also necessary to acquire the Cancel spin lock and hold it until all the IRPs in the Device Queue have been processed.

❷ See if there are any IRPs in the Device Queue. If it's empty, there's no work to do, so just quit.

❸ Loop until every IRP has been removed from the Device Queue. For each IRP, decide whether to cancel it or requeue it. At the end of this loop, the Device Queue has been emptied, hence its state will be Not Busy.

❹ If the IRP's File object pointer is the same as the one in the IRP_MJ_CLEANUP IRP, set the IRP's various **CancelXxx** fields. Then put the IRP into a holding queue of requests to be canceled.

❺ If the File object pointer doesn't match, this IRP should not be canceled. In that case, add it to the list of IRPs to be put back in the Device Queue.

❻ The IRPs have been divided. Run the list of IRPs to be requeued and put them all back in the Device Queue.

❼ Scanning the Device Queue emptied it, which put it in the Not Busy state. This means it will take two insertion calls to reinsert the first IRP: One to make the Device Queue Busy and the second to actually insert the IRP.

❽ Finally, run the list of IRPs to be canceled and send all of them back to the I/O Manager.

XxCancelAlternateIrp   The I/O Manager calls this function to cancel a single IRP_MJ_READ IRP. The IRP might either be sitting in the Device Queue or it may have just been removed from the queue, but not quite started yet. By the time this function runs, the I/O Manager has set the IRP's **Cancel** flag and cleared its **CancelRoutine** field.[7]

```
VOID
XxCancelAlternateIrp(
  IN PDEVICE_OBJECT DeviceObject,
  IN PIRP Irp
  )
{
  PDEVICE_EXTENSION DeviceExtension =
              DeviceObject->DeviceExtension;

  if( Irp == DeviceObject->CurrentAlternateIrp ) ❶
  {
        IoReleaseCancelSpinLock( Irp->CancelIrql ); ❷

        Irp->IoStatus.Status = STATUS_CANCELLED;
        Irp->IoStatus.Information = 0;

        IoCompleteRequest( Irp, IO_NO_INCREMENT );
        XxAlternateStartNextPacket( ❸
                        DeviceObject,
                        TRUE );
  }
  else ❹
  {
```

---

[7] **CANCEL.C** contains a similar function for canceling IRP_MJ_WRITE IRPs.

```
KeRemoveEntryDeviceQueue(
        &DeviceObject->AlternateIrpQueue,
        &Irp->Tail.Overlay.DeviceQueueEntry );

IoReleaseCancelSpinLock( Irp->CancelIrql );

Irp->IoStatus.Status = STATUS_CANCELLED;
Irp->IoStatus.Information = 0;

//
// Complete this IRP, but don't start the
// next one.
//
IoCompleteRequest( Irp, IO_NO_INCREMENT );
    }
}
```

❶ If the IRP is already in the **CurrentAlternateIrp** slot, but not yet started, it can still be canceled.

❷ Release the Cancel spin lock *before* completing the IRP. Notice that the I/O Manager has loaded the **CancelIrql** field of the IRP with the IRQL to which the driver should return when it releases the lock.

❸ Since the current alternate IRP has been removed, it's necessary to see if another one is waiting in the wings.

❹ The IRP wasn't current, so it must still be sitting in the Device Queue. Simply remove it from the queue and complete it. In this case, the driver *doesn't* try to start the next IRP.

11.7 SUMMARY

This chapter has presented a slightly different driver architecture that allows you to process more than one IRP at a time. Implementing this architecture required that we set up a Device Queue object to hold alternate IRPs. CustomDpc and Cancel routines also proved helpful, although their usefulness goes far beyond full-duplex drivers.

So much for drivers that manage Programmed I/O devices. The next step is to see what kind of support NT provides for DMA hardware. That will be the subject of the coming chapter.

CHAPTER 12

DMA Drivers

One way or another, all the drivers we've seen so far have depended on the CPU to move data between memory and the peripheral device. This technique is fine for slower hardware, but for fast devices that transfer large amounts of data, it would introduce too much overhead. Such devices are usually capable of directly accessing system memory and transferring data without the CPU's intervention. This chapter explains how to write drivers for these kinds of devices.

12.1 How DMA Works Under Windows NT

As you saw in Chapter 1, insulating drivers from CPU- and platform-dependencies was a major design goal of the NT I/O subsystem. One way that NT does this is by using an abstract model of DMA operations. Drivers that perform DMA work within the framework of this abstract model and can ignore many of the hardware-specific aspects of what's going on. This section presents the major features of the NT DMA framework.

Hiding DMA Hardware Variations with Adapter Objects

The purpose of using DMA is to minimize the CPU's involvement in data transfer operations. To do this, DMA devices use an auxiliary processor (called a DMA controller) to move data between memory and the peripheral device. This allows the CPU to continue doing other useful work in parallel with the I/O operation.

Although the exact details will vary, most DMA controllers have a very similar architecture. In its simplest form, this consists of an address register for the starting address of the DMA buffer, and a count register for the number of bytes or words to transfer. When you set these registers and start the attached device, the DMA controller begins moving data on its own. With each transfer, it increments the memory address register and decrements the count register. When the count register empties out, the DMA controller generates an interrupt, and the device is ready for another transfer.

Unfortunately, the needs of real-world hardware design complicate this simple picture. Consider the DMA implementation on ISA-based machines, described back in Chapter 2. These systems use a pair of Intel 8237 controller chips cascaded to provide four primary and three secondary DMA data channels. The primary channels (identified as zero through three) can perform single-byte transfers, while the secondary channels (five through seven) always transfer two bytes at a time. Since the 8237 uses a 16-bit transfer counter, the primary and secondary channels can handle only 64K bytes or 128K bytes per operation, respectively. Due to limitations of the ISA architecture, the DMA buffer must be located in the first sixteen megabytes of physical memory.

Contrast this with the DMA architecture used by EISA systems. The Intel 82357 EISA I/O controller extends ISA capabilities by supporting one-, two-, or four-byte transfers on any DMA channel, as well as allowing DMA buffers to be located anywhere in a 32-bit address space. In addition, EISA introduces three new DMA bus-cycle formats (known as types A, B, and C) that give peripheral designers the ability to work with faster devices.

Even on the same ISA or EISA bus, different devices can use different DMA techniques. Remember the discussion of DMA slaves and bus masters from Chapter 2. Slave devices compete for shareable system DMA hardware on the motherboard, while bus masters avoid bottlenecks by using their own built-in DMA controllers.

The problem with all this variety is that it tends to make DMA drivers very platform dependent. To avoid this trap, NT drivers don't manipulate DMA hardware directly. Instead, they work with an abstract representation of the hardware in the form of an NT Adapter object. Chapter 4 briefly introduced these objects and said they help with orderly sharing of system DMA resources. It turns out that Adapter objects also simplify the task of writing platform-independent drivers by hiding many of the details of setting up the DMA hardware. The rest of this section will explain more about what Adapter objects do and how to use them in a driver.

Solving the Scatter/Gather Problem with Mapping Registers

Although virtual memory simplifies the lives of application developers, it introduces two major complications for DMA-based drivers. The first problem is that the buffer address passed to the I/O Manager is a *virtual* address. Since the DMA controller works with *physical* addresses, DMA drivers need some way to determine the physical pages making up a virtual buffer. You'll see how this works when we look at Memory Descriptor Lists in the next section.

The other problem (illustrated in Figure 12.1) is that a process doesn't necessarily occupy consecutive pages of physical memory, and what appears to be a contiguous buffer in virtual space is probably scattered throughout physical memory. The NT Virtual Memory Manager uses the platform's address translation hardware (represented by a generic page table in the diagram) to give the process the illusion of a single, unbroken virtual address space. Unfortunately, the DMA controller doesn't participate in this illusion.

Since most DMA controllers can only generate sequential physical addresses, buffers that span virtual page boundaries present a serious challenge. Consider what happens if a DMA controller starts at the top of a multi-page buffer and simply increments its way through successive pages of physical memory. It's unlikely that any page after the first will actually correspond to one of the caller's virtual buffer pages. In fact, the pages touched by the DMA controller probably won't even belong to the process issuing the I/O request.

All virtual memory systems have to deal with the problem of scattering and gathering physical buffer pages during a DMA operation. Support for scatter/gather capabilities can come either from system DMA hardware or from hardware built into a smart bus master device. Once again, NT tries to simplify things by presenting drivers with a unified, abstract view of whatever scatter/gather hardware happens to exist on the system. This model consists of a contiguous range of addresses (called *logical space*) used by the DMA hardware and a

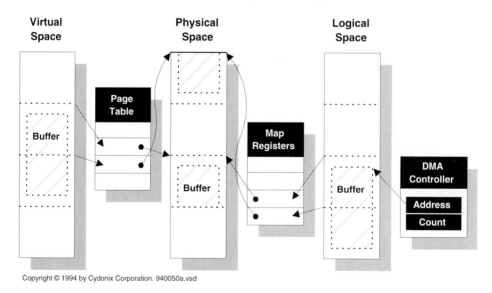

Copyright © 1994 by Cydonix Corporation. 940050a.vsd

Figure 12.1   Address spaces involved in DMA operations

set of *mapping registers* that translate logical space addresses into physical space addresses.

Here's how it works. Referring to Figure 12.1, each mapping register corresponds to one page of DMA logical space, and a group of consecutively numbered registers represents a contiguous range of logical addresses. To perform a DMA transfer, a driver first allocates enough contiguous mapping registers to account for all the pages in the caller's buffer. It then loads consecutive mapping registers with the physical addresses of the caller's buffer pages. This has the effect of mapping the physically noncontiguous user buffer into a contiguous area of logical space. Finally, the driver loads the DMA controller with the starting address of the buffer in *logical* space and starts the device. While the operation is in progress, the DMA controller generates sequential, logical addresses that the scatter/gather hardware maps to appropriate physical page references.

So much for the conceptual view of mapping registers. Like the DMA controller, the actual implementation depends on the platform, the bus, and the I/O device. To minimize the driver's awareness of these details, NT lumps the mapping registers into the Adapter object and provides a set of routines for managing them.

Managing I/O Buffers with Memory Descriptor Lists

As you've just seen, loading physical addresses into mapping registers is an important part of setting up a DMA transfer. To make this process easier, the I/O Manager uses a structure called a *Memory Descriptor List* (MDL). An MDL keeps track of the physical pages associated with a virtual buffer. The buffer described by an MDL can be in either user- or system-address space.

Direct I/O operations are one place where MDLs play a major role. If a Device object has the DO_DIRECT_IO bit set in its **Flags** field, the I/O Manager automatically builds an MDL describing the caller's buffer each time an I/O request is sent to the device. It stores the address of this MDL in the IRP's **MdlAddress** field, and the driver uses it to prepare the DMA hardware for a transfer.

As you can see from Figure 12.2, the MDL consists of a header describing the virtual buffer, followed by an array that lists the physical pages associated with the buffer. Given a virtual address within the buffer, it's possible to determine the corresponding physical page. Some of the fields in the header help clarify the use of an MDL.

StartVa and ByteOffset The **StartVa** field contains the address of the buffer described by the MDL, rounded down to the nearest virtual page boundary. Since the buffer doesn't necessarily start on a page boundary, the **ByteOffset** field specifies the distance from this page boundary to the actual beginning of the buffer. Keep in mind that if the buffer is in user space, your driver can use the **StartVa** field to calculate indexes into the MDL but *not* as an actual address pointer.

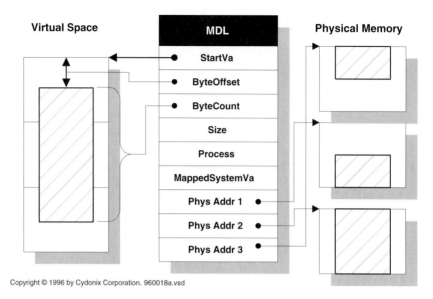

Copyright © 1996 by Cydonix Corporation. 960018a.vsd

Figure 12.2   Structure of a Memory Descriptor List (MDL)

MappedSystemVa   If the buffer described by the MDL is in user space and you need to access the contents of the buffer itself, you first have to map the buffer into system space with **MmGetSystemAddressForMdl**. This field of the MDL is used to hold the system-space address where the user-space buffer has been mapped.[1]

ByteCount and Size   These fields contain the number of bytes in the buffer described by the MDL and the size of the MDL itself, respectively.

Process   If the buffer lives in user space, the **Process** field points to the Process object that owns the buffer. The I/O Manager will use this information when it cleans up the I/O operation.

Keep in mind that MDLs are opaque data objects defined by the NT Virtual Memory Manager. Their actual contents may vary from platform to platform and they might also change in future versions of NT. Consequently, you must access an MDL using system support functions. Any other approach could lead to disaster. Table 12.1 lists the MDL functions you're most likely to encounter in a driver. See the DDK documentation for others. It's worth pointing out that some of the functions in this table are implemented as macros for speed.

---

[1] Using doubly-mapped buffers is generally a bad idea. Unmapping the buffer can cause a great deal of system overhead.

Table 12.1   Functions that work with Memory Descriptor Lists

MDL access functions

Function	Description
IoAllocateMdl	Allocates an empty MDL
IoFreeMdl	Releases MDL allocated by **IoAllocateMdl**
MmBuildMdlForNonPagedPool	Builds MDL for an existing nonpaged pool buffer
MmGetSystemAddressForMdl	Returns a nonpaged system space address for the buffer described by an MDL
IoBuildPartialMdl	Builds an MDL describing part of a buffer
MmGetMdlByteCount	Returns count of bytes in buffer described by MDL
MmGetMdlByteOffset	Returns page-offset of buffer described by MDL
MmGetMdlVirtualAddress	Returns starting VA of buffer described by MDL

MDLs give drivers a convenient, platform-independent way of describing buffers located either in user- or system-address space. For drivers that perform DMA operations, MDLs are important because they make it easier to set up an Adapter object's mapping registers. Later parts of this chapter will show you how to use MDLs to set up DMA transfers.

Maintaining Cache Coherency

The final thing we need to consider is the impact of various caches on DMA operations. During a DMA transfer, data may be getting cached in various places, and if everything isn't coordinated properly, someone might end up with stale data. Figure 12.3 shows who the players are in this drama.

CPU data cache   Modern CPUs support both on-chip and external caches for holding copies of recently-used data. When the CPU wants something from physical memory, it first looks for the data in the cache. If the CPU finds what it wants, it doesn't have to make the long, slow trip down the system memory bus. For write operations, data moves from the CPU to the cache, where (depending on the caching policy) it may stay for awhile before making its way out to main memory.

The problem is that, on some architectures (primarily RISC platforms), the CPU's cache controller and the DMA hardware are unaware of each other. This lack of awareness can lead to incoherent views of memory. For instance, if the CPU cache is holding part of a buffer and that buffer is overwritten in physical memory by a DMA input, the CPU cache will contain stale data. Similarly, if modified data hasn't been flushed from the CPU cache when a DMA output begins,

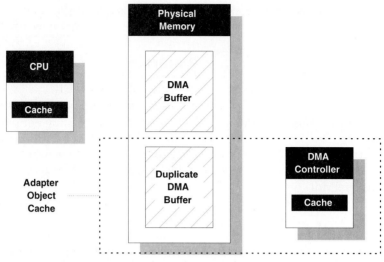

Figure 12.3   Caches involved in DMA processing

the DMA controller will be sending stale data from physical memory out to the
device.

One way of handling this problem is to make sure that any portions of a
DMA buffer residing in the CPU's data cache are flushed before a DMA operation
begins.[2] Your driver can do this by calling **KeFlushIoBuffers** and giving it the
MDL describing the DMA buffer. This function flushes any pages in the MDL
from the data cache of every processor on the system. The code example later in
this chapter shows how this works.

If you know something about hardware, you may be horrified by the overhead of flushing every CPU's data cache before every DMA transfer. It's important to emphasize that the cache coherency problem described above is only an
issue on some platforms. On machines that automatically maintain cache coherency, **KeFlushIoBuffers** is a no-op. You should always call it, however, just in case
your driver ends up on a platform that doesn't handle caching properly.

Adapter object cache   The Adapter object is another place where data
may be cached during a DMA transfer. Unlike the CPU cache, which is always a
real piece of hardware, the Adapter object's cache is an abstraction representing
platform-dependent hardware or software. It might be an actual cache in a system
DMA controller or a software buffer maintained by the I/O Manager. In fact, for
some combinations of hardware, there might not even be a cache, but your driver
has to act as if there were in order to guarantee portability.

---
[2] Another option is to use non-cached memory for your DMA buffers.

If this sounds strange, consider a DMA controller attached to an ISA bus. Such a controller can access only the first sixteen megabytes of physical memory. If the pages of a user buffer are outside this range, the I/O Manager allocates another buffer in low memory when your driver sets up its DMA mapping registers. If you're setting up an output operation, the I/O Manager also copies the contents of the user buffer pages into this Adapter object buffer.

You need to flush the Adapter object cache of this ISA DMA controller in two cases. First, after an input operation, your driver must tell the I/O Manager to copy data from the Adapter buffer back to the user buffer. Second, when you complete any data transfer, you have to let the I/O Manager know that it can release the memory in the Adapter buffer. The function that does the work is **IoFlushAdapterBuffers**.

Categorizing DMA Drivers

The NT DMA model divides drivers into two categories, based on the location of the DMA buffer itself. In *packet-based DMA*, data moves directly between the device and the locked-down pages of a user-space buffer. This is the type of DMA associated with Direct I/O operations. The main thing to notice here is that each new I/O request will probably use a different set of physical pages for its buffer. This has an impact on the kinds of setup and cleanup steps the driver will have to take for each I/O.

The other possibility is that the driver sets up a single nonpaged buffer in system space and uses it for all DMA transfers. This is referred to as *common buffer DMA*.

Packet-based and common-buffer DMA are not mutually exclusive categories. Some complex devices perform both kinds of DMA. One example is the Adaptec AHA-1742 controller, which uses packet-based DMA to transfer data between SCSI devices and user buffers. This same controller exchanges command and status information with its driver using a set of mailboxes kept in a common-buffer area.

Although DMA drivers are all rather similar, certain implementation details will depend on whether you're performing packet-based or common-buffer DMA. Later sections of this chapter will present the specifics of writing each kind of driver.

Limitations of the NT DMA Architecture

Although NT's use of an abstract DMA model makes some things easier, it does have its drawbacks. For one thing, it tends to favor the notion of shared-system DMA controllers. Much of the setup that goes on in an NT DMA driver is based on the idea of passing a shared DMA channel from driver to driver. In an age of dumb peripherals, this made sense, but as more bus-mastering devices have appeared, the slave DMA model has become a little out of date.

A more significant problem is that NT doesn't allow you to perform DMA operations directly from device to device. Instead, you have to read data from one device, buffer it in system memory, and from there write it out to another device.[3] This puts severe limitations on the available bandwidth and wastes one of the main architectural features of modern buses like PCI. Sadly, Microsoft appears to be adamantly opposed to direct device-to-device data transfers.

12.2 WORKING WITH ADAPTER OBJECTS

Although the specific details will vary according to the nature of the device and the architecture of the driver, DMA drivers generally have to perform several kinds of operations on Adapter objects.

- Locate the Adapter object associated with a specific device.
- Acquire and release ownership of Adapter objects and their mapping registers.
- Load the Adapter object's mapping registers at the start of a transfer.
- Flush the Adapter object's cache after a transfer completes.

The following subsections discuss these topics in general terms. Later sections of this chapter will add more detail.

Finding the Right Adapter Object

All DMA drivers need to locate an Adapter object before they can perform any I/O operations. To find the right one, a driver's initialization code needs to call the **HalGetAdapter** function described in Table 12.2.

Given a description of some DMA hardware, **HalGetAdapter** returns a pointer to the corresponding Adapter object and a count of the maximum number of map-

Table 12.2 Function prototype for HalGetAdapter

PADAPTER_OBJECT HalGetAdapter	IRQL == PASSIVE_LEVEL
Parameter	**Description**
IN PDEVICE_DESCRIPTION DeviceDescription	Points to a structure describing device capabilities
IN OUT PULONG NumberOfMapRegisters	• IN — requested number of registers • OUT — maximum allowable number
Return value	• Non-NULL — address of Adapter object • NULL — no such Adapter object available

---

[3] Part of the problem here is that you can only build MDLs for physical memory that's known to the system at bootstrap time. There's simply no way to create an MDL describing memory that's actually located on a peripheral or that's just a range of address space on some bus.

ping registers available for a single transfer. The driver needs to save both these items in nonpaged storage (usually the Device or Controller Extension) for later use.

The main input to **HalGetAdapter** is the DEVICE_DESCRIPTION block pictured in Table 12.3. It's important to set up this structure correctly, since most

Table 12.3   The DEVICE_DESCRIPTION structure describes a piece of DMA hardware

DEVICE_DESCRIPTION, *PDEVICE_DESCRIPTION

Field	Contents
ULONG Version	• DEVICE_DESCRIPTION_VERSION • DEVICE_DESCRIPTION_VERSION1
BOOLEAN Master	• TRUE — device is a bus master • FALSE — devices uses system DMA
BOOLEAN ScatterGather	Slave device supports scatter/gather
BOOLEAN DemandMode	Slave device uses demand-mode
BOOLEAN AutoInitialize	Slave device uses autoinitialize mode
BOOLEAN Dma32BitAddresses	DMA logical space uses 32-bit addressing
BOOLEAN IgnoreCount	Platform's DMA controller doesn't maintain an accurate DMA count*
BOOLEAN Reserved1	—*
BOOLEAN Reserved2	—*
ULONG BusNumber	System-assigned bus number
ULONG DmaChannel	Slave device DMA channel number
INTERFACE_TYPE InterfaceType	Bus architecture • Internal • Isa • Eisa • MicroChannel • PCIBus
DMA_WIDTH DmaWidth	Width of a single transfer operation • Width8Bits • Width16Bits • Width32Bits
DMA_SPEED DmaSpeed	DMA bus-cycle speed • Compatible • TypeA • TypeB • TypeC
ULONG MaximumLength	Largest transfer size (in bytes) device can perform
ULONG DmaPort	Micro Channel DMA port number

*Requires the use of DEVICE_DESCRIPTION_VERSION1

of the failures of **HalGetAdapter** are due to bogus device descriptions. Also be sure to clear the structure with **RtlZeroMemory** before you fill it in.

Most of these fields are self-explanatory, but the following ones may need a little clarification.

ScatterGather   For bus master devices, this says that the hardware has some sort of built-in support for transferring data to and from noncontiguous ranges of physical memory. A later section of this chapter will explain how to write drivers that can take advantage of these capabilities.

For slave devices, setting this field to TRUE implies that the device can stop and wait in the middle of a transfer while the I/O Manager reprograms the DMA controller. Since the system DMA controllers on some platforms have only one mapping register per channel, setting **ScatterGather** to TRUE would mean stopping after each page of memory is transferred.

Demand transfer mode   Some devices need to stop and "catch their breath" during a DMA transfer. This gives them the chance to finish working with one chunk of data before the next comes through. If your device behaves this way, the DMA controller has to be programmed to work in demand mode. Otherwise, the system DMA controller won't stop, no matter how much the device screams.

Autoinitialization   System DMA channels can be programmed to reinitialize themselves when a transfer completes. In this mode, the DMA controller's count and address registers are automatically reloaded from a pair of base count and address registers at the end of each operation. This causes another transfer to begin immediately. Typically, drivers using this mode of operation will also use a common buffer for the data transfer.

IgnoreCount   Setting this field to TRUE says that the platform's DMA hardware doesn't maintain an accurate running count of the number of bytes transferred. This forces the HAL to do some extra work during DMA operations, which slows things down.

Acquiring and Releasing the Adapter Object

There's no guarantee that the DMA resources needed for a transfer will be free when a driver's Start I/O routine runs. For example, a slave-device's DMA channel may already be in use by another device, or there may not be enough mapping registers to handle the request. Consequently, all packet-based DMA drivers and drivers for common-buffer slave devices have to request ownership of the Adapter object before starting a data transfer.

Since a Start I/O routine runs at DISPATCH_LEVEL IRQL, there's no way it can stop and wait for the Adapter object. Instead, it calls the **IoAllocateAdapterChannel** function (see Table 12.4) and then returns control to the I/O Manager.

Table 12.4 Prototype for IoAllocateAdapterChannel

NTSTATUS IoAllocateAdapterChannel	IRQL == DISPATCH_LEVEL
Parameter	**Description**
IN PADAPTER_OBJECT AdapterObject	Adapter object from **HalGetAdapter**
IN PDEVICE_OBJECT DeviceObject	Target device for DMA operation
IN ULONG NumberOfMapRegisters	Count of map registers to allocate
IN PDRIVER_CONTROL ExecutionRoutine	Address of **XxAdapterControl**
IN PVOID Context	Argument for **XxAdapterControl**
Return value	• STATUS_SUCCESS
	• STATUS_INSUFFICIENT_ RESOURCES

When the requested DMA resources become available, the I/O Manager notifies the driver by calling its Adapter Control routine. It's important to keep in mind that this is an asynchronous callback. It may happen as soon as Start I/O calls **IoAllocateAdapterChannel** or it may not occur until some other driver releases the Adapter resources.

Notice that you have to be at DISPATCH_LEVEL IRQL when you call this function. Since you normally call it from the Start I/O routine, this poses no problem. However, if you're using it in some weird way and you happen to be at PASSIVE_LEVEL, make sure you use **KeRaiseIrql** and **KeLowerIrql** before and after your call to **IoAllocateAdapterChannel**.

The Adapter Control routine in a DMA driver is responsible for calling **IoMapTransfer** to set up the DMA hardware and starting the actual device operation. Table 12.5 contains a prototype of the Adapter Control callback.

The MapRegisterBase argument is an opaque value that identifies the mapping registers assigned to your I/O request. In a sense, it's a kind of handle to a specific group of registers. You use this handle to set up the DMA hardware for

Table 12.5 Function prototype for an Adapter Control routine

IO_ALLOCATION_ACTION XxAdapterControl	IRQL == DISPATCH_LEVEL
Parameter	**Description**
IN PDEVICE_OBJECT DeviceObject	Target device for DMA operation
IN PIRP Irp	IRP describing this operation
IN PVOID MapRegisterBase	Handle to a group of mapping registers
IN PVOID Context	Driver-determined context
Return value	• DeallocateObjectKeepRegisters
	• KeepObject

the transfer. Normally, you should save this value in the Device or Controller extension because you'll need it in later parts of the DMA operation.

Watch out for the Irp argument. The IRP address sent to your Adapter Control routine comes from the **CurrentIrp** field of the Device object. Since the **CurrentIrp** field only gets set when the Start I/O routine is called, you can only use this passed IRP pointer if **IoAllocateAdapterChannel** is called from the Start I/O routine. If you're calling it from some other context, this pointer will be NULL. In that case, you'll have to find another way to pass the IRP (and its associated MDL address) to the Adapter Control routine.

After it programs the DMA controller and starts the data transfer, the Adapter Control routine gives control back to the I/O Manager. Drivers of slave devices should return a value of KeepObject from this function so that no one else will be able to use the Adapter object until this request is finished. Bus master drivers return DeallocateObjectKeepRegisters instead.

When the DpcForIsr routine in a DMA driver completes an I/O request, it needs to release any Adapter resources it owns. Drivers of slave devices do this by calling **IoFreeAdapterChannel**; bus master drivers call **IoFreeMapRegisters**.

Setting Up the DMA Hardware

All packet-based drivers, as well as common-buffer drivers for slave devices, have to program the DMA hardware at the beginning of each data transfer. In terms of the abstract DMA model used by NT, this means loading the Adapter object's mapping registers with physical-page addresses taken from the MDL. This set up work is done by the **IoMapTransfer** function described in Table 12.6.

Table 12.6   Prototype for IoMapTransfer

PHYSICAL_ADDRESS IoMapTransfer	IRQL £ DISPATCH_LEVEL
Parameter	**Description**
IN PADAPTER_OBJECT AdapterObject	Allocated Adapter object
IN PMDL Mdl	Memory Descriptor List for DMA buffer
IN PVOID MapRegisterBase	Handle to a group of mapping registers
IN PVOID CurrentVa	Virtual address of buffer within the MDL
IN OUT PULONG Length	• IN — count of bytes to be mapped
	• OUT — actual count of bytes mapped
IN BOOLEAN WriteToDevice	• TRUE — send data to device
	• FALSE — read data from device
Return value	DMA logical address of the mapped region

IoMapTransfer uses the CurrentVa and Length arguments to figure out what physical page addresses to put into the mapping registers. These values must fall somewhere within the range of addresses described by the MDL.

Keep in mind that **IoMapTransfer** may actually move the contents of a DMA output buffer from one place to another in memory. For example, on an ISA machine, if the pages in the MDL are outside the 16-megabyte DMA limit, calling this function results in data being copied to a buffer in low physical memory. Similarly, if a DMA input buffer is out of range, **IoMapTransfer** will allocate a buffer in low memory for the transfer. On buses that support 32-bit DMA addresses, no copying or duplicate buffers are required.

Drivers of bus master devices also need to call **IoMapTransfer**. In this case, however, the function behaves a little differently, since it doesn't know how to program the bus master's control registers. Instead, **IoMapTransfer** simply returns address and length values that your driver then loads into the device's registers. For bus masters with built-in scatter/gather support, this same mechanism allows your driver to create a scatter/gather list for the device. Later sections of this chapter will explain how all this works.

Flushing the Adapter Object Cache

At the end of a data transfer, all packet-based DMA drivers and drivers for common-buffer slave devices have to call **IoFlushAdapterBuffers** (see Table 12.7). For devices using the system DMA controller, this function flushes any hardware caches associated with the Adapater object.

In the case of ISA devices doing packet-based DMA, this call releases any low memory used for auxiliary buffers. For input operations, it also copies data back to the physical pages of the caller's input buffer. Refer back to the section on cache coherency for a discussion of this process.

Table 12.7 Prototype for IoFlushAdapterBuffers

BOOLEAN IoFlushAdapterBuffers	IRQL £ DISPATCH_LEVEL
Parameter	**Description**
IN PADAPTER_OBJECT AdapterObject	Adapter object used for this I/O
IN PMDL Mdl	MDL describing the buffer
IN PVOID MapRegisterBase	Handle passed to **XxAdapterControl**
IN PVOID CurrentVa	Starting VA where I/O operation took place
IN ULONG Length	Length of buffer
IN BOOLEAN WriteToDevice	• TRUE — operation was an output
	• FALSE — operation was an input
Return value	• TRUE — Adapter buffers flushed
	• FALSE — an error occurred

12.3 WRITING A PACKET-BASED SLAVE DMA DRIVER

In packet-based slave DMA, the device transfers data to or from the locked-down pages of the caller's buffer using a shared DMA controller on the motherboard. The system is also responsible for providing scatter/gather support.

How Packet-Based Slave DMA Works

Although the specifics will depend on the nature of your device, most packet-based slave DMA drivers conform to a very similar pattern. The following subsections describe what goes on in the routines making up one of these drivers.

DriverEntry routine   Along with its usual duties, the DriverEntry routine has some extra work to do:

1. It finds the DMA channel used by the device. This can come either from auto-detected hardware information in the Registry or it can be hard-coded in the **Parameters** subkey of the driver's service key.

2. **DriverEntry** uses its hardware information to build a DEVICE_DESCRIP-TION structure and calls **HalGetAdapter** to locate the Adapter object associated with the device.

3. It saves the address of the Adapter object and the count of mapping registers returned by **HalGetAdapter** for later use. Usually these are stored in the Device Extension.

4. It sets the DO_DIRECT_IO bit in the **Flags** field of any Device objects it creates. This causes the I/O Manager to lock user buffers in memory and create MDLs for them.

Start I/O routine   Unlike its counterpart in a programmed I/O driver, this Start I/O routine doesn't actually start the device. Instead, it just requests ownership of the Adapter object and leaves the rest of the work to the Adapter Control callback routine. Specifically, the Start I/O routine does the following:

1. It calls **KeFlushIoBuffers** to flush data from the CPU's cache out to physical memory.

2. Start I/O decides how many mapping registers to request. Initially, it calculates the number of registers needed to cover the entire user buffer. If this turns out to be more mapping registers than the Adapter object has, it will ask for as many as are available.

3. Based on the number of mapping registers and the size of the user buffer, Start I/O calculates the number of bytes to transfer in the first device opera-

tion. This may be the entire buffer or it may be only the first portion of a split transfer.

4. Next, it calls **MmGetMdlVirtualAddress** to recover the virtual address of the user buffer from the MDL. It stores this address in the Device Extension. Later parts of the driver will use this address as an offset into the MDL to set up the actual DMA transfer.

5. Start I/O then calls **IoAllocateAdapterChannel** to request ownership of the Adapter object. If this function succeeds, the rest of the setup work will be done by the AdapterControl routine, so Start I/O simply returns control to the I/O Manager.

6. If **IoAllocateAdapterChannel** returns an error, Start I/O puts an error code in the IRP's **IoStatus** block, calls **IoCompleteRequest**, and starts processing the next IRP.

Adapter Control routine The I/O Manager calls the Adapter Control routine whenever the necessary Adapter resources have become available. Its job is to initialize the DMA controller for the transfer and start the device itself. This routine does the following:

1. It stores the value of the MapRegisterBase argument in the Device Extension for later use.

2. The Adapter Control routine then calls **IoMapTransfer** to load the Adapter object's mapping registers. To make this call, it uses the buffer's virtual address and the transfer size calculated by the Start I/O routine.

3. Next, it sends appropriate commands to the device to begin the transfer operation.

4. Finally, the Adapter Control routine returns the value KeepObject to retain ownership of the Adapter object.

At this point, the transfer is actually in progress, and the system can go off and do other things until an interrupt arrives from the device.

Interrupt Service routine Compared to a programmed I/O driver, the ISR in a packet-based DMA driver is not very complicated. Unless hardware limitations force the driver to split a large transfer request across several device operations, there will be only a single interrupt to service when the whole transfer completes. When this interrupt arrives, the ISR does the following:

1. It issues whatever commands are necessary to acknowledge the device and prevent it from generating any more interrupts.

2. The ISR then stores device status (and any relevant error information) in the Device Extension.

3. It calls **IoRequestDpc** to continue processing the request in the driver's Dpc-
    ForIsr routine.

4. The ISR returns a value of TRUE to indicate that it serviced the interrupt.

DpcForIsr routine   The DpcForIsr routine is triggered by the ISR at the
end of each partial data transfer operation. Its job is to start the next partial transfer (if there is one) or to complete the current request. Specifically, the DpcForIsr
routine in a packet-based DMA driver does the following:

1. It calls **IoFlushAdapterBuffers** to force any remaining data from the Adapter
    object's cache.

2. The DpcForIsr routine checks the Device Extension to see if there were any
    errors during the operation. If there were, it completes the request with an
    appropriate status code and length, and starts the next request.

3. Otherwise, it decrements the count of bytes remaining by the size of the last
    transfer. If the whole buffer has been processed, it completes the current
    request and starts the next.

4. If more data remains, the DpcForIsr routine increments the user-buffer
    address pointer (stored in the Device Extension) by the size of the last opera-
    tion. It then calculates the number of bytes to transfer in the next device oper-
    ation, calls **IoMapTransfer** to reset the mapping registers, and starts the
    device.

   If the DpcForIsr routine started another partial transfer, the I/O Manager
will return control to the driver again when the device generates an interrupt.

Splitting DMA Transfers

   When a packet-based DMA driver receives a buffer, it may not be able to
transfer all the data in a single device operation. It could be that the Adapter
object doesn't have enough mapping registers to handle the whole thing at once,
or there could be limitations on the device itself. In any event, the driver has to be
prepared to split the request across multiple data-transfer operations.

   There are two solutions to this problem. One is have the driver reject any
requests that it can't handle in a single I/O. With this approach, anyone using the
driver is responsible for breaking the request into chunks that are small enough to
process. Of course, the driver will have to provide some mechanism for letting its
clients know the maximum allowable buffer size (an IOCTL, for example). If you
decide to do things this way, you might want to write a higher-level driver that
sits on top of the DMA device driver and splits the requests. This has the advantage of shielding application programs from the details of splitting the request.

   Another approach is to write a single, monolithic driver that accepts
requests of any size and splits them into several I/O operations. This is the strategy used by the sample driver in the next section of this chapter.

To do things this way, you need to maintain a pointer that tracks your position in the user buffer as you transfer successive chunks of data. You also need to maintain a count of the number of bytes left to process, as well as calculating the amount of data to transfer in the current I/O operation. The following subsections explain how to initialize and update these data items during an I/O request.

First transfer   The Start I/O routine normally sets things up for the first transfer. Initially, it tries to grab enough mapping registers to do everything in one I/O. If the Adapter object doesn't have enough mapping registers for this to work, Start I/O asks for as many as it can get and sets up the current transfer accordingly. The following code fragment shows how it's done.

```
pDE->TransferVA =
        MmGetMdlVirtualAddress( Irp->MdlAddress );

pDE->BytesRemaining =
        MmGetMdlByteCount( Irp->MdlAddress );

pDE->TransferSize = pDE->BytesRemaining;

MapRegsNeeded = ADDRESS_AND_SIZE_TO_SPAN_PAGES(
                    pDE->TransferVA,
                    pDE->TransferSize );

if( MapRegsNeeded > pDE->MapRegsAvailable )
{
  MapRegsNeeded = pDE->MapRegsAvailable;
  pDE->TransferSize =
      MapRegsNeeded * PAGE_SIZE -
          MmGetMdlByteOffset( Irp->MdlAddress );
}
IoAllocateAdapterChannel(. . .);
```

Additional transfers   After each interrupt, the DpcForIsr checks to see if there's any data left to process. If there is, it calculates the number of mapping registers needed to transfer all the remaining bytes in a single I/O operation. If there aren't enough mapping registers available, it sets up another partial transfer. The following code fragment illustrates the procedure.

```
pDE->BytesRemaining -= pDE->TransferSize;

if( pDE->BytesRemaining > 0 )
{
  pDE->TransferVA += pDE->TransferSize;

  pDE->TransferSize = pDE->BytesRemaining;

  MapRegsNeeded = ADDRESS_AND_SIZE_TO_SPAN_PAGES(
                    pDE->TransferVA,
                    pDE->TransferSize );
```

```
      if( MapRegsNeeded > pDE->MapRegsAvailable )
      {
            MapRegsNeeded = pDE->MapRegsAvailable );

            pDE->TransferSize =
                  MapRegsNeeded * PAGE_SIZE -
                        BYTE_OFFSET( pDE->TransferVA );
      }
      IoMapTransfer(...);
}
```

12.4 CODE EXAMPLE: A PACKET-BASED SLAVE DMA DRIVER

This example is a skeleton of a packet-based driver for a generic slave DMA device. Although it doesn't actually manage a specific kind of hardware, it will help you to understand how these drivers work. You can find the complete code for this example in the **CH12\PACKT-S** directory on the disk that accompanies this book.

XXDRIVER.H

This excerpt from the driver-specific header file shows the changes that need to be made to support a DMA device.

DEVICE_EXTENSION   The modified Device Extension structure contains some extra items that are necessary for packet-based DMA.

```
      typedef struct _DEVICE_EXTENSION {
        PDEVICE_OBJECT DeviceObject;   // Back pointer

        ULONG NtDeviceNumber;          // Zero-based device num

        PUCHAR PortBase;               // First control register

        PKINTERRUPT pInterrupt;        // Interrupt object

        PADAPTER_OBJECT AdapterObject; ❶
        ULONG MapRegisterCount;

        PVOID MapRegisterBase; ❷

        ULONG BytesRequested; ❸
        ULONG BytesRemaining;
        ULONG TransferSize;
        PUCHAR TransferVA;

        BOOLEAN WriteToDevice; ❹
        UCHAR DeviceStatus;

      } DEVICE_EXTENSION, *PDEVICE_EXTENSION;
```

❶ These are returned by **HalGetAdapter**. They identify the specific Adapter object and its maximum transfer size.

❷ This identifies a particular group of mapping registers that have been assigned to our driver during the course of an I/O request.

❸ These bookkeeping fields keep track of our progress through a split transfer operation.

❹ These items hold the direction of the current data transfer and the status of the DMA device itself.

REGCON.C

This sample uses the version of **XxGetHardwareInfo** that extracts hard-coded information from the **Parameters** subkey of the driver's service key. You could just as easily use auto-detected information.

XxGetDmaInfo   This function uses information pulled from the Registry, supplemented with a few assumptions about the hardware, to find the device's Adapter object.

```
static NTSTATUS
XxGetDmaInfo(
  IN INTERFACE_TYPE BusType,
  IN ULONG BusNumber,
  IN PDEVICE_BLOCK pDevice
  )
{
  DEVICE_DESCRIPTION Descrip;

  RtlZeroMemory(
        &Descrip,
        sizeof( DEVICE_DESCRIPTION )); ❶

  Descrip.Version = DEVICE_DESCRIPTION_VERSION1;

  Descrip.Master            = FALSE; ❷
  Descrip.ScatterGather     = FALSE;
  Descrip.DemandMode        = FALSE;
  Descrip.AutoInitialize    = FALSE;
  Descrip.Dma32BitAddresses = FALSE;

  Descrip.InterfaceType     = BusType;
  Descrip.BusNumber         = BusNumber;

  Descrip.DmaChannel        = pDevice->DmaChannel;
  Descrip.MaximumLength     = XX_MAX_DMA_LENGTH;
  Descrip.DmaWidth          = Width16Bits;
  Descrip.DmaSpeed          = Compatible;
```

```
pDevice->MapRegisterCount =
     (XX_MAX_DMA_LENGTH / PAGE_SIZE) + 2; ❸

pDevice->AdapterObject =
          HalGetAdapter(
               &Descrip,
               &pDevice->MapRegisterCount ); ❹

if( pDevice->AdapterObject == NULL ) ❺
     return STATUS_INSUFFICIENT_RESOURCES;
else
     return STATUS_SUCCESS;
}
```

❶ It's important to make sure that there aren't any spurious bits set in the DEVICE_DESCRIPTION structure.

❷ From this point on, start to build a description of the DMA device. In this case, it's a slave device that performs 16-bit transfers and needs an ISA-compatible bus cycle speed.

❸ Calculate the number of mapping registers that correspond to the largest possible transfer the device can handle. In the worst case, a buffer could occupy some integral number of pages plus one byte before the first page and one byte after the last page. To account for this possibility, request two additional mapping registers.

❹ Try to find the Adapter object for the device. Later parts of the driver will need a pointer to the object and information about the maximum number of available mapping registers.

❺ If **HalGetAdapter** fails, it usually means that the DEVICE_DESCRIPTION had some inconsistencies.

TRANSFER.C

This portion of the example performs the actual data transfers. If an I/O request is too large for a single device operation, these routines split the request over several transfers.

XxStartIo   This function gets control at the beginning of each request. It calculates the size of the first data transfer and requests ownership of the Adapter object.

```
VOID
XxStartIo(
  IN PDEVICE_OBJECT DeviceObject,
  IN PIRP Irp
  )
```

```
{
  PIO_STACK_LOCATION IrpStack =
        IoGetCurrentIrpStackLocation( Irp );

  PDEVICE_EXTENSION pDE =
        DeviceObject->DeviceExtension;

  PMDL Mdl = Irp->MdlAddress;
  ULONG MapRegsNeeded;
  NTSTATUS status;

  switch( IrpStack->MajorFunction ) {

        case IRP_MJ_WRITE:
        case IRP_MJ_READ:
            pDE->BytesRequested =
                MmGetMdlByteCount( Mdl ); ❶

        pDE->BytesRemaining =
            pDE->BytesRequested;

        pDE->TransferVA =
            MmGetMdlVirtualAddress( Mdl );

        //
        // Set the direction flag
        //
        if( IrpStack->MajorFunction
            == IRP_MJ_WRITE )
        {
            pDE->WriteToDevice = TRUE;
        }
        else
        {
            pDE->WriteToDevice = FALSE;
        }

        pDE->TransferSize =
                pDE->BytesRemaining; ❷

        MapRegsNeeded =
            ADDRESS_AND_SIZE_TO_SPAN_PAGES(
                pDE->TransferVA,
                pDE->TransferSize );

        if( MapRegsNeeded >
            pDE->MapRegisterCount )
        {
            MapRegsNeeded =
                pDE->MapRegisterCount;
```

```
            pDE->TransferSize =
                 MapRegsNeeded * PAGE_SIZE -
                     MmGetMdlByteOffset( Mdl );
        }

        status = IoAllocateAdapterChannel( ❸
                     pDE->AdapterObject,
                         DeviceObject,
                         MapRegsNeeded,
                         XxAdapterControl,
                         pDE );

        if( !NT_SUCCESS( status )) ❹
        {
                Irp->IoStatus.Status = status;
                Irp->IoStatus.Information = 0;

                    IoCompleteRequest(
                        Irp,
                        IO_NO_INCREMENT );

                    IoStartNextPacket(
                        DeviceObject,
                        FALSE );
        }
        break;
    //
    // Should never get here -- just get rid
    // of the packet...
    //
    default:
        Irp->IoStatus.Status =
                    STATUS_NOT_SUPPORTED;
        Irp->IoStatus.Information = 0;
        IoCompleteRequest(
            Irp,
            IO_NO_INCREMENT );
        IoStartNextPacket( DeviceObject, FALSE );
        break;
    } // end switch
}
```

❶ Set up various bookkeeping values. The size and address of the user
buffer come from the MDL built by the I/O Manager. Keep in mind that
you can use the virtual address as an index into the user buffer but you
can't actually dereference it.

❷ This section calculates the size of the first partial transfer. First, the driver
tries to transfer everything in a single DMA. If there aren't enough map-

ping registers to handle the whole buffer, the driver asks for as many mapping registers as it can get. Based on this smaller number, it calculates a smaller size for the current transfer.

❸ Ask for the Adapter object using an asynchronous call. The Adapter Control routine will execute when the DMA channel is available. It will start the actual device operation.

❹ If the call to **IoAllocateAdapaterChannel** fails, it usually means there aren't enough mapping registers. In that case, the driver simply fails the IRP and starts the next request.

XxAdapterControl   This function programs the system DMA hardware and starts the device itself. The I/O Manager calls it when the Adapter object belongs to our device and there are enough mapping registers to handle the request.

```
static IO_ALLOCATION_ACTION
XxAdapterControl(
  IN PDEVICE_OBJECT DeviceObject,
  IN PIRP Irp,  ❶
  IN PVOID MapRegisterBase,
  IN PVOID Context
  )
{
  PDEVICE_EXTENSION pDE = Context;

  pDE->MapRegisterBase = MapRegisterBase;  ❷

  KeFlushIoBuffers(
        Irp->MdlAddress,
        !pDE->WriteToDevice,
        TRUE );  ❸

  IoMapTransfer(
        pDE->AdapterObject,
        Irp->MdlAddress,
        pDE->MapRegisterBase,
        pDE->TransferVA,
        &pDE->TransferSize,
        pDE->WriteToDevice );  ❹

  //
  // Start the device
  //
  XxWriteControl(
        pDE,
        XX_CTL_INTENB | XX_CTL_DMA_GO );

  return KeepObject;  ❺
}
```

❶ The I/O Manager gets this IRP pointer from the **CurrentIrp** field of the Device object. Normally, this field gets set when your driver uses **IoStart-Packet** or **IoStartNextPacket** to call a standard Start I/O routine. If your driver doesn't have a Start I/O routine, it's up to you to make sure that the **CurrentIrp** field gets set before you call **IoAllocateAdapterChannel**. Or, you'll have to have some other way of getting the IRP pointer (and it's associated MDL address) into the Adapter Control routine.

❷ Save the value of the MapRegisterBase argument for use by later parts of the driver.

❸ Flush any processor caches that might be holding parts of the DMA buffer. This is a no-op on CPUs that handle their own cache coherency. Notice the perverse way that the direction argument for this function is **TRUE** for a *read*. Other I/O Manager functions use **TRUE** for *write* requests.

❹ Set up the system DMA channel associated with the device.

❺ Return a value of **KeepObject** in order to retain ownership of the Adapter object until the whole buffer has been transferred.

XxIsr   This function processes interrupts from the device. Normally, there will be a single interrupt at the end of each partial transfer, or when an error occurs.

```
BOOLEAN
XxIsr(
  IN PKINTERRUPT Interrupt,
  IN PVOID ServiceContext
  )
{
  PDEVICE_EXTENSION pDE = ServiceContext;
  PDEVICE_OBJECT DeviceObject = pDE->DeviceObject;
  UCHAR Status = XxReadStatus( pDE );
  UCHAR Control;

  //
  // See if this device requested an interrupt
  //
  if(( Status & XX_STS_IRQ ) == 0 )
        return FALSE;

  Control = XxReadControl( pDE ); ❶

  Control &= ~( XX_CTL_INTENB |
            XX_CTL_DMA_GO );

  XxWriteControl( pDE, Control);
```

```
    pDE->DeviceStatus = Status;  ❷

    IoRequestDpc(
          DeviceObject,
          DeviceObject->CurrentIrp,
          (PVOID)pDE );  ❸

          return TRUE;
}
```

❶ When an interrupt arrives, issue some device-specific commands to acknowledge the interrupt and prevent any further ones from coming in.

❷ Save the status of the hardware so that the DpcForIsr routine can figure out whether the transfer was successful.

❸ There's not much more that can be done up at DIRQL. Issue a DPC request and let the rest of the work happen at DISPATCH_LEVEL IRQL.

XxDpcForIsr This function executes after the Interrupt Service routine runs. It either sets up the next partial transfer or it completes the current request and starts the next one.

```
VOID
XxDpcForIsr(
   IN PKDPC Dpc,
   IN PDEVICE_OBJECT DeviceObject,
   IN PIRP Irp,
   IN PVOID Context
   )
{
   PDEVICE_EXTENSION pDE = Context;
   ULONG MapRegsNeeded;
   PMDL Mdl = Irp->MdlAddress;

   IoFlushAdapterBuffers(
          pDE->AdapterObject,
          Mdl,
          pDE->MapRegisterBase,
          pDE->TransferVA,
          pDE->TransferSize,
          pDE->WriteToDevice );  ❶

   if( !XX_STS_OK( pDE->DeviceStatus ))  ❷
   {
   IoFreeAdapterChannel( pDE->AdapterObject );

          Irp->IoStatus.Status =
                    STATUS_DEVICE_DATA_ERROR;
```

```
        Irp->IoStatus.Information =
                    pDE->BytesRequested -
                          pDE->BytesRemaining;
        //
        // Complete this request and
        // start the next
        //
        IoCompleteRequest( Irp, IO_NO_INCREMENT );
        IoStartNextPacket( DeviceObject, FALSE );
        return;
}

pDE->BytesRemaining -= pDE->TransferSize;

if( pDE->BytesRemaining > 0 ) ❸
{
        //
        // Update the pointer and try to
        // do all of it in one operation
        //
        pDE->TransferVA += pDE->TransferSize;
        pDE->TransferSize = pDE->BytesRemaining;

        MapRegsNeeded =
              ADDRESS_AND_SIZE_TO_SPAN_PAGES(
                          pDE->TransferVA,
                          pDE->TransferSize );
        //
        // If the remainder of the buffer is more
        // than we can handle in one I/O. Reduce
        // our expectations.
        //
        if( MapRegsNeeded > pDE->MapRegisterCount )
        {
              MapRegsNeeded = pDE->MapRegisterCount;

              pDE->TransferSize =
                    MapRegsNeeded * PAGE_SIZE -
                        BYTE_OFFSET( pDE->TransferVA );
        }

        IoMapTransfer(
              pDE->AdapterObject,
              Mdl,
              pDE->MapRegisterBase,
              pDE->TransferVA,
              &pDE->TransferSize,
              pDE->WriteToDevice ); ❹
```

```
                XxWriteControl(
                        pDE,
                        XX_CTL_INTENB | XX_CTL_DMA_GO );
        }
        else  ❺
        {
                IoFreeAdapterChannel( pDE->AdapterObject );

                Irp->IoStatus.Status = STATUS_SUCCESS;
                Irp->IoStatus.Information =
                                pDE->BytesRequested;

        IoCompleteRequest( Irp, IO_DISK_INCREMENT );  ❻
                IoStartNextPacket( DeviceObject, FALSE );
        }
}
```

❶ Flush any data out of the Adapter object's cache. On platforms with DMA address limitations (ISA buses, for example), this may result in data being copied from place to place in memory.

❷ Check for device errors. This driver simply fails the IRP if an error occurred. A real driver might retry the operation some number of times before failing it.

❸ At this point, the driver can assume the previous operation was a success. It checks to see if there are any bytes left in the buffer, and if there are, it sets up the next partial transfer. The logic here is similar to what goes on in the Start I/O routine: Try to transfer all the remaining bytes, or as much as the Adapter object can handle, whichever is less.

❹ Set up the system DMA controller for the next partial transfer, then start the device.

❺ This **else** clause executes when the entire user buffer has been transferred. It simply completes the IRP and starts the next one.

❻ Pick a priority-boost value that's appropriate for your device. Slower devices can probably get by with **IO_DISK_INCREMENT**, while faster hardware may need a heftier boost.

12.5 WRITING A PACKET-BASED BUS MASTER DMA DRIVER

In packet-based bus master DMA, the device transfers data to or from the locked-down pages of the caller's buffer using DMA hardware that's part of the device itself. Depending on the capabilities of the device, it might be providing its own scatter/gather support as well.

The architecture of a packet-based bus master driver is almost identical to that of a driver for a slave device. The only difference is the way the driver sets up the bus master hardware. The following subsections describe these differences.

Setting Up Bus Master Hardware

A bus master device complicates things because the system doesn't know how to program the device's onboard DMA controller. The most the I/O Manager can do is to give the driver two things: An address in DMA logical space where a contiguous segment of the buffer begins and a count indicating the number of bytes in that segment. It then becomes the driver's responsibility to load this information into the address and length registers of the device and start the transfer.

The function that performs this little miracle is none other than our old friend, **IoMapTransfer**. When you pass NULL for its AdapterObject pointer, its return value will be the address in DMA logical space that corresponds to the CurrentVa and Mdl arguments. You put this logical address into the device's address register.

Furthermore, when AdapterObject is NULL, Length becomes both an input and output argument. On input, you ask it to map all the bytes remaining between CurrentVa and the end of the buffer. On output, Length contains the number of contiguous bytes starting at the logical address returned by **IoMapTransfer**. This number goes into your device's count register. Figure 12.4 shows how this works.

Supporting bus master devices requires some changes to the driver's Adapter Control and DpcForIsr routines. The following subsections contain frag-

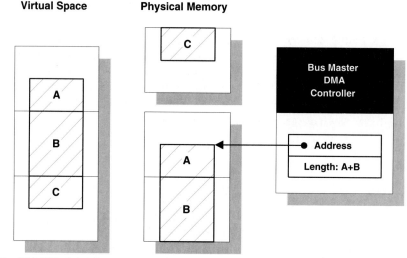

Figure 12.4   For bus masters, IoMapTransfer scans for contiguous buffer segments

ments of these routines. Compare them with the corresponding routines in the
packet-based slave DMA driver in the previous section of this chapter.

Adapter Control routine Being optimistic, the Adapter Control routine
asks **IoMapTransfer** to map the entire buffer at the start of the first transfer.
Instead, it tells the driver how much contiguous memory is actually available in
the first segment of the buffer.

```
PHYSICAL_ADDRESS DmaAddress;

pDE->TransferVA =
        MmGetMdlVirtualAddress( Irp->MdlAddress );

pDE->BytesRemaining =
        MmGetMdlByteCount( Irp->MdlAddress );

pDE->TransferSize = pDE->BytesRemaining;

DmaAddress = IoMapTransfer(
                NULL,
                Irp->MdlAddress,
                pDE->MapRegisterBase,
                pDE->TransferVA,
                &pDE->TransferSize,
                pDE->WriteRequest );

XxWriteAddress( pDE, (PUCHAR)DmaAddress.LowPart );
XxWriteCount( pDE, pDE->TransferSize );
XxWriteControl( XX_CTL_DMA_GO );

return DeallocateObjectKeepRegisters;
```

DpcForIsr routine After each partial transfer, the DpcForIsr routine increments the CurrentVa pointer by the previously returned Length value. It then
calls **IoMapTransfer** with this updated pointer and asks to map all the bytes
remaining in the buffer. **IoMapTransfer** returns another logical address and a new
Length value indicating the size of the next contiguous buffer segment. This continues until the whole buffer has been processed.

```
PHYSICAL_ADDRESS DmaAddress;

IoFlushAdapterBuffers(
                NULL,
                Irp->MdlAddress,
                pDE->MapRegisterBase,
                pDE->TransferVA,
                pDE->TransferSize,
                pDE->WriteRequest );

pDE->BytesRemaining -= pDE->TransferSize;
```

```
if( pDE->BytesRemaining > 0 )
{
  pDE->TransferVA += pDE->TransferSize;

  pDE->TransferSize = pDE->BytesRemaining;

  DmaAddress = IoMapTransfer(
                  NULL,
                  Irp->MdlAddress,
                  pDE->MapRegisterBase,
                  pDE->TransferVA,
                  &pDE->TransferSize,
                  pDE->WriteRequest );

  XxWriteAddress( pDE, (PUCHAR)DmaAddress.LowPart );
  XxWriteCount( pDE, pDE->TransferSize );
  XxWriteControl( XX_CTL_DMA_GO );
}
```

Hardware with Scatter/Gather Support

Some bus master devices contain multiple pairs of address and length registers, each one describing a single contiguous buffer segment. This allows the device to perform I/O using buffers that are scattered throughout DMA address space. These multiple address and count registers are often referred to as a *scatter/gather list*, but you can also think of these bus masters as having their own built-in mapping registers. Figure 12.5 shows how this works.

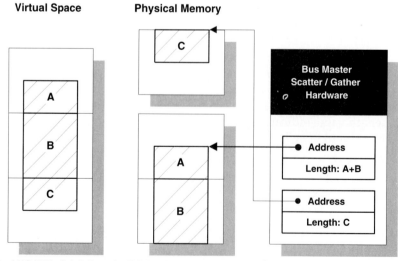

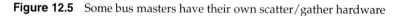

Figure 12.5   Some bus masters have their own scatter/gather hardware

Before each transfer, the driver loads as many pairs of address and count registers as there are segments in the buffer. When the device is started, it walks through the scatter/gather list entries in sequence, filling or emptying each segment of the buffer and then moving on to the next. When all the list entries have been processed, the device generates an interrupt.

Building Scatter/Gather Lists with IoMapTransfer

Once again, IoMapTransfer will be used to find contiguous segments of the DMA buffer. In this case, however, the driver will call it several times before each data transfer operation — once for each entry in the hardware scatter/gather list. These fragments of an Adapter Control and a DpcForIsr routine show how it's done.

Adapter Control routine   Before the first transfer operation, the Adapter Control routine loads the hardware scatter/gather list and starts the device. The remainder of the buffer will be handled by the ISR and DpcForIsr routines.

```
PHYSICAL_ADDRESS DmaAddress;
ULONG BytesLeftInBuffer;
ULONG SegmentSize;
PUCHAR SegmentVA;

pDE->TransferVA =
        MmGetMdlVirtualAddress( Irp->MdlAddress );

pDE->BytesRemaining =
        MmGetMdlByteCount( Irp->MdlAddress );

pDE->TransferSize = 0;

BytesLeftInBuffer = pDE->BytesRemaining;
SegmentVA = pDE->TransferVA;

XxClearSgList( pDE );

while( pDE->AvailableSgEntries > 0 &&
        BytesLeftInBuffer > 0 )
{
   SegmentSize = BytesLeftInBuffer;
   DmaAddress = IoMapTransfer(
                   NULL,
                   Irp->MdlAddress,
                   pDE->MapRegisterBase,
                   pDE->TransferVA,
                   &SegmentSize,
                   pDE->WriteRequest );
```

```
XxAddToSgList(
        pDE,
        DmaAddress.LowPart,
        SegmentSize );

  pDE->TransferSize += SegmentSize;
  SegmentVA += SegmentSize;
  BytesLeftInBuffer -= SegmentSize;
  AvailableSgEntries--;
}

XxWriteControl( XX_CTL_DMA_GO );

return DeallocateObjectKeepRegisters;
```

DpcForIsr routine   After each transfer is finished, the ISR issues a DPC request. The DpcForIsr routine flushes the previous request, and if there are more bytes left to transfer, it rebuilds the scatter/gather list.

```
PHYSICAL_ADDRESS DmaAddress;
ULONG BytesLeftInBuffer;
ULONG SegmentSize;
PUCHAR SegmentVA;

IoFlushAdapterBuffers(
                NULL,
                Irp->MdlAddress,
                pDE->MapRegisterBase,
                pDE->TransferVA,
                pDE->TransferSize,
                pDE->WriteRequest );

pDE->BytesRemaining -= pDE->TransferSize;

if( pDE->BytesRemaining > 0 )
{
  pDE->TransferVA += pDE->TransferSize;

  pDE->TransferSize = 0;

  BytesLeftInBuffer = pDE->BytesRemaining;
  SegmentVA = pDE->TransferVA;

  XxClearSgList( pDE );

  while( pDE->AvailableSgEntries > 0 &&
         BytesLeftInBuffer > 0 )
  {
        SegmentSize = BytesLeftInBuffer;
        DmaAddress = IoMapTransfer(
```

```
                                  NULL,
                                  Irp->MdlAddress,
                                  pDE->MapRegisterBase,
                                  pDE->TransferVA,
                                  &SegmentSize,
                                  pDE->WriteRequest );

                 XxAddToSgList(
                         pDE,
                         DmaAddress.LowPart,
                         SegmentSize );

                 pDE->TransferSize += SegmentSize;
                 SegmentVA += SegmentSize;
                 BytesLeftInBuffer -= SegmentSize;
                 AvailableSgEntries--;

         } // end while

         XxWriteControl( XX_CTL_DMA_GO );
     }
     else
     {
         IoFreeMapRegisters( . . . );
         IoCompleteRequest( . . . );
         IoStartNextPacket( . . . );
     }
```

12.6 WRITING A COMMON BUFFER SLAVE DMA DRIVER

In common buffer slave DMA, the device transfers data to or from a contiguous buffer in nonpaged pool using a system DMA channel. Although originally intended for devices that use the system DMA controller's autoinitialize mode, common buffers can also improve throughput for some types of ISA-based slave devices.

Allocating a Common Buffer

Memory for a common buffer has to be physically contiguous and visible in the DMA logical space of a specific device. To guarantee that both these conditions are met, you use the **HalAllocateCommonBuffer** function described in Table 12.8 to allocate memory for the buffer.

Notice the CacheEnabled argument to this function. It's usually a good idea to request non-cached memory for the common buffer since it eliminates the need to call **KeFlushIoBuffers**. On some platforms, this can improve the performance of both your driver and the system.

Table 12.8   Prototype for HalAllocateCommonBuffer

PVOID HalAllocateCommonBuffer	IRQL == PASSIVE_LEVEL
Parameter	**Description**
IN PADAPTER_OBJECT Adapter object	AdapterObject associated with DMA device
IN ULONG Length	Requested size of buffer in bytes
OUT PPHYSICAL_ADDRESS LogicalAddress	Address of the common buffer in the DMA controller's logical space
IN BOOLEAN CacheEnabled	• TRUE — memory is cacheable by the CPU
	• FALSE — memory is not cached
Return value	• Non-NULL — system VA of common buffer
	• NULL — error

In the case of common buffer *slave* DMA, you'll need to build an MDL for the buffer.[4] This MDL is a required argument for **IoMapTransfer** and **IoFlush-AdapterBuffers**. To set up the MDL, call **IoAllocateMdl** followed by **MmBuildMdlForNonPagedPool**. When your driver unloads, call IoFreeMdl to release the memory used for the MDL.

Using Common Buffer Slave DMA to Maintain Throughput

Common buffer slave DMA is useful if a driver can't afford to have **IoMapTransfer** copy a DMA buffer from one place to another during a data transfer. On ISA buses, this kind of copying is always a possibility with packet-based DMA. Since common buffers are guaranteed to be accessible by their associated DMA devices, there's never any danger of **IoMapTransfer** moving data from one place to another.

For example, drivers of some ISA-based tape drives need to maintain very high throughput if they want to keep the tape streaming. They won't be able to do this if a buffer copy happens during a call to **IoMapTransfer**. To prevent this, the driver uses a ring of common buffers for the actual DMA operation. Other, less time-critical portions of the driver move data between these common buffers and the actual user buffers.

To see how this might work, lets consider the operation of a driver for a hypothetical ISA output device. To maintain a high DMA data rate, it uses a series of common buffers that are shared between the driver's Dispatch and DpcForIsr routines. The Dispatch routine copies user-output data into an available common buffer and attaches the buffer to a queue of pending DMA requests. Once a DMA

---

[4] The MDL is unnecessary if you plan to use the common buffer for *bus master* DMA.

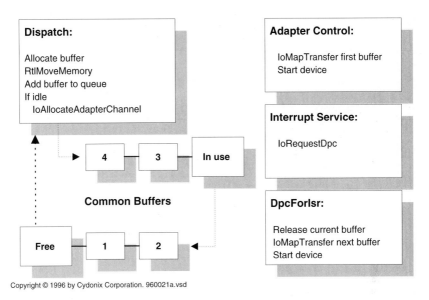

Figure 12.6 Using common buffers allows some ISA drivers to maintain higher throughput

is in progress, the DpcForIsr removes buffers from the queue and processes them as fast as it can. Figure 12.6 shows the organization of this driver, and the subsections below describe various driver routines.

DriverEntry routine As always the DriverEntry routine has to find and allocate the driver's hardware. Along with its usual responsibilities, DriverEntry also does the following:

1. When it creates its Device object, it sets the DO_BUFFERED_IO bit in the **Flags** field. Although the underlying common buffers will be processed using DMA, the user data will initially be copied into system-space buffers.

2. **DriverEntry** initializes two queues in the Device Extension. One holds a list of free common buffers. The other is for work requests in progress.

3. Next, it creates separate spin locks to guard each queue. The spin lock for the work list also protects a flag in the Device Extension called **DmaInProgress**.

4. Then, **DriverEntry** calls **HalGetAdapter** to find the Adapter object associated with its device. It uses the count of mapping registers returned by this function to determine the size of its common buffers.

5. It allocates some number of common buffers and adds them to the free list in the Device Extension. (As an implementation detail, some of the space in each common buffer is used for a linked-list pointer, a pointer to the IRP associated with this request, and a pointer to the MDL for the common buffer.) For each

buffer, it also calls **IoAllocateMdl** and **MmBuildMdlForNonPagedPool** to create an MDL.

6.   Finally, **DriverEntry** initializes a Semaphore object and sets its initial count to the number of common buffers it has just created.

Dispatch routine   The Dispatch routine of this driver works differently than the ones you've seen so far. Since the driver has no Start I/O routine, the Dispatch routine is actually responsible for queuing or starting each request. This is what the Dispatch routine does to process an output request:

1.   It calls **KeWaitForSingleObject** to wait for the Semaphore object associated with the driver's list of free buffers. The thread issuing the call will freeze until there's at least one buffer in the queue.[5]

2.   The Dispatch routine removes an available common buffer from the free list and (since we're only considering outputs here) uses **RtlMoveMemory** to fill it with data from the user's buffer.

3.   It prevents the I/O Manager from completing the request by calling **IoMarkIrpPending**.

4.   Next, it acquires the spin lock associated with the queue of active requests. As a side-effect, acquiring the spin lock raises IRQL up to DISPATCH_LEVEL. After it owns the spin lock, the Dispatch routine adds the new request to the list of buffers to be output.

5.   Still holding the spin lock, the Dispatch routine checks an internal **DmaInProgress** flag to see if other parts of the driver are already doing an output. If the flag is TRUE, it simply releases the spin lock. If the flag is FALSE, the Dispatch routine sets it to TRUE and calls **IoAllocateAdapterChannel** to start the device. It then releases the spin lock.

6.   Finally, it returns a value of STATUS_PENDING.

At this point, the work request for this buffer has been either started or queued. The next phase of the transfer will take place after the device generates an interrupt.

Adapter Control routine   If the device was idle, the Adapter Control is called to get it going. This is what it does:

1.   It removes the first request from the work queue and saves its address in the Device Extension as the current request.

---

[5] Chapter 14 will explain how to use Semaphore objects. If you're familiar with Win32 programming, you already have a good idea of how they work.

2. Next, the Adapter Control routine saves the value of the MapRegisterBase argument in the Device Extension for later use.

3. It then calls **IoMapTransfer** to load the system DMA controller with the address of the current request's common buffer.

4. Finally, the Adapter Control routine starts the device and returns a value of **KeepObject**.

Once the driver owns the Adapter object, it will hold on to it as long as there are work requests in the queue.

Interrupt Service routine As with packet-based DMA, the ISR in a common-buffer driver for a slave device just saves hardware status in the Device Extension. It then calls **IoRequestDpc** to continue processing at DISPATCH_LEVEL IRQL.

DpcForIsr routine In this driver, the DpcForIsr routine sets up each additional work request after the first. Here's how it works:

1. It calls **IoFlushAdapterBuffers** to flush any data from the system DMA controller's hardware cache.

2. The DpcForIsr routine tries to remove the next I/O request from the work queue. If there is another request, the driver makes it the new current request, maps its buffer with **IoMapTransfer**, and starts the device. On the other hand, if the work queue is empty, the driver calls **IoFreeAdapterChannel** to release the Adapter object and clears the **DmaInProgress** flag in the Device Extension.

3. Next, it puts appropriate status information in the IRP for the just-completed request and calls **IoCompleteRequest** to give it back to the I/O Manager.

4. Finally, the DpcForIsr routine puts the just-completed common buffer back in the free list and calls **KeRleaseSemaphore** to increment the count of available buffers.

Each completed DMA operation causes another interrupt that brings the driver back through the DpcForIsr routine. This loop continues until all the requests in the work queue have been processed.

Unload routine When a common buffer bus master driver is unloaded, it first needs to stop the device from trying to use the buffer. Once the device is silent, the Unload routine calls **HalFreeCommonBuffer** to release the memory associated with the ring of buffers. It also calls **IoFreeMdl** to release memory used for each buffer's MDL.

12.7 WRITING A COMMON-BUFFER BUS MASTER DMA DRIVER

In common-buffer bus master DMA, the device transfers data to or from a contiguous nonpaged pool buffer using a DMA controller that's part of the device itself. Frequently, this kind of hardware will treat the common buffer as a mailbox for exchanging control and status messages with the driver.

How Common-Buffer Bus Master DMA Works

The exact operation of a common-buffer bus master driver will depend on the whims of the hardware designer. The description that follows is based on a typical architecture. It assumes the device uses one mailbox for commands and another to return status information. Figure 12.7 illustrates this arrangement.

DriverEntry routine The DriverEntry routine does the following to set up a common buffer:

1. It calls **HalGetAdapter** to find an Adapter object for the device.

2. **DriverEntry** next calls **HalAllocateCommonBuffer** to get a block of contiguous, nonpaged memory that both the driver and the device can access. It usually simplifies things if the common buffer is allocated from non-cached memory.

3. It stores the virtual address of the common buffer in the Device Extension for later use.

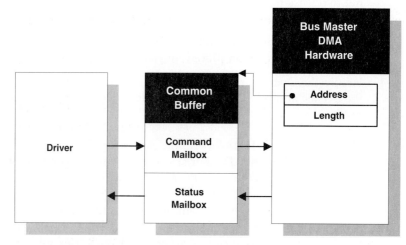

Copyright © 1996 by Cydonix Corporation. 960022a.vsd

Figure 12.7 The driver and the device exchange messages using a common buffer

4.   **DriverEntry** also makes the device itself aware of the common buffer. This usually means storing the logical address and size of the buffer in a pair of device control registers.

Start I/O routine   When it wants to send a command to the device, the Start I/O routine does the following:

1.   It builds a command structure in the common buffer using the virtual address stored in the Device Extension.

2.   If **DriverEntry** specified **TRUE** for the CacheEnabled parameter of **HalAllocateCommonBuffer**, Start I/O needs to call **KeFlushIoBuffers** to force data from the CPU's cache out to physical memory.

3.   Finally, Start I/O sets a bit in a device control register to notify the device that there is a command waiting for it.

In response to the notification bit being set, the device begins processing the command in the common buffer.

Interrupt Service routine   When the device has finished processing the command in the common buffer, it puts a message in the status mailbox and generates an interrupt. In response to this interrupt, the driver's Interrupt Service routine does the following:

1.   It copies the contents of the status mailbox into various fields of the Device Extension.

2.   If necessary, the ISR sets another bit in the device control register to acknowledge that it has read the status message.

3.   It calls **IoRequestDpc** to continue processing the request at a lower IRQL.

Unload routine   When a common-buffer bus master driver is unloaded, it first needs to stop the device from trying to use the buffer. Once the device is silent, the Unload routine calls **HalFreeCommonBuffer** to release the memory associated with the buffer.

12.8 SUMMARY

Without a doubt, drivers for DMA devices are more complicated than drivers for programmed I/O hardware. In return for this added complexity, the system achieves greater throughput by overlapping CPU activity with data transfers. The I/O Manager tries to simplify things by providing a generic framework in which to perform DMA. This chapter has presented the details of NT's abstract DMA model and shown how to perform various styles of DMA.

So far, we've been assuming that things have gone well during device operations. But suppose something terrible happens? Something so terrible, in fact, that you think the system administrator should hear about it. In the next chapter, you'll see how to add error-logging capabilities to a driver.

Logging Device Errors

System administrators are a nervous and para-
noid lot. Like small mammals in the Jurassic period, they scurry about — imagin-
ing the worst and waiting for it to happen. Adding to their anxiety may seem
cruel, but if you're writing a commercial-quality driver, you really should tell
someone when serious hardware and software errors occur. This chapter explains
how to generate these notifications using NT's event-logging mechanism.

13.1 EVENT LOGGING IN WINDOWS NT

Built into Windows NT is a mechanism that allows software components to keep
a record of interesting events. This event-logging capability can help you monitor
the behavior of a piece of software that's under development. It can also give support personnel crucial information once the software is out in the field. The
remainder of this section presents guidelines for deciding what information to log
and then describes how event logging works.

Deciding What to Log

For the most part, error logging is something that's best done by lowest-level
device drivers. Higher-level drivers usually don't have anything to say that's
worth putting in the log file, except possibly startup and shutdown notifications.
There are several kinds of events that a device driver might log:

- Hard device errors that result in an IRP failing
- Soft errors that are corrected after some number of retries
- Device timeouts
- Driver startup and shutdown

Along with various pieces of standard information, you're allowed to add your own data to the messages in the event log. Useful items to include are

- The contents of any device control or status registers that might indicate the cause of the problem
- Any fields from the Device or Controller Extension that indicate the state of the driver when the error occurred
- Any additional information about the request that would help with the diagnosis. For example, logging the transfer size might lead you to discover that large requests always fail.

Two points are worth mentioning. First, don't get carried away with the idea of adding driver-specific data to event-log messages. The amount of space available for private data in a kernel-mode event-log message is rather limited. So, stick to the essentials and only add things to your log packets that will be of true diagnostic value.

Second, hardware that's on its last legs can generate a lot of error messages as it fails and can easily overwhelm the log file. It's important to have some strategy for dealing with this situation. For example, you might keep track of how many messages a device is generating, and if it exceeds some threshold, reduce the level of detail reported by your driver.

How Event Logging Works

The developers of Windows NT had several goals for the event-logging architecture. The first was to provide application programs, drivers, and the operating system with a unified framework for recording information. This framework includes a simple yet flexible standard for the binary format of event-log entries.

Another goal was to give system administrators an easy way to view these messages. As part of this goal, viewing utilities must be able to display event messages in the currently selected national language. Under the American version of NT, the message text should appear in English, while the French version of NT should display French text. Figure 13.1 shows how it all works.

The following describes what happens when a kernel-mode driver decides to log an error. The process is similar for a user-mode Win32 application, although the specific API calls are different.[1]

---

[1] The data-collection DLL in Chapter 18 contains an example of using the Win32 event-logging API.

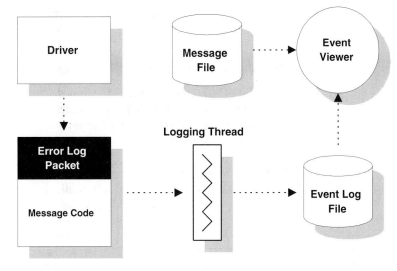

Figure 13.1   NT event-logging components

1. All event messages take the form of packets in Windows NT. When a kernel-mode driver wants to log an event, it first calls the I/O Manager to allocate a message packet from nonpaged pool.

2. The driver fills in this packet with various pieces of descriptive information. One of the key items is a 32-bit message code number that identifies the text to be displayed for this packet. Once the packet's ready, the driver gives it back to the I/O Manager.

3. The I/O Manager takes the message packet and sends it to the system event-logging thread. This thread accumulates packets and periodically writes them to the proper event-log file.[2]

4. The Event Viewer utility reads binary packets from the log files. To translate a packet's 32-bit message code into text, the Viewer goes to the Registry. There it finds the path names of one or more message files associated with the packet. These message files contain the actual message text (possibly in multiple languages) which the Viewer displays.

13.2 WORKING WITH MESSAGES

As you've just seen, your driver doesn't include the actual text for its messages in an event-log entry. Instead, it identifies messages using code numbers. The text associated with these code numbers takes the form of a message resource stored

---

[2] If the system crashes before a group of log packets have been written out, you can still see them by using WINDBG's !errlog command. See Chapter 17 for more details.

somewhere on disk. This section describes how these message codes work and explains how to generate your own message resources.

How Message Codes Work

The code number identifying a specific message is a 32-bit value consisting of several fields. Figure 13.2 shows the layout of a message code.

Table 13.1 gives a little more detail about the meaning of each of these fields. Although you'll probably never need to decode these fields on sight, it's always nice to be able to impress your friends.

The I/O Manager provides a number of standard messages that your driver can use. The header file, **NTIOLOGC.H**, defines symbolic names for these message codes, all of which begin with IO_ERR_ (for example, IO_ERR_TIMEOUT or

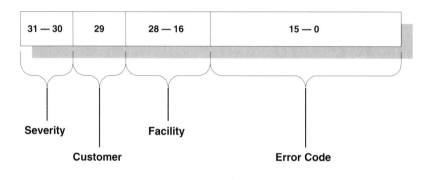

Copyright © 1996 by Cydonix Corporation. 960023a.vsd

Figure 13.2   Layout of a message-code number

Table 13.1   The meaning of message-code fields

Message-code fields		
Field	**Bits**	**Description**
Code	0–15	Code number identifying the error
Facility	16–28	Software component generating the message
Customer	29	If set, this is a customer-generated (non-Microsoft) message
Severity	30–31	One of the following: • 0 — success • 1 — information • 2 — warning • 3 — error

IO_ERR_NOT_READY). Browse through this header file for a complete list of standard messages.

If you want to use these standard messages, you have to add your driver to the list of event-logging system components in the Registry. You also have to identify the file where the text for these messages is located (**%System Root%\SYSTEM32\IOLOGMSG.DLL**). The procedure for doing this is described a little later in this chapter.

If the standard messages don't meet all your needs, you can supplement them with driver-defined messages. To do this, you need to follow these steps:

1. Write a message definition file that associates your message codes with specific text strings.

2. Compile this file using the message compiler (MC) utility.

3. Incorporate the message resources generated by MC into your driver.

4. Register your driver as an event-logging system component and identify the driver executable as the file containing the text for these private messages.

Writing Message Definition Files

To use the MC utility, you first need to write a definition file describing all your messages. This definition file is divided into two major sections.

Header section   Keywords in the header define names for values that will be used in the actual message definitions. Table 13.2 contains the keywords that you can use in the header section of a message definition file.

Message section   This portion of the message definition file contains the actual text of the messages. Each message begins with the keywords listed in Table 13.3.

Table 13.2   Keywords used in the header section of a message definition file

Header section keywords

Keyword	Description
MessageIdTypedef = *DataType*	Typecast applied to all message codes
SeverityNames = (*name=number*[*:name*])	Up to four severity values used in the Message section
FacilityNames = (*name=number*[*:name*])	Facility names used in the Message section
LanguageNames = (*name=number:filename*)	Language names used in Message section

Table 13.3   Keywords used in the message section of a message definition file

Message section keywords

Keyword	Description
MessageId = [*number* | *+number*]	16-bit value assigned to this message*
Severity = *SeverityName*	Severity level of this message
Facility = *FacilityName*	Facility generating the message
SymbolicName = *SymbolName*	Name of message code in generated header file
Language = *LanguageName*	Language ID associated with the message

*Required.

The message text itself begins after the last keyword. The text of a message can occupy several lines. You end a message with a line containing only a single period character.

The message compiler ignores any whitespace or carriage returns in a message definition. If you want explicit control over the appearance of a message when the Event Viewer displays it, you can include various escape sequences (listed in Table 13.4) in the body of the message.

The **%1–%99** escape codes represent Unicode strings (embedded in the event log packet) that will be inserted in the message when the Event Viewer displays it.[3] If a kernel-mode driver associates an event packet with a Device object, **%1** will automatically contain the NT name of the device; if the driver associates the packet with the Driver object, **%1** will be blank. In either case, your first real insertion string will be **%2**, your second one will be **%3**, and so on. The code example appearing later in this chapter will explain how to add insertion strings to an event packet.

Table 13.4   The effects of various escape codes on displayed message text

Message formatting escape codes

IF you use...	THEN it's replaced with...
%b	A single space character
%t	A single tab character
%r%n	Carriage return and linefeed
%1–%99	An insertion string

---

[3] Remember that these insertion strings will always be displayed as raw text. There's no way for the Event Viewer to translate them into the local language.

A Small Example: XXMSG.MC

Here is the message definition file for the example that goes with this chapter. You can find it in the **CH13\DRIVER** directory on the floppy that accompanies this book.

Header section   The first part of the message definition file contains header information.

```
MessageIdTypedef = NTSTATUS❶

SeverityNames = (
    Success          = 0x0:STATUS_SEVERITY_SUCCESS
    Informational    = 0x1:STATUS_SEVERITY_INFORMATIONAL
    Warning          = 0x2:STATUS_SEVERITY_WARNING
    Error            = 0x3:STATUS_SEVERITY_ERROR
)

FacilityNames = (❷
    System      = 0x0
    RpcRuntime  = 0x2:FACILITY_RPC_RUNTIME
    RpcStubs    = 0x3:FACILITY_RPC_STUBS
    Io          = 0x4:FACILITY_IO_ERROR_CODE
    XxDriver    = 0x7:FACILITY_XX_ERROR_CODE
)
```

❶ The definitions of any symbolic names generated by MC will include a typecast to NTSTATUS.

❷ You can find codes for Microsoft-defined facilities in the **NTSTATUS.H** header file. For your own facility number, pick something that isn't in use.

Message section   Here's the message section of the file. It defines the actual text to be associated with message code number.

```
MessageId=0x0001❶
Facility=XxDriver
Severity=Informational
SymbolicName=XX_MSG_LOGGING_ENABLED❷
Language=English
Event logging enabled for XxDriver. ❸
.

MessageId=+1❹
Facility=XxDriver
```

```
Severity=Informational
SymbolicName=XX_MSG_DRIVER_STARTING
Language=English
XxDriver has successfully initialized.
.

MessageId=+1
Facility=XxDriver
Severity=Informational
SymbolicName=XX_MSG_DRIVER_STOPPING
Language=English
XxDriver has unloaded.
.

MessageId=+1
Facility=XxDriver
Severity=Informational
SymbolicName=XX_MSG_OPENING_HANDLE
Language=English
Opening handle to %1.
.

MessageId=+1
Facility=XxDriver
Severity=Informational
SymbolicName=XX_MSG_CLOSING_HANDLE
Language=English
Closing handle to %1.
.

MessageId=+1
Facility=XxDriver
Severity=Warning
SymbolicName=XX_MSG_MULTIPLE_OCCUPANCY
Language=English
%1 contains multiple life-forms. Data
specifies number of occupants.
.

MessageId=+1
Facility=XxDriver
Severity=Informational
SymbolicName=XX_MSG_MERGING_DNA
Language=English
Merging DNA from %2 and %3 in %1. ❺
.
```

❶ The **MessageId** keyword is required at the start of a message. This form of the keyword assigns an absolute number to the 16-bit **Code** field of the generated message code.

❷ This keyword tells the message compiler to define a symbol called XX_MSG_LOGGING_ENABLED in the header file it generates.

❸ The actual message text begins after the last keyword. A line containing only a single period character ends the text.

❹ This form of the **MessageId** keyword assigns a **Code** value to the message that's one greater than the previous message.

❺ This message contains placeholders for insertion strings. **%1** will become the device name; **%2** and **%3** will be replaced with whatever insertion strings are embedded in the event-log packet.

Compiling a Message Definition File

Once you've written the message definition file, you use the message compiler (MC) to process it. MC is another quirky little command-line utility that comes with the Win32 SDK and Visual C++.[4] Table 13.5 shows the syntax of the MC command.

Table 13.5   Syntax of the MC command

MC [-?cdosvw] [-herx argument] [-uU] filename.MC

Parameter	Description
-c	Set Customer bit in all message codes.
-d	Use decimal definitions of facility and severity codes in header.
-o	Generate OLE2 header file.
-s	Insert symbolic name as first line of each message.
-v	Generate verbose output.
-w	Give warning if message-text is not OS/2 compatible.
-h *pathname*	Location of generated header file. (Default is current directory.)
-e *extension*	One- to three-character extension for header file.
-r *pathname*	Location of generated RC and binary message files.
-x *pathname*	Location of generated debug file.
-u	Input file is Unicode.
-U	Message text in binary—output binary file should be Unicode.
filename	Name of the message definition file to compile.

---

[4] Documentation for MC is rather sparse. One of the best sources is the **MC.HLP** help file that comes with the compiler.

When you run the message compiler, it automatically generates the follow-ing files:

- **filename.RC** — This is a resource control script that identifies all the lan-guages used in the message definition file. For each language, it also iden-tifies the binary message file containing the message text.

- **filename.H** — This header file contains **#define** statements for all the message code numbers in the MC input file. The compiler also puts a lot of inline commentary in the header, including the text of the correspond-ing message.

- **MSGnnnnn.BIN** — This binary file holds all the text for messages in one language. MC will generate separate files (beginning with **MSG00001.BIN**) for each national language used in the message definition file.

Although you can specify the paths where the header and RC files will go, the actual names of these files will always be the same as the name of the message definition file. You have no control over the names of the binary message file.

Adding Message Resources to a Driver

After you run the message compiler, you still need to do something with the binary message resources it generates. You could put them in a separate DLL, the way the I/O Manager does with **IOLOGMSG.DLL**, but for most drivers it makes more sense to add the message resources to the driver executable itself. That way, you won't have to worry about keeping track of multiple files when you send your driver out into the world.

The BUILD utility (described in Chapter 16) understands how to process resource control scripts. So, all you have to do is to add the name of the script to the list of source files making up the driver. BUILD will then run the resource compiler and link the resulting resources into your driver. For example, if you've just compiled a message definition file called **XXMSG.MC**, you'll have a resource script called **XXMSG.RC**. The following excerpt from a BUILD **SOURCES** file shows how you would add this resource script to your driver.

```
      :
SOURCES= init.c unload.c  \
         dispatch.c       \
         eventlog.c       \
         xxmsg.rc
      :
```

There's one glitch in all this. BUILD doesn't know what to do with message definition files, so you can't just add **XXMSG.MC** itself to the list of driver sources. This means you need to run the message compiler by hand any time you modify your message definition file. Fortunately, there's a way to extend the capabilities of BUILD so that it will automatically maintain message resources for you. Chapter 17 explains how to perform this little bit of magic.

Registering a Driver as an Event Source

So now you have a header file containing message codes, and a bunch of message resources stuffed into your driver. But there's still a question: Just how does the system know that it should look in your driver executable when it wants to translate a particular message code into text? Once again, we're saved by the Registry.

Any software component that plans to generate log entries must identify itself to the system as an *event source*. Further, every event source has to specify the location of the message files needed to translate any message codes appearing in its log entries. Figure 13.3 shows the Registry entries that identify a driver as an event source.[5]

To register your driver as an event source, make the following changes to the Registry:

1. Under **...Services\EventLog\System**, add the name of your driver's executable (without the extension) to the REG_MULTI_SZ value called **Sources**.

2. Under **...Services\EventLog\System**, add a key with the same name as your driver.

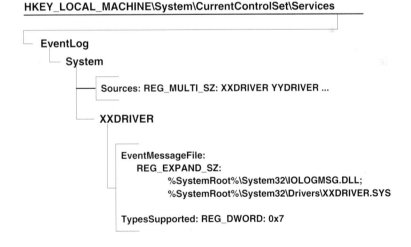

HKEY_LOCAL_MACHINE\System\CurrentControlSet\Services

   EventLog
      System
         Sources: REG_MULTI_SZ: XXDRIVER YYDRIVER ...

         XXDRIVER

            EventMessageFile:
              REG_EXPAND_SZ:
                %SystemRoot%\System32\IOLOGMSG.DLL;
                %SystemRoot%\System32\Drivers\XXDRIVER.SYS

            TypesSupported: REG_DWORD: 0x7

Figure 13.3 Registering a kernel-mode driver as an event source

---

[5] These entries apply only to kernel-mode event sources. Chapter 18 shows how to register a user-mode component as an event source.

3. In this key, create a value called **EventMessageFile**. This is a REG_EXPAND_SZ containing the full path names of any message files used by your driver. If your driver uses multiple files, separate them with a semicolon. If you're using standard messages defined in **NTIOLOGC.H**, you'll also need to add **IOLOGMSG.DLL** to this list.

4. In this same key, create a value called **TypesSupported**. This is a REG_DWORD bit mask identifying the types of messages generated by your driver. A value of 0x7 gets everything.

13.3 GENERATING LOG ENTRIES

The final piece of the puzzle is to add code to your driver that actually generates event-log entries. This is a relatively straightforward process that involves allocating an empty packet, filling it in, and sending it off to the system logging thread. The rest of this section describes the major steps along the way.

Preparing a Driver for Error Logging

If you plan to support error logging, there a few small changes you'll want to make to your driver. In particular, it's a good idea to add the following items to your Device Extension:

- A sequence number field that your driver increments for each IRP processed by the device. This value should remain constant for the life of the request.

- A retry count for the current request, if you retry device operations when an error occurs. Set it to zero each time you start processing an IRP and increment it for each repeated attempt.

- Copies of any device registers that would help diagnose the error. If your ISR decides to log an error, it should take a snapshot of the hardware registers for the logging routine.

You should also adopt some convention that assigns a unique identifying number to each stage of processing an IRP. This number becomes part of the error-log information, and it will help you figure out where in your driver the error occurred. This fragment of a driver's header file shows how you might do this:

```
     :
#define XX_ERRORLOG_STARTIO                 1
#define XX_ERRORLOG_CONTROLLER_CONTROL      2
#define XX_ERRORLOG_ADAPTER_CONTROL         3
#define XX_ERRORLOG_ISR                     4
#define XX_ERRORLOG_DPC_FOR_ISR             5
     :
```

Finally, you might want to define a value in the **Parameters** subkey of your driver's Registry service key to control driver error logging. This could either be a Boolean that simply enables and disables logging, or it could be an actual value that determines the level of logging detail. The code example appearing later in this chapter uses a value called **EventLogLevel** to control the quantity event messages it generates.

Allocating an Error-Log Packet

When your driver uncovers some terrible sin that needs reporting, it has to prepare an error-log packet. There are three sections to an error-log packet:

- A standard header
- An array of driver-defined ULONGs (referred to as *dump data*)
- One or more NULL-terminated Unicode insertion strings[6]

Both the dump-data and insertion strings are variable in length and are optional. Figure 13.4 shows the structure of an error-log packet.

Before you can allocate an error-log packet, you need to determine how big the packet should be. Remember to leave room for any dump-data and insertion

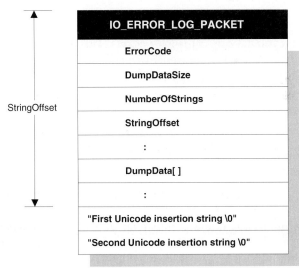

Figure 13.4 Layout of an error-log packet

---

[6] Don't confuse these with the counted UNICODE_STRING data structures used in other parts of NT.

strings. You can calculate the size of the packet using a variation on the following piece of code:

```
PacketSize =
        sizeof( IO_ERROR_LOG_PACKET ) +
        (sizeof( ULONG ) * ( DumpDataCount - 1 )) +
        sizeof( InsertionStrings );
```

Here, **DumpDataCount** is the number of driver-specific ULONG data items, and **InsertionStrings** are any driver-supplied UNICODE strings to be inserted in the error message. The requested size of the packet cannot exceed ERROR_LOG_MAXIMUM_SIZE.

Use the **IoAllocateErrorLogEntry** function (described in Table 13.6) to allocate the packet. As you can see from the table, you're allowed to associate the packet either with the Driver object or with a particular Device object. Your choice will determine how the Event Viewer utility displays your message. Overall initialization and shutdown are good choices for Driver-level messages, while problems involving specific IRPs or pieces of hardware ought to be associated with a Device object.

Low memory conditions could make it impossible for the system to get a packet for you, so don't assume that your allocation request will always succeed. One easy way to handle these situations is just to forget about logging the error, with the hope that it will happen again when the system isn't so pressed for memory.

Finally, notice that you have to be at or below DISPATCH_LEVEL IRQL when you allocate error-log packets. This means that if your ISR decides to log an error (a common occurrence), you'll need a CustomDpc routine to do the actual work.

Logging the Error

Once you've allocated the packet, you need to fill in all the relevant fields. In addition to the fields listed in Table 13.7, you should also copy any driver-specific data and strings into the packet.

Table 13.6   Use this function to allocates an error-log packet

PVOID IoAllocateErrorLogEntry	IRQL ≤ DISPATCH_LEVEL
Parameter	**Description**
IN PVOID IoObject	• Address of a Device object generating an error
	• Address of a Driver object reporting an error
IN UCHAR EntrySize	Size in bytes of packet to be allocated
Return value	• PIO_ERROR_LOG_PACKET — success
	• NULL — allocation failure

Table 13.7   Layout of an IO_ERROR_LOG_PACKET

IO_ERROR_LOG_PACKET, *PIO_ERROR_LOG_PACKET

Field	Description
UCHAR MajorFunctionCode	IRP_MJ_XXX code of current IRP
UCHAR RetryCount	Zero-based count of consecutive retries
USHORT DumpDataSize	Bytes of driver-specific data
USHORT NumberOfStrings	Number of insertion strings
USHORT StringOffset	Byte offset of first insertion string
USHORT EventCategory	Event category from driver's message file
NTSTATUS ErrorCode	IO_ERR_XXX (see **NTIOLOGC.H**)
ULONG UniqueErrorValue	Indicates where in the driver the error occurred
NTSTATUS FinalStatus	STATUS_XXX value from the IRP
ULONG SequenceNumber	Driver-assigned number for current IRP
ULONG IoControlCode	IOCTL_XXX if this is a DeviceIoControl request
LARGE_INTEGER DeviceOffset	Device offset where error occurred, or zero
ULONG DumpData[1]	Driver-specific data if DumpDataSize is nonzero

When the packet is ready, call **IoWriteErrorLogEntry** to send it to the system logging thread. The packet doesn't belong to you once you call this function, so don't touch it again. As with packet allocation, you can only write an error-log packet if you're at or below DISPATCH_LEVEL IRQL.

13.4 CODE EXAMPLE: AN ERROR-LOGGING ROUTINE

This example illustrates how to log event messages from a kernel-mode driver. The complete example includes a driver that uses these event-logging functions, as well as a test program that exercises the driver. You can find all of this in the **CH13** directory on the disk that accompanies this book.

EVENTLOG.C

This module provides a general event-logging mechanism that any driver can use. In addition to the functions listed below, **EVENTLOG.C** also defines a global variable called **LogLevel** that determines logging verbosity. Although globals are generally a bad idea in drivers, this one's okay because its value doesn't change once driver initialization is done.

XxInitializeEventLog   This function is called from **DriverEntry** to set up the driver's event-logging mechanism. Its main purpose is to retrieve a value called **EventLogLevel** from the driver's Registry service key and store it in the **LogLevel** variable.

```
VOID
XxInitializeEventLog(
  IN PDRIVER_OBJECT DriverObject
  )
{
  RTL_QUERY_REGISTRY_TABLE QueryTable[2]; ❶

  //
  // Fabricate a Registry query.
  //
  RtlZeroMemory( QueryTable, sizeof( QueryTable )); ❷

  QueryTable[0].Name = L"EventLogLevel";
  QueryTable[0].Flags = RTL_QUERY_REGISTRY_DIRECT;
  QueryTable[0].EntryContext = &LogLevel;

  //
  // Look for the EventLogLevel value
  // in the Registry.
  //
  if( !NT_SUCCESS(
              RtlQueryRegistryValues(❸
                  RTL_REGISTRY_SERVICES,
                  XX_DRIVER_NAME
                      L"\\Parameters",
                  QueryTable,
                  NULL, NULL )))
  {
      LogLevel = DEFAULT_LOG_LEVEL;
  }

  //
  // Log a message saying that logging
  // is enabled.
  //
  XxReportEvent(❹
      LOG_LEVEL_DEBUG,
      XX_MSG_LOGGING_ENABLED,
      XX_ERRORLOG_INIT,
      (PVOID)DriverObject,
      NULL,                          // No IRP
      NULL, 0,                       // No dump data
      NULL, 0 );                     // No strings
}
```

❶ This function uses our old friend **RtlQueryRegistryValues** to set the event-logging verbosity level. We need a query table with one entry for the value and another (NULL) entry for a terminator.

❷ It's a good idea to clear the table before using it. Otherwise, you can get some strange error messages resulting from random bit settings.

❸ Query the Registry. RTL_REGISTRY_SERVICES says that the path name (**xxdriver\Parameters**) should be treated as a subkey of the **…\Services** key.

❹ If verbose logging is enabled, log a message indicating that logging is enabled.

XxReportEvent   This function does the actual grunt work of allocating an error-log packet, filling it in, and sending it off to the system logging thread. You can only call this function from DISPATCH_LEVEL IRQL.

```
BOOLEAN
XxReportEvent(
   IN ULONG MessageLevel,
   IN NTSTATUS ErrorCode,
   IN ULONG UniqueErrorValue,
   IN PVOID IoObject,
   IN PIRP Irp,
   IN ULONG DumpData[],
   IN ULONG DumpDataCount,
   IN PWSTR Strings[],
   IN ULONG StringCount
   )
{
   PIO_ERROR_LOG_PACKET Packet;
   PDEVICE_EXTENSION pDE;
   PIO_STACK_LOCATION IrpStack;
   PUCHAR pInsertionString;
   UCHAR PacketSize;
   UCHAR StringSize[ XX_MAX_INSERTION_STRINGS ];
   ULONG i;

   if( ( LogLevel == LOG_LEVEL_NONE ) ||❶
         ( MessageLevel > LogLevel ))
   {
         return TRUE;
   }

   PacketSize = sizeof( IO_ERROR_LOG_PACKET ); ❷

   if( DumpDataCount > 0 ) ❸
         PacketSize +=
               (UCHAR)( sizeof( ULONG ) *
                           ( DumpDataCount - 1 ));

   if( StringCount > 0 ) ❹
```

```
{
    if( StringCount > XX_MAX_INSERTION_STRINGS )
        StringCount = XX_MAX_INSERTION_STRINGS;

    for( i=0; i<StringCount; i++ )  ❺
    {
        StringSize[i] =
        (UCHAR)XxGetStringSize( Strings[i] );

        PacketSize += StringSize[i];
    }
}
//
// Try to allocate the packet
//
Packet = IoAllocateErrorLogEntry(
                    IoObject,
                    PacketSize );

if( Packet == NULL ) return FALSE;

//
// Fill in standard parts of the packet
//
Packet->ErrorCode = ErrorCode;
Packet->UniqueErrorValue = UniqueErrorValue;

if( Irp != NULL )  ❻
{
    IrpStack
        = IoGetCurrentIrpStackLocation( Irp );

    pDE = (PDEVICE_EXTENSION)
            ((PDEVICE_OBJECT)IoObject)->
                            DeviceExtension;

    Packet->MajorFunctionCode =
                    IrpStack->MajorFunction;

    Packet->RetryCount = pDE->IrpRetryCount;

    Packet->FinalStatus = Irp->IoStatus.Status;

    Packet->SequenceNumber =
                    pDE->IrpSequenceNumber;

    if( IrpStack->MajorFunction ==
                IRP_MJ_DEVICE_CONTROL ||
            IrpStack->MajorFunction ==
                IRP_MJ_INTERNAL_DEVICE_CONTROL )
```

```
            {
                    Packet->IoControlCode =
                            IrpStack->Parameters.
                                        DeviceIoControl.
                                            IoControlCode;
            }
            else Packet->IoControlCode = 0;
    }
    else // No IRP
    {
            Packet->MajorFunctionCode = 0;
            Packet->RetryCount = 0;
            Packet->FinalStatus = 0;
            Packet->SequenceNumber = 0;
            Packet->IoControlCode = 0;
    }

    //
    // Add the dump data
    //
    if( DumpDataCount > 0 )
    {
            Packet->DumpDataSize =
                    (USHORT)( sizeof( ULONG ) *
                                        DumpDataCount );

            for( i=0; i<DumpDataCount; i++ )
                    Packet->DumpData[i] = DumpData[i];
    }
    else Packet->DumpDataSize = 0;

    //
    // Add the insertion strings
    //
    Packet->NumberOfStrings = (USHORT)StringCount;

    if( StringCount > 0 )
    {
            Packet->StringOffset =
                    sizeof( IO_ERROR_LOG_PACKET ) +
                    ( DumpDataCount - 1 ) * sizeof( ULONG );

            pInsertionString =
                    (PUCHAR)Packet + Packet->StringOffset; ❼

            for( i=0; i<StringCount; i++ ) ❽
            {
                    //
```

```
                     // Add each new string to the end
                     // of the existing stuff
                     //
                     RtlCopyBytes(
                          pInsertionString,
                          Strings[i],
                          StringSize[i] );

                     pInsertionString += StringSize[i];
               }
          }
          //
          // Log the message
          //
          IoWriteErrorLogEntry( Packet );

          return TRUE;
     }
```

❶ If we're not logging or the message is out of range, return without doing anything.

❷ Begin calculating the packet size. Start with the minimum required number of bytes.

❸ Add in any dump data. Remember that the standard error-log packet already has one slot in its **DumpData** array.

❹ Determine the total space needed for any insertion strings. If the caller has sent too many strings, process only as many as this function can handle.

❺ Build a table containing the length of each individual string using **XxGet-StringSize**, a local helper function. This table will be used again later to copy the insertion strings into the error-log packet. Also add the size of each string to the total packet requirement.

❻ If there's an IRP, then the IoObject argument must point to a Device object. In that case, use the IRP and the Device Extension to fill in additional parts of the error-log packet. If there's no IRP, then set the additional fields to 0.

❼ Insertion strings always go just after the **DumpData** array in the error-log packet. After setting the offset of the first string, calculate the address where the first string should go in the packet.

❽ This loop simply adds each new string to the end of the packet using **Rtl-CopyBytes**. It takes advantage of the table of string sizes generated earlier in the routine.

XxGetStringSize   This little helper function calculates the amount of space needed by a NULL-terminated Unicode string. The size includes space for the (2 bytes) UNICODE_NULL at the end of the string.

```
ULONG
XxGetStringSize(
  IN PWSTR String
  )
{
  UNICODE_STRING TempString;

  //
  // Use an RTL routine to get the length
  //
  RtlInitUnicodeString( &TempString, String );

  //
  // Size is actually two greater because
  // of the UNICODE_NULL at the end.
  //
  return( TempString.Length + sizeof( WCHAR));
}
```

13.5 SUMMARY

This chapter has presented NT's event-logging mechanisms. As you can see, it isn't terribly difficult for drivers to leave a little trail when devices start generating errors. These audit trails can be a useful diagnostic aid to system administrators.

This chapter also finishes our look at basic kernel-mode device driver techniques. In the next chapter, you'll see the first of several variations on the driver architecture we've developed so far.

CHAPTER 14

System Threads

Some types of legacy hardware can have a bad effect on system performance if you manage them using the driver model we've developed so far. System threads give you a way to keep these devices out of everyone's way.

14.1 SYSTEM THREADS

A system thread is a thread that runs exclusively in kernel mode. It has no user-mode context and can't access user address space. Just like a Win32 thread, a system thread executes at or below APC_LEVEL IRQL and it competes for use of the CPU based on its scheduling priority.

When to Use Threads

There are several reasons why you might use threads in a driver. The first possibility is that you're working with a piece of hardware that has the following characteristics:

- The device is slow and infrequently accessed.
- It takes a long time (more than 50 microseconds) for the device to make a state transition, and the driver has to wait for the transition to occur.

- The device needs to make several state transitions in order to complete a single operation.

- The device doesn't generate interrupts for some kinds of interesting state transitions, and the driver has to poll the device for extended periods.

You could, of course, manage a device like this using a CustomTimerDpc routine. Depending on the amount of device activity, this approach could clog up the DPC queues and slow down other drivers. Threads, on the other hand, run at PASSIVE_LEVEL and won't interfere with DPC routines.

Fortunately, there aren't too many categories of hardware that behave this rudely, and most of them are legacy devices that date from the early days of the personal computer. The most notable examples are floppy disks and QIC tapes attached to floppy controllers.

The second possibility is that you've got a device which takes a very long time to initialize itself, and which your driver has to monitor throughout the initialization. Certain kinds of optical jukeboxes behave this way. So might a computer-controlled pottery kiln.

This kind of behavior is a problem because the Service Control Manager gives a driver only about 30 seconds to execute its DriverEntry routine. If **DriverEntry** hasn't returned by then, the Service Control Manager forcibly unloads the driver. The only solution is to put the long-running device start-up code in a separate thread, and return immediately from the DriverEntry routine with STATUS_SUCCESS.[1]

Finally, you might need to perform some kind of operation that will only work at PASSIVE_LEVEL IRQL. For example, if your driver had to access the Registry on a regular basis, or write something to a file, a thread might be the answer.

Creating and Terminating System Threads

Call **PsCreateSystemThread**, described in Table 14.1, when you want to create a system thread. Since you can only call this function at PASSIVE_LEVEL IRQL, you will usually create driver threads in your DriverEntry routine.

When your driver unloads, it must kill any system threads it may have created. The only way to do this is to have the thread itself call **PsTerminateSystemThread** with an appropriate exit status. Unlike Win32 user-mode threads, there is no way to forcibly terminate a system thread. This means you need to set up some kind of signaling mechanism to let a thread know that it should exit. As you'll see later in this chapter, Event objects provide a convenient way to do this.

---

[1] Of course, you'll have to figure out what to do if the device fails to initialize successfully. Once **DriverEntry** has returned, there's no way for a driver to unload itself, so any cleanup will have to be done by the thread itself. This includes things like deleting Device objects, freeing resources, etc. If the driver finds it has *no* initialized devices, it might also make itself entirely paged in order to reduce its impact on the system.

Table 14.1   Prototype for function that creates a system thread

NTSTATUS PsCreateSystemThread	IRQL == PASSIVE_LEVEL
Parameter	**Description**
OUT PHANDLE ThreadHandle	Handle of new thread
IN ULONG DesiredAccess	0 for a driver-created thread
IN POBJECT_ATTRIBUTES Attrib	NULL for a driver-created thread
IN HANDLE ProcessHandle	NULL for a driver-created thread
OUT PCLIENT_ID ClientId	NULL for a driver-created thread
IN PKSTART_ROUTINE StartAddr	Entry point for thread
IN PVOID Context	Argument passed to thread routine
Return value	• STATUS_SUCCESS — thread was created • STATUS_XXX — an error code

Managing Thread Priority

In general, system threads running in a driver should set their thread priority to the low end of the real-time range. The following code fragment shows how to do this.

```
VOID ThreadStartRoutine( PVOID Context )
{
        :
  KeSetPriorityThread(
        KeGetCurrentThread(),
        LOW_REALTIME_PRIORITY );
        :
}
```

Remember that real-time threads have no quantum timeout. This means that they only give up the CPU when they voluntarily go into a wait state, or when they're preempted by a thread of higher priority. So don't design any drivers that depend on automatic round-robin thread scheduling.

System Worker Threads

For occasional, quick operations at PASSIVE_LEVEL IRQL, creating and terminating a separate thread may not be very efficient. The alternative is to have one of NT's *system worker threads* perform the task. These threads use a callback mechanism to do work on behalf of any driver.

It's not difficult to use system worker threads. First, allocate storage for a WORK_QUEUE_ITEM structure. The system will use this block to keep track of your work request. Next, call **ExInitializeWorkItem** to associate a callback function in your driver with the WORK_QUEUE_ITEM.

Later, when you want a system thread to execute your callback function, call **ExQueueWorkItem** to insert the request block into one of the system work queues. You can choose to have your request executed either by a worker thread with a real-time priority, or by one with a variable priority.

Keep in mind that all drivers are sharing the same group of system worker threads. Requests that take a very long time to complete may delay the execution of requests from other drivers. If you need to perform tasks involving lengthy operations or long time delays, use a private driver thread rather than the system work queues.

14.2 THREAD SYNCHRONIZATION

Like user-mode threads in a Win32 application, system threads may need to suspend their execution until some other condition has been satisfied. This section describes the basic synchronization techniques available to system threads.

Time Synchronization

The simplest kind of synchronization involves stopping a thread's execution until a specific time interval elapses. Although you can use the Timer objects described later in this chapter, the Kernel provides a convenience function (described in Table 14.2) that's easier to use.

Table 14.2 Prototype for the KeDelayExecutionThread function

NTSTATUS KeDelayExecutionThread	IRQL == PASSIVE_LEVEL
Parameter	**Description**
IN KPROCESSOR_MODE WaitMode	KernelMode for drivers
IN BOOLEAN Alertable	FALSE for drivers
IN PLARGE_INTEGER Interval	Absolute or relative duetime
Return value	STATUS_SUCCESS — wait completed

General Synchronization

System threads can synchronize their activities in more general ways by waiting for things called *dispatcher objects*. Thread synchronization depends on the fact that a dispatcher object is always in either the *Signaled* or *Nonsignaled* state. When a thread asks to wait for a Nonsignaled dispatcher object, the thread's execution stops until the object becomes Signaled. (Waiting for a dispatcher object that's already Signaled is a no-op.) There are two different functions you can use to wait for a dispatcher object.

KeWaitForSingleObject   This function, described in Table 14.3, puts the calling thread into a wait state until a specific dispatcher object is set to the Signaled state.

Optionally, you can also specify a timeout value that will cause the thread to awaken even if the dispatcher object is Nonsignaled. If you don't pass a timeout argument, **KeWaitForSingleObject** will wait indefinitely.

Table 14.3   Prototype for the single object wait function

NTSTATUS KeWaitForSingleObject

Parameter	Description
IN PVOID Object	Pointer to an initialized dispatcher object
IN KWAIT_REASON Reason	Executive for drivers
IN KPROCESSOR_MODE WaitMode	KernelMode for drivers
IN BOOLEAN Alertable	FALSE for drivers
IN PLARGE_INTEGER Timeout	• Absolute or relative timeout value
	• NULL for an infinite wait
Return value	• STATUS_SUCCESS
	• STATUS_ALERTED
	• STATUS_TIMEOUT

KeWaitForMultipleObjects   This function, described in Table 14.4, puts the calling thread into a wait state until any or all of a group of dispatcher objects

Table 14.4   Prototype for the multiple-object wait function

NTSTATUS KeWaitForMultipleObjects

Parameter	Description
IN ULONG Count	Number of objects to wait for
IN PVOID Object[ ]	Array of pointers to dispatcher objects
IN WAIT_TYPE WaitType	• WaitAll — wait until all are Signaled
	• WaitAny — wait until one is Signaled
IN KWAIT_REASON Reason	Executive for drivers
IN KPROCESSOR_MODE WaitMode	KernelMode for drivers
IN BOOLEAN Alertable	FALSE for drivers
IN PLARGE_INTEGER Timeout	• Absolute or relative timeout value
	• NULL for an infinite wait
IN PKWAIT_BLOCK WaitBlocks[ ]	Array of wait blocks for this operation
Return value	• STATUS_SUCCESS
	• STATUS_ALERTED
	• STATUS_TIMEOUT

are set to the Signaled state. Again, you have the option of specifying a timeout value for the wait.

Be aware that there are limits on how many objects your thread can wait for at one time. Each thread has a built-in array of Wait blocks that it uses for concurrent wait operations. The thread can use this array to wait for THREAD_WAIT_OBJECTS number of objects. If you need to wait for more than this number of objects, you must supply your own array of Wait blocks when you call **KeWaitForMultipleObjects**. In either case, the number of objects you wait for cannot exceed MAXIMUM_WAIT_OBJECTS.

You can call the **KeWaitForXxx** functions either from PASSIVE_LEVEL or DISPATCH_LEVEL IRQL. If you call them from DISPATCH_LEVEL IRQL, however, you *must* specify a zero timeout value.[2] This can be useful when your real goal is to cause some side effect produced by the **KeWaitForXxx** functions.

14.3 USING DISPATCHER OBJECTS

Except for Thread objects, it's up to you to allocate storage for any dispatcher objects you plan to use. The objects must be permanently resident, so you have to put them in the Device or Controller Extension, or in some other piece of non-paged memory.

You also have to initialize the dispatcher object once with the proper **KeInitializeXxx** function before you use it. Since you can only call these functions at PASSIVE_LEVEL IRQL, you should usually initialize all dispatcher objects in your DriverEntry routine.

The following subsections describe each category of dispatcher object in greater detail.

Event Objects

An Event is a dispatcher object that must be explicitly set to the Signaled or Nonsignaled state. They are useful for notifying one or more threads of some specific occurrence. You can see this behavior in Figure 14.1, where thread A awakens B, C, and D by setting an Event object.

These objects actually come in two different flavors: Notification Events and Synchronization Events. You choose the type when you initialize the object. These two types of Events exhibit different behavior when they're put into the Signaled state. As long as a Notification Event remains Signaled, all threads waiting for the Event come out of their wait-state. You have to explicitly reset a Notification Event to put it into the Nonsignaled state. This is the same behavior exhibited by Win32 manual-reset Events.

When you put a Synchronization Event into the Signaled state, it remains there only long enough for one call to **KeWaitForXxx** to be satisfied. It then resets

---

[2] Keep in mind that specifying a timeout value of 0 is not the same as passing a NULL pointer for the Timeout argument.

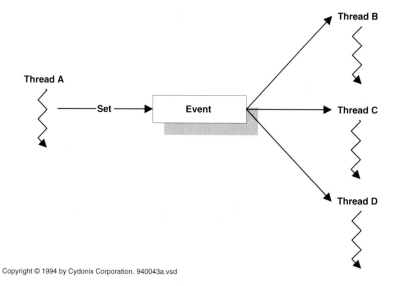

Figure 14.1   How Event objects synchronize system threads

itself to the Nonsignaled state automatically. In other words, the gate stays open until one thread passes through, and then it slams shut. This is equivalent to a Win32 auto-reset Event.

To use an Event, you need to declare some nonpaged storage for an item of type KEVENT, and then call the functions listed in Table 14.5.

Notice that you can use either of two functions to put an Event object into the Nonsignaled state. The difference is that **KeResetEvent** returns the state of the Event before it became Nonsignaled, and **KeClearEvent** does not. **KeClearEvent** is somewhat faster, so you should use it unless you specifically need to know the previous state of the Event.

Table 14.5   Use these functions to work with Event objects

How to use Event objects

IF you want to...	THEN call...	IRQL
Create an Event	KeInitializeEvent	PASSIVE_LEVEL
Create a named Event	IoCreateSynchronizationEvent	PASSIVE_LEVEL
	IoCreateNotificationEvent	
Modify Event state	KeSetEvent	≤ DISPATCH_LEVEL
	KeClearEvent	
	KeResetEvent	
Wait for a Timer	KeWaitForSingleObject	PASSIVE_LEVEL
	KeWaitForMultipleObjects	
Interrogate an Event	KeReadStateEvent	≤ DISPATCH_LEVEL

The driver that we'll be examining later in this chapter provides a good example of using Events. It has a worker thread that needs to pause until an interrupt arrives, so the thread waits for an Event object. The driver's DpcForIsr routine sets the Event into the Signaled state, waking up the worker thread.

Sharing Events between Drivers

Normally, it's rather awkward for two unrelated drivers to share an Event object created with **KeInitializeEvent**. These Event objects are referenced only by pointer, and without some kind of explicit agreement (an internal IOCTL for example), there's no simple way to pass a pointer from one driver to another. Even then, there's the issue of making sure that the driver creating the Event object doesn't unload while some other driver is using the object. Overall, it's a very messy problem. The **IoCreateNotificationEvent** and **IoCreate-SynchronizationEvent** functions make things easier by allowing you to create named Event objects. As long as two drivers use the same Event name, they will be able to get pointers to the same Event object.

Both **IoCreateXxxEvent** functions behave very much like the Win32 **CreateEvent** system service. In other words, the first driver to make a call with a specific Event name causes the Event object to be created. Each additional call using the same name simply returns a handle to the existing Event object.

There are two things to notice when you use the **IoCreateXxxEvent** functions. First, you don't supply any memory to hold the KEVENT object itself. Storage for these objects is provided by the system. When everyone using the Event releases it, the system deletes the object automatically.

The second little twist is that **IoCreateXxxEvent** calls return a handle to the Event object. If you want to use the Event object in calls to the **KeXxx** functions listed in Table 14.5, you need a pointer to the object rather than a handle. To convert a handle into an object pointer, do the following:

1. First, call **ObReferenceObjectByHandle**. This function gives you a pointer to the Event object itself and increments the object's pointer reference count.

2. If you don't need the handle for anything (and you probably don't), call **ZwClose** to release it. This reduces the object's handle reference count. (Don't do this until after you increment the pointer count; otherwise the object may be deleted.)

3. When you have finished using the Event object (normally in the driver's Unload routine), call **ObDereferenceObject** to decrement the Event object's pointer reference count and possibly delete the Event object.

You can call these functions only from PASSIVE_LEVEL IRQL which limits the places in your driver where you can use them.

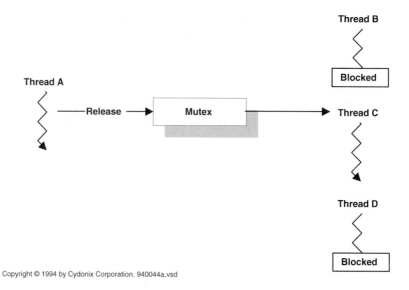

Figure 14.2   How Mutex objects synchronize system threads

Mutex Objects

A Mutex (short for mutual exclusion) is a dispatcher object that can be owned by only one thread at a time. The object becomes Nonsignaled when a thread owns it and Signaled when it's available. Mutexes provide an easy mechanism for coordinating mutually exclusive access to some shared resource, usually memory.

Figure 14.2 shows threads B, C, and D waiting for a Mutex owned by thread A. When A releases the Mutex, one of the waiting threads will wake up and become its new owner.

To use a Mutex, you need to declare some nonpaged storage for an item of type KMUTEX, and then call the functions listed in Table 14.6. Be aware that when you initialize a Mutex, it is always set to the Signaled state.

Table 14.6   Use these functions to work with Mutex objects

How to use Mutex objects

IF you want to...	THEN call...	IRQL
Create a Mutex	KeInitializeMutex	PASSIVE_LEVEL
Request Mutex ownership	KeWaitForSingleObject KeWaitForMultipleObjects	PASSIVE_LEVEL
Give up Mutex ownership	KeReleaseMutex	PASSIVE_LEVEL
Interrogate Mutex	KeReadStateMutex	≤ DISPATCH_LEVEL

If a thread calls **KeWaitForXxx** on a Mutex it already owns, the thread never waits. Instead, the Mutex increments an internal counter to record the fact that this thread is making recursive ownership requests. When the thread wants to free the Mutex, it has to call **KeReleaseMutex** as many times as it requested ownership. Only then will the Mutex go into the Signaled state. This is the same behavior exhibited by Win32 Mutex objects.

It's also crucial that your driver release any Mutexes it might be holding before it makes a transition back into user mode. The NT Kernel will bugcheck if any of your driver threads attempt to return control to the I/O Manager while owning a Mutex. So, for example, a DriverEntry or Dispatch routine isn't allowed to acquire a Mutex which would later be released by some other Dispatch routine or by a system thread.

Semaphore Objects

A Semaphore is a dispatcher object that maintains a count. The object remains Signaled as long as its count is greater than zero, and Nonsignaled when the count is zero.

Figure 14.3 shows the operation of a Semaphore. Threads B, C, and D are all waiting for a Semaphore whose count is zero. When thread A calls **KeRelease-Semaphore** twice, the count increments to two, and two of the waiting threads are allowed to resume execution. Waking up the threads also causes the Semaphore to decrement back to zero.

Again, the driver in Section 14.4 provides a good example. Its Dispatch routines increment a Semaphore each time they add an IRP to an internal work queue. As a worker thread removes IRPs from the queue, it decrements the Semaphore and finally goes into a wait state when the queue is empty.

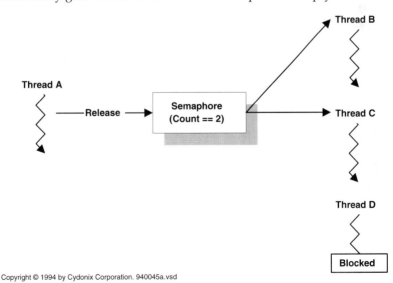

Figure 14.3   How Semaphore objects synchronize system threads

Table 14.7   Use these functions to work with Semaphore objects

How to use Semaphore objects

IF you want to...	THEN call...	IRQL
Create a Semaphore	KeInitializeSemaphore	PASSIVE_LEVEL
Decrement Semaphore	KeWaitForSingleObject KeWaitForMultipleObjects	PASSIVE_LEVEL
Increment Semaphore	KeReleaseSemaphore	≤ DISPATCH_LEVEL
Interrogate Semaphore	KeReadStateSemaphore	Any

To use a Semaphore, you need to allocate some storage for an item of type KSEMAPHORE, then call the functions listed in Table 14.7.

Timer Objects

A Timer is a dispatcher object with a timeout value. When you start a Timer, it goes into the Nonsignaled state until its timeout value expires. At that point, it becomes Signaled. In Chapter 10, you saw that Timer objects can cause Custom-TimerDpc routines to execute. Since they are just Kernel dispatcher objects, you can also use them in calls to **KeWaitForXxx**.

Figure 14.4 illustrates the operation of a Timer object. Thread A starts a Timer and then calls **KeWaitForSingleObject**. The thread blocks until the Timer expires. At that point, the Timer goes into the Signaled state and the thread wakes up.

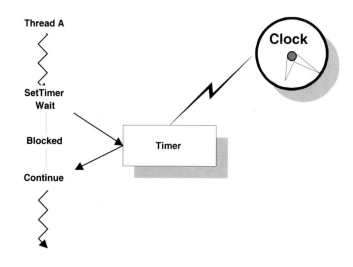

Figure 14.4   How Timer objects synchronize system threads

Timer objects actually come in two different flavors: Notification Timers and Synchronization Timers. You choose the type when you initialize the object. Although both types of Timer go into the Signaled state when their timeout value expires, their behavior from that point on is different.

When a Notification Timer times out, it remains in the Signaled state until it's explicitly reset. While the Timer is Signaled, all threads waiting for the Timer are awakened. Earlier versions of Windows NT supported only Notification Timers.

When a Synchronization Timer expires, it remains in the Signaled state only long enough to satisfy a single **KeWaitForXxx** request. At that point, the Timer becomes Nonsignaled automatically. Synchronization Timers are a new feature of Windows NT 4.0.

To use a Timer, you need to allocate some storage for an item of type KTIMER and then call the functions listed in Table 14.8.

Thread Objects

System threads are also dispatcher objects, which means they have a signal state. When a system thread terminates, its Thread object changes from the Non-signaled to the Signaled state. This allows your driver to synchronize its cleanup operations by waiting for the Thread object.

One thing to notice is that when you call **PsCreateSystemThread**, you get a *handle* to the Thread object. If you want to use a Thread object in a call to **KeWait-ForXxx**, you need a *pointer* to the object rather than a handle. To convert a handle into an object pointer, do the following:

1. Call **ObReferenceObjectByHandle**. This function gives you a pointer to the Thread object itself and increments the object's pointer reference count.

2. If you don't need the handle for anything (and you probably don't), call **ZwClose** to release it. This decrements the object's handle reference count.

3. After the thread terminates, call **ObDereferenceObject** to decrement the Thread object's pointer reference count and possibly delete the Thread object.

Table 14.8 Use these functions to work with Timer objects

How to use Timer objects

IF you want to...	THEN call...	IRQL
Create a Timer	KeInitializeTimerEx	PASSIVE_LEVEL
Start a one-shot Timer	KeSetTimer	$\leq$ DISPATCH_LEVEL
Start a repeating Timer	KeSetTimerEx	$\leq$ DISPATCH_LEVEL
Stop a Timer	KeCancelTimer	$\leq$ DISPATCH_LEVEL
Wait for a Timer	KeWaitForSingleObject	PASSIVE_LEVEL
	KeWaitForMultipleObjects	
Interrogate a Timer	KeReadTimerState	$\leq$ DISPATCH_LEVEL

You can call these functions only from PASSIVE_LEVEL IRQL which limits the places in your driver where you can use them.

Variations on the Mutex

The NT Executive supports two variations on Mutex objects. The following subsections describe them briefly. In general, using these objects instead of Kernel Mutexes can result in better driver performance. See the NT DDK documentation for more complete information.

Fast Mutexes   A Fast Mutex is a synchronization object that acts like a Kernel Mutex, except that it doesn't allow recursive ownership requests. By removing this feature, the Fast Mutex doesn't have to do as much work and its speed improves.

The Fast Mutex itself is an object of type FAST_MUTEX that you associate with one or more data items needing protection. Any code touching the data items must acquire ownership of the corresponding FAST_MUTEX first. Use the functions listed in Table 14.9 to work with Fast Mutexes. Notice that these objects have their own functions for requesting ownership. You can't use **KeWaitForXxx** to acquire Fast Mutexes.

Table 14.9   Use these functions to work with Fast Mutexes

How to use Fast Mutexes

IF you want to...	THEN call...	IRQL
Create a Fast Mutex	ExInitializeFastMutex	≤ DISPATCH_LEVEL
Request Fast Mutex ownership	ExAcquireFastMutex	< DISPATCH_LEVEL
Give up Fast Mutex ownership	ExReleaseFastMutex	< DISPATCH_LEVEL

Executive Resources   Another synchronization object that behaves very much like a Kernel Mutex is an Executive Resource. Here, the main difference is that a Resource can either be owned exclusively by a single thread, or shared by multiple threads for read access. Since it's common (in the real world) for multiple readers to request simultaneous access to a resource, Executive Resource objects provide better throughput than standard Kernel Mutexes.

The Executive Resource itself is just an object of type ERESOURCE that you associate with one or more data items needing protection. Any code planning to touch the data items has to acquire ownership of the corresponding ERESOURCE first. Table 14.10 lists the functions that work with Executive Resources. Notice that these objects have their own functions for requesting ownership. You can't use **KeWaitForXxx** to acquire Executive Resources.

Table 14.10 Use these functions to work with Executive Resources

How to use Executive Resources

IF you want to...	THEN call...	IRQL
Create	ExInitializeResourceLite	≤ DISPATCH_LEVEL
Acquire	ExAcquireResourceExclusiveLite	< DISPATCH_LEVEL
	ExAcquiredResourceSharedLite	< DISPATCH_LEVEL
	ExTryToAcquireResourceExclusiveLite	< DISPATCH_LEVEL
	ExConvertExclusiveToSharedLite	< DISPATCH_LEVEL
Release	ExReleaseResourceForThreadLite	≤ DISPATCH_LEVEL
Interrogate	ExIsResourceAcquiredSharedLite	≤ DISPATCH_LEVEL
	ExIsResourceAcquiredExclusiveLite	≤ DISPATCH_LEVEL
Delete	ExDeleteResourceLite	≤ DISPATCH_LEVEL

Synchronization Deadlocks

Deadlock situations can occur whenever multiple threads compete for simultaneous ownership of multiple resources. Figure 14.5 shows the simplest form of this problem:

1. Thread A acquires resource X.

2. Thread B acquires resource Y.

3. Thread A requests ownership of resource Y and goes into a wait state until B releases Y.

4. Thread B then requests ownership of resource X. This causes B to go into a wait state until A releases X. Deadlock.

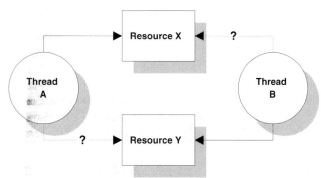

Figure 14.5 How a multiple-resource deadlock occurs

You can cause this kind of deadlock using Events, Mutexes, or Semaphores. Even Thread objects can deadlock waiting for each other to terminate. There are two general approaches to solving deadlock problems:

- Use the Timeout argument of the **KeWaitForXxx** functions to limit the time you wait. While this technique may help you detect a deadlock, it doesn't really correct the underlying problem.

- Force all the threads using a given set of resources to acquire them in the same order. In the previous example, if A and B had both gone after resource X first and then Y second, there would have been no deadlock.

Mutex objects give you some protection against deadlocks through the use of level numbers. When you initialize a Mutex, you have to assign a level number to it. Later, when a thread attempts to acquire the Mutex, the Kernel will not grant ownership if that thread is holding any Mutex with a lower level number. By enforcing this policy, the Kernel avoids deadlocks involving multiple Mutexes.

14.4 CODE EXAMPLE: A THREAD-BASED DRIVER

This section presents a modified version of the packet-based slave DMA driver that you saw back in Chapter 12. What's different about this driver is that it uses a system thread to do most of the I/O processing. As a result, it spends very little time at DISPATCH_LEVEL IRQL or DIRQL and doesn't interfere as much with other system components. You can find the code for this example in the **CH14\DRIVER** directory on the disk that accompanies this book.

How the Driver Works

The driver you're about to see is unlike anything that's appeared so far in this book. Figure 14.6 gives a high-level view of its inner workings. One of the first things to notice is that the driver has no Start I/O routine. When a user-mode I/O request arrives, one of the driver's Dispatch routines simply adds the IRP to a work queue associated with the Device object. Then the Dispatch routine calls KeReleaseSemaphore to increment a Semaphore object that keeps track of the number of IRPs in the work queue.

Each Device object has its own system thread that processes these I/O requests. This thread is in an endless loop that begins with a call to KeWaitForSingleObject on the Semaphore. If the Semaphore object has a nonzero count, the thread will remove an IRP from the work queue and perform the I/O operation. On the other hand, if the count is zero the thread will go into a wait state until the Dispatch routine inserts another IRP in the queue.

When the thread needs to perform a data transfer, it starts the device and then uses **KeWaitForSingleObject** to wait for an Event object. The driver's Dpc-ForIsr routine will set this Event into the Signaled state after an interrupt arrives.

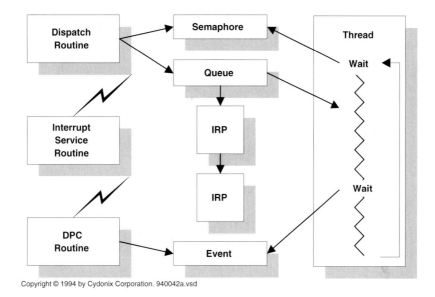

Copyright © 1994 by Cydonix Corporation. 940042a.vsd

Figure 14.6   Architecture of the thread-based DMA driver

When the driver's Unload routine needs to kill the system thread it sets a flag in the Device Extension and increments the Semaphore object. If the thread was asleep waiting for the Semaphore object, it will wake up, see the flag, and terminate itself. If it's in the middle of an I/O operation, it won't see the flag until it completes the current IRP.

The DEVICE_EXTENSION Structure in XXDRIVER.H

This file contains all the usual driver-defined data structures. The following excerpt shows only those fields that driver needs in order to manage the system thread and its work queue. Other fields are identical to those in the packet-based slave DMA example of Chapter 12.

```
typedef struct _DEVICE_EXTENSION
{
            :
        PETHREAD ThreadObject;  ❶
        BOOLEAN ThreadShouldStop;

        KEVENT AdapterObjectIsAcquired;  ❷
        KEVENT DeviceOperationComplete;

        KSEMAPHORE IrpQueueSemaphore;  ❸
        LIST_ENTRY IrpQueueListHead;
        KSPIN_LOCK IrpQueueSpinLock;

} DEVICE_EXTENSION, *PDEVICE_EXTENSION;
```

❶ Once the thread is running, other parts of the driver can use the Thread object pointer synchronize with it. The BOOLEAN flag tells the thread when it's time to shut down.

❷ The thread waits for these Event objects at appropriate places in its processing cycle. Other parts of the driver set them into the Signaled state when interesting things happen.

❸ The work queue consists of a doubly-linked list guarded by a spin lock and a Semaphore object that keeps track of the number of IRPs in the queue.

The XxCreateDevice Function in INIT.C

This portion of the example shows the initialization code for the Thread object, the work queue, and the various synchronization objects used to process an I/O request. Remember that **DriverEntry** calls **XxCreateDevice** once for each Device object.

```
static NTSTATUS
XxCreateDevice (
        IN PDRIVER_OBJECT DriverObject,
        IN INTERFACE_TYPE BusType,
        IN ULONG BusNumber,
        IN PDEVICE_BLOCK DeviceBlock,
        IN ULONG NtDeviceNumber
        )
{
                :
        KeInitializeSpinLock(
            &pDevExt->IrpQueueSpinLock ); ❶

        InitializeListHead(
            &pDevExt->IrpQueueListHead );

        KeInitializeSemaphore(
            &pDevExt->IrpQueueSemaphore,
            0,
            MAXLONG );

        KeInitializeEvent( ❷
            &pDevExt->AdapterObjectIsAcquired,
            SynchronizationEvent,
            FALSE );

        KeInitializeEvent(
            &pDevExt->DeviceOperationComplete,
            SynchronizationEvent,
            FALSE );
```

```
       pDevExt->ThreadShouldStop = FALSE;

       status = PsCreateSystemThread( ❸
                  &ThreadHandle,
                  (ACCESS_MASK)0,
                  NULL,
                  (HANDLE) 0,
                  NULL,
                  XxThreadMain,
                  pDevExt );

       if( !NT_SUCCESS( status ))
       {
             IoDeleteSymbolicLink( &linkName );
             IoDeleteDevice( pDevObj );
             return status;
       }

       ObReferenceObjectByHandle( ❹
             ThreadHandle,
             THREAD_ALL_ACCESS,
             NULL,
             KernelMode,
             &pDevExt->ThreadObject,
             NULL );

       ZwClose( ThreadHandle );

       IoConnectInterrupt(...);
                  :
}
```

❶ This section of code sets up the work queue used by the thread.

❷ These calls initialize the Event objects that signal ownership of the Adapter object and the arrival of a device interrupt. Notice that they're both synchronization (i.e., auto-reset) Events.

❸ The call to **PsCreateSystemThread** starts the thread. The entry point function is **XxThreadMain** and it will receive a pointer to the Device Extension as its Context argument. Because this is an asynchronous operation, the status of **PsCreateSystemThread** is only telling you that the thread was started successfully. It says nothing about what happens to the thread afterwards.

❹ **PsCreateSystemThread** gives back a handle to Thread rather than a pointer to the Thread object itself. This section of code gets a pointer to the object and then releases the (unneeded) handle.

The XxDispatchReadWrite Function in DISPATCH.C

This portion of the example shows how the Dispatch routine of this driver works. Its operation is relatively straightforward: After checking for a zero-length transfer, it puts the IRP into the pending state and inserts it into the work queue attached to the target Device object. It then increments the count in the work queue's Semaphore object. Notice that there are no calls to **IoStartPacket** because there is no Start I/O routine.

```
NTSTATUS
XxDispatchReadWrite(
        IN PDEVICE_OBJECT pDO,
        IN PIRP Irp
        )
{
        PIO_STACK_LOCATION IrpStack =
                    IoGetCurrentIrpStackLocation( Irp );

        PDEVICE_EXTENSION pDE = pDO->DeviceExtension;

        //
        // Check for zero-length transfers
        //
        if( IrpStack->Parameters.Read.Length == 0 )
        {
                Irp->IoStatus.Status = STATUS_SUCCESS;
                Irp->IoStatus.Information = 0;
                IoCompleteRequest( Irp, IO_NO_INCREMENT );
                return STATUS_SUCCESS;
        }

        //
        // Start device operation
        //
        IoMarkIrpPending( Irp );

        //
        // Add the IRP to the thread's work queue
        //
        ExInterlockedInsertTailList(
                &pDE->IrpQueueListHead,
                &Irp->Tail.Overlay.ListEntry,
                &pDE->IrpQueueSpinLock );

        KeReleaseSemaphore(
                &pDE->IrpQueueSemaphore,
                0,                      // No priority boost
                1,              // Increment semaphore by 1
```

```
                        FALSE );  // No WaitForXxx after this call
            return STATUS_PENDING;
    }
```

THREAD.C

This module contains the main thread function and any routines needed to manage the thread.

XxThreadMain   Here is the IRP-processing engine itself. Its job is to pull I/O requests from the work queue in the Device Extension and perform the data transfer operation. This function continues to wait for new IRPs until the Unload routine tells it to shut down.

```
VOID
XxThreadMain(
        IN PVOID Context
        )
    {
        PDEVICE_EXTENSION DevExtension = Context;

        PDEVICE_OBJECT DeviceObject =
                DevExtension->DeviceObject;

        PLIST_ENTRY ListEntry;
        PIRP Irp;
        CCHAR PriorityBoost;

        KeSetPriorityThread(
                KeGetCurrentThread(),
                LOW_REALTIME_PRIORITY );  ❶

        //
        // Now enter the main IRP-processing loop
        //
        while( TRUE )
        {
                KeWaitForSingleObject( ❷
                        &DevExtension->IrpQueueSemaphore,
                        Executive,
                        KernelMode,
                        FALSE,
                        NULL );

                if( DevExtension->ThreadShouldStop )  ❸
                PsTerminateSystemThread( STATUS_SUCCESS);
```

```
                //
                // It must be a real request. Get an IRP
                //
                ListEntry =
                        ExInterlockedRemoveHeadList(
                          &DevExtension->IrpQueueListHead,
                          &DevExtension->IrpQueueSpinLock );

                Irp = CONTAINING_RECORD(
                            ListEntry,
                            IRP,
                            Tail.Overlay.ListEntry );

                PriorityBoost =
                        XxPerformDataTransfer( ❹
                            DeviceObject,
                            Irp );

                IoCompleteRequest( Irp, PriorityBoost );
            }
        }
```

❶ System threads normally start running down in the variable priority range. The usual practice is to move the thread to the lowest of the time-critical scheduling priorities.

❷ The thread will wait here indefinitely for an IRP to appear in the work queue or for the Unload routine to stop the thread.

❸ When the thread awakens, it has to see whether the wake-up call was the result of an I/O request or a thread shutdown signal. The flag in the Device Extension will give a clue.

❹ This function processes the IRP. This is a synchronous call which doesn't return until the data transfer operation is done. It returns a priority boost value which the thread then uses when it completes the IRP. After releasing the IRP, the thread goes back to the top of the loop and waits for the Semaphore object again.

XxKillThread   This function notifies the thread associated with a particular Device object that it's time to quit. To simplify things, this function stops and waits until the target thread is gone. Consequently, it can only be called from PASSIVE_LEVEL IRQL.

```
    VOID
    XxKillThread(
            IN PDEVICE_EXTENSION pDE
            )
    {
```

```
        //
        // Set the Stop flag
        //
        pDE->ThreadShouldStop = TRUE;

        //
        // Make sure the thread wakes up
        //
        KeReleaseSemaphore(
                &pDE->IrpQueueSemaphore,
                0,              // No priority boost
                1,              // Increment semaphore by 1
                TRUE );         // WaitForXxx after this call

        //
        // Wait for the thread to terminate
        //
        KeWaitForSingleObject(
                &pDE->ThreadObject,
                Executive,
                KernelMode,
                FALSE,
                NULL );

        ObDereferenceObject( &pDE->ThreadObject );
    }
```

TRANSFER.C

This portion of the example contains the support routines that perform I/O operations. A great deal of what's in here is derived from the packet-based slave DMA driver in Chapter 12. Consequently, only those features that differ significantly will be described in detail.

The main thing to notice is that very little work actually happens inside the Adapter Control or DpcForIsr routines. Instead of doing their usual jobs, these functions just set Event objects to signal the thread's data transfer routines that they can proceed.

XxPerformDataTransfer   This function moves an entire buffer of data to or from the device. This may include splitting the transfer over several device operations if there aren't enough mapping registers to handle it all at once. This routines runs at PASSIVE_LEVEL IRQL and doesn't return to the caller until everything is done.

```
CCHAR
XxPerformDataTransfer(
        IN PDEVICE_OBJECT DeviceObject,
```

```
        IN PIRP Irp
        )
{

        PIO_STACK_LOCATION IrpStack =
            IoGetCurrentIrpStackLocation( Irp );

        PDEVICE_EXTENSION pDE =
            DeviceObject->DeviceExtension;

        PMDL Mdl = Irp->MdlAddress;
        ULONG MapRegsNeeded;
        NTSTATUS status;

        //
        // Set the I/O direction flag
        //
        if( IrpStack->MajorFunction
            == IRP_MJ_WRITE )
        {
            pDE->WriteToDevice = TRUE;
        }
        else
        {
            pDE->WriteToDevice = FALSE;
        }

        //
        // Set up bookkeeping values
        //
        pDE->BytesRequested =
            MmGetMdlByteCount( Mdl );

        pDE->BytesRemaining =
            pDE->BytesRequested;

        pDE->TransferVA =
            MmGetMdlVirtualAddress( Mdl );

        //
        // Flush CPU cache if necessary
        //
        KeFlushIoBuffers(
            Irp->MdlAddress,
            !pDE->WriteToDevice,
            TRUE );

        //
        // Calculate size of first partial
```

```
                    // transfer
                    //
                    pDE->TransferSize = pDE->BytesRemaining;

                    MapRegsNeeded =
                            ADDRESS_AND_SIZE_TO_SPAN_PAGES(
                                    pDE->TransferVA,
                                    pDE->TransferSize );
                    if( MapRegsNeeded > pDE->MapRegisterCount )
                    {
                            MapRegsNeeded =
                                    pDE->MapRegisterCount;

                            pDE->TransferSize =
                                    MapRegsNeeded * PAGE_SIZE -
                                    MmGetMdlByteOffset( Mdl );
                    }
                    //
                    // Acquire the adapter object.
                    //
                    status = XxAcquireAdapterObject( ❶
                                    pDE,
                                    MapRegsNeeded );
                    if( !NT_SUCCESS( status ))
                    {
                            Irp->IoStatus.Status = status;
                            Irp->IoStatus.Information = 0;
                            return IO_NO_INCREMENT;
                    }
                    //
                    // Try to perform the first partial
                    // transfer
                    //
                    status =
                            XxPerformSynchronousTransfer( ❷
                                    DeviceObject,
                                    Irp );
                    if( !NT_SUCCESS( status ))
                    {
                            IoFreeAdapterChannel( pDE->AdapterObject
            );
                            Irp->IoStatus.Status = status;
                            Irp->IoStatus.Information = 0;
                            return IO_NO_INCREMENT;
```

```
            }
            //
            // It worked. Update the bookkeeping
            // information.
            //
            pDE->TransferVA += pDE->TransferSize;
            pDE->BytesRemaining -= pDE->TransferSize;

            while( pDE->BytesRemaining >0 )  ❸
            {
                    //
                    // Try to do all of it in one operation
                    //
                    pDE->TransferSize = pDE->BytesRemaining;

                    MapRegsNeeded =
                            ADDRESS_AND_SIZE_TO_SPAN_PAGES(
                                    pDE->TransferVA,
                                    pDE->TransferSize );

                    //
                    // If the remainder of the buffer is more
                    // than we can handle in one I/O. Reduce
                    // our expectations.
                    //
                    if( MapRegsNeeded > pDE->MapRegisterCount
)
                    {
                            MapRegsNeeded =
                                    pDE->MapRegisterCount;

                            pDE->TransferSize =
                                    MapRegsNeeded * PAGE_SIZE -
                                    BYTE_OFFSET( pDE->TransferVA
);
                    }
                    //
                    // Try to perform a device operation.
                    //
                    status =
                            XxPerformSynchronousTransfer(
                                    DeviceObject,
                                    Irp );

                    if( !NT_SUCCESS( status )) break;
                    //
                    // It worked. Update the bookkeeping
```

```
                        // information for the next cycle.
                        //
                        pDE->TransferVA += pDE->TransferSize;
                        pDE->BytesRemaining -= pDE->TransferSize;
               }

               IoFreeAdapterChannel( pDE->AdapterObject ); ❹

               Irp->IoStatus.Status = status; ❺
               Irp->IoStatus.Information =
                            pDE->BytesRequested -
                                  pDE->BytesRemaining;
               //
               // Since there has been at least one I/O
               // operation, give the IRP a priority boost.
               //
               return IO_DISK_INCREMENT; ❻
     }
```

❶ Before starting a data transfer, the Device object has to acquire its Adapter object. The thread calls this synchronous helper function to grab the Adapter object. This is different from the callback model used by the DMA driver in Chapter 12.

❷ Once the Adapter object is secured, the driver can try to perform the first partial data transfer. Again, since this code is running in the context of a system thread, it can stop and wait for the I/O operation to complete. If there's an error, processing stops and the IRP is sent back with no priority boost.

❸ If there's more data to transfer, continue to step through the buffer and perform partial DMA transfers.

❹ When the last partial transfer is done, release the DMA Adapter object.

❺ The final status of the IRP will be the status of the last data transfer operation. Also calculate the number of bytes actually transferred.

❻ Tell the caller to apply a priority boost to the IRP. This makes sense since there has been at least one actual device operation.

XxAcquireAdapterObject and XxAdapterControl These two functions work together to give the thread a synchronous mechanism for acquiring ownership of the Adapter object. **XxAcquireAdapterObject** runs in the context of a system thread so it can stop and wait for a nonzero time interval.

```
static NTSTATUS
XxAcquireAdapterObject(
        IN PDEVICE_EXTENSION pDE,
        IN ULONG MapRegsNeeded
```

```
            )
    {
            KIRQL OldIrql;
            NTSTATUS status;

            KeRaiseIrql( DISPATCH_LEVEL, &OldIrql ); ❶

            status = IoAllocateAdapterChannel(
                    pDE->AdapterObject,
                    pDE->DeviceObject,
                    MapRegsNeeded,
                    XxAdapterControl,
                    pDE );

            KeLowerIrql( OldIrql );

            //
            // If the call failed, it's because there
            // weren't enough mapping registers.
            //
            if( !NT_SUCCESS( status ))
            {
                    return status;
            }

            KeWaitForSingleObject( ❷
                    &pDE->AdapterObjectIsAcquired,
                    Executive,
                    KernelMode,
                    FALSE,
                    NULL );

            return STATUS_SUCCESS;
    }

    static IO_ALLOCATION_ACTION
    XxAdapterControl(
            IN PDEVICE_OBJECT DeviceObject,
            IN PIRP Irp,
            IN PVOID MapRegisterBase,
            IN PVOID Context
            )
    {
            PDEVICE_EXTENSION pDE = Context;

            pDE->MapRegisterBase = MapRegisterBase; ❸

            KeSetEvent( ❹
                    &pDE->AdapterObjectIsAcquired,
                    0,
                    FALSE );
```

```
        return KeepObject;  ❺
}
```

❶ Only code running at DISPATCH_LEVEL IRQL can request ownership of the Adapter object. Consequently, this routine raises its IRQL level before calling **IoAllocateAdapterChannel**. Once it makes the call, it returns to PASSIVE_LEVEL IRQL.

❷ The function then stops and waits for the Adapter Control routine to set a synchronization Event. That will be the signal that Adapter object has been acquired.

❸ It's important for the Adapter Control routine to store the mapping register handle because the thread will need it to set up any DMA data transfers.

❹ Next, let the waiting thread know that it can use the DMA hardware.

❺ Finally, return a value of KeepObject in order to hold on to the Adapter Object.

XxPerformSynchronousTransfer   Running in the context of the system thread, this function performs a single data transfer operation. It doesn't return to the caller until the transfer finishes. The main thing to notice here is that the function uses an Event object to wait for the arrival of a device interrupt.

```
static NTSTATUS
XxPerformSynchronousTransfer(
        IN PDEVICE_OBJECT DeviceObject,
        IN PIRP Irp
        )
  {
        PDEVICE_EXTENSION pDE =
                DeviceObject->DeviceExtension;

        //
        // Set up the system DMA controller
        // attached to this device.
        //
        IoMapTransfer(
                pDE->AdapterObject,
                Irp->MdlAddress,
                pDE->MapRegisterBase,
                pDE->TransferVA,
                &pDE->TransferSize,
                pDE->WriteToDevice );

        //
        // Start the device
        //
```

```
XxWriteControl(
      pDE,
      XX_CTL_INTENB | XX_CTL_DMA_GO );

//
// The DPC routine will set an Event
// object when the I/O operation is
// done. Stop here and wait for it.
//
KeWaitForSingleObject(
      &pDE->DeviceOperationComplete,
      Executive,
      KernelMode,
      FALSE,
      NULL );

//
// Flush data out of the Adapater
// object cache.
//
IoFlushAdapterBuffers(
      pDE->AdapterObject,
      Irp->MdlAddress,
      pDE->MapRegisterBase,
      pDE->TransferVA,
      pDE->TransferSize,
      pDE->WriteToDevice );

//
// Check for device errors
//
if( !XX_STS_OK( pDE->DeviceStatus ))
      return STATUS_DEVICE_DATA_ERROR;
else
      return STATUS_SUCCESS;
}
```

XxDpcForIsr   When the device generates an interrupt, the Interrupt Service routines (not shown here) saves the status of the hardware and requests a DPC. Eventually, **XxDpcForIsr** executes and just sets an Event object into the Signaled state. **XxPerformSynchronousTransfer** (which has been waiting for this Event object) wakes up and continues processing the current IRP.

```
VOID
XxDpcForIsr(
      IN PKDPC Dpc,
      IN PDEVICE_OBJECT DeviceObject,
```

```
        IN PIRP Irp,
        IN PVOID Context
        )
{
        PDEVICE_EXTENSION pDE = Context;

        KeSetEvent(
                &pDE->DeviceOperationComplete,
                0,
                FALSE );

        return;
}
```

14.5 SUMMARY

This chapter has presented you with an alternative driver architecture based on the use of system threads. Although it's not a good choice for most drivers, this model can be useful if you're trying to manage certain kinds of legacy devices, or devices that would interfere with normal system operation if you used the standard interrupt-driven architecture.

Now that you have a good understanding of how to work at the hardware level, it's time to see how higher-level drivers are organized. That's the subject of the next chapter.

Higher-Level Drivers

One of the I/O Manager's nifty features is that it lets you stack drivers on top of one another. This permits one driver to use another as a prepackaged component and send requests to it just as a user-mode thread might. As you saw back in Chapter 1, NT's SCSI and network driver architectures both rely on this building-block approach. This chapter describes the techniques you need to use if you want to design your own driver hierarchies.

15.1 AN OVERVIEW OF INTERMEDIATE DRIVERS

Before getting into a discussion of writing intermediate drivers, it's a good idea to define just what they are. This section also explores some of the trade-offs inherent in using a hierarchical driver architecture.

What Are Intermediate Drivers?

For the purposes of this chapter, an *intermediate driver* is any kernel-mode driver that issues I/O requests to another driver. Intermediate drivers are not usually responsible for any direct, register-level manipulation of hardware resources. Instead, they often depend on a lower-level device driver to perform hardware operations. This may seem like an overly broad definition, but the truth is that intermediate drivers can assume a wide variety of shapes.

From an implementation standpoint, you can classify an intermediate driver according to its relationship with the driver directly below it. Taking this approach, you end up with three distinct groups:

- **Layered drivers** — This generic category includes just about any driver that uses the I/O Manager's standard calling mechanism to send requests to another driver.

- **Filter drivers** — This is a special category of intermediate drivers that transparently intercept requests intended for some other driver. These drivers also use the I/O Manager's standard calling mechanism.

- **Tightly coupled drivers** — This category includes any pair of drivers that define a private interface between themselves — one that doesn't use the I/O Manager's calling mechanism for the bulk of the communication.

Later parts of this chapter will explain how to develop drivers in each of these families.

Should You Use a Layered Architecture?

One important thing to decide is whether your driver design would benefit from being broken into a series of layers, or whether it should be structured as a single monolithic unit. The following will help you understand the trade-offs of taking a layered approach.

Why you should Depending on your goals, using multiple driver layers can provide a number of benefits. For example, it allows you to separate higher-level protocol issues from management of the specific underlying hardware. This makes it possible to support a wider variety of hardware without having to rewrite large amounts of code. It also promotes flexibility by allowing the same protocol driver to plug into different hardware drivers at runtime. This is the approach taken by NT network drivers.

If several different kinds of peripherals can all be attached to the same controller (as in the case of a SCSI adapter), layering allows you to decouple management of the peripheral from management of the controller. To do this, you write a single device driver for the controller (the *port driver*) and separate higher-level *class drivers* for each type of attached peripheral. The two main benefits here are that the class drivers are smaller and simpler and (assuming a well-defined protocol) the class and port drivers can come from different vendors.[1]

---

[1] This is exactly what NT's SCSI architecture does. Expect to see more of this kind of thing in future versions of Windows NT when buses like the IEEE 1394 bus and the Universal Serial Bus make their appearance.

Layering also makes it possible to hide hardware limitations from users of a device, or to add features not supported by the hardware itself. For example, if a given piece of hardware can only handle transfers of a certain size, you might stack another driver on top of it that would break oversized transfers into smaller pieces. Users of the device would be unaware of the device's shortcomings.

Inserting driver layers gives you a transparent way to add or remove features from a product without having to maintain multiple code bases for the same product. NT's fault-tolerant disks are one example of this. They're implemented as a separate driver layer which is shipped with NT Server but not with NT Workstation.

Why you shouldn't   Of course, there are costs you have to consider if you're thinking about a layered architecture. First of all, I/O requests incur some extra overhead because each IRP has to take a trip through the I/O Manager every time it passes from one driver to another. To some extent, you can reduce this overhead by defining a private interdriver interface that partially bypasses the I/O Manager.

It also takes somewhat more design effort to make sure that the separate driver components fit together seamlessly. In the absence of an external standard, this can be especially painful if some of the drivers are coming from different vendors.

Since the overall functionality is no longer contained in a single driver executable, there's somewhat more bookkeeping involved in managing the drivers. This also has some impact on maintaining version compatibility between various members of the hierarchy.

Finally, installing layered drivers is a little more involved since each one will need its own area in the Registry. In addition, it's necessary to set up dependency relationships among the various drivers in the hierarchy to make sure they start in the proper order.[2]

15.2 WRITING LAYERED DRIVERS

Layered drivers are the most general type of intermediate driver. They depend for their operation on a well-defined interdriver calling mechanism provided by the I/O Manager. This is the first of three sections that explain how this mechanism works, and what a driver needs to do if it wants to use another driver as a component.

How Layered Drivers Work

As you can see from Figure 15.1, a layered driver exposes one or more named Device objects to which clients send I/O requests. When an IRP representing one of these requests arrives, the layered driver can process it in two different ways: In some cases, it might send the IRP directly to a lower-level driver.

---

[2] See Chapter 16 for more information about creating startup dependencies among drivers.

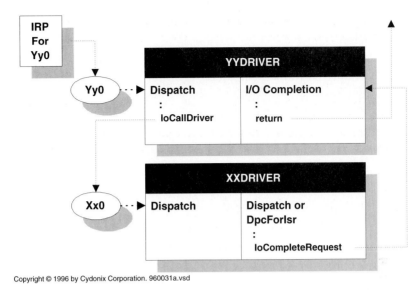

Copyright © 1996 by Cydonix Corporation. 960031a.vsd

Figure 15.1 How a layered driver works

Alternatively, the layered driver might hold the IRP in a pending state while it allocates additional IRPs and sends them to one or more lower-level drivers.

   If the layered driver needs to regain control after a lower-level driver finishes with an IRP, it can attach an I/O Completion routine to the IRP. This routine will execute when the lower driver calls **IoCompleteRequest**.

Initialization and Cleanup in Layered Drivers

   Like every other kernel-mode driver, a layered driver must have a main entry point called **DriverEntry**. If the driver is to be unloaded while the system is running, it needs an Unload routine as well. The following subsections describe what these routines have to do.

   DriverEntry routine   The initialization steps performed by a layered driver are similar to those of a regular device driver. The main difference is that a layered driver doesn't have any direct contact with hardware, so all the hardware detection and allocation code that you saw in Chapter 7 will be missing. In general, the DriverEntry routine of a layered driver will do the following:

1. It uses **IoCreateDevice** to build the upper-level Device object that will be seen by the outside world. Like the Device objects created by hardware drivers, this one has its own unique name.

2. **DriverEntry** then calls **IoGetDeviceObjectPointer**. Given a device name, this function returns the address of the target Device object and a pointer to a File object associated with the target Device. Normally, **DriverEnry** saves the

target Device object pointer in the Device Extension of the upper-level Device object.

3.   Next, it increments the pointer reference count on the target Device object by calling **ObReferenceObjectByPointer**. This is necessary because **IoGetDeviceObjectPointer** automatically increments the reference count on the File object pointer, but not the reference count on the target Device object.

4.   Then, **DriverEntry** calls **ObDereferenceObject** to decrement the pointer reference count on the File object associated with the target Device object.

5.   If the layered driver forwards incoming IRPs to the target Device object, **DriverEntry** should set the layered Device object's **StackSize** field to a value one greater than the **StackSize** field of the target Device object. This guarantees that there will be enough stack slots for all the drivers in the hierarchy.

6.   If the lower-level driver requires it, **DriverEntry** can fabricate an IRP with IRP_MJ_CREATE as its major function code and send it to the target Device object.

7.   If the Device object is going to be visible to Win32 applications, **DriverEntry** calls **IoCreateSymbolicLink** to add its Win32 name to the **\DosDevices** area of the Object Manager's namespace.

The layered driver can now use the target Device object pointer to make calls to the lower-level driver.

Unload routine   When a layered driver unloads itself, it basically reverses the sequence of operations it performed at initialization time. Once again, since the driver is not working directly with the hardware, it won't need to release any hardware resources. Although the exact steps may vary, a layered driver's Unload routine will generally do the following:

1.   It calls **IoDeleteSymbolicLink** to remove the upper-level Device object's Win32 name from the Object Manager's namespace.

2.   If the lower-level driver requires it, the layered driver's Unload routine can fabricate an IRP with IRP_MJ_CLOSE as its major function code and send it to the target Device object.

3.   Next, the Unload routine decrements the target Device object's pointer reference count by calling **ObDereferenceObject**. This effectively breaks the connection with the target Device object.

4.   Finally, it destroys the upper-level Device object by calling **IoDeleteDevice**.

Code Fragment: Connecting to Another Driver

The following code fragment (taken from somewhere in the flow of a DriverEntry routine) shows how one driver might layer itself on top of another. In this example, the lower-level driver XXDRIVER exposes a device called (what else) **XX0** and the layered driver (YYDRIVER) exposes **YY0**.

```
UNICODE_STRING UpperDeviceName;
DEVICE_OBJECT UpperDeviceObject;
PDEVICE_EXTENSION UpperExtension;

UNICODE_STRING LowerDeviceName;
DEVICE_OBJECT LowerDeviceObject;
FILE_OBJECT LowerFileObject;

NTSTATUS status;

RtlInitUnicodeString( ❶
    &UpperDeviceName,
    L"\device\YY0" );

RtlInitUnicodeString(
    &LowerDeviceName,
    L"\device\XX0" );

status = IoCreateDevice(
                :
            &UpperDeviceName,
                :
            &UpperDeviceObject );

UpperExtension = UpperDeviceObject->DeviceExtension;

status = IoGetDeviceObjectPointer( ❷
            &LowerDeviceName,
            FILE_ALL_ACCESS,
            &LowerFileObject,
            &LowerDeviceObject );

status = ObReferenceObjectByPointer( ❸
            LowerDeviceObject,
            FILE_ALL_ACCESS,
            NULL,
            KernelMode );

ObDereferenceObject( LowerFileObject );

UpperExtension->LowerDevice = LowerDeviceObject; ❹

UpperDeviceObject->StackSize =
            LowerDeviceObject->StackSize + 1; ❺

UpperDeviceObject->Flags |=
        ( LowerDeviceObject->Flags &
            ( DO_BUFFERED_IO | DO_DIRECT_IO ));

UpperDeviceObject->AlignmentRequirement =
            LowerDeviceObject->AlignmentRequirement;
```

❶ The upper driver prepares Unicode names for both the upper and lower devices. Be careful: These names are case-sensitive.

❷ It then retrieves a pointer to the lower Device object. This function returns pointers to both a Device object *and* a File object.

❸ **IoGetDeviceObjectPointer** doesn't increment the pointer count on the Device object. The upper driver has to do that itself. Then, it decrements the pointer count on the lower driver's File object, since this isn't needed anymore.

❹ The upper driver needs to save the address of the lower Device object in its own Device Extension so that other routines will be able to find it.

❺ If the upper driver plans to forward IRPs directly to the lower one, these IRPs have to have enough I/O stack locations for all the drivers in the hierarchy. In this case, it's also important for the upper driver to duplicate the buffering strategy and alignment of the lower driver.

Other Initialization Concerns for Layered Drivers

You've just seen the general steps a layered driver needs to perform if it wants to connect to another driver. Depending on how the layered driver operates, there may be some other issues that the initialization code has to deal with. There are basically two cases to consider.

Transparent layer   Some layered drivers are intended to slip transparently between some lower-level driver and its clients. Here, it's important for the Device objects exposed by the layered driver to mimic the behavior of the lower driver's Device objects. NT Server's fault-tolerant disk driver is one example of a transparent layer.

To guarantee that the layered driver can be added or removed transparently, its **DriverEntry** routine needs to perform the following extra initialization:

- It should copy the **DeviceType** and **Characteristics** fields from the target Device object to the layered Device object.

- **DriverEntry** should also copy the DO_DIRECT_IO and DO_BUF-FERED_IO bits from the target Device's **Flags** field. This ensures that the layered Device object will use the same buffering strategy as the target.

- It should copy the **AlignmentRequirement** field from the target to the upper-level Device object.

- Finally, the **MajorFunction** table in the layered Driver object has to support the exact same set of IRP_MJ_XXX function codes as the lower-level Driver object.[3]

---

[3] The sample filter driver that appears later in this chapter shows how to set up a layered driver's **MajorFunction** table dynamically.

Virtual or logical device layer   The other possibility is that the layered driver exposes virtual or logical Device objects.[4] For example, NT's TDI network protocol drivers present Device objects that have no particular similarity to the network interface cards below them. Likewise, SCSI class drivers export Device objects whose characteristics are those of the peripheral attached to the SCSI bus — not those of the SCSI interface card.

In this case, the layered driver should pick appropriate values for the **Type** and **Characteristics** fields of the layered Device object. Also, the exact set of IRP_MJ_XXX functions supported by the layered driver will be ones appropriate to the layered Device object. There's also no requirement for the layered and target Device objects to use the same buffering strategy.

I/O Request Processing in Layered Drivers

Since layered drivers don't directly manage any hardware, they don't need any Start I/O, Interrupt Service, or DPC routines. Instead, most of the code in a layered driver consists of Dispatch routines and I/O Completion routines. Because they deserve some extra attention, I/O Completion routines get their own section later in this chapter.

The subsections below describe the operation of a layered driver's Dispatch routines. When one of these Dispatch routines receives an IRP, it can do one of three things.

Complete the original IRP   The simplest case is the one where the Dispatch routine is able to process the request all by itself and return either success or failure notification to the original caller. The Dispatch routine does the following:

1. It calls **IoGetCurrentIrpStackLocation** to get a pointer to this driver's I/O stack slot.

2. The Dispatch routine processes the request using various fields in the IRP and the I/O stack location.

3. It puts an appropriate value in the **IoStatus.Information** field of the IRP.

4. The Dispatch routine also fills the **IoStatus.Status** field of the IRP with a suitable STATUS_XXX code.

5. Then, it calls **IoCompleteRequest** with a priority-boost value of IO_NO_IN-CREMENT to send the IRP back to the I/O Manager.

---

[4] A *virtual device* is one whose behavior is not tied to the characteristics of the underlying peripheral hardware. This also includes things like RAM disks which have no associated peripheral device.

A *logical device* is a temporary construct that maintains the context for a specific series of transactions — usually occurring over a shared communication medium. For example, when a client requests a connection to a Named Pipe object, the pipe driver creates a separate instance of the pipe just for that client. This pipe instance is a logical device. Logical devices normally have a limited lifespan; the driver creates them when a series of transactions begins, and destroys them when the last transaction is finished.

6. As its return-value, the Dispatch routine passes back the same STATUS_XXX code that it put into the IRP.

There's nothing at all mysterious going on here. In fact, it's the same procedure any Dispatch routine follows when it wants to end the processing of a request.

Pass the IRP to another driver   The second possibility is that the layered driver's Dispatch routine needs to pass the IRP to the next lower driver. The Dispatch routine does the following:

1. It calls **IoGetCurrentIrpStackLocation** to get a pointer to its own I/O stack location.

2. The Dispatch routine also calls **IoGetNextIrpStackLocation** to retrieve a pointer to the I/O stack location belonging to the next lower driver.

3. It sets up the next lower driver's I/O stack location, including the **Major-Function** field and various members of the **Parameters** union.

4. The Dispatch routine calls **IoSetCompletionRoutine** to associate an I/O Completion routine with the IRP. At the very least, this I/O Completion routine is going to be responsible for marking the IRP as pending.

5. It sends the IRP to a lower-level driver using **IoCallDriver**. This is an asynchronous call that returns immediately regardless of whether the lower-level driver completed the IRP.

6. As its return value, the Dispatch routine passes back whatever status code was returned by **IoCallDriver**. This will be either STATUS_SUCCESS, STATUS_PENDING, or some STATUS_XXX error code.

Notice that the Dispatch routine does not call **IoMarkIrpPending** to put the original IRP in the pending state before sending it to the lower driver. This is because the Dispatch routine doesn't know whether the IRP should be marked pending until after **IoCallDriver** returns. Unfortunately, by that time **IoCallDriver** has already pushed the I/O stack pointer in the IRP, so a call to **IoMarkIrpPending** (which always works with the current stack slot) would mark the wrong stack location. The solution is to call **IoMarkIrpPending** in an I/O Completion routine, after the IRP stack pointer has been reset to the proper level.

Allocate additional IRPs   Finally, the layered driver's Dispatch routine may need to allocate one or more additional IRPs which it then sends to lower-level drivers. The Dispatch routine has the option of waiting for these additional IRPs to complete, or of issuing asynchronous requests to the lower driver. In the asynchronous case, cleanup of the additional IRPs occurs in an I/O Completion routine. The discussion of driver-allocated IRPs (appearing later in this chapter) will explain how to use both these techniques.

Code Fragment: Calling a Lower-Level Driver

The code fragment below shows how the Dispatch routine in one driver might forward an IRP to a lower-level driver. For purposes of example, it also shows how the upper driver could store some context (in this case, a retry count) in an unused field of its own I/O stack location.

```
NTSTATUS
YyDispatchRead(
  IN PDEVICE_OBJECT DeviceObject,
  IN PIRP Irp
  )
{
  PDEVICE_EXTENSION Extension =
        DeviceObject->DeviceExtension;

  PIO_STACK_LOCATION ThisIrpStack =
        IoGetCurrentIrpStackLocation( Irp );

  PIO_STACK_LOCATION NextIrpStack =
        IoGetNextIrpStackLocation( Irp );

  *NextIrpStack = *ThisIrpStack;  ❶

  ThisIrpStack->
        Parameters.Read.Key =
                YY_RETRY_COUNT_MAXIMUM_VALUE;  ❷

  IoSetCompletionRoutine(  ❸
        Irp,
        YyReadCompletion,
        NULL,
        TRUE, TRUE, TRUE );

        return IoCallDriver(  ❹
                Extension->LowerDevice,
                Irp );
}
```

❶ In this simple example, the upper driver just copies the entire I/O stack location from its own slot to the slot of the next lower driver. This is essentially just a pass-through operation.

❷ The upper driver's I/O Completion routine is going to use the count stored in the **Parameters.Read.Key** field of the upper driver's I/O stack slot to keep track of attempted retries. Since the upper driver isn't using this field for its intended purpose, it can get away with this trick.

❸ To recapture this IRP after the lower driver completes it, the upper driver attaches an I/O Completion routine. Since all three InvokeOnXxx arguments are TRUE, the I/O Manager will call this routine no matter what happens to the IRP.

❹ Finally, the upper driver sends the IRP to the lower driver. Notice that the return value of **IoCallDriver** becomes the return value of the Dispatch routine. Also, notice that the Dispatch routine doesn't call **IoMarkIrp-Pending** with the IRP; that will happen in the I/O Completion routine.

15.3 WRITING I/O COMPLETION ROUTINES

An I/O Completion routine is an I/O Manager callback that lets you recapture an IRP after a lower-level driver has completed it. This section explains how to use I/O Completion routines in intermediate drivers.

Requesting an I/O Completion Callback

If you want to regain control of an IRP after it's been processed, you need to call **IoSetCompletionRoutine** (described in Table 15.1). This function puts the address of an I/O Completion routine in the IRP stack location associated with the next lower driver. When some lower-level driver calls **IoCompleteRequest**, the I/O Completion routine will execute as the IRP bubbles its way back to the top of the driver hierarchy.

Except for the driver on the bottom, each driver in the hierarchy can attach its own I/O Completion routine to an IRP. This allows everyone to receive notification when an IRP completes. The I/O Completion routines will execute in driver-stacking order, from bottom to top.

Also notice the three BOOLEAN InvokeOnXxx arguments. These allow you to specify the situations in which a particular I/O Completion routine will run. The I/O Manager uses the **IoStatus.Status** field of the IRP to decide whether it should call the I/O Completion routine.

Table 15.1   Function prototype for IoSetCompletionRoutine

VOID IoSetCompletionRoutine	IRQL ≤ DISPATCH_LEVEL
Parameter	**Description**
IN PIRP Irp	Address of IRP the driver wants to track
IN PIO_COMPLETION_ROUTINE CompletionRoutine	Routine to call when a lower driver completes the IRP
IN PVOID Context	Argument passed to I/O Completion routine
IN BOOLEAN InvokeOnSuccess	Call routine if IRP completes successfully
IN BOOLEAN InvokeOnError	Call routine if IRP completes with error
IN BOOLEAN InvokeOnCancel	Call routine if IRP is canceled
Return value	—

Execution Context

By the time it calls your I/O Completion routine, the I/O Manager has already popped the I/O stack pointer, so that the current stack location is the one belonging to your driver. Table 15.2 lists the arguments passed to an I/O Completion routine.

One tricky item is the IRQL level at which an I/O Completion routine executes. If the lower-level driver calls **IoCompleteRequest** from PASSIVE_LEVEL IRQL, then higher-level I/O Completion routines will also run at PASSIVE_LEVEL. On the other hand, if the lower-level driver completes the request from DISPATCH_LEVEL IRQL (from a DPC routine, for example), then higher-level I/O Completion routines will execute at DISPATCH_LEVEL. Since DISPATCH_LEVEL IRQL has more restrictions associated with it than PASSIVE_LEVEL IRQL, it's a good idea to limit the actions of an I/O Completion routine to things that can safely be done at DISPATCH_LEVEL.[5]

When an I/O Completion routine is finished, it should return one of two status codes. Returning STATUS_SUCCESS causes the IRP to continue its journey back toward the original caller. This includes the execution of any other I/O Completion routines attached by drivers above this one. This is normally the appropriate value to use if this is the original IRP that came from some caller outside the driver.

To stop any further processing of this IRP, an I/O Completion routine can return STATUS_MORE_PROCESSING_REQUIRED. This value blocks the execution of any higher-level I/O Completion routines attached to the IRP. It also prevents the original caller from receiving notification that the IRP has completed. An I/O Completion routine should return this code if it either plans to send the IRP back down to a lower-level driver (as in the case of split transfer), or if the IRP was allocated by this driver and the I/O Completion routine is going to deallocate it.

Table 15.2 Function prototype for an I/O Completion routine

NTSTATUS XxIoCompletion	IRQL == PASSIVE_LEVEL I DISPATCH_LEVEL
Parameter	**Description**
IN PDEVICE_OBJECT DeviceObject	Device object that just completed the request
IN PIRP Irp	The IRP that's being completed
IN PVOID Context	Context that was passed to **IoSetCompletionRoutine**
Return value	One of the following: • STATUS_MORE_PROCESSING_REQUIRED • STATUS_SUCCESS

---

[5] For example, don't mark any I/O Completion routines as paged in an alloc_text pragma.

What I/O Completion Routines Do

An intermediate driver can attach an I/O Completion routine to any IRP it sends to another driver. This includes the original IRP that the driver received from some outside caller, as well as any IRPs that the driver allocates on its own. When an I/O Completion routine executes, there are three general kinds of tasks it may need to perform.

Release the original IRP If the completed IRP is one that came from an outside caller, it may require some driver-specific cleanup. At the very least, the I/O Completion routine for one of these IRPs needs to do the following:

1. It tests the value of the IRP's **PendingReturned** flag.

2. If this flag is TRUE, the I/O Completion routine puts the current I/O stack location into the pending state with a call to **IoMarkIrpPending**.

3. Finally, it returns a value of STATUS_SUCCESS to allow completion processing to continue.

Deallocate the IRP If the IRP was allocated by the driver, the I/O Completion routine may be responsible for releasing it. Once again, this is a rather involved topic because the I/O Manager supports several different IRP allocation strategies. The next section of this chapter will explain all the gory details of releasing driver-allocated IRPs.

Recycle the IRP Some intermediate drivers have to split a transfer into smaller pieces before sending it to a lower-level driver. Normally, the most efficient way to do this is to send each partial transfer to the lower driver by reusing the same IRP. To recycle an IRP, the I/O Completion routine does the following:

1. It checks the context information stored with the IRP to see if this was the last partial transfer. If the whole transfer is finished and the IRP came from an outside caller, the driver performs any necessary cleanup and returns STATUS_SUCCESS to allow further completion processing.

2. If the whole transfer is finished and this is a driver-allocated IRP, the I/O Completion routine performs any necessary cleanup, frees the IRP, and returns STATUS_MORE_PROCESSING_REQUIRED to prevent any further completion processing.

3. If there's more work to be done, the I/O Completion routine calls **IoGetNext-IrpStackLocation** and sets up the I/O stack slot for the next lower driver.

4. Next, it uses **IoSetCompletionRoutine** to attach the address of this I/O Completion routine to the IRP.

5. It passes the IRP to the target Device object using **IoCallDriver**.

6. Finally, it returns STATUS_MORE_PROCESSING_REQUIRED to prevent any further completion processing of this IRP.

An implementation detail: During each partial transfer, an intermediate driver has to keep track of how much of the original caller's request has been satisfied. One clever way to maintain this context information is to store it in unused fields of the intermediate driver's I/O stack location. For example, if the intermediate driver doesn't need the **ByteOffset** or **Key** fields, it can use them to hold three longwords of context data. Of course, if your driver *does* use these fields for their intended purpose, you can always allocate a private block and pass it as the Context argument to **IoSetCompletionRoutine**.

Code Fragment: An I/O Completion Routine

Below you'll find a fragment of an I/O Completion routine. It complements the **YyDispatchRead** function presented in the previous section of this chapter. If the request completed normally, it sends it back to the original caller. If something failed at a lower level, it retries the operation a fixed number of times.

```
NTSTATUS
YyReadCompletion(
  IN PDEVICE_OBJECT DeviceObject,
  IN PIRP Irp,
  IN PVOID Context
  )
{
  PIO_STACK_LOCATION ThisIrpStack =
        IoGetCurrentIrpStackLocation( Irp );

  PIO_STACK_LOCATION NextIrpStack =
        IoGetNextIrpStackLocation( Irp );

  PDEVICE_EXTENSION Extension =
        DeviceObject->DeviceExtension;

  if(( NT_SUCCESS( Irp->IoStatus.Status ))
  || ( ThisIrpStack->Parameters.Read.Key == 0 ))  ❶
  {
        if( Irp->PendingReturned )  ❷
            IoMarkIrpPending( Irp );

            return STATUS_SUCCESS;
  }

  ThisIrpStack->Parameters.Read.Key--;  ❸

  *NextIrpStack = *ThisIrpStack;
  NextIrpStack->Parameters.Read.Key = 0;

  IoSetCompletionRoutine(  ❹
        Irp,
        YyReadCompletion,
```

```
                    NULL,
                    TRUE,  TRUE,  TRUE );

        IoCallDriver( Extension->LowerDevice, Irp ); ❺

        return STATUS_MORE_PROCESSING_REQUIRED;
    }
```

❶ If the lower driver completed the IRP with a successful status code, or if the IRP failed and it has run out of retries, this driver is about to send it on its way back up the driver hierarchy.

❷ It's necessary to see if the current I/O stack location should be marked pending. Because of the asynchronous nature of **IoCallDriver**, this can't be done until the completion routine runs.

❸ The lower driver failed the IRP but it still has some retries left. At this point, the upper driver decrements the retry count and prepares to send the IRP back down for another try.

❹ The I/O Completion routine address has to be reset each time the IRP is recycled.

❺ Finally, the I/O Completion routine sends the IRP back to the lower driver. As its return value, the I/O Completion routine sends back STATUS_MORE_PROCESSING_REQUIRED. This prevents the I/O Manager from continuing to complete the IRP.

15.4 ALLOCATING ADDITIONAL IRPS

There are some situations where an intermediate driver may need to allocate additional IRPs to send to another driver. For example, the initialization code in one driver might want to query the capabilities of a lower-level driver by issuing an IOCTL request. The filter driver appearing later in this chapter does exactly this.

Or, for purposes of fault tolerance, the intermediate driver might want to duplicate an incoming request and send redundant copies to multiple lower-level drivers. The fault-tolerant disk driver that comes with NT Server uses this technique.

Finally, a command exposed by an intermediate driver might require lower-level drivers to perform a complex sequence of operations. For example, the class driver for a particular kind of SCSI device has to issue a whole series of commands to the SCSI port driver to implement one of the class driver's operations.

The IRP's I/O Stack Revisited

When you start to allocate additional IRPs, it's important to have a clear understanding of just how the IRP's I/O stack works. As you already know, when any driver receives an IRP from an outside caller, the I/O stack pointer points to

the stack location belonging to that driver. To retrieve this pointer, the driver simply calls **IoGetCurrentIrpStackLocation**.

If an intermediate driver plans to pass an incoming IRP to a lower-level
driver, it has to set up the I/O stack location for the lower driver. To get a pointer
to the lower driver's I/O stack slot, the intermediate driver makes a call to **IoGet-
NextIrpStackLocation**. After setting up the lower stack slot, the intermediate
driver uses **IoCallDriver** to pass the IRP on. This function automatically pushes
the I/O stack pointer so that when the lower driver calls **IoGetCurrentIrpStack-
Location**, it will get the right address.

When the lower driver calls **IoCompleteRequest**, the completed IRP's I/O
stack is popped. This allows an I/O Completion routine belonging to the intermediate driver to call **IoGetCurrentIrpStackLocation** if it needs to access its own
stack location. As the IRP bubbles its way back up to the original caller, the I/O
stack is automatically popped again for each driver in the hierarchy. Table 15.3
summarizes the effects of these functions on an IRP's I/O stack pointer.

To maintain consistent behavior with driver-allocated IRPs, the I/O Manager plays a little trick. When a driver allocates an IRP, the I/O Manager initializes the new IRP's I/O stack pointer so that it points at a nonexistent slot one
location beyond the end of the stack. This guarantees that when the driver passes
the IRP to a lower-level driver, **IoCallDriver**'s push operation will set the stack
pointer to the first real slot in the stack. This means the higher-level driver must
call **IoGetNextIrpStackLocation** to retrieve a pointer to the I/O stack slot
intended for the target driver.

Controlling the Size of the IRP Stack

When a driver receives an IRP from an outside caller, the number of I/O
stack slots is determined by the **StackSize** field of the driver's Device object. If
an intermediate driver plans to pass incoming IRPs to a lower-level driver, it
needs to set this field equal to one more than the **StackSize** value of the lower
driver. This ensures that there will be enough I/O stack for all the drivers in the
hierarchy.

Table 15.3 What various functions do to the IRP's I/O stack pointer

Working with the IRP stack pointer

Function	Effect on the IRP stack pointer
IoGetCurrentIrpStackLocation	No change
IoGetNextIrpStackLocation	No change
IoSetNextIrpStackLocation	Pushes stack pointer one location
IoCallDriver	Pushes stack pointer one location
IoCompleteRequest	Pops stack pointer one location

If an intermediate driver calls **IoBuildAsynchronousFsdRequest**, **IoBuild-DeviceIoControlRequest**, or **IoBuildSynchronousFsdRequest** to create an IRP, the I/O Manager uses the **StackSize** field of the target Device object (passed as an argument to all three functions) to determine the number of I/O stack locations in the new IRP. These IRPs will have enough I/O stack slots for the target driver and any drivers below it. There will *not* be a slot in the I/O stack for the intermediate driver itself.

If an intermediate driver uses **IoAllocateIrp**, **ExAllocatePool**, or some privately managed memory to create an IRP, the driver must explicitly specify the number of I/O stack slots in the new IRP. Again, the common practice is to use the **StackSize** field of the target Device object to determine the proper number of slots.

Ordinarily, an intermediate driver won't need a stack slot for itself in any IRPs it allocates. The one exception would be if the intermediate driver needed to associate some per-request context with the IRP. In that case, the driver could allocate an IRP with one extra stack slot and use the extra slot for holding private context data. This code fragment shows how it's done:

```
NewIrp = IoAllocateIrp( LowerDevice->StackSize + 1 );

//
// Push the I/O stack pointer so that it points
// at the first valid slot. Use this slot to hold
// context information needed by the upper driver.
//
IoSetNextIrpStackLocation( NewIrp );
ContextArea = IoGetCurrentIrpStackLocation( NewIrp );
NextDriverSlot = IoGetNextIrpStackLocation( NewIrp );

//
// Set up next driver's I/O stack slot
//
NextDriverSlot->MajorFunction = IRP_MJ_XXX;
   :

//
// Attach an I/O Completion routine and
// send the IRP to someone else
//
IoSetCompletionRoutine(
        NewIrp,
        YyIoCompletion,
        NULL,
        TRUE, TRUE, TRUE );

IoCallDriver( LowerDevice, NewIrp );
```

Creating IRPs with IoBuildSynchronousFsdRequest

The I/O Manager provides three convenience functions that simplify the process of building IRPs for standard kinds of I/O request. The first one is **IoBuildSynchronousFsdRequest**, and it fabricates read, write, flush, or shutdown IRPs. See Table 15.4 for a description of this function.

The number of I/O stack locations in IRPs created with this function is equal to the **StackSize** field of the TargetDevice argument. There's no straightforward way to leave room in the I/O stack for the intermediate driver itself.

The Buffer, Length, and StartingOffset arguments to this function are required for read and write operations. They must be NULL, 0, and NULL (respectively) for flush or shutdown operations.

IoBuildSynchronousFsdRequest automatically sets up various fields in the **Parameters** area of the next lower I/O stack location, so there's rarely any need to touch the I/O stack. For read or write requests, this function also allocates system buffer space or builds an MDL, depending on whether the TargetDevice does Buffered or Direct I/O. For buffered outputs, it also copies the contents of the caller's buffer into the system buffer; at the end of a buffered input, data is automatically copied from the system buffer to the caller's buffer.

As the function name suggests, you make requests for synchronous I/O operations with the IRPs returned by **IoBuildSynchronousFsdRequest**. In other words, the thread that calls **IoCallDriver** normally blocks itself until the I/O operation completes. To do this, just pass the address of an initialized Event object

Table 15.4 Function prototype for IoBuildSynchronousFsdRequest

PIRP IoBuildSynchronousFsdRequest	IRQL == PASSIVE_LEVEL
Parameter	**Description**
IN ULONG MajorFunction	One of the following: • IRP_MJ_READ • IRP_MJ_WRITE • IRP_MJ_FLUSH_BUFFERS • IRP_MJ_SHUTDOWN
IN PDEVICE_OBJECT TargetDevice	Device object where IRP will be sent
IN OUT PVOID Buffer	Address of I/O buffer
IN ULONG Length	Length of buffer in bytes
IN PLARGE_INTEGER StartingOffset	Device offset where I/O will begin
IN PKEVENT Event	Event object used to signal I/O completion
OUT PIO_STATUS_BLOCK Iosb	Receives final status of I/O operation
Return value	• Non-NULL — address of new IRP • NULL — IRP could not be allocated

when you allocate the IRP. Then, after sending the IRP to a lower-level driver with **IoCallDriver**, use **KeWaitForSingleObject** to wait for the Event object. When a lower-level driver completes the IRP, the I/O Manager will put this Event object into the Signaled state, which will awaken your driver. The I/O status block will tell you whether everything worked.

Two points about intermediate drivers issuing synchronous I/O requests to other drivers. First, drivers that perform blocking I/O can be rather sluggish because they prevent the calling thread from overlapping its I/O operations. This is contrary to the philosophy of the NT I/O architecture, so you shouldn't do it unless you really need to.

Second, the Event object used to wait for I/O completion needs to be synchronized properly or there could be a nasty collision. Consider the case where two threads in the same process issue a read request using the same handle. The **YyDispatchRead** routine executes in the context of the first thread and blocks itself waiting for the Event object. Then the same **YyDispatchRead** routine executes in the context of the other thread and reuses the same Event object to issue a second request. When the IRP for either request completes, the Event object will be set, both threads will awaken, and nothing good will happen.[6] The solution is to guard the Event object with a Fast Mutex.

The I/O Manager automatically cleans up and deallocates IRPs created with **IoBuildSynchronousFsdRequest** after their completion processing is done. This includes releasing any system buffer space or MDL attached to the IRP. To trigger this cleanup, a lower-level driver simply has to call **IoCompleteRequest**.

Normally, there won't be any need to attach an I/O Completion routine to one of these IRPs, unless you need to do some driver-specific postprocessing. If you do attach an I/O Completion routine, it should return STATUS_SUCCESS when it's done. This lets the I/O Manager free the IRP.

Creating IRPs with IoBuildAsynchronousFsdRequest

The second convenience function, **IoBuildAsynchronousFsdRequest**, is quite similar to the first. It lets you build read, write, flush, and shutdown requests without worrying about too many of the details. The main difference is that you have to process these IRPs asynchronously. You don't have the option of stopping and waiting for the I/O to complete. Table 15.5 contains the prototype for this function.

As with **IoBuildSynchronousFsdRequest**, the Buffer, Length, and Starting-Offset parameters to **IoBuildAsynchronousFsdRequest** are required for read and write operations. They must be NULL, 0, and NULL (respectively) for flush or shutdown operations.

---

[6] This problem isn't limited to threads in the same process, by the way. If the intermediate driver's Device object is shareable, the same issue arises if threads in two separate processes issue simultaneous requests that travel through the **YyDispatchRead** routine.

Table 15.5 Function prototype for IoBuildAsynchronousFsdRequest

PIRP IoBuildAsynchronousFsdRequest	IRQL ≤ DISPATCH_LEVEL
Parameter	**Description**
IN ULONG MajorFunction	One of the following: • IRP_MJ_READ • IRP_MJ_WRITE • IRP_MJ_FLUSH_BUFFERS • IRP_MJ_SHUTDOWN
IN PDEVICE_OBJECT TargetDevice	Device object where IRP will be sent
IN OUT PVOID Buffer	Address of I/O buffer
IN ULONG Length	Length of buffer in bytes
IN PLARGE_INTEGER StartingOffset	Device offset where I/O will begin
OUT PIO_STATUS_BLOCK Iosb	Receives final status of I/O operation
Return value	• Non-NULL — address of new IRP • NULL — IRP could not be allocated

Notice that you can call **IoBuildAsynchronousFsdRequest** at or below DISPATCH_LEVEL IRQL. **IoBuildSynchronousFsdRequest** works only at PASSIVE_LEVEL.

Unlike the IRPs from **IoBuildSynchronousFsdRequest**, the ones from this function are *not* released automatically when a lower-level driver completes them. Instead, you *must* attach an I/O Completion routine to any IRP created with **IoBuildAsynchronousFsdRequest**. The I/O Completion routine calls **IoFreeIrp** which releases the system buffer or MDL associated with the IRP and then deallocates the IRP itself. The return value of the I/O Completion routine should be STATUS_MORE_PROCESSING_REQUIRED.

Creating IRPs with IoBuildDeviceIoControlRequest

The last convenience function, **IoBuildDeviceIoControlRequest**, (described in Table 15.6) simplifies the task of building IOCTL IRPs. This is useful because it's a fairly common practice for drivers of odd pieces of hardware to expose an interface composed almost entirely of IOCTLs. Some higher-level drivers (like NT's TDI network protocol drivers) take this same approach.

The InternalDeviceIoControl argument lets you specify the major function code in the target driver's I/O stack slot. FALSE produces an IRP with IRP_MJ_DEVICE_CONTROL, while TRUE causes it to be set to IRP_MJ_INTERNAL_DEVICE_CONTROL.

Also notice that you can make either synchronous or asynchronous calls with the IRPs returned by this function. If you want your Dispatch routine to stop

Table 15.6   Function prototype for IoBuildDeviceIoControlRequest

PIRP IoBuildDeviceIoControlRequest	IRQL == PASSIVE_LEVEL
Parameter	**Description**
IN ULONG IoControlCode	IOCTL code recognized by target driver
IN PDEVICE_OBJECT TargetDevice	Device object where IRP will be sent
IN PVOID InputBuffer	Buffer of data passed to lower driver
IN ULONG InputBufferLength	Size of data buffer in bytes
OUT PVOID OutputBuffer	Data buffer filled by lower driver
IN ULONG OutputBufferLength	Size of data buffer in bytes
IN BOOLEAN InternalDeviceIoControl	(See below)
IN PKEVENT Event	Event object used to signal I/O completion
OUT PIO_STATUS_BLOCK Iosb	Receives final status of I/O operation
Return value	• Non-NULL — address of new IRP
	• NULL — IRP could not be allocated

and wait until an I/O control operation completes, simply pass the address of an initialized Event object when you allocate the IRP. Then, after sending the IRP to a lower-level driver with **IoCallDriver**, use **KeWaitForSingleObject** to wait for the Event object. When a lower-level driver completes the IRP, the I/O Manager will put this Event object into the Signaled state, which awakens your driver. The I/O status block will tell you how everything went. As with **IoBuildSynchronousFsdRequest**, you have to be careful about multiple threads using this Event object at the same time.

The I/O Manager automatically cleans up and deallocates IRPs created with **IoBuildDeviceIoControlRequest** after their completion processing is done. This includes releasing any system buffer space or MDL attached to the IRP. To trigger this cleanup, a lower-level driver simply has to call **IoCompleteRequest**.

Normally, there's no need to attach an I/O Completion routine to one of these IRPs, unless you need to do some driver-specific post-processing. If you do attach an I/O Completion routine, it should return STATUS_SUCCESS when it's done. This lets the I/O Manager free the IRP.

The one problem with this function is the way it handles the buffering-method bits embedded in the IOCTL code. If an IOCTL code contains METHOD_BUFFERED, **IoBuildDeviceIoControl** allocates a nonpaged pool buffer and copies the contents of the InputBuffer to it; when the IRP completes, the contents of the nonpaged pool buffer are automatically copied to OutputBuffer. So far, it behaves exactly like a Win32 **DeviceIoControl** call coming from a user-mode application.

But, if you specify an IOCTL code containing one of the Direct I/O methods, a nasty bug appears: **IoBuildDeviceIoControl** *always* builds an MDL for the OutputBuffer address and *always* uses a nonpaged pool buffer for the InputBuffer address, regardless of whether the IOCTL code specifies METHOD_IN_DIRECT or METHOD_OUT_DIRECT.

Creating IRPs from Scratch

The I/O Manager routines described above are the most convenient way to work with driver-allocated IRPs. Every once in awhile, however, they may not be the right thing to use. For example, if you're trying issue a request other than read, write, flush, shutdown, or device I/O control, these functions aren't very helpful. At that point, your only option is allocate a blank IRP and set it up by hand. The following subsections describe several ways to do this.

IRPs from IoAllocateIrp   The **IoAllocateIrp** function will allocate an IRP from an I/O Manager zone buffer and perform certain basic kinds of initialization.[7] Your driver has to fill in the I/O stack location for the target driver and set up whatever kind of buffer the target driver is expecting to find. The following code fragment illustrates the use of this function.

```
PMDL NewMdl;
PIRP NewIrp;
PIO_STACK_LOCATION NextIrpStack;

NewIrp = IoAllocateIrp( LowerDevice->StackSize );

NewMdl = IoAllocateMdl(
            MmGetMdlVirtualAddress(
                OriginalIrp->MdlAddress ),
            XX_SIZE_OF_BIGGEST_TRANSFER,
            FALSE, // Primary buffer
            FALSE, // No quota charge
            NewIrp );

IoBuildPartialMdl(
  OriginalIrp->MdlAddress,
  NewMdl,
  MmGetMdlVirtualAddress( OriginalIrp->MdlAddress ),
  XX_SIZE_OF_BIGGEST_TRANSFER );

NextIrpStack = IoGetNextIrpStackLocation( NewIrp );

NextIrpStack->MajorFunction = IRP_MJ_XXX;

NextIrpStack->
  Parameters.Xxx.Length =
                XX_SIZE_OF_BIGGEST_TRANSFER;
```

---

[7] There's a very serious error in the DDK documentation that's worth knowing about: The documentation clearly states that you *must* pass any IRPs created with **IoAllocateIrp** to **IoInitializeIrp** before you can use them. This turns out to be a lie. If you pass an IRP returned from **IoAllocateIrp** to **IoInitializeIrp**, the system will crash when your driver tries to release the IRP. So, don't do that.

```
NewIrp->
  Tail.Overlay.Thread =
                OriginalIrp->Tail.Overlay.Thread;

IoSetCompletionRoutine(
        NewIrp,
        YyIoCompletion,
        NULL,
        TRUE, TRUE, TRUE );

IoCallDriver( LowerDevice, NewIrp );
```

One thing to mention here: If the new IRP is targeted at a disk device or a device with removable media, the intermediate driver needs to copy the contents of the original IRP's **Tail.Overlay.Thread** field into the new IRP. This guarantees that the system will be able to pop up a dialog box for the user if the underlying device driver calls **IoSetHardErrorOrVerifyDevice**.

Your driver is responsible for releasing any IRPs created with **IoAllocateIrp**. It also has to free any other resources (MDLs or system buffers, for example) associated with the IRP. Normally, this cleanup occurs in the IRP's I/O Completion routine. The following code fragment shows what you need to do.

```
NTSTATUS
YyIoCompletion(
  IN PDEVICE_OBJECT DeviceObject,
  IN PIRP Irp,
  IN PVOID Context
  )
{
  :
  IoFreeMdl( Irp->MdlAddress );
  IoFreeIrp( Irp );

  return STATUS_MORE_PROCESSING_REQUIRED;
}
```

IRPs from ExAllocatePool   If, for some odd reason, you'd prefer to get your IRPs directly from nonpaged pool, you can allocate them with the standard **ExAllocatePool** function. Once you have the block of pool, you still need to turn it into an IRP using **IoInitializeIrp**. (This is the correct place to call this function.) Filling in the I/O stack location and setting up appropriate buffers or MDLs is still left to you.

Here's an example of what to do; in this fragment, the lower Device object is expecting a nonpaged pool buffer rather than an MDL.

```
NewIrp = ExAllocatePool(
            NonPagedPool,
```

```
                    IoSizeOfIrp(
                          LowerDevice->StackSize ));
    IoInitializeIrp(
          NewIrp,
          IoSizeOfIrp( LowerDevice->StackSize ),
          LowerDevice->StackSize );

    NextIrpStack = IoGetNextIrpStackLocation( NewIrp );

    NextIrpStack ->MajorFunction = IRP_MJ_XXX;

    NextIrpStack->
      Parameters.Xxx.Length = XX_BUFFER_SIZE;

    NewIrp->
      AssociatedIrp.SystemBuffer =
          ExAllocatePool( NonPagedPool, XX_BUFFER_SIZE );

    NewIrp->
      Tail.Overlay.Thread =
                  OriginalIrp->Tail.Overlay.Thread;

    IoSetCompletionRoutine(
          NewIrp,
          YyIoCompletion,
          NULL,
          TRUE, TRUE, TRUE );

    IoCallDriver( LowerDevice, NewIrp );
```

Once again, it's the job of the I/O Completion routine attached to the IRP to do all the cleanup and release the IRP. The following code fragment shows you how.

```
NTSTATUS
YyIoCompletion(
  IN PDEVICE_OBJECT DeviceObject,
  IN PIRP Irp,
  IN PVOID Context
  )
{
  :
  ExFreePool( Irp->AssociatedIrp.SystemBuffer );
  IoFreeIrp( Irp );

  return STATUS_MORE_PROCESSING_REQUIRED;
}
```

Notice that you use **IoFreeIrp** to get rid of the IRP, even though you allocated it with **ExAllocatePool**. This is because a field in the IRP tells the I/O Manager whether this IRP came directly from the pool, or whether it came from the I/O Manager's private zone buffer.

IRPs from driver-managed memory   Finally, there's always the chance that you're keeping a private collection of IRPs that you've carved out of a driver-specific zone buffer or a look-aside list. This is really the same as the case where you allocate IRPs using **ExAllocatePool**, in that you still need to initialize each IRP using **IoInitializeIrp**.

The big difference is the way you release these privately managed IRPs. Since the I/O Manager doesn't know anything about your driver's memory management strategy for these IRPs, the **IoFreeIrp** function wouldn't know what to do with one of them. So, instead of calling **IoFreeIrp**, the I/O Completion routine needs to call whatever internal driver function is responsible for releasing the IRP.

Setting Up Buffers for Lower Drivers

If you use any of the preceding techniques to create IRPs from scratch, it's also your responsibility to initialize and clean up any buffers needed by those IRPs.[8] How you do this will depend on whether the target Device object does Buffered or Direct I/O.

Buffered I/O requests   Here, the Dispatch routine in the intermediate driver has to call **ExAllocatePool** to allocate the buffer. It stores the address of this buffer in **AssociatedIrp.SystemBuffer** field of the driver-allocated IRP. Later, an I/O Completion routine attached to the IRP has to release the buffer with a call to **ExFreePool**.

Direct I/O requests   Handling these requests means the intermediate driver has to set up an MDL describing the I/O buffer. In this case, the intermediate driver's Dispatch routine would do the following:

1. It calls **IoAllocateMdl** to create an empty MDL large enough map the buffer. It stores the address of this MDL in the **MdlAddress** field of the driver-allocated IRP.

2. The Dispatch routine fills in the MDL. To map a portion of the buffer associated with the original caller's IRP, it calls **IoBuildPartialMdl**. To map system memory into the MDL, it uses **MmBuildMdlForNonPagedPool**.

3. It then attaches an I/O Completion routine to the driver-allocated IRP using **IoSetCompletionRoutine**.

4. Finally, the Dispatch routine sends the IRP to a lower-level driver with **IoCallDriver**.

---

[8] This is one of the arguments in favor of using the convenience routines to build IRPs, since they handle all this nastiness on their own.

When the lower-level driver completes the IRP, the intermediate driver's I/O Completion routine uses **IoFreeMdl** to release the MDL.

Keeping Track of Driver-Allocated IRPs

Intermediate drivers have to be careful about how they handle incoming I/O requests that result in multiple IRPs being sent simultaneously to some other drivers. In particular, it's important for the original incoming IRP *not* to be completed until all the allocated IRPs have finished their work. Exactly how the intermediate driver does this will depend on whether it performs synchronous or asynchronous I/O with the driver-allocated IRPs.

Synchronous I/O   This is the simpler of the two cases, since the intermediate driver's Dispatch routine just has to stop and wait until all the allocated IRPs have been completed. In general, the Dispatch routine would do the following:

1. It calls **IoBuildSynchronousFsdReqest** to create some number of driver-allocated IRPs.

2. Next, the Dispatch routine uses **IoCallDriver** to pass all the driver-allocated IRPs to other drivers.

3. It then calls **KeWaitForMultipleObjects** and freezes until all the allocated IRPs have completed.

4. Finally, it calls **IoCompleteRequest** with the original IRP to send it back to the caller.

Notice here that, since the original request is blocking inside the Dispatch routine itself, there's no need to mark the original IRP pending.

Asynchronous I/O   This is a somewhat more complex case because there's no central point of control where the driver can stop and wait for everything to finish. Instead, the intermediate driver has to attach I/O Completion routines to each driver-allocated IRP, and the completion routine will have to decide whether it's time to complete the original caller's IRP.

Here's what happens in the Dispatch routine of an intermediate driver using this kind of freewheeling approach:

1. It puts the original caller's IRP in the pending state by calling **IoMarkPending**.

2. Next the Dispatch routine uses one of the methods described in the previous section to allocate some additional IRPs.

3. It attaches an I/O Completion routine to each of these IRPs with **IoSetCompletionRoutine**. When it makes this call, the Dispatch routine passes a pointer to the original caller's IRP as the Context argument.

4. The Dispatch routine stores a count of outstanding allocated IRPs in an unused field of the original IRP. The **Key** field in the current I/O stack location's **Parameters** union is one possible place.

5. Next, it uses **IoCallDriver** to pass all the IRPs to other drivers.

6. Finally, the Dispatch routine passes back STATUS_PENDING as its return value. This is necessary because the original IRP isn't yet ready for completion processing.

As each of the other drivers completes one of these IRPs, the intermediate driver's I/O Completion routine executes. That routine does the following:

1. First, it performs whatever cleanup is necessary and deletes the driver-allocated IRP.

2. The I/O Completion routine calls **ExInterlockedDecrementLong** to decrement the count of outstanding IRPs contained in the original caller's IRP. (Remember, it received a pointer to this original IRP as its Context argument.)

3. If the count equals zero, then this is the last outstanding driver-allocated IRP. In that case, the I/O Completion routine completes the original IRP by calling **IoCompleteRequest**.

4. Finally, it returns STATUS_MORE_PROCESSING_REQUIRED to prevent any further completion processing of the driver-allocated IRP (which has just been deleted).

15.5 WRITING FILTER DRIVERS

A filter driver is a special type of intermediate driver. What sets filters apart from the layered drivers described earlier in this chapter is that they are invisible. They sit on top of some other driver and intercept requests directed at the lower driver's Device objects. Users of the lower driver are completely unaware that this is going on. Some of the things you can do with filters include the following:

- Filters let you modify some aspects of an existing driver's behavior without rewriting the whole thing. SCSI filter drivers (described back in Chapter 1) work this way.

- They make it easier to hide the limitations of lower-level device drivers. For example, a filter could split large transfers into smaller pieces before passing them on to a driver with transfer size limits.

- Filters allow you to add features like compression or encryption to a device without modifying the underlying device driver or the programs that use the device.

- They let you add or remove expensive behavior like performance monitoring that you don't want included in a driver all the time. The disk performance monitoring tools in NT work this way.

The rest of this section explains how to write filter drivers. As you read it, keep in mind that things like driver-allocated IRPs and I/O Completion routines work the same way in a filter driver as they do in a regular layered driver.

How Filter Drivers Work

The main difference between filter drivers and other layered drivers is in the Device objects they create. Whereas a layered driver exposes Device objects with their own unique names, a filter driver's Device objects have no names at all. Filter drivers work by attaching one of these nameless Device objects to a Device object created by some lower-level driver. Figure 15.2 illustrates this relationship.

In the diagram, **YYDRIVER** has attached a filter Device object to **XX0**, one of **XXDRIVER**'s Device objects. Any IRPs sent to **XX0** are automatically rerouted to the Dispatch routines in **YYDRIVER**. Here's how it works.

1. The DriverEntry routine in the filter driver creates an invisible Device object and attaches it to a named Device object belonging to another driver.

2. A client of the lower-level driver opens a connection to **XX0**. This can be a user-mode program calling **CreateFile** to get a handle, or a kernel-mode client

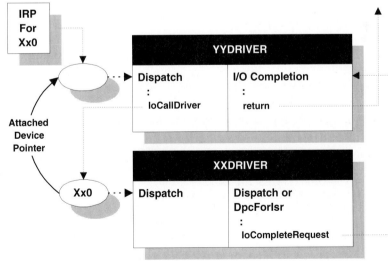

Copyright © 1996 by Cydonix Corporation. 960032a.vsd

Figure 15.2 How filter drivers work

calling **IoGetDeviceObjectPointer**. In either case, the I/O Manager actually opens a connection between the client and the filter driver's invisible Device object.

3. When the client sends an I/O request to **XX0**, the I/O Manager sends it to the filter driver's unnamed Device object instead. The I/O Manager uses the **MajorFunction** table of the filter's Driver object to select an appropriate Dispatch routine.

4. The Dispatch routines in the filter driver either process the IRP on their own and complete it immediately, or they send the IRP down to **XX0** with **IoCall-Driver**. If the filter driver needs to regain control of the IRP when the lower-level driver completes it, the filter can associate an I/O Completion routine with the IRP.

Filters can also be layered above other filters. If you try to attach a filter to an already filtered Device object, the new filter simply gets layered on top of the highest existing filter. So, you can have essentially any number of filter levels.

Initialization and Cleanup in Filter Drivers

Like every other kernel-mode driver, a filter driver must have a main entry point called **DriverEntry**. If the driver is to be unloaded while the system is running, it needs an Unload routine as well. The following subsections describe what these routines have to do.

DriverEntry routine   The initialization sequence in a filter driver will follow one of two basic patterns. The first possibility is that the filter needs to intercept IRPs directed at all the Device objects created by a lower-level driver. In that case, the filter's DriverEntry routine will perform these steps:

1. It calls **IoGetDeviceObjectPointer** to get a pointer to one of the Device objects belonging to the lower-level driver.

2. From this Device object, the filter's DriverEntry routine gets a pointer to the target Driver object. It uses this pointer to scan the **MajorFunction** table of the target Driver object and make sure that every function code supported by the target is also supported by the filter driver.

3. Next, **DriverEntry** uses the **DeviceObject** field of the target Driver object to get the first target Device object.

4. The filter calls **IoCreateDevice** to create a filter Device object for this target Device object. This filter Device object has no NT name, nor does it have a symbolic link to give it a Win32 name.

5. It then calls **IoAttachDeviceByPointer** to attach the new filter Device object to the target Device object.

6. It stores the address of the target Device object in the Device Extension of the filter Device object. Other parts of the filter driver will need this pointer to call the target driver.

7. Next, **DriverEntry** copies the **DeviceType** and **Characteristics** fields from the target Device object to the filter Device object. It also copies the DO_DIRECT_IO and DO_BUFFERED_IO bits from the target Device object's **Flags** field. This guarantees that the filter will look the same and have the same buffering strategy as the target driver.

8. It uses the **NextDevice** field of the target Device object to get the next Device object in the chain and repeats steps 4–7.

9. Finally, it calls **ObDereferenceObject** to decrement the reference count on the File object returned by **IoGetDeviceObjectPointer**.

The second possibility is that the filter driver only wants to capture I/O requests sent a specific Device object belonging to a lower-level driver. In that case, the filter's DriverEntry routine performs the following steps.

1. It calls **IoCreateDevice** to create a filter Device object. This object has no NT name, nor does it have a symbolic link to give it a Win32 name.

2. **DriverEntry** uses **IoAttachDevice** to connect the filter Device object to a specific target Device object. This function takes the case-sensitive NT name of the target device (for example, **\Device\XX0**) and a pointer to the filter Device object. After making the attachment, it returns a pointer to the target Device object.

3. It stores the address of the target Device object in the Device Extension of the filter Device object.

4. Next, **DriverEntry** copies the **DeviceType** and **Characteristics** fields from the target Device object to the filter Device object. It also copies the DO_DIRECT_IO and DO_BUFFERED_IO bits from the target Device object's **Flags** field.

5. From the target Device object, the filter's DriverEntry routine gets a pointer to the target Driver object. It uses this pointer to scan the **MajorFunction** table of the target Driver object and make sure that every function code supported by the target is also supported by the filter driver.

Unload routine A filter driver's Unload routine has to disconnect the filter and target Device objects. It does this by calling **IoDetachDevice** and passing a pointer to the target Device object. Once the filter Device object has been detached, the Unload routine calls **IoDeleteDevice** to get rid of it. If the filter driver has attached itself to a number of target Device objects, it needs to repeat this procedure for each filter Device object.

What Happens behind the Scenes

A lot of undocumented activity occurs when a filter driver attaches itself to a target Device object. In response to an **IoAttachDeviceByPointer** call, the I/O Manager performs the following steps.

1. It sends an IRP to the target Device object. This IRP contains the function code IRP_MJ_CREATE. There are enough I/O stack locations in this IRP for the target driver plus any other drivers layered beneath it. This IRP does *not* pass through the filter driver's **MajorFunction** dispatch table.

2. Next, the I/O Manager sets the filter Device object's **StackSize** field to one greater than the **StackSize** field of the target Device object. This guarantees that IRPs created for the filter will have enough I/O stack locations for any lower-level drivers in the hierarchy.

3. It also sets the **AlignmentRequirement** field of the filter Device object equal to the **AlignmentRequirement** field of the target Device object.

4. The I/O Manager then sends an IRP to the filter Device object. This IRP contains the function code IRP_MJ_CLOSE. Regardless of what Dispatch routines are registered in the filter driver's **MajorFunction** table, this IRP_MJ_CLOSE IRP is *not* preceded by an IRP_MJ_CLEANUP IRP.

5. Finally, the I/O Manager returns the address of the target Device object to the caller of **IoAttachDeviceByPointer**.

Unlike the attach function, **IoDetachDevice** function doesn't send any self-generated IRPs to the target Device object, nor does it reset the **StackSize** field of the filter Device object.

Making the Attachment Transparent

Once a filter has attached itself to a target driver, any I/O requests sent to the target have to pass through the Dispatch routines of the filter driver first. If the **MajorFunction** table of the filter Driver object doesn't support the same set of IRP_MJ_XXX codes as the target driver, clients of the target may experience problems when the filter is attached. Specifically, some types of requests that work without the filter will be rejected as illegal operations when the filter is in place.

To avoid this kind of inconsistency, the filter driver's **MajorFunction** table must contain a Dispatch routine for every IRP_MJ_XXX function supported by the target driver. Even if the filter isn't interested in modifying a particular major function code, it still has to supply a dummy Dispatch routine that just passes the IRP on to the target driver.

The best way to set this up is for the filter driver to scan the **MajorFunction** table of the target Driver object. If an entry in the target driver's table contains a pointer to **_IopInvalidDeviceRequest**,[9] then the corresponding IRP_MJ_XXX code is unsupported; if it contains anything else, then the target driver supports the function code. In that case, the filter driver has to put a Dispatch routine in the corresponding **MajorFunction** slot of its own Driver object. The sample driver in the next section shows how to do this.

15.6 CODE EXAMPLE: A FILTER DRIVER

This example shows how a basic filter driver (called YYDRIVER) intercepts all requests intended for a lower-level driver (XXDRIVER). The purpose of the filter is to hide the lower driver's limited output transfer size. To do this, it breaks large outputs into smaller pieces. It also overrides an IOCTL from the lower driver that returns the maximum size of an output buffer. All other major function codes supported by the lower driver are simply passed through from the filter.

You can find the code for this example in the **CH15\FILTER\DRIVER** directory on the disk that accompanies this book. Code for the dummy device driver sitting below it is in **CH15\LOWER\DRIVER**.

YYDRIVER.H — Driver Data Structures

Here's the Device Extension used by the filter driver. Notice that it contains a pointer to the lower driver's Device object. The filter uses this to send IRPs to the lower driver.

```
typedef struct _DEVICE_EXTENSION {
    PDEVICE_OBJECT DeviceObject; // Back pointer

    PDEVICE_OBJECT TargetDevice;
    XX_BUFFER_SIZE_INFO BufferInfo;
} DEVICE_EXTENSION, *PDEVICE_EXTENSION;
```

INIT.C — Initialization Code

Initialization in this filter follows the pattern described in the previous section of this chapter. This driver takes the general approach of intercepting I/O requests for all the Device objects created by the lower driver.

DriverEntry   This function is responsible for driver-level initialization. It uses one of the lower driver's Device objects to locate all Device objects belonging to the lower driver. It uses a helper function to attach filter Device objects to each one. It also sets up the filter's **MajorFunction** table by scanning the slots in the lower driver's table.

---

[9] Remember from Chapter 8 that this is the I/O Manager routine that rejects an IRP with an unwanted function code. This is the default value for any slot in the **MajorFunction** table.

```
NTSTATUS
DriverEntry(
  IN PDRIVER_OBJECT DriverObject,
  IN PUNICODE_STRING RegistryPath
  )
{
  PDEVICE_OBJECT TargetDevice;
  UNICODE_STRING TargetDeviceName;
  PDRIVER_OBJECT TargetDriver;
  PDRIVER_DISPATCH EmptyDispatchValue;

  XX_BUFFER_SIZE_INFO BufferInfo;
  PFILE_OBJECT FileObject;

  NTSTATUS status;
  ULONG i;

  EmptyDispatchValue =
        DriverObject->MajorFunction[ IRP_MJ_CREATE ]; ❶
//
// Export other driver entry points...
//
  DriverObject->DriverUnload = YyDriverUnload;

  DriverObject->
        MajorFunction[ IRP_MJ_WRITE ] =
              YyDispatchWrite; ❷

  DriverObject->
        MajorFunction[ IRP_MJ_DEVICE_CONTROL ] =
              YyDispatchDeviceIoControl;

  RtlInitUnicodeString(
        &TargetDeviceName,
        TARGET_DEVICE_NAME );

  status = IoGetDeviceObjectPointer( ❸
              &TargetDeviceName,
              FILE_ALL_ACCESS,
              &FileObject,
              &TargetDevice );

  if( !NT_SUCCESS( status ))
  {
        return status;
  }

  YyGetBufferLimits( TargetDevice, &BufferInfo );
  TargetDriver = TargetDevice->DriverObject;
```

```
for( i=0; i<=IRP_MJ_MAXIMUM_FUNCTION; i++ )  ❹
{
        if(( TargetDriver->MajorFunction[i]
        != EmptyDispatchValue )
        && ( DriverObject->MajorFunction[i]
        == EmptyDispatchValue ))
        {
                DriverObject->MajorFunction[i] =
                                YyDispatchPassThrough;
        }
}

TargetDevice = TargetDriver->DeviceObject;  ❺

while( TargetDevice != NULL )
{
        status = YyAttachFilter(
                DriverObject,
                TargetDevice,
                &BufferInfo );

        if( !NT_SUCCESS( status ))
        {
                YyDriverUnload( DriverObject );
                break;
        }
        TargetDevice = TargetDevice->NextDevice;
}

ObDereferenceObject( FileObject );  ❻

return status;
}
```

❶ The first step is to get the contents of an empty slot in the filter's **Major-Function** table. This is actually the address of an internal system routine called **_IopInvalidDeviceRequest**. We can find its current value by looking in any slot of the filter's own table that it hasn't filled in yet.

❷ Next, overwrite slots in the filter's **MajorFunction** table that correspond to functions the filter wants to intercept and modify. In this driver, only write and IOCTL functions are being fooled with.

❸ Using the NT name of any device belonging to the lower driver, get a pointer to the Device object itself. It doesn't really matter which one, since it's only being used to query buffer size limits and to get a pointer to the lower Driver object.

❹ In this loop, see which IRP_MJ_XXX function codes the lower driver responds to. If the lower driver processes a given code and the filter doesn't explicitly intercept that code, fill the corresponding slot in the filter's **MajorFunction** table with the address of a generic pass-through Dispatch routine.

❺ Now, run the list of all Device objects attached to the lower Driver object. For each one, create and attach an invisible filter Device object.

❻ Finally, decrement the reference count on the unused File object and return the most recent status value. This is either STATUS_SUCCESS or some error code from **YyAttachFilter**.

YyAttachFilter   This is a little helper function that does the grunt work associated with creating and attaching a filter Device object to a specific lower-level Device object.

```
static NTSTATUS
YyAttachFilter(
  IN PDRIVER_OBJECT FilterDriver,
  IN PDEVICE_OBJECT TargetDevice,
  IN PXX_BUFFER_SIZE_INFO BufferInfo
  )
{
  PDEVICE_OBJECT FilterDevice;
  PDEVICE_EXTENSION FilterExtension;

  ULONG TargetMethod;
  NTSTATUS status;

  status = IoCreateDevice( ❶
            FilterDriver,
            sizeof( DEVICE_EXTENSION ),
            NULL,
            FILE_DEVICE_UNKNOWN,
            0,
            TRUE,
            &FilterDevice );

  if( !NT_SUCCESS( status ))
  {
        return status;
  }

  status = IoAttachDeviceByPointer(❷
              FilterDevice,
              TargetDevice );
  if( !NT_SUCCESS( status ))
  {
```

```
            IoDeleteDevice( FilterDevice );
            return status;
      }

    FilterExtension = FilterDevice->DeviceExtension;  ❸
    FilterExtension->DeviceObject = FilterDevice;
    FilterExtension->TargetDevice = TargetDevice;

    FilterExtension->
          BufferInfo.MaxWriteLength =
                        BufferInfo->MaxWriteLength;

    FilterExtension->
             BufferInfo.MaxReadLength =
                        BufferInfo->MaxReadLength;

    FilterDevice->DeviceType =
                        TargetDevice->DeviceType;  ❹

    FilterDevice->Characteristics =
                        TargetDevice->Characteristics;

    FilterDevice->Flags |=
          ( TargetDevice->Flags &
             ( DO_BUFFERED_IO | DO_DIRECT_IO ));  ❺

    return STATUS_SUCCESS;
}
```

❶ Create a Device object without an NT name. It doesn't matter what its type or characteristics are, since they'll be copied from the lower-level Device object.

❷ Attach the invisible Device object to the lower-level Device object. See the previous section in this chapter for a description of all the things that happen when you make this call.

❸ Set up the filter Device object's Device Extension structure. This includes storing the transfer size limitations queried from the lower driver.

❹ Copy various items from the lower-level Device object into the filter Device object. This is necessary to make the presence of the filter as transparent as possible.

❺ Last, select the same buffering strategy as the one used by the lower-level Device object.

YyGetBufferLimits   This is an even tinier helper function that queries the lower-level driver for information about its buffer size limits. It shows how to make a synchronous IOCTL call from one driver to another.

```
static VOID
YyGetBufferLimits(
  IN PDEVICE_OBJECT TargetDevice,
  IN OUT PXX_BUFFER_SIZE_INFO BufferInfo
  )
{
  KEVENT IoctlComplete;
  IO_STATUS_BLOCK Iosb;
  PIRP Irp;
  NTSTATUS status;

  KeInitializeEvent(
        &IoctlComplete,
        NotificationEvent,
        FALSE );

  Irp = IoBuildDeviceIoControlRequest(
                IOCTL_XX_GET_MAX_BUFFER_SIZE,
                TargetDevice,
                NULL,
                0,
                BufferInfo,
                sizeof( XX_BUFFER_SIZE_INFO ),
                FALSE,
                &IoctlComplete,
                &Iosb );

  IoCallDriver( TargetDevice, Irp );

  KeWaitForSingleObject(
        &IoctlComplete,
        Executive,
        KernelMode,
        FALSE,
        NULL );
}
```

DISPATCH.C — Filter Dispatch Routines

Here are the Dispatch routines for the filter driver. Only two major function codes are actually modified by the filter. All the others are passed directly to the lower-level driver.

YyDispatchWrite   The lower driver has a limit on the maximum size of an output operation. The filter hides this by breaking writes into smaller pieces. This Dispatch routine and the corresponding I/O Completion routine do the work of splitting the transfer.

```
NTSTATUS
YyDispatchWrite(
  IN PDEVICE_OBJECT DeviceObject,
  IN PIRP Irp
  )
{
  PDEVICE_EXTENSION FilterExtension =
        DeviceObject->DeviceExtension;

  PIO_STACK_LOCATION IrpStack =
        IoGetCurrentIrpStackLocation( Irp );

  PIO_STACK_LOCATION NextIrpStack =
        IoGetNextIrpStackLocation( Irp );

  ULONG MaxTransfer =
        FilterExtension->
                     BufferInfo.MaxWriteLength;

  ULONG BytesRequested =
        IrpStack->Parameters.Write.Length;

  if( BytesRequested == 0 )  ❶
  {
        Irp->IoStatus.Status = STATUS_SUCCESS;
        Irp->IoStatus.Information = 0;
        IoCompleteRequest( Irp, IO_NO_INCREMENT );
        return STATUS_SUCCESS;
  }
  if( BytesRequested <= MaxTransfer )  ❷
  {
        return YyDispatchPassThrough(
                               DeviceObject,
                               Irp );
  }
  NextIrpStack->
        MajorFunction = IRP_MJ_WRITE;  ❸

  NextIrpStack->
        Parameters.Write.Length = MaxTransfer;

  IrpStack->
        Parameters.Write.
             ByteOffset.HighPart = BytesRequested;  ❹

  IrpStack->
        Parameters.Write.
             ByteOffset.LowPart =
```

```
                              (ULONG)Irp->AssociatedIrp.
                                         SystemBuffer;  ➎

       IoSetCompletionRoutine(  ➏
               Irp,
               YyWriteCompletion,
               NULL,
               TRUE, TRUE, TRUE );

       //
       // Pass the IRP to the target device
       //
           return IoCallDriver(  ➐
                   FilterExtension->TargetDevice,
                   Irp );
   }
```

➊ Check for zero-length transfers and complete them right here.

➋ If the requested length is within the lower driver's acceptable limits, just
   send the IRP right on through.

➌ Otherwise, set up the lower driver's I/O stack location in this IRP to
   transfer as much as possible in a single operation.

➍ Use the high-order part of the **ByteOffset** field in the filter driver's I/O
   stack location to hold the number of bytes remaining in the original
   caller's request. This is all right because this field isn't being used for anything else in this driver. Initially, this is the same as the number of bytes
   requested in the whole transfer.

➎ Save the original system buffer address in the low-order (unsigned) part
   of the **ByteOffset** field.

➏ Set up an I/O Completion routine to continue working on the split transfer. All the necessary context is stored somewhere in the IRP, so there's no
   need to pass any other context block.

➐ Finally, pass the IRP to the lower-level driver and begin the first partial
   transfer operation.

YyDispatchDeviceIoControl   To further hide the limitations of the lower-
level driver, the filter intercepts IOCTL queries about the driver's maximum
transfer size. Instead of returning the lower-level driver's limit values, it lies and
says there are no limits. Any other kind of IOCTL function is passed through.

```
NTSTATUS
YyDispatchDeviceIoControl(
  IN PDEVICE_OBJECT DeviceObject,
```

```
    IN PIRP Irp
    )
{
  PIO_STACK_LOCATION IrpStack =
        IoGetCurrentIrpStackLocation( Irp );

  PXX_BUFFER_SIZE_INFO BufferInfo;

  if( IrpStack->
        Parameters.
              DeviceIoControl.IoControlCode
  == IOCTL_XX_GET_MAX_BUFFER_SIZE ) ❶
  {
        BufferInfo =
              (PXX_BUFFER_SIZE_INFO)Irp->
                    AssociatedIrp.SystemBuffer;

        BufferInfo->
              MaxWriteLength = XX_NO_BUFFER_LIMIT;

        BufferInfo->
              MaxReadLength = XX_NO_BUFFER_LIMIT;

        Irp->IoStatus.Information =
                          sizeof( XX_BUFFER_SIZE_INFO );

        Irp->IoStatus.Status = STATUS_SUCCESS;
        IoCompleteRequest( Irp, IO_NO_INCREMENT );
        return STATUS_SUCCESS;
  }
  else ❷
  {
        return YyDispatchPassThrough(
                          DeviceObject,
                          Irp );
  }
}
```

❶ Intercept the buffer-size IOCTL code used by the lower-level driver and tell the caller that there are no size limits.

❷ If it's any other kind of IOCTL, just send it on to the lower driver for processing.

YyDispatchPassThrough   This is the "none of the above" Dispatch routine. It simply passes everything on to the lower-level driver. It attaches a generic I/O Completion routine to handle making the IRP pending.

```
NTSTATUS
YyDispatchPassThrough(
```

```
  IN PDEVICE_OBJECT DeviceObject,
  IN PIRP Irp
  )
{
  PDEVICE_EXTENSION FilterExtension =
        DeviceObject->DeviceExtension;

  PIO_STACK_LOCATION IrpStack =
        IoGetCurrentIrpStackLocation( Irp );

  PIO_STACK_LOCATION NextIrpStack =
        IoGetNextIrpStackLocation( Irp );

  NTSTATUS status;
//
// Copy args to next level
//
  *NextIrpStack = *IrpStack;
//
// Set up Completion routine to handle
// marking the IRP pending.
//
  IoSetCompletionRoutine(
        Irp,
        YyGenericCompletion,
        NULL,
        TRUE, TRUE, TRUE );
//
// Pass the IRP to the target
//
  return IoCallDriver(
            FilterExtension->TargetDevice,
            Irp );
}
```

COMPLETE.C — I/O Completion Routines

The functions in this file handle all the I/O completion performed by the filter driver.

YyWriteCompletion   This is the real workhorse routine. Its job is to perform all the additional partial transfers needed to satisfy the original caller's request. If there's an error, or when the whole transfer is finished, it allows the IRP to continue its journey back up the driver stack. Otherwise, it sets up the IRP for another small transfer and sends it to the lower driver.

```
NTSTATUS
YyWriteCompletion(
  IN PDEVICE_OBJECT DeviceObject,
  IN PIRP Irp,
  IN PVOID Context
  )
{
  PDEVICE_EXTENSION FilterExtension =
        DeviceObject->DeviceExtension;

  PIO_STACK_LOCATION IrpStack =
        IoGetCurrentIrpStackLocation( Irp );

  PIO_STACK_LOCATION NextIrpStack =
        IoGetNextIrpStackLocation( Irp );

  ULONG TransferSize =
        Irp->IoStatus.Information;

  ULONG BytesRequested =
        IrpStack->Parameters.Write.Length;

  ULONG BytesRemaining =
        (ULONG)IrpStack->
                Parameters.Write.ByteOffset.HighPart;

  ULONG MaxTransfer =
        FilterExtension->BufferInfo.MaxWriteLength;

  NTSTATUS status;

  if( NT_SUCCESS( Irp->IoStatus.Status )) ❶
  {
        BytesRemaining -= TransferSize;

        IrpStack->
                Parameters.Write.
                    ByteOffset.HighPart =
                                        BytesRemaining;
  }
  if( NT_SUCCESS( Irp->IoStatus.Status ) ❷
  && BytesRemaining > 0 )
  {
        (PUCHAR)Irp->
                AssociatedIrp.SystemBuffer +=
                                        TransferSize; ❸

        TransferSize = BytesRemaining; ❹

        if( TransferSize > MaxTransfer )
```

```
        {
                TransferSize = MaxTransfer;
        }
        NextIrpStack->MajorFunction = IRP_MJ_WRITE;

        NextIrpStack->
                Parameters.Write.Length =
                                        TransferSize;

        IoSetCompletionRoutine( ❺
                Irp,
                YyWriteCompletion,
                NULL,
                TRUE, TRUE, TRUE );

        IoCallDriver( ❻
                FilterExtension->TargetDevice,
                Irp );

        return STATUS_MORE_PROCESSING_REQUIRED;
    }
    else ❼
    {
        Irp->AssociatedIrp.SystemBuffer =
            (PVOID)IrpStack->
                    Parameters.Write.
                            ByteOffset.LowPart; ❽

        Irp->IoStatus.Information =
                BytesRequested - BytesRemaining; ❾

        if( Irp->PendingReturned ) ❿
        {
                IoMarkIrpPending(Irp);
        }
        return STATUS_SUCCESS;
    }
}
```

❶ If the current transfer worked, reduce the count of bytes left to send and save the new count in an unused part of the filter driver's I/O stack location.

❷ If there's more data left to transfer, set up the next partial output operation.

❸ Increment the pointer into the system buffer to account for the data transfer that's just completed.

❹ Calculate the size of the next partial transfer. Start by assuming it can all be done in a single operation. Reduce that expectation if it proves to be too optimistic.

❺ After setting up the I/O stack location for the lower-level driver, attach this I/O Completion routine to catch the operation when it finishes.

❻ Pass the IRP to the lower-level driver. The return value from the call doesn't matter since the I/O Completion routine will clean up after everything. Then prevent any further processing of this IRP by the **IoCompleteRequest**. After all, the IRP has just been given away.

❼ At this point, there was either an error or all the bytes have been transferred. In either case, get rid of the IRP.

❽ Before the IRP continues its journey up the driver stack, it's very important to restore the original system buffer pointer. The I/O Manager is going to use this pointer to release the buffer, so it must contain its original value.

❾ The **IoStatus.Information** field contains the size of the most recent partial transfer. Change that to show the true number of bytes transferred in all the partial transfers up to this point.

❿ See if the current I/O stack location needs to be put in the pending state. Finally, return STATUS_SUCCESS to let the IRP continue traveling back up the driver hierarchy to the original caller.

YyGenericCompletion   This is another one of those "none of the above" functions. It is used by any kind of I/O request that doesn't need driver-specific completion processing by the filter. Its main purpose is to mark the current I/O stack location pending after the IRP's been released by the lower driver.

```
NTSTATUS
YyGenericCompletion(
  IN PDEVICE_OBJECT DeviceObject,
  IN PIRP Irp,
  IN PVOID Context
  )
{

  if( Irp->PendingReturned )
  {
        IoMarkIrpPending(Irp);
  }
  return STATUS_SUCCESS;
}
```

15.7 WRITING TIGHTLY COUPLED DRIVERS

Unlike layered and filter driver, tightly coupled drivers don't use the I/O Manager's **IoCallDriver** function for most of their communications. Instead, they define some kind of private calling interface. The advantage of this approach is that it's usually faster than the IRP-passing model supported by the I/O Manager. In trade for improved performance, however, you have to pay much more attention to the mechanics of the interface. Also, unless the details of the interface are well documented, it's difficult for drivers from different vendors to work with each other this way.

How Tightly Coupled Drivers Work

Since the interface between two tightly coupled drivers is completely determined by the driver designer, it's impossible to give a single, unified description of how all tightly coupled drivers work. Instead, this subsection presents some general architectural guidelines.[10] Figure 15.3 shows one common method of tightly coupling a pair of drivers.

In this picture, the lower driver has exposed a special setup function in the form of a IRP_MJ_INTERNAL_DEVICE_CONTROL IOCTL. During the upper driver's initialization, it calls this IOCTL function to retrieve a table of function

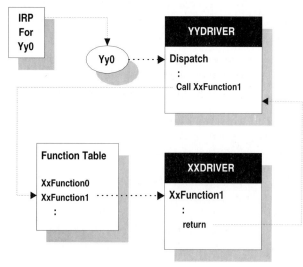

Figure 15.3 How tightly coupled drivers work

---

[10] For some concrete examples, see source code for the mouse and keyboard drivers that comes with the DDK.

pointers from the lower driver. When the upper driver needs the services of the lower driver, it calls one of the functions in this table directly, rather than using **IoCallDriver**. Before unloading, the upper driver calls another function in the function table to disconnect it from the lower driver.

Initialization and Cleanup in Tightly Coupled Drivers

The following subsections describe in general terms how a pair of tightly coupled drivers might initialize and unload. Of course, the exact steps will depend on the architecture chosen by the driver designer.

Lower DriverEntry routine   Assuming the lower driver manages some specific piece of hardware, its DriverEntry routine will perform the following steps.

1. Using the techniques described in Chapter 7, it finds and allocates any hardware for which it is responsible.

2. **DriverEntry** adds an IRP_MJ_INTERNAL_DEVICE_CONTROL Dispatch routine to the Driver object's **MajorFunction** table. One of the IOCTLs supported by this function code will be to export a table of pointers to various functions in the lower driver.

3. Next, it calls **IoCreateDevice** to build a Device object. Although this object has an NT name, it does *not* have a Win32 symbolic link. This Device object is used by the upper driver to establish its initial connection with the lower driver.

4. Finally, **DriverEntry** does any other driver-specific initialization. For example, it might set up a ring of buffers that it will share with its higher-level clients.

Upper DriverEntry routine   The upper driver makes its initial contact with the lower driver using the standard I/O Manager interface described earlier in this chapter. This is what its DriverEntry routine does.

1. It calls **IoGetDeviceObjectPointer** to get a pointer to the lower driver's Device object. As with a layered driver, this is followed by a call to **ObReferenceObjectByPointer** to increment the pointer reference count of the lower Device object, and a call to **ObDereferenceObject** to decrement the reference count of the File object returned by **IoGetDeviceObjectPointer**.

2. Next, **DriverEntry** issues a synchronous IOCTL request to the lower Device object. This IOCTL returns the address of the lower driver's table of exported functions.

3. It creates one or more Device objects with **IoCreateDevice**. If the upper driver is exposing these objects to user-mode applications, it calls **IoCreateSymbolicLink** to give them Win32 names.

4.   Finally, **DriverEntry** stores the address of the lower driver's function table in the Device Extension of the upper Device objects.

Upper Unload routine   When the upper driver is stopped, its Unload routine should perform the following general steps.

1.   It releases any resources it might have acquired from the lower driver. For example, if it received a buffer from the lower driver, it returns it.

2.   Next, the Unload routine issues a synchronous IOCTL to the lower Device object. This notifies the lower driver that the upper one is disconnecting and gives the lower driver a chance to release resources acquired from the upper driver.

3.   It then calls **ObDereferenceObject** to decrement the pointer reference count on the lower Device object. This effectively breaks the connection with the lower driver.

4.   Finally, the Unload routine performs the usual cleanup tasks, such as deleting its own Device objects and symbolic links.

Lower Unload routine   There's nothing particular exciting about the lower driver's Unload routine. It simply releases any hardware it might be holding, releases any other system resources it has allocated, and deletes the Device object that it exposed to the upper driver.

I/O Request Processing in Tightly Coupled Drivers

When a client of the upper driver issues an I/O request, the I/O Manager sends an IRP representing the transaction to one of the upper driver's Dispatch routines. Rather than using **IoCallDriver** to send this IRP to the lower driver, the Dispatch routine directly calls one or more functions in the lower driver to service the request. The exact processing sequence will depend on whether the request is handled synchronously or asynchronously.

Synchronous I/O   For input operations, the upper driver uses a **GetBuffer** function in the lower driver to dequeue a buffer of data from the ring of shared buffers. Following the model described in Chapter 14, this queue has a Semaphore object that keeps track of the number of full buffers. If the queue of ready buffers is empty, the Semaphore will be in the Non-signaled state, and the upper driver's Dispatch routine will wait. When the lower driver adds a full buffer to the queue, it increments the Semaphore, which awakens the waiting Dispatch routine. The Dispatch routine then formats and copies data from the shared buffer into the buffer associated with the original caller's IRP, completes the IRP, and releases the shared buffer using a **PutBuffer** function exposed by the lower driver.

Synchronous output operations just reverse the sequence. Here, the upper driver's Dispatch routine calls a **GetBuffer** function in the lower driver to get an empty buffer from the queue. Again, the queue has an attached Semaphore object that counts the number of available buffers. If there are no empty buffers, the upper driver's Dispatch routine waits until the lower driver adds one to the queue and increments the Semaphore. Once it gets an empty buffer, the upper driver fills it with data from the buffer associated with the original IRP. It then calls a **PutBuffer** function exposed by the lower driver.

The **PutBuffer** function begins the actual data transfer and then waits for a synchronization Event object embedded in the buffer. This causes the upper driver's Dispatch routine to go to sleep. When the transfer operation completes, some other part of the lower driver (a DPC routine, for example) sets the Event object and returns the buffer to the queue of available blocks. At that point, the upper driver's Dispatch routine wakes up and completes the original caller's IRP.

Asynchronous I/O   In this case, the upper driver's Dispatch routine calls **IoMarkIrpPending** to put the original caller's IRP into the pending state. It then calls a **QueueRequest** function exported by the lower driver. As arguments, this function takes the address of the original IRP and a pointer to a callback routine in the upper driver. **QueueRequest** stores the IRP address and callback pointer in a driver-defined context block and adds it to a private queue of pending requests. It then returns control to the upper driver, and the upper driver's Dispatch routine returns STATUS_PENDING to the I/O Manager.

Meanwhile, the lower driver is busily pulling context blocks from its private queue and performing I/O requests. As each one finishes, the lower driver invokes the upper driver's callback routine and passes it the address of the processed IRP. The callback routine in the upper driver does any postprocessing needed by the request and calls **IoCompleteRequest** with the original caller's IRP.

15.8 SUMMARY

The layered architecture in Windows NT allows you to simplify the design of drivers that might otherwise be extremely complex. Breaking a monolithic driver into smaller, logically distinct pieces makes implementation and maintenance easier, reduces debugging time, and increases the likelihood that some of the software will be reusable.

In this chapter, you've seen a number of different ways to stack drivers on top of one another. Most of these techniques depend on the I/O Manager's standard calling mechanism to send IRPs from one driver to another. If this proves not to be fast enough, you can also define private interfaces between a pair of drivers. In general, these privately-defined interfaces are a bad idea because they make the design more fragile and harder to maintain.

Regardless of how your drivers communicate with one another, you still have to guarantee that they load in the proper order. Getting that to happen is one of the topics discussed in the next chapter.

Building and Installing Drivers

*T*here's always a certain amount of grunt work associated with any interesting activity. This chapter is about the mundane details of building drivers and installing them on a system. Some of this information is pretty straightforward stuff. Other bits of it have been teased painfully from various header files, online sources, and tedious experimentation. So, even if you're familiar with the DDK documentation, you may find something of value here.

16.1 BUILDING DRIVERS

One difficult aspect of writing drivers for Windows NT is that you need to maintain separate versions of the driver for each hardware platform that you support. Generating and keeping track of multiple binaries is especially troublesome because you may need different sets of compiler and linker options for each platform. The BUILD utility supplied with the NT DDK insulates you from most of these platform dependencies.

What BUILD Does

The BUILD utility is just an elaborate wrapper around NMAKE. Using a set of keywords, you describe the operation you want to perform. BUILD then scans your source files for dependencies and constructs an appropriate set of NMAKE commands. Next, it runs NMAKE to execute these commands, and the result is

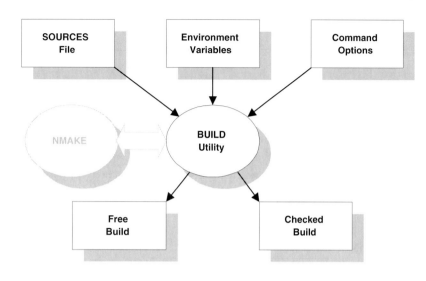

Figure 16.1 How the BUILD utility works

one or more binary output files (referred to as *BUILD products*). Figure 16.1 shows how this process works.

BUILD itself is actually a rather simple-minded piece of software. Most of the build process is controlled by a set of standard command files that BUILD passes to NMAKE. These files contain all the platform-specific rules and option settings needed to create a BUILD product. Keeping these rules in a separate file allows Microsoft to modify the build process without having to rewrite the whole BUILD utility. Currently, BUILD uses these command files (located in **...\DDK\INC**):

- **MAKEFILE.DEF** is the master control file. It uses several other files to do some of its work.

- **MAKEFILE.PLT** selects the target platform for a build operation.

- **I386MK.INC**, **ALPHAMK.INC**, **MIPSMK.INC**, and **PPCMK.INC** contain platform-specific compiler and linker switches for Intel, Alpha, MIPS, and PowerPC systems.

BUILD helps you manage multiplatform projects by separating binary files according to their platform type. To do this, it uses different directories for Intel, MIPS, Alpha, and PowerPC binaries. If you have cross-hosted compilers and linkers, you can produce the binaries for all the supported platforms on one system using a single BUILD command. Figure 16.2 shows the directory structure that BUILD uses.

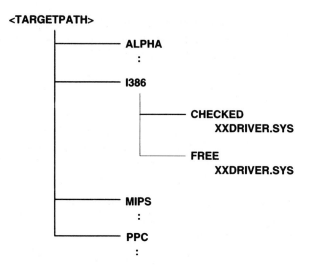

Figure 16.2   Directory structure for BUILD products

Notice that BUILD also uses separate directories for the *checked* and *free* versions of your binaries. In the checked version, compiler optimization is disabled, extra debugging information is added to the file, and the **DBG** symbol is defined as 1 (allowing you to include conditional debugging code in your driver). By contrast, free BUILD products are compiled with optimization turned on and the **DBG** symbol is defined as 0. Checked builds are useful when you're debugging; free builds are generally smaller and faster and should be used for the commercial release of a driver.

One of BUILD's odd little quirks is that, while it creates the platform-specific directories automatically, for some reason it doesn't create the **CHECKED** and **FREE** subdirectories. This results in an error message from the linker when it tries to create your driver. The easiest solution is to set up the directory structure by hand.

How to Build a Driver

Once you have some source code ready, follow these steps to generate your driver. You only need to perform steps 1–3 the first time you build the driver.

1.   In the directory where you keep your driver source code, create a file called **SOURCES** that identifies the components of the final driver. A discussion of what to put in this file appears later in this section.

2.   In the same directory, create a file called **MAKEFILE** that contains only the following line:

```
!INCLUDE $(NTMAKEENV)\MAKEFILE.DEF
```

This stub invokes the standard makefile needed by any driver created with BUILD. Don't edit this stub makefile. If you want to add more source files to this driver, add them to the **SOURCES** file.

3. Use the File Manager or the MKDIR command to set up the directory tree for your BUILD products. Refer back to Figure 16.2.

4. In the Program Manager group for the Windows NT DDK, double-click on the icon for either the Checked Build or the Free Build environment. A command window will appear with the appropriate BUILD environment variables set for a debug or release version of your driver. It's important that you run the BUILD utility only from one of these windows.

5. When the Checked or Free command window opens, its default directory is the same as the installation directory for the NT DDK itself. Use the CD command to move to the directory where your driver's **SOURCES** file is located.

6. Run the BUILD utility to create the driver executable.

If all goes well, your driver will be in the **CHECKED** or **FREE** subdirectory of the appropriate platform directory. If something goes awry, look at the various BUILD log files to determine the problem.

You might be wondering whether you can build NT drivers on a Windows 95 system. The VC++ tools all run under Windows 95, so in theory it should work. Unfortunately, when BUILD spawns NMAKE, it uses a command line that's too long for Windows 95 to handle and the operation fails. Consequently, you have to do your BUILDing on a Windows NT system.

Writing a SOURCES File

You describe your BUILD operation using a series of keywords. These keywords specify things like the type of driver you want to generate, the source files making up the BUILD product, and the directories for various files. Although you can pass these keywords to BUILD as command-line options or environment variables, the usual procedure is to put them in a **SOURCES** file. Keep the following points in mind when you write one of these files:

- The filename must be **SOURCES** (without any extension).

- The file should contain some number of commands, each having the following format:

  ```
  keyword=value
  ```

- You can break a single BUILD command over multiple lines in the **SOURCES** file by putting a \ character at the end of each line except the last.

- The value of a BUILD keyword must be pure text. BUILD itself does only very limited processing of NMAKE macros and doesn't handle conditional statements at all.

- Make sure you don't leave any whitespace between a BUILD keyword and the = character. Whitespace after the = is acceptable.

- You can put comments in a **SOURCES** file by starting the line with a # character.

Table 16.1 lists the **SOURCES** keywords that you're most likely to use for building drivers. If you're the sort of person who enjoys going to the dentist for root-canal work, you may want to use the BUILD utility for maintaining user-mode applications as well as drivers. In that case, see the BUILD documentation for a list of additional keywords.

Table 16.1　BUILD utility keywords for maintaining drivers and libraries

Selected BUILD keywords

Keyword	Meaning
INCLUDES	List of paths containing header files
SOURCES	List of source files making up the BUILD product*
TARGETPATH	Top-level directory for BUILD product tree*
TARGETNAME	Name of the BUILD product, without an extension*
TARGETEXT	File extension for the BUILD product
TARGETTYPE	Case-sensitive keyword describing BUILD product* • DRIVER • GDI_DRIVER • MINIPORT • LIBRARY (for static libraries) • DYNLINK (for DLLs)
TARGETLIBS	List of libraries to be linked with the driver
LINKER_FLAGS	Linker options of the form *–flag:value* **Example:** –MAP:XXDRIVER.MAP
PRECOMPILED_INCLUDE	File containing **#include** directives
NTTARGETFILE0	List of nonstandard components to be built with MAKEFILE.INC after initial dependency scan
NTTARGETFILE1	List of nonstandard components to be built with MAKEFILE.INC before linking
NTTARGETFILES	List of nonstandard components to be built with MAKEFILE.INC both before and after the link

*Required.

The following is an example of a minimal SOURCES file for building a kernel-mode driver.

```
TARGETNAME= XXDRIVER

TARGETTYPE= DRIVER
TARGETPATH= .

INCLUDES= $(BASEDIR)\inc;..\inc

SOURCES= init.c config.c resalloc.c \
         dispatch.c xfer.c unload.c
```

One item to point out in this file is the INCLUDES= keyword. For some reason, neither the DDK installation procedure nor the Free/Checked build icons add the DDK header directory to the INCLUDE-path environment variable. By naming it explicitly in **SOURCES**, you can avoid a number of miscellaneous BUILD error messages.

Log Files Generated by BUILD

In addition to its screen output, the BUILD utility generates several text files that you can use to determine the status of a BUILD product. These files are:

- **BUILD.LOG** — Lists the commands invoked by NMAKE.

- **BUILD.WRN** — Contains any warnings generated during the build.

- **BUILD.ERR** — Contains a list of errors generated during the build.

BUILD puts these files in the same directory as the **SOURCES** file. The warning and error files appear only if something bad happened during the BUILD operation.

One other point worth mentioning is BUILD's nasty habit of filtering out some compiler and linker messages. These filtered messages don't appear on the screen display, but they will show up in the log files. For that reason, it's important to check the log files after each BUILD.

Recursive BUILD Operations

You can use BUILD to maintain an entire source code tree by creating a file called **DIRS**. You put this file in a directory that contains nothing but subdirectories. Each subdirectory can be a source directory (containing a **SOURCES** file) or the root of another source tree (containing another **DIRS** file). When you run BUILD from the topmost DIRS directory, it creates all the BUILD products described in each **SOURCES** file.

The rules for writing a **DIRS** file are the same as those for a **SOURCES** file, with the restriction that you're only allowed to use the following two keywords:

- **DIRS** — Lists subdirectories that should always be built. Entries in this list are separated by spaces or tabs.

- **OPTIONAL_DIRS** — Lists subdirectories that should be built only if they are named on the original BUILD command line.

This recursive BUILD feature can be useful for maintaining things like video drivers that have both a user-mode and a kernel-mode component.

16.2 MISCELLANEOUS BUILD-TIME ACTIVITIES

Along with the basic operations of getting your driver to compile and link, there are several other kinds of activities that you may want to perform at BUILD time. This section presents the ones that have proven to be the most useful.

Using Precompiled Headers

Much of the time consumed by a BUILD operation is spent compiling various large header files. During a normal development cycle, your driver's code will change frequently, but these headers will be relatively static. This leads to a lot of wasted time as the headers are compiled again and again. By taking advantage of the C compiler's precompiled header feature, you can significantly reduce the BUILD time of your driver (at the expense of some disk space).

To use precompiled headers, you'll need to make some changes to your driver sources and add a new keyword to the BUILD control file. Follow these steps:

1. Create a header file containing nothing but **#include** directives for any other headers used by your driver. For example, if you called this file **PRECOMP.H**, it would contain the following:

   ```
   #include <ntddk.h>
   #include "xxdriver.h"
   #include "hardware.h"
   :
   ```

2. In all your other driver source files, replace all **#include** directives with

   ```
   #include "precomp.h"
   ```

3. Add the following statement to your **SOURCES** file:

   ```
   PRECOMPILED_INCLUDE= PRECOMP.H
   ```

When you run BUILD for the first time, the C compiler will save the precompiled header information in a binary file called **PRECOMP.PCH**. As long as you don't change the contents of your headers, the compiler will be able to save itself some work by reusing the precompiled binary version.

Including Version Information in a Driver

How much time have you spent tracking down weird bugs, only to find that the real problem was a software version mismatch? This can be a real time waster, especially if you're trying to support a commercial product used by hundreds of customers. You can avoid this situation altogether by putting explicit version information in your drivers and checking it before you start looking for more complex explanations.

You add version information to a driver using a resource script that defines a version structure. An example later in this section shows how to do this, but the basic steps you need to follow are:

1. Separate your version data into two categories: things that relate to your company as a whole (like the company name), and things that are product-specific.

2. Use the generic company information to write a header that can be included in the version resource scripts of all your products.

3. Write a resource script for your driver that contains product-specific version information. This file should be updated each time you release a version of your driver for testing.

4. Add the name of the resource script to the list of driver components identified by the SOURCES keyword in your **SOURCES** file.

When you want to examine the driver's version data, you can use the File Manager's File Properties... menu item. To display this information in a more complete form, you could also write a little Win32 program to read the version data. The following Win32 API calls are relevant.

- **GetFileVersionInfoSize** — This tells you the number of bytes of version data are associated with the driver.

- **GetFileVersionInfo** — This returns a buffer of version data.

- **VerQueryValue** — This extracts a specific piece of version information from the buffer returned by **GetFileVersionInfo**.

To make all this more concrete, here are examples of a vendor header file and the corresponding product resource script.

Vendor information file. This header file contains version information common to all the products from one vendor. Although you could include this stuff in the RC file itself, if you're maintaining several products, it's less work to keep it in one place for all of them. Below is a copy of **CYDNXVER.H**, the vendor information file for Cydonix Corporation.

```
#define VER_COMPANYNAME_STR      "Cydonix Corporation"

#define VER_LEGALTRADEMARKS_STR          \
"Cydonix\256 is a trademark of Cydonix Corporation."

#define VER_LEGALCOPYRIGHT_YEARS "1994-1995"

#define VER_LEGALCOPYRIGHT_STR           \
  "Copyright \251 Cydonix Corp. "        \
  VER_LEGALCOPYRIGHT_YEARS

/* default is nodebug */
#if DBG
#define VER_DEBUG                VS_FF_DEBUG
#else
#define VER_DEBUG                0
#endif

/* default is release */
#if BETA
#define VER_PRERELEASE           VS_FF_PRERELEASE
#else
#define VER_PRERELEASE           0
#endif

#define VER_FILEFLAGSMASK VS_FFI_FILEFLAGSMASK
#define VER_FILEOS        VOS_NT_WINDOWS32
#define VER_FILEFLAGS     (VER_PRERELEASE | VER_DEBUG)
```

Product information file   This is the actual resource control script that sets product-specific fields in the version resource. Notice that it includes the vendor default values defined above. The actual version resource is built by including the system-supplied **COMMON.VER** file. Any version information not defined by the time you include **COMMON.VER** will be filled in with Microsoft-specific information. The following is a copy of **XXDRIVER.RC**, the version resource script for XXDRIVER.

```
#include <windows.h>

/*-------------------------------------------------------*/
/* Include default values for generic vendor info */
/*                                               */
/*-------------------------------------------------------*/
#include "cydnxver.h"

/*-------------------------------------------------------*/
/* The following values should be modified only by */
/* the official builder, and they should be updated */
/* for each release */
/*-------------------------------------------------------*/
```

```
#define VER_PRODUCTBUILD 42
#define VER_PRODUCTVERSION_STR "1.01"
#define VER_PRODUCTVERSION 1,01,VER_PRODUCTBUILD,1
#define VER_PRODUCTBETA_STR ""

/*-------------------------------------------------*/
/* Include product-specific default values */
/*                                         */
/*-------------------------------------------------*/

#define VER_PRODUCTNAME_STR"XXDRIVER"
#define VER_FILETYPEVFT_DRV
#define VER_FILESUBTYPEVFT2_UNKNOWN
#define VER_FILEDESCRIPTION_STR"Driver for XX"
#define VER_INTERNALNAME_STR"xxdriver.sys"
#define VER_ORIGINALFILENAME_STR"xxdriver.sys"

/*-------------------------------------------------*/
/* Define the version resource itself */
/*                                    */
/*-------------------------------------------------*/
#include <common.ver>
```

Including Nonstandard Components in a BUILD

Even though BUILD is the epitome of software maintenance technology, there are still some things it doesn't do very well. For example, if you have a nonstandard driver component (like a custom message file), BUILD won't know what to do. It's your job to help BUILD out of these sticky situations by writing an auxiliary makefile that tells it how to process the nonstandard components. These are the steps you need to follow:

1. Decide what nonstandard target files need to be part of the driver.

2. In the same directory as the **SOURCES** file for your driver, create a makefile called **MAKEFILE.INC**. This makefile describes the dependencies among your driver's nonstandard components and gives instructions for building these components.

3. For each nonstandard component, decide when during the BUILD operation the component should be created.

4. Add the component to the list of files in the NTTARGEFILE0, NTTARGETFILE1, or NTTARGETFILES keyword of your BUILD control file. See Table 16.1 for a description of these keywords.

5. Run the BUILD utility.

Back in Chapter 13, you saw an example of a driver that defined some private messages for logging events. Here are the auxiliary NMAKE and BUILD control files that generate this driver's executable. You can find the complete example in the **CH13\DRIVER** directory on the floppy that accompanies this book.

MAKEFILE.INC   Recall from Chapter 13 that the message compiler generates a tiny resource script along with a binary message file and a header. You include this stub resource script in the driver's main resource file, which leads to the following dependencies in the auxiliary makefile:

```
xxmsg.rc xxmsg.h msg00001.bin: xxmsg.mc
    mc -v -c xxmsg.mc
```

SOURCES   Since the dependent files must be generated before BUILD runs the resource compiler or the C compiler, you use the NTTARGETFILE0 keyword. Identifying any one of the dependent files is enough to get BUILD to invoke **MAKEFILE.INC**.

```
TARGETTYPE= DRIVER
TARGETNAME= xxdriver
TARGETPATH= .

INCLUDES= $(BASEDIR)\inc;..\inc;.

SOURCES= init.c unload.c          \
        dispatch.c                \
        eventlog.c                \
        xxmsg.rc

NTTARGETFILE0= xxmsg.h
```

Moving Driver Symbol Data into .DBG Files

Contrary to what the DDK documentation claims, both checked and free versions of your driver contain symbol data, which greatly increases the size of your driver executable. This section explains how to strip symbols from your driver and put them into a separate file. Follow this procedure.

1. Use the following command to examine the header information in your driver's executable:

    ```
    DUMPBIN/HEADERS XXDRIVER.SYS | MORE
    ```

2. In the **OPTIONAL HEADER VALUES** section, look for the image base address. Usually this will be 0x10000 for kernel-mode drivers.

3. Strip symbol information from your driver and put it in a separate file using this command:

    ```
    REBASE -B 0x10000 -X .\SYMBOLS XXDRIVER.SYS
    ```

    The B option specifies the new base address for the driver (in this case, the same as the original value). The X option identifies the directory where the

Table 16.2 Effect of removing symbols on driver file sizes

Driver sizes with and without symbols

Version	Before REBASE	After REBASE
Checked build	376,476 bytes	96,544 bytes
Free build	77,600 bytes	46,368 bytes

symbol file should go. The symbol file will have the same name as the driver executable, with the extension **.DBG**.

4. To use the symbol file for debugging, move it to the directory where you keep other **.DBG** files on the host machine.

If you look at Table 16.2, you'll see the impact symbol data can have on the size of a driver. This table compares the sizes of checked and free builds of the standard NT serial port driver with and without symbols.

16.3 INSTALLING DRIVERS

This section explains how to install a driver by hand, which is something you'll need to do while you're developing your driver. It also presents some guidelines for automating the driver installation process once the retail version is ready for the world.

How to Install a Driver by Hand

Installing an NT driver is just a matter of copying some files to the right directory and making a few entries in the system Registry. These are the basic steps you need to follow:

1. Copy the driver to the **%SystemRoot%\SYSTEM32\DRIVERS** directory on the target system.

2. Add appropriate entries to the Registry of the target system using the REGEDT32 utility. These entries are described below.

3. Reboot the target system to make the Service Control Manager aware of the new driver. If the driver's Registry entries specify automatic startup, the driver will load during system boot.

4. If the driver's Registry entries specify manual startup, use the Control Panel Devices applet to start the driver.

If you find a nonfatal bug in your driver, you can load a corrected copy without rebooting the system. Just use the Control Panel Devices applet to stop the driver. Then, overwrite the driver executable in the **...\DRIVERS** directory and restart it using the Devices applet. Of course, this only works if the driver has an XxUnload routine and if it isn't crucial to the operation of the system.

Driver Registry Entries

During system bootstrap, NT builds a list of available drivers by scanning the Registry. This list identifies both the drivers that start automatically as well as those that need to be started manually. To add your driver to this list, you need to build the Registry entries that appear in Figure 16.3.

Table 16.3 describes these Registry keys and values. To bring a driver online, you only need the driver's service key plus the **Start**, **Type**, and **ErrorControl** values. The service key should have the same name as the driver executable, without the file extension. As you saw in Chapter 7, the **Parameters** subkey is normally used for device information that doesn't auto-detect, although you can really put anything in it.

End-User Installation of Standard Drivers

Manual installation is fine while you're still developing a driver, but once your code is ready for commercial release, it's a good idea to automate the whole procedure. If your driver manages a standard piece of hardware (like a video or network card), you can take advantage of NT's built-in driver installation mechanisms. These built-in mechanisms run in three different situations.

During text setup   When end users perform a full installation of Windows NT, the first piece of setup software runs in text mode. During this text phase, the

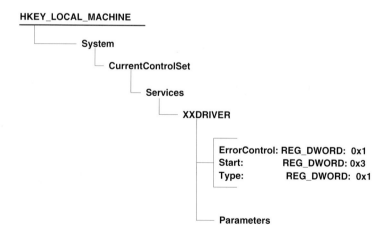

Figure 16.3   Structure of a driver's Registry service key

Table 16.3 Kernel-driver Registry entries

Driver service key Registry entries		
Name	**Data type**	**Description**
XXDRIVER	(Key)	Driver service key*
Type	REG_DWORD	What kind of driver this is*
		• 1 — kernel-mode driver
		• 2 — file-system driver
Start	REG_DWORD	When to start the driver (see below)*
ErrorControl	REG_DWORD	System response if driver fails to load*
		• 0 — log error and ignore
		• 1 — log error and put up a message box
		• 2 — log error and reboot with last-known good configuration
		• 3 — log error and fail if already using last-known good configuration
Group	REG_SZ	Driver's group name (see below)
DependOnGroup	REG_MULTI_SZ	Drivers needed by this one (see below)
Tag	REG_BINARY	Driver load order within a group (see below)
Parameters	(Key)	Key to hold driver-specific parameters

*These entries are required.

setup program installs drivers for the keyboard, the mouse, SCSI HBAs, and video devices. If it can't find a driver for one of these devices (or if the user chooses to replace the standard driver), the setup program will prompt the user for an installation diskette.

The diskette contains a copy of the driver itself and a control script called **TXTSETUP.OEM**. This script is just a text file that identifies the type of hardware supported by the driver, lists the files that need to be copied from the floppy, and names the keys and values that should be added to the Registry. The Windows NT DDK *Programmer's Guide* describes the exact contents and format of a **TXT-SETUP.OEM** file.

During GUI setup Once the text phase of Windows NT installation finishes, a GUI-based setup program takes over. This GUI setup program can install drivers for the keyboard and mouse, video and network cards, tape drives, and SCSI HBAs. Just like its text-based counterpart, the GUI setup program prompts the user for the location of any drivers it can't find; it also allows the user to supply replacements for the standard drivers.

To install a driver during GUI setup, once again you'll need to write a control file. This one is called **OEMSETUP.INF**, and it uses a much more full-featured scripting language than **TXTSETUP.OEM**. The GUI scripting language supports dialog boxes, message text in multiple national languages, elaborate flow control, and commands for a variety of common installation tasks. If the built-in commands aren't enough, you can call functions in DLLs or run external programs from within the script. See the Windows NT DDK *Programmer's Guide* for a description of the GUI scripting language.

After NT installation   Users can also install drivers for standard devices after NT itself has been set up. This is referred to as *maintenance mode installation*, and it uses the same **OEMSETUP.INF** script as the GUI setup phase of NT. Depending on the type of hardware, the end user will have to run either the Windows NT Setup program or a Control Panel applet to execute the script. Table 16.4 shows the various options.

End-User Installation of Nonstandard Drivers

If your device isn't one of the types supported by **TXTSETUP.OEM** or **OEMSETUP.INF**, you'll have to provide your own installation program. You can either use commercial installation software, or you can roll your own using some of the following Win32 API calls:

- **CopyFile** to move the driver file to the appropriate directory.
- **RegCreateKeyEx** and **RegSetValueEx** to set up the proper keys and values in the Registry.
- **CreateProcess** to run any external programs needed during installation.
- **CreateService** and **StartService** if you want to bring the driver online without rebooting the system.[1]

As you've seen elsewhere in this book, you can customize the behavior of your driver using values stored in the **Parameters** subkey of the driver's Registry

Table 16.4   How to install standard drivers in maintenance mode

Installation tools for standard drivers

Type of driver	Installation tool
Keyboard	Windows NT Setup
Mouse	Windows NT Setup
Multimedia device	Control Panel Drivers applet
Net-card and network protocol	Control Panel Network applet
SCSI HBA	Windows NT Setup
Tape drive	Windows NT Setup
Video	Control Panel Display applet

---

[1] See the INSTDRV sample that comes with the NT DDK for an example of using the Service Control Manager API to install a driver without forcing the user to reboot.

service key. If you have many of these parameters and you expect end users to change them, you should consider writing either a Control Panel applet or a standalone program to modify the Registry. This is much safer than asking an end user to work with REGEDT32.

Finally, you'll make everyone's life easier if you supply software that allows users to remove your driver from the system. This means cleaning up the Registry as well as deleting any relevant files.

16.4 CONTROLLING DRIVER LOAD SEQUENCE

There are times when you may need to control the sequence in which NT loads multiple drivers. For example, class drivers usually have to be loaded after the port drivers that manage their underlying hardware. If your drivers load automatically when the system boots, you can use various Registry entries to control their load sequence. This section explains how.

Changing the Driver's Start Value

You can control when a driver loads by setting the **Start** value in the driver's Registry service key. The number you assign to **Start** corresponds to one of the Service startup types recognized by the NT Service Control Manager. Currently, **Start** can take one of the following values.

0x0 (SERVICE_BOOT_START)   This value specifies that a driver should be started by the operating system loader. Since much of the system isn't available, this value should be used only for drivers that are necessary to the bootstrap operation itself (for example, the driver for the boot device).

0x1 (SERVICE_SYSTEM_START)   This value identifies drivers that should be started after the operating system has been loaded, but while it is still initializing itself.

0x2 (SERVICE_AUTO_START)   Drivers with this **Start** value are loaded by the Service Control Manager after the entire system is up and running. Unless your driver is crucial to the system bootstrap or initialization, this is probably the most appropriate value to choose.

0x3 (SERVICE_DEMAND_START)   These drivers have to be started manually, either by using the Control Panel Devices applet or by making direct calls to the Win32 Service Control Manager API.

0x4 (SERVICE_DISABLED)   Disabled drivers cannot be started until their **Start** value is changed to something else. Again, you change this value using the Control Panel Devices applet or the Service Control Manager API, or by modifying the Registry directly.

NT guarantees that drivers with lower **Start** values will be loaded ahead of drivers with higher values. So all drivers with a value of 0 will load ahead of any drivers with values of 1 or 2. Keep in mind that this only works for **Start** values of 0, 1, or 2, because drivers with other **Start** values require some kind of manual intervention to get them going.

Creating Explicit Dependencies between Drivers

Setting **Start** values is fine if your drivers need to be loaded during different phases of system startup, but what if you need to control the load order of multiple drivers with the same **Start** value? For example, a SCSI class driver won't be able to load successfully until all the SCSI miniport HBA drivers are available. One solution to this problem is to use the **Group** and **DependOnGroup** values in the driver service keys.

These are the steps you should follow if you want to establish an explicit load-order dependency between two drivers:

1. Decide which driver needs to load first and choose a group name for this driver. In some cases (like the SCSI miniport), you may need to use a standard, system-defined group name. Otherwise, use a name of your own choosing.

2. Add a value called **Group** to the service key of the driver that loads first. The **Group** value is a REG_SZ containing the group name you've assigned to this driver.

3. Add a value called **DependOnGroup** to the service key of the driver that should load second. The **DependOnGroup** value is a REG_MULTI_SZ containing the names of any groups on which this driver depends. At least one driver in each named group must be started before the system will start any dependent driver.

Keep in mind that you can have as many drivers as you like with the same **Group** value. This guarantees that all the members of the group will get a chance to load ahead of any drivers depending on that group name. Again, SCSI miniports are a good example.

To see how all this works, imagine that you have two drivers, XXDRIVER and YYDRIVER, and that XXDRIVER is a member of the group called "Group W." If you wanted XXDRIVER to load ahead of YYDRIVER, you'd need to set up the following Registry entries:

```
HKEY_LOCAL_MACHINE\...\Services\XXDRIVER
  Start: REG_DWORD: 2
  Group: REG_SZ: Group W

HKEY_LOCAL_MACHINE\...\Services\YYDRIVER
  Start: REG_DWORD: 2
  DependOnGroup: REG_MULTI_SZ: Group W
```

With these values, both drivers will load during final stages of system startup, after everything is running. Further, all the drivers in "Group W" will be given a chance to load before YYDRIVER.

Establishing Global Group Dependencies

Another way to control the load order of your drivers is to modify the **ServiceGroupOrder** key in the Registry. This key contains a single REG_MULTI_SZ value called **List** that identifies group names in the order that they will be loaded. The earlier a driver's group name appears in this list, the sooner it loads. NT will try to load all the drivers in an earlier group ahead of any driver in a later group.

Figure 16.4 shows an excerpt of this part of the Registry. In this example, drivers in the group "SCSI class" load after all drivers in the group "Primary disk" and before any drivers in the group "SCSI CDROM class."

Although you could achieve the same results using **DependOnGroup**, this technique is useful for situations where you don't want to modify the Registry values of some of the drivers. For example, if you wanted one of your drivers to load earlier than a particular system-supplied driver group, you could simple modify the **ServiceGroupOrder** key. There would be no need to change the **DependOnGroup** value of each system-supplied driver.

The **ServiceGroupOrder** list is actually scanned several times during system startup. First, at bootstrap time, all drivers with a **Start** value of 0 load according to their **ServiceGroupOrder** sequence. Next, during system initialization, drivers with a **Start** value of 1 load. Finally, when the system is up and running, any drivers with a **Start** value of 2 are loaded. So, drivers with lower **Start** values load

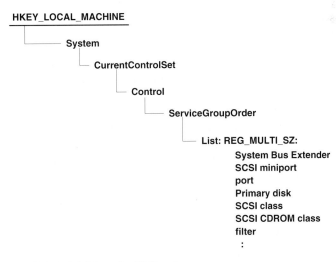

Figure 16.4 The layout of the ServiceGroupOrder Registry key

before any drivers with higher **Start** values, no matter what their positions in the **ServiceGroupOrder** list.

As an example, suppose you had a SCSI disk that needed a special driver. Unfortunately, the standard SCSI disk class driver is going to allocate anything that looks like a SCSI disk, including yours. The only way to prevent this is to make sure that your driver loads ahead of the standard driver. You can do this by modifying the **ServiceGroupOrder** list.

First, add a **Group** value to the Registry key for the driver that manages the special disk. If this driver were XXDRIVER, and you wanted to add it to "Group W," the Registry key would be

```
HKEY_LOCAL_MACHINE\...\Services\XXDRIVER
  Group: REG_SZ: Group W
  Start: REG_DWORD: 0
```

Examining the Registry service key for the standard SCSI disk driver (SCSIDISK), you find that it belongs to the group "SCSI class." So, you need to edit the **ServiceGroupOrder** list and add "Group W" ahead of "SCSI class." The Registry would then look like this:

```
HKEY_LOCAL_MACHINE\...\Control\ServiceGroupOrder
  List: REG_MULTI_SZ:     System Bus Extender
                          SCSI miniport
                          :
                          Group W
                          SCSI class
                          :
```

Controlling Load Sequence within a Group

The techniques presented so far allow you to set up load-order relationships among groups of drivers, but they make no promises about the load order of drivers in the same group. By adding **Tag** values to the Registry keys of drivers within a group, you can control their loading sequence. Here's what you need to do:

1. Modify the **...\CurrentControlSet\Control\GroupOrderList** key in the Registry by adding a value with the same name as your driver group. Give this value a data type of REG_BINARY and make sure its contents follow the pattern described below. This value defines a series of tag numbers and their sequence.

2. Add a REG_DWORD value called **Tag** to the Registry service key of each driver in the group. Set this value to one of the tag numbers you defined for your group in **GroupOrderList**.

Within a single group, NT will load drivers according to the sequence of their **Tag** values, as defined in the **GroupOrderList**. Drivers without a **Tag** value

Figure 16.5   Layout of a tag definition in the GroupOrderList key

(and drivers whose **Tag** value is not in the **GroupOrderList**) load after the drivers with valid **Tag** values. For these drivers, the order of loading is not guaranteed, other than that all drivers in a group load before the next group loads.

The tag definitions in the **GroupOrderList** are REG_BINARY data, and their format needs a little explanation. As you can see from Figure 16.5, each definition contains several fields. The first field is a 1-byte count of the number of tag values to follow. Next come the tag numbers themselves, each one taking up a DWORD. These are followed by 3 null bytes that round the whole entry up to an integral number of DWORDs.

The following example of one of these values defines two tags: one with a value of 0x44 and another with a value of 0x28.

```
02 00 00 00 44 00 00 00 28 00 00 00
```

Note that it's the sequence of the tags (and not their actual numerical values) that determines driver load order. With the example above, drivers in this group with a **Tag** of 0x44 would load ahead of those with a **Tag** value of 0x28.

As an example of using these tags, imagine that you have two drivers, XXDRIVER and YYDRIVER, both belonging to "Group W" and you want XXDRIVER to load ahead of YYDRIVER. The first step is to add a value to the **GroupOrderList** that defines the tags:

```
HKEY_LOCAL_MACHINE\...\Control\GroupOrderList
   :
   Group W: REG_BINARY: 02 00 00 00 44 00 00 00 28...
   :
```

Next, modify the service keys for XXDRIVER and YYDRIVER by adding **Tag** values to them. The Registry entries would look like this:

```
HKEY_LOCAL_MACHINE\...\Services\XXDRIVER
   Start: REG_DWORD: 2
   Group: REG_SZ: Group W
   Tag: REG_DWORD: 0x44

HKEY_LOCAL_MACHINE\...\Services\YYDRIVER
   Start: REG_DWORD: 2
   Group: REG_SZ: Group W
   Tag: REG_DWORD: 0x28
```

One final point: Not every group shows up in the **GroupOrderList** key. When a group is not in the **GroupOrderList**, the order in which drivers load within the group is undetermined.

16.5 SUMMARY

This chapter has presented a variety of different topics, all of which had to do with building a driver and getting it online. But what if the driver has personal problems? What if, in an occasional psychotic fit, it crashes the system or mutilates some data? In the next chapter, you'll see some techniques you can use to track down and eliminate bugs from your driver.

CHAPTER 17

Testing and Debugging Drivers

Where do they come from, these driver bugs? Do they hide beneath the bed like mutant dust bunnies, scheming and plotting — waiting for nightfall so they can sneak into our code? No, driver bugs are not random events. Instead, they represent some coding or logic error, or some lack of understanding about how the hardware or the system actually works. This chapter presents a number of testing and debugging techniques you can use to catch both catastrophic and subtle flaws in your driver.

17.1 SOME GUIDELINES FOR DRIVER TESTING

As in other areas of software development, a great deal of thought has gone into the practice of software testing over the last three decades. It's a good idea to take advantage of this thinking when you start to design a testing strategy for your driver. The following sections present some of the major issues you should consider. (See the Bibliography for some other references on software testing.)

The General Approach to Testing Drivers

The first thing to do is to accept the hopelessness of your situation. It's simply not possible to verify that a driver is free of bugs. To begin with, even trivial pieces of software can have so many code paths that there's just no way to exercise every one of them. Add to that all the various hardware and system-load conditions your driver might encounter in the real world, and your chances of catching every bug disappear pretty quickly.

As a tester, the best you can do is to show that a driver doesn't exhibit any of the bugs detectable by your tests. If your tests represent a reasonable model of conditions in the driver's target environment, then you'll probably be in good shape. This points to the fact that designing good tests is just as important as designing a good driver.

When to do the testing   Experience shows that it's more effective to test individual driver components as they're developed, rather than waiting until the whole driver is written to perform a single "big bang" test. Although incremental testing means writing a larger number of small test programs, this strategy makes it much easier to locate the source of a problem. The tiny test programs are also helpful when you want to make sure that changes to a driver's code base haven't introduced any new bugs.

Another advantage of testing during development is that it can point out basic design flaws in the driver which might otherwise go undetected until the end of the project. Correcting these kinds of fundamental errors late in the project cycle is usually much more expensive than catching them early.

What to test   Later in this chapter, you'll see some specific types of driver failures to watch out for, but you can generally divide driver tests into the following categories:

- **Hardware tests** — These verify the operation of the hardware. This is especially important if both the device and the driver are being developed together. In some cases, this may actually mean using a logic analyzer to see what's going on.

- **Normal response tests** — These confirm that the driver executes the full range of commands it will have to perform once it's out in the real world.

- **Error response tests** — These check the reaction of the driver to bad input from a user program, as well as to device errors and timeout conditions.

- **Boundary tests** — If the device has any limitations on its maximum transfer size or speed, these tests make sure that the driver can handle them.

- **Stress tests** — These subject the driver and its devices to high levels of sustained activity. This category also includes tests where the overall system experiences high levels of CPU, memory, and I/O activity, or where resources like memory are in very short supply.

How to develop the tests   Writing test software is an art. Good tests must be thorough enough to have a high probability of actually uncovering errors in the driver. This means you need to analyze the kinds of errors you think the driver *might* generate, and then write a test suite that will produce them.

Good test software also gives the tester enough information to pinpoint the cause of the failure easily. The output generated by a test program should be easy to read and should be formatted in such a way that important details aren't hidden somewhere in a pile of extraneous information.

Finally, test software needs to be complex enough to model a real-world situation, yet simple enough that it's easy to develop. If a test program is too complex, it may take a long time just to write and debug the test itself.

How to perform the tests   It's important to automate the test procedure itself. This makes it easier to guarantee that the same sequence of tests are being performed each time.

It's also a good idea to do regression testing. In other words, if you fix something in the driver, run the tests again to make sure you haven't broken anything else. This is another good reason to automate the test procedure.

When you run the tests, log the results and keep the output. This will give you a good idea of whether or not you're actually getting closer to fixing things or not.

Who should do the testing   Remember that the goal of testing is to tear the driver to shreds. To find bugs lurking under every line of code. To prove that only angelic intervention keeps the driver working at all. This is very different from the goal of the driver writer, who generally assumes that what he or she is producing will work properly. Because coding and testing have this kind of adversarial relationship, it's usually best if these jobs are performed by different people. It's almost always unreasonable to expect a single person to be objective about their own code.

Using the Microsoft Hardware Compatibility Tests (HCTs)

The hardware compatibility test suite (or simply, the HCTs), is a collection of programs which allow platform vendors to see whether their systems will run Windows NT. This suite contains a number of different components, including

- General system tests that exercise the FPU, the onboard serial and parallel ports, the keyboard interface, and the HAL.
- Tests that exercise drivers for specific kinds of hardware like video adapters, multimedia devices, network interface cards, tape drives, SCSI devices, etc.
- General stress tests that put unusually high loads on system resources and I/O bandwidth.
- A GUI-based test manager that automates test execution and data collection.

Even if you're not developing a driver for one of the types of hardware with its own test, you can use the HCTs as part of your stress-testing strategy.

You can find the HCTs in the **\HCT...** directory tree on the CD containing the NT DDK. Although they're distributed with the DDK, the HCTs are not automatically installed. For installation instructions, see the **README.TXT** file in the **\HCT** directory. Remember to put the HCTs on the target machine (where your driver will be running), *not* on the host. For more information about using the HCTs, look in the **\HCT\DOC** directory on the DDK CD. This directory contains all the HCT documentation in Word for Windows format.

Finally, if you're writing a driver for a commercial product and you want it to be logo-branded by Microsoft, you'll need to send your driver (and its hardware) to the Microsoft Compatibility Labs for testing. Microsoft offers Windows NT certification programs for several hardware categories including video cards, network adapters, SCSI adapters, multimedia audio cards, and printers. Once a driver passes the Microsoft certification tests, it's added to the driver library that's distributed with Windows NT. At that point, you're allowed to display a special logo on any product packaging. Contact your friends at Microsoft for details and pricing.

17.2 SOME THOUGHTS ABOUT DRIVER BUGS

As you saw in the last section, successful testing and debugging depend on figuring out ahead of time what might go wrong. The goal of this section is to get you thinking about the specific kinds of problems drivers can have. It also presents some techniques that can make bugs easier to detect and manage.

Categories of Driver Errors

Drivers can fail in any number of interesting ways. Although it's not possible to give a complete list, the following subsections describe some of the more common types of driver pathology.

Hardware problems   There's always a chance that the hardware itself might be causing problems. This becomes even more likely if both the device and the driver are being developed at the same time. Symptoms of hardware problems include

- Errors occurring during data transmission.
- Device status codes indicating an error.
- Interrupts not arriving.
- The device not responding properly to commands.

The cause might be as simple as undocumented behavioral quirks in the device (for example, some kind of restriction on command timing or sequencing). If it's a complex device, it might have bugs in its firmware (there simply is no bug-free SCSI firmware in the world). It could also be the result of some low-level bus contention or external signal noise. The device might just be broken.

The best approach to these problems is to make the error reproducible and then get as much information as you can. See if the manufacturer has any more information on the behavior of the device, or on known bugs. Use any available hardware diagnostics to verify that the device itself is working properly.

System crashes   It's easy for failures in kernel-mode code to kill the entire system. Many kinds of driver logic errors can produce a crash, although the most common problem seems to be access violations caused by a bogus pointer. It's also possible for things like bad DMA addresses to corrupt system memory. The next section of this chapter will have more to say about interpreting system crashes.

Resource leaks   The system doesn't perform any resource tracking or automatic cleanup for kernel-mode components. When a driver unloads, it's responsible for releasing whatever it may have allocated. This includes both memory from the pool areas plus any hardware the driver manages.

Even while a driver is running, it can leak memory if it regularly grabs pool space for temporary use and doesn't release it. Higher-level drivers can also be a source of leaks if they allocate their own IRPs and forget to free them. These kinds of driver errors can lead to bad system performance, as the pools slowly dry up, or to a complete system crash.

You can use the pool-tagging mechanism and sanity counters (described later in this chapter) to catch pool leakage and lost IRPs. By examining the **RESOURCEMAP** section of the Registry with REGEDT32, you can check for hardware allocation problems.

Thread hangs   Another kind of failure involves synchronous I/O requests that don't return. In this case, the user-mode thread issuing the request is blocked forever and never comes out of its wait state. This type of behavior can result from several different driver problems.

The most obvious cause is not calling **IoCompleteRequest** to send the IRP back to the I/O Manager. Not so obvious is the need to call **IoStartNextPacket**. Even if there are no pending requests to be processed, your driver has to call this function because it marks the Device object as idle. Without this call, all new IRPs will go into the pending queue, rather than going to the Start I/O routine.

The calling thread can hang in a driver's Dispatch routine if the driver is trying to recursively acquire a Fast Mutex or an Executive Resource. Similarly, if a kernel-mode thread acquires a Mutex or Executive Resource without releasing it, Dispatch routines may hang up if they try to acquire the same object.

DMA drivers that don't release the Adapter object or its mapping registers can prevent IRPs from being processed. In the case of slave DMA devices, the offending driver might even cause other drivers using the same DMA channel to lock up.

Drivers that manage multiunit controllers can cause similar trouble by not releasing the Controller object. In this case, new IRPs sent to any Device object using the Controller object will freeze up.

Unfortunately, there's no convenient way to see who currently owns Adapter or Controller objects, Mutexes or Executive resources. About the best you can do is to use a counter to make sure you're releasing these objects as many times as you're acquiring them. In some cases, the checked build of NT may flag some of these errors with a crash.

System hangs   Occasionally, a driver error can cause the entire system to lock up. For example, deadly embraces involving multiple spin locks (or attempts to acquire the same spin lock multiple times on the same CPU) will bring everything to a grinding halt. Endless loops in a driver's Interrupt Service routine or a DPC routine could cause a similar failure.

Once this kind of collapse occurs, it's difficult (if not impossible) to regain control of the system. The best approach is usually to debug the driver interactively and see if you can trace the exact sequence of steps that lead to the hang.

Reproducing Driver Errors

One of the keys to correcting a driver bug is being able to reproduce the problem. Intermittent errors are the bane of a driver writer's existence. Be as meticulous as possible in recording the exact circumstances at the time a bug appears, so that you can track and correct it. Several factors can make bugs intermittent.

Time dependencies   Some kinds of problems only show themselves when a driver is running at full speed. This could mean large numbers of I/O requests per second, high data rates, or both. Stress testing is usually a good way to make these kinds of bugs appear.

Multiprocessor dependencies   Things don't behave the same way on single- and multiprocessor systems. For example, ISR, DPC, and I/O Timer routines can all run simultaneously on an SMP machine. This can lead to various problems that don't show up on a single CPU. For this reason, it's important to make multiprocessor testing part of your driver verification strategy. One warning: SMP debugging is very painful, so it's a good idea to do the initial debugging on a single processor.

Multithreading dependencies   If your driver manages shareable Device objects, it's important to see what happens when multiple threads are issuing requests at the same time.

Miscellaneous causes   Finally, intermittent errors can depend on a whole universe of other factors. This includes sensitivity to system load conditions, problems caused by specific combinations of hardware on the same machine, or specific combinations of devices on the same bus. Once again, a detailed log is your best hope of determining the factors that make the bug appear.

Coding Strategies That Reduce Debugging

There are several things you can do during the coding phase of driver development that will reduce debugging time. Here are some of them:

- Get someone else to look at your code. It's amazing how quickly an unbiased eye can sometimes see the cause of a problem that you haven't been able to find.

- Use assertions (described later in this chapter) to check for various kinds of inconsistencies.

- Leave the debug code in your driver, surrounded with appropriate **#if** and **#end**if statements.

- Add a version resource to the driver so that you can determine exactly which version of the driver is having problems. Chapter 16 explains how to do this.

- If you're working on a large driver project with other people, using version control software will help to maintain everyone's sanity.

Keeping Track of Driver Bugs

Research has shown that bugs are not evenly distributed throughout a piece of code. Rather, they tend to cluster in a few specific routines. Usually, this will be some very complex piece of code, or code with complex (or questionable) logic. A bug log can help you track these errors by drawing your attention to the places where your driver tends to fail.

Such a log can also help you spot patterns of system loading or driver usage that result in failures. Finally, you can use the bug log to decide which errors are worth fixing (not all of them are) and to keep track of which errors have already been corrected.

Individual needs vary, but at the very least, you should keep the following kinds of information in a bug log:

- An exact description of the failure.

- As much detail as possible about the prevailing conditions at the time of the failure. This includes the version of the operating system and the driver and a description of the hardware configuration,

- The importance of fixing this bug.

- Current status of the bug.

17.3 READING CRASH SCREENS

System crashes (which Microsoft documentation euphemistically calls "STOP messages") are perhaps the most dramatic sign that your driver has a bug. This section describes how STOP messages are generated and explains how to get useful information from them.

What Happens When the System Crashes

In spite of its name, a system crash is really a very orderly thing. It is NT's way of telling you that something in the operating system has become so unstable that rebooting is the only safe thing to do. Oddly enough, a crash actually improves NT's reliability by preventing further damage to the system, and by drawing attention to problems that might otherwise go unnoticed.

Two different sequences of events can lead to a system crash. In the first scenario, some kernel-mode component happens to notice a horribly inconsistent state of affairs and decides to take the system down. For example, the I/O Manager might discover that a driver is trying to pass an already completed IRP to **IoCompleteRequest**. The I/O Manager responds by initiating a crash.

The second path to a system crash is less direct. Here, a kernel-mode component causes an exception which it does not or cannot handle. Code in the Kernel traps the exception and initiates a crash. For example, a buggy driver that generated an access violation would produce this kind of crash. So would a driver that caused a page fault at an elevated IRQL level.

Regardless of who decides to crash the system, the deed is done by making one of the following calls:[1]

```
VOID KeBugCheck( Code );
VOID KeBugCheckEx( Code, Arg1, Arg2, Arg3, Arg4 );
```

These functions generate the STOP screen itself and (optionally) save a crash file to disk. Then, depending on various system settings, they either reboot, halt the system, or start up the Kernel's debug client.

The *Code* argument to **KeBugCheck** and **KeBugCheckEx** identifies the cause of the crash. **KeBugCheckEx** takes an additional four arguments that appear as part of the STOP message. **KeBugCheck** sets these values to zero. The **BUG-CODES.H** header file in the DDK defines all the standard bugcheck codes. You'll find descriptions of the more common codes and their parameters in Appendix B of this book.

---

[1] You can also call **KeBugCheck** and **KeBugCheckEx** in your own code if you discover some terrible error. If you do make these functions part of your debugging strategy, use conditional compilation to keep them out of the retail version of the driver. Very, very few situations are serious enough to warrant a system crash in a commercial driver.

Layout of a STOP Message

It's hard to miss the bright blue, character-mode screen on which STOP messages appear. If you look at one of these "blue screens of death," you'll see four distinct sections.[2]

Bugcheck information   The first part of the display identifies the cause of the crash. This includes the bugcheck code, zero to four bugcheck parameters, and (if the bugcheck code is one of Microsoft's) the symbolic name associated with the error. Here's a sample:

```
*** STOP: 0x0000000A (0x00000000,0x00000002,0x00000000,0xFCE10796)
IRQL_NOT_LESS_OR_EQUAL*** Address fce10796 has base at fce10000 - XxDriver.SYS

p4-300 irql:1f SYSVER 0xf0000522
```

In this example, the bugcheck code is 0x0000000A and the associated symbolic name is IRQL_NOT_LESS_OR_EQUAL. Fine, but just what does it mean? If you look in Appendix B, you'll find that 0x0000000A is saying that the driver caused a page fault at or above DISPATCH_LEVEL IRQL.

The four numbers in parentheses after the bugcheck code are the extra arguments passed to **KeBugCheckEx**. Their significance depends on the bugcheck code itself. Again consulting Appendix B, you'll see that the first parameter contains the paged address (0), the second is the IRQL level at the time of the reference (2), the third indicates the type of access (0 means "read"), and the fourth is the address of the instruction that caused the fault (0xFCE10796). Very thoughtfully, the display tells us that this address falls within the range of the **XXDRIVER.SYS** module.

Next comes a line that seems to say something about the IRQL level of the crash. This would be very useful to know, if it were correct. Sadly, **KeBugCheck** always raises IRQL to HIGHEST_LEVEL for synchronization purposes so the value in a STOP message is always 0x1F.

On this same line, the SYSVER field tells you what version of NT was running. This is just the build-number in hex, with a 0xF or a 0xC in the highest nibble to indicate whether it's the free or checked build of NT. In the sample above, converting 0x522 to decimal says that this crash occurred under the free version of build 1314.

Most of the useful information comes from this section of the STOP message. All by itself, it's often enough to give you a good idea of what caused the crash. You should always take note of this part of the STOP screen before rebooting the system.

---

[2] Under some conditions, the Kernel won't be able to display the entire screen. This usually means that the services it needs to output some of the information are not available.

Module list   Next comes a two-column display naming all the operating system modules and drivers loaded at the time of the crash. It also lists each module's base address in memory and a date-stamp indicating the module's file date.

```
Dll Base DateStmp - Name            Dll Base DateStmp - Name
80100000 2fc653bc - ntoskrnl.exe    80400000 2fb24f4a - hal.dll
80010000 2faae8b0 - Atdisk.sys      80686000 2fc15d19 - Fastfat.sys
fcc20000 00000000 - Floppy.SYS      fcc30000 00000000 - Fs_rec.SYS
fcc40000 00000000 - Null.SYS        fcc50000 00000000 - Beep.SYS
fcc60000 2faae8d9 - Sermouse.SYS    fcc70000 2faae8b2 - i8042prt.SYS
fcc80000 2faae8b5 - Mouclass.SYS    fcc90000 2faae8b4 - Kbdclass.SYS
fccb0000 2faae88d - VIDEOPRT.SYS    fcca0000 2faae892 - vga.sys
fccc0000 2faae8fd - Msfs.SYS        fccd0000 2faae8ec - Npfs.SYS
fccf0000 2fc12af6 - NDIS.SYS        fcce0000 2faae92d - am1500t.sys
fcd30000 2faae945 - TDI.SYS         fcd10000 2fae6a5f - nbf.sys
fcd40000 2faae94f - netbios.sys     fcd50000 00000000 - Parport.SYS
fcd60000 00000000 - Parallel.SYS    fcd70000 2faae8d8 - Serial.SYS
fcd80000 00000000 - afd.sys         fcd90000 2fba6818 - rdr.sys
fcdd0000 2fc3e3eb - srv.sys         fce10000 316aa594 - XxDriver.SYS
```

Occasionally, this part of the display can help you detect hostile interactions between drivers. If driver X crashes the system if (and only if) driver Y is loaded, there may be something going on between them. A written crash log will help you to see these kinds of patterns.

Stack trace   The third part is a listing of the function calls on the stack that preceded the STOP message.

```
Address dword dump Build [1314]- Name
ff416d18 fce10796 fce10796 ff4f9c10 e1304018 801862e3 00000246 - XxDriver.SYS
ff416d24 801862e3 801862e3 00000246 801316e6 ff416d4c ff4f9c10 - ntoskrnl.exe
ff416d2c 801316e6 801316e6 ff416d4c ff4f9c10 80175de6 ff538288 - ntoskrnl.exe
ff416d38 80175de6 80175de6 ff538288 ff416f04 00000000 00000000 - ntoskrnl.exe
ff416d84 fce10796 fce10796 fce10008 00010246 ff567ee8 00000000 - XxDriver.SYS
ff416d88 fce10008 fce10008 00010246 ff567ee8 00000000 ff58bc40 - XxDriver.SYS
ff416da4 fce1061f fce1061f 00000004 ff567ee8 00000000 ff58bc40 - XxDriver.SYS
ff416db8 80119b69 80119b69 ff58bcf8 ff567f58 ff416de4 80114d69 - ntoskrnl.exe
ff416dc8 80114d69 80114d69 ff58bc40 ff567ee8 ff567ee8 ff58bc40 - ntoskrnl.exe
ff416de8 fce105d3 fce105d3 ff58bc40 ff567ee8 00000000 00000000 - XxDriver.SYS
ff416e08 804042ac 804042ac 80102f48 ff58bc40 ff567ee8 ff567ee8 - hal.dll
ff416e0c 80102f48 80102f48 ff58bc40 8010d544 ff567ee8 804042a0 - ntoskrnl.exe
ff416e1c 804042a0 804042a0 8015b943 ff416ed8 ff593d8c 00403054 - hal.dll
ff416e20 8015b943 8015b943 ff416ed8 ff593d8c 00403054 ff567f64 - ntoskrnl.exe
ff416e3c 8010d544 8010d544 8015a348 ff58bc40 ff567ee8 ff4f9c28 - ntoskrnl.exe
ff416e40 8015a348 8015a348 ff58bc40 ff567ee8 ff4f9c28 00000001 - ntoskrnl.exe
ff416e68 80159c9c 80159c9c 00000000 00120196 01040864 ff416e08 - ntoskrnl.exe
ff416e84 80134f30 80134f30 80100c60 ffffffff ff416ed0 8015612d - ntoskrnl.exe
ff416e88 80100c60 80100c60 ffffffff ff416ed0 8015612d 0012ff30 - ntoskrnl.exe
ff416e94 8015612d 8015612d 0012ff30 40100080 00120196 0012ff14 - ntoskrnl.exe
ff416ecc 80134f30 80134f30 80100ec0 ffffffff ff416f04 80137fb5 - ntoskrnl.exe
```

Each line in this display represents one frame on the stack, with the most recent frame being at the top of the display. This top frame is the one that was active at the time of the crash. Reading down the display gives you a history of the function calls that led to the crash.

On each line, the first column is the address of the stack frame itself. The second two columns both contain the return address of the function. The remaining columns are the first four DWORD arguments passed to the function. If a particular function takes more arguments, you won't see anything beyond the fourth. If it takes less than four DWORDs, the information in some of the rightmost columns will be bogus. The last column identifies the module in which the return address (from column two) falls.

In the crash pictured above, you can see that code somewhere around 0xFCE10796 in **XXDRIVER.SYS** was executing at the time of the crash. This code was called by a routine in **NTOSKRNL.EXE** (at 0x801862E3), which in turn was called by another system routine at 0x801316E6. Unfortunately, without a linker map, there's no way to turn these hideous addresses back into function names. This seriously limits the value of this display.

Also keep in mind that the call frames on the stack show you where the problem was *detected*, not necessarily where it was caused. It's possible for a driver to do horrible damage to a seldom-used part of the system and be long gone before NT discovers it and crashes.

Recovery instructions   There's very little useful information in this part of the display. It basically confirms the communication settings of the Kernel's debug client (if it's enabled), lets you know when the crash dump is finished, and recommends a response to the STOP message.

```
Beginning dump of physical memory
Physical memory dump complete. Contact your system administrator or
technical support group.
```

The actual text of this message will depend on the current option settings selected for the system. For example, if you have disabled crash dumps, you'll see a slightly different display.

Deciphering STOP Messages

If the truth be told, there's not all that much helpful information in a STOP message. The top few lines, containing the bugcheck information are perhaps the most useful things to know. The stack trace (which at first glance looks so promising) actually has very little to say, unless you can determine the identities of the functions listed in the trace.

To do this, you need linker maps for the modules containing the functions. This means you're out of luck if the functions are located in a Microsoft module like **NTOSKRNL.EXE** or **HAL.DLL**, since these linker maps don't come with the

DDK. You can, however, generate a linker map for your own driver using the following BUILD command:

```
BUILD -cef -nmake LINKER_FLAGS=-MAP:xxdriver.map
```

This is all a rather tedious process, and it still doesn't give you a great deal of information. Fortunately, if you have a crash file handy, you can find out much more with far less work. The next two sections of this chapter will explain how to work with crash files.

17.4 AN OVERVIEW OF WINDBG

WINDBG is a kernel-mode debugger you can use to analyze both crash files and running driver code. This section gives a brief overview of WINDBG. For more information, see WINDBG's online help and the NT DDK *Programmer's Reference*.

Although WINDBG is a helpful tool, it does have some problems. For one thing, it's actually an amalgamation of an older console-based kernel-mode debugger (KD) and a GUI-based source-code debugger that came with early versions of the Win32 SDK. This double ancestry can make WINDBG a little confusing to use, since there may be a console command, a menu option, and a toolbar button that all do the same thing.

You may also experience occasional unexplainable WINDBG crashes from time to time, as well as several other kinds of quirky behavior. For a complete list of known (or at least, acknowledged) WINDBG bugs, look for an article on the Microsoft Developers CD in the Win32 SDK Knowledge Base.[3]

The Key to Source-Code Debugging

One of WINDBG's most powerful features is its ability to debug kernel-mode components at the source-code level. Sadly, the documentation isn't real clear about how to accomplish this little miracle. Proper configuration of two sets of directories is the key to making it all work.

Symbol directories   WINDBG gets very cranky if it can't find the symbol files for the modules you're trying to debug. This includes both the symbols for your driver and those for various operating system modules. See Appendix A for a description of how to set up WINDBG symbol directories.

Source code directories   On the machine where you're running WINDBG, the directory path to your driver's source code must *exactly* match the source-code

---

[3] Search for "WINDBG near bug" to find this article.

path *on the machine where the driver was compiled and linked*. Even the drive letter has to be the same. The Linker stores this path information in the driver executable, and WINDBG uses it to find the source code.[4]

If you don't know the original source-code path for a kernel-mode component, don't worry. As long as you have a checked build of your driver (and its symbols haven't been stripped out), you can use the DUMPBIN utility to find the path names. The command looks like this:

```
DUMPBIN /SYMBOLS XXDRIVER.SYS | MORE
```

This generates a lot of output. The important information is at the top of the listing. The following excerpts show the things you should look for.

```
Dump of file xxdriver.sys

File Type: EXECUTABLE IMAGE

COFF SYMBOL TABLE
000 0000000B DEBUG notype Filename | .file
    D:\users\art\drivers\ch18\crash\driver\crash.c
        :
00B 00000015 DEBUG notype Filename | .file
    D:\users\art\drivers\ch18\crash\driver\transfer.c
        :
015 0000001D DEBUG notype Filename | .file
    D:\users\art\drivers\ch18\crash\driver\dispatch.c
        :
01D 00000023 DEBUG notype Filename | .file
    D:\users\art\drivers\ch18\crash\driver\unload.c
        :
023 00000000 DEBUG notype Filename | .file
    D:\users\art\drivers\ch18\crash\driver\init.c
        :
```

A Few WINDBG Commands

Although WINDBG is a GUI program, you really can't avoid using its command-line window. This text-based interface supports several dozen built-in commands, and as you'll see later, you can add extensions of your own. Table 17.1 gives an overview of the more helpful WINDBG commands. See the online documentation and the WINDBG Help file for more information.

---

[4] WINDBG has a menu option that supposedly lets you change the source-code path, but it doesn't seem to work.

Table 17.1   Some useful WINDBG commands

WINDBG commands and extensions	
Command	**Description**
help	Print help on basic WINDBG commands
k, kb, and kv	Print a trace of the current kernel-mode stack
dd *address*	Dump the contents of memory
ln	Print symbol names nearby a given value
.logopen	Open a log file, replacing a previous version
.logappend	Add new log information to an existing file
.logclose	Close the debug log file
!help	Print help on standard WINDBG extensions
!handle 0 3 *CID*	Print verbose information about process handles
!process 0 0	List all processes on system
!process *address flags*	Print information about a process object
!process *CID* –1	Print detailed information about specific process
!thread *address*	Print information about a thread
!pcr	Print context information for 80x86 CPU
!vm	Print Virtual memory statistics
!sysptes 1	Print summary of system page table usage
!drivers	List currently-loaded kernel-mode modules
!irpzone	List IRPs in use in NT's IRP zone buffer
!irpzone full	(Same as above, but with more information)
!errlog	List any unflushed messages in errorlog buffer
!bugdump *ComponentName*	Dump contents of bugcheck callback buffer
!irp *address*	Print formatted contents of an IRP
!devobj *address*	Print formatted contents of a Device object
!drvobj *address*	Print formatted contents of a Driver object
!srb *address*	Print formatted contents of an SRB
!trap *address*	Print formatted contents of 80x86 trap frame
!poolfind *Tag*	Print information about pool with a given tag
!poolused	Print information about tagged pool
!reload	Reload a particular module
!load *ExtensionName*	Load an extension DLL
!unload *ExtensionName*	Unload an extension DLL

17.5 ANALYZING A CRASH DUMP

When a crash occurs, Windows NT can save the state of the system in a dump file on the boot partition.[5] Crash dumps allow you to reboot almost immediately and determine the cause of the crash at a later time. This section explains how to analyze a system crash dump.

Goals of the Analysis

Using WINDBG, you can poke around in the remains of a dead system and find out almost as much as if it were still running. This kind of forensic pathology can help you develop a convincing explanation of what led to the crash. Some of the questions you should ask when you're analyzing a crash include:

- Was my driver executing at the time of the crash?
- Was my driver responsible for the crash?
- What was the sequence of events that led to the crash?
- What operation was the driver trying to perform when the system crashed?
- Is there any information in the Device Extension that might tell me what was going on?
- What Device object was it working with?

Starting the Analysis

To begin analyzing a crash file, run WINDBG from the command line with the -y and -z options. These specify the location of the crash symbols and the dump file. For example,

```
WINDBG -y c:\wnt\symbols -z c:\wnt\memory.dmp
```

For the crash that produced the STOP message you saw earlier, the initial output from WINDBG looks like this:

```
Thread Create: Process=0, Thread=0
Module Load: d:\users\art\drivers\symbols\free\NTOSKRNL.DBG (symbols loaded)
Kernel Debugger connection established for G:\WINNT\MEMORY.DMP
Kernel Version 1314 Free loaded @ 0x80100000
Bugcheck 0000000a : 00000000 00000002 00000000 fce10796
Stopped at an unexpected exception: code=80000003 addr=8013b416
Hard coded breakpoint hit
  :
```

---

[5] See Appendix A for instructions on enabling crash dumps.

You'll recognize some of this information from the STOP message. The bugcheck code is 0xA, which means the fourth parameter (0xFCE10796 in this case) is the address where the problem occurred. To see where this instruction is in your source code, choose Goto Address from the View menu, and enter the address from the bugcheck parameter. In this particular crash, 0xFCE10796 turns out to be a function called **XxTryToCrash**.

The second parameter for bugcheck 0xA is the true IRQL level at the time of the crash. From **NTDDK.H**, two turns out to be DISPATCH_LEVEL, which gives us a hint about what parts of the driver might have been executing at the time of the crash.

One point: Don't be mislead by the message about the unexpected exception with a code of 0x80000003. This is just the breakpoint used by **KeBugCheck** itself to halt the system, so it has no significance.

Tracing the Stack

The stack trace is like a time line, showing you the sequence of function calls leading up to the crash. By reading the trace from the oldest frame (at the bottom) to the crash frame (at the top), you can come up with a coherent story describing what happened. The trick is to find the stack.

High-IRQL crashes   If the system crashed while it was running at or above DISPATCH_LEVEL IRQL, you can use the **k** command to get a trace of the stack at the time of the bugcheck.

```
KDx86> k
ff416d1c  fce10796  NT!KiTrap0E+0x252
ff416da0  fce1061f  XXDRIVER!XxTryToCrash+0x26(0x00000004)
ff416dc4  80114d69  XXDRIVER!XxStartIo+0x2f(0xFF58BC40, 0xFF567EE8)
ff416de4  fce105d3  NT!IoStartPacket+0x9b
ff416e08  80102f48  XXDRIVER!XxDispatchWrite+0x43(0xFF58BC40, 0xFF567EE8)
ff416e1c  8015b943  NT!@IofCallDriver@8+0x38
ff416e3c  8015a348  NT!IopSynchronousServiceTail+0x6f
ff416ed8  80137fb5  NT!NtWriteFile+0x6ac
ff416ed8  77f89427  NT!KiSystemService+0xa5
0012ff6c  00000000  NTDLL!ZwWriteFile+0xb
```

Each line shows the address of the stack frame, the return address of the function, the name of the function, and (in parentheses) the arguments passed to the function. You generally won't see any arguments for system functions. To make them show up, use the **kv** version of the stack-trace command.

In this trace, a call to **ZwWriteFile** eventually found its way to XXDRIVER's **XxDispatchWrite** routine. The first argument for a Dispatch routine is always the Device object (here, 0xFF58BC40) and the second (0xFF567EE8) is the IRP. **XxDispatchWrite** called **IoStartPacket**, which called the Start I/O routine in XXDRIVER. Just before it died, **XxStartIo** made a call to **XxTryToCrash** and passed it an argument with a value of four.

Another way to see the current stack is by selecting Calls from the WINDBG Window menu. Double-clicking on one of the frames in the Calls display will take you to the line of source code where the call originated. Once you've entered a stack frame this way, you can examine the function's local variables at the time of the crash by selecting Locals from the WINDBG Window menu.

Crashes below DISPATCH_LEVEL   When the system crashes because of an unhandled exception below DISPATCH_LEVEL IRQL, the stack trace from the **k** command won't tell you much about what was going on.[6] Instead, you need to find the trap frame associated with the crash.

On 80x86 platforms, you can find the trap frame by using the **kb** command. First, look for the stack frame associated with a function called **KiDispatch-Exception**.[7]

```
KDx86> kb
FramePtr RetAddr Param1 Param2 Param3 Function Name
fccccab8 80138f59 fccccad4 00000000 fccccb28 NT!KiDispatchException+0x366
fcccc10 8015c542 80102f48 ff564410 ff4ebc88 NT!CommonDispatchException+0x4d
fccccb28 ff56c860 ff50c1e8 00000000 00000006 NT!IopErrorLogQueueRequest+0x5c
```

Next, look down the left-hand column (the one labeled "FramePtr") for the address of the frame two earlier than the **KiDispatchException** frame. In this crash, the frame of interest has the address 0xFCCCCB28. What you've just found is called the trap frame, and you can use the **!trap** command to format it.

```
KDx86> !trap fccccb28
eax=00000000 ebx=00000000 ecx=fccccb88 edx=00000000 esi=ff4ebec0 edi=ff567ee8
eip=fce10796 esp=fccccb9c ebp=fccccbac iopl=0 nv up ei pl zr na po nc
vip=0 vif=0
cs=0008 ss=0010 ds=0023 es=0023 fs=0030 gs=0000 efl=00010246
ErrCode = 00000000
```

From the formatted trap frame, note the contents of the EBP (0xFCCCCBAC), ESP (0xFCCCCB9C), and EIP (0xFCE10796) registers. Use these values in the **k** command to specify the stack address. This displays the true stack trace at the time of the crash.

```
KDx86> k =fccccbac fccccb9c fce10796
fccccbac fce1046a XXDRIVER!XxTryToCrash+0x26(0x00000002)
fccccbc4 80102f48 XXDRIVER!XxDispatchOpenClose+0x1a(0xFF4EBEC0, 0xFF567EE8)
fccccbd8 8015ccca NT!@IofCallDriver@8+0x38
fccccc9c 80179b00 NT!IopParseDevice+0x77e
fcccccd0c 80175cf6 NT!ObpLookupObjectName+0x480
fccccde4 80151e33 NT!ObOpenObjectByName+0xa2
fcccce90 8015612d NT!IoCreateFile+0x43d
fccccced0 80137fb5 NT!NtCreateFile+0x2f
```

---

[6] If you have WINDBG connected to the target system and it catches the exception, the stack trace *will* give you useful information.

[7] This sample output is from a different crash than the one we've been examining.

```
fccced0 77f889b3 NT!KiSystemService+0xa5
fccccb98 ff567ee8 0x77f889b3
```

In this trace, it's obvious that the problem occurred during a call to **NtCreateFile** in the driver's **XxDispatchOpenClose** function.

Using trap frames Another way to find the proper stack on 80x86 machines is to use the **kv** command. This displays a more detailed view of each frame. Look for a function with **KiTrap** in its name. Next to this function, you'll find the address of the trap frame.

```
KDx86> kv
ff416d1c fce10796 NT!KiTrap0E+0x252 (FPO: [0,0] TrapFrame @ ff416d1c)
ff416da0 fce1061f XXDRIVER!XxTryToCrash+0x26(0x00000004)
ff416dc4 80114d69 XXDRIVER!XxStartIo+0x2f(0xFF58BC40, 0xFF567EE8)
ff416de4 fce105d3 NT!IoStartPacket+0x9b
    :
```

On the line for **KiTrap**, you'll find the address of the trap frame (in this case, 0xFF416D1C). Use the **!trap** command to format its contents.

```
KDx86> !trap ff416d1c
eax=00000000 ebx=ff58bc40 ecx=ff416d7c edx=00000000 esi=00000000 edi=ff567ee8
eip=fce10796 esp=ff416d90 ebp=ff416da0 iopl=0     nv up ei pl zr na po nc
vip=0          vif=0
cs=0008 ss=0010 ds=0023 es=0023 fs=0030 gs=0000                efl=00010246
ErrCode = 00000000
0xfce10796 8a00             mov          al,byte ptr [eax]
```

From the trap frame, note the contents of the EBP (0xFF416DA0), ESP (0xFF416D90), and EIP (0xFCE10796) registers. Use these values in the **k** command to specify the stack address. This displays the true stack trace at the time of the crash.

```
KDx86> k =ff416da0 ff416d90 fce10796
ff416da0 fce1061f XXDRIVER!XxTryToCrash+0x26(0x00000004)
ff416dc4 80114d69 XXDRIVER!XxStartIo+0x2f(0xFF58BC40, 0xFF567EE8)
ff416de4 fce105d3 NT!IoStartPacket+0x9b
ff416e08 80102f48 XXDRIVER!XxDispatchWrite+0x43(0xFF58BC40, 0xFF567EE8)
ff416e1c 8015b943 NT!@IofCallDriver@8+0x38
ff416e3c 8015a348 NT!IopSynchronousServiceTail+0x6f
ff416ed8 80137fb5 NT!NtWriteFile+0x6ac
ff416ed8 77f89427 NT!KiSystemService+0xa5
ff416d8c ff567ee8 0x77f89427
```

You can see that this display matches the one generated by the **k** command, verifying that we've found the right stack.

Indirect Methods of Investigation

If your driver wasn't running at the time of the crash, the stack trace won't contain any useful information and you'll need to take a more indirect approach to find the problem. The goal is to gather as much information as possible about what the driver was doing when the system crashed. This involves a certain amount of creativity and imagination.

Finding I/O requests   One approach is to track down any IRPs the driver was processing at the time it died, and then try to puzzle out what was happening. Begin by getting a list of all the active IRPs on the system with the **!irpzone** command:

```
KDx86> !irpzone
Small Irp list
ff567ee8 Thread ff599be0 current stack belongs to \Driver\XxDriver
Large Irp list
ff56a708 Thread ff519620 current stack belongs to \Driver\Mouclass
ff56ab08 Thread ff547a60 current stack belongs to \Driver\Kbdclass
    :
ff56bd08 Thread ff500500 current stack belongs to \FileSystem\Rdr
```

From this list, select the IRPs currently belonging to your driver. Next, use the **!irp** command to format each one (this can be a rather tedious process if there are a lot of IRPs). This is what the formatted IRP looks like:

```
KDx86> !irp ff567ee8
Irp is from zone and active with 1 stacks 1 is current
 No Mdl System buffer = ff593d88 Thread ff599be0: Irp stack trace.
 cmd flg cl Device File Completion-Context
> 4 0 1 ff58bc40 ff4f9c28 00000000-00000000 pending
    \Driver\XxDriver
        Args: 00000004 00000000 00000000 00000000
```

The **cmd** field shows the major function, and the **Args** field displays the **Parameters** union of the I/O stack location. The **flg** and **cl** fields show the stack location flags and control bits, which you can find in **NTSTATUS.H**.

Here, you can see that the function code was a four (IRP_MJ_WRITE) and **Parameters.Write.Length** was 4 bytes. Furthermore, no Completion routine (or completion context) was associated with this I/O stack location, and it had already been marked pending at the time of the crash.

Finally, there is a system buffer associated with the IRP (at location 0xFF593D88) which you can examine using the **dd** command or the Memory option in the WINDBG Window menu. This tells us that the Device object is doing Buffered I/O.

To see exactly which device the IRP was sent to, use the **!devobj** command on the address of the Device object from the IRP display. Here you can see that the target device was **Crash0**, and that the IRP had already been made current when the system crashed.

```
KDx86> !devobj ff58bc40
Device object is for:
 Crash0 \Driver\XxDriver DriverObject ff53e1d0
Current Irp ff567ee8 RefCount 1 Type 00000022 DevExt ff58bcf8
DeviceQueue:
```

Sometimes, you can find out even more information about what was going on by dumping the contents of the Device Extension with the **dd** command. Later in this chapter, you'll see how to write a WINDBG extension that makes the Device Extension easier to dump.

Of course, this doesn't give us nearly as much information as the stack trace, but it does tell us that the driver was trying to process a Buffered I/O IRP_MJ_WRITE command. Since the IRP had been made current, we know that it got at least as far the driver's Start I/O routine. Often the best approach in this case is to set up the system for interactive debugging and try to make the error repeat.

Examining processes   Occasionally, it's helpful to know what processes were running on a system at the time of a crash. This could help you spot patterns of system usage or even specific user programs that cause your driver to fail. For general information, you can use the **!process** command like this:

```
KDx86> !process 0 0
**** NT ACTIVE PROCESS DUMP ****
PROCESS ff578940 Cid: 0002 Peb: 00000000 ParentCid: 0000
  DirBase: 00030000 ObjectTable: e1000f88 TableSize: 64.
  Image: System

PROCESS ff554360 Cid: 0013 Peb: 7ffdf000 ParentCid: 0002
  DirBase: 012ec000 ObjectTable: e10017c8 TableSize: 48.
  Image: smss.exe
    :
PROCESS ff58b6c0 Cid: 0090 Peb: 7ffdf000 ParentCid: 007b
  DirBase: 003b9000 ObjectTable: e11feee8 TableSize: 16.
  Image: Xxtest.exe
```

For more information, you can use the CID number of a specific process and increase the level of verbosity with some flags.[8]

```
KDx86> !process 90 -1
Searching for Process with Cid == 90
PROCESS ff58b6c0 Cid: 0090 Peb: 7ffdf000 ParentCid: 007b
    DirBase: 003b9000 ObjectTable: e11feee8 TableSize: 16.
    Image: Xxtest.exe
    VadRoot ff4fa668 Clone 0 Private 33. Modified 0. Locked 0.
    FF58B87C MutantState Signalled OwningThread 0
    Token                            e1304030
    ElapsedTime                      0:00:00.0110
    UserTime                         0:00:00.0020
    KernelTime                       0:00:00.0030
    QuotaPoolUsage[PagedPool]        6892
    QuotaPoolUsage[NonPagedPool]     1096
```

---
[8] Kernel-mode threads always run in the process whose CID is 2.

```
        Working Set Sizes (now,min,max)    (146, 50, 345)
        PeakWorkingSetSize                 153
        VirtualSize                        8 Mb
        PeakVirtualSize                    8 Mb
        PageFaultCount                     159
        MemoryPriority                     FOREGROUND
        BasePriority                       9
        CommitCharge                       38
```

```
THREAD ff599be0 Cid 90.88 Teb: 7ffde000 Win32Thread: 801448c0 RUNNING
IRP List:
    ff567ee8: (0006,0094) Flags: 00000a30 Mdl: 00000000
Not impersonating
Owning Process ff58b6c0
WaitTime (seconds) 107578
Context Switch Count 12
UserTime 0:00:00.0010
KernelTime 0:00:00.0030
Start Address 0x77f270a4
Initial Sp ff417000 Current Sp ff416bec
Priority 9 BasePriority 9 PriorityDecrement 0 DecrementCount 124

ChildEBP RetAddr Args to Child
0012f750 00000000 00000000 00000000 00000000
```

For multithreaded processes, this form of the **!process** command will tell you things about all the threads, including any objects they might be waiting for. It also gives information about the I/O requests issued by a given thread, so if a thread seems to be getting hung, you can see what IRPs it issued.

Analyzing Crashes with DUMPEXAM

DUMPEXAM is a command-line utility that you can use to analyze a crash dump file. When you run this utility, it uses the kernel-mode debugger to execute a standard series of commands and produces an output file called **MEMORY.TXT**. The analysis performed by DUMPEXAM is intended to give support personnel a fairly detailed snapshot of the state of the system at the time of the crash. This can be useful if you're trying to support a driver out in the field.

You'll find DUMPEXAM on the Windows NT distribution CD in the **\SUPPORT\DEBUG**<*platform*> directory. Along with the DUMPEXAM executable, you have to install the **KD**<*platform*>**EXTS.DLL** extension DLL for the target platform. Normally, these DLLs are copied along with everything else when you install WINDBG from the Win32 SDK. You also need to copy **IMAGEHLP.DLL** from the Windows NT distribution CD. It's in the same directory as the DUMPEXAM executable.

Finally, make sure you mirror the debug symbol tree that's on the CD when you run DUMPEXAM. Unfortunately, this tool isn't smart enough to handle the situation where everything is in the same directory.

17.6 INTERACTIVE DEBUGGING

Poking around in the remains of a dead system can tell you a great deal, but some problems are easier to diagnose while a driver is still running. This section briefly describes how to debug driver code interactively.

Starting and Stopping a Debug Session

WINDBG is the primary tool for interactive debugging. To use it, you'll need to set up host and target systems as described in Appendix A. As with crash dump analysis, make certain the source-code path on the host exactly matches the source-code path on the machine where the driver was built. Once everything is configured, follow these steps to begin an interactive debug session:

1. Move a copy of your driver's executable (or the corresponding **.DBG** symbol file) into the symbol directory on the host. Repeat this step each time you rebuild the driver, or the symbols will be out of sync.

2. From the command line, run WINDBG using the **-k** and **-y** options, for example,

    ```
    WINDBG -k i386 com1 9600 -y c:\wnt\symbols ntoskrnl.exe
    ```

3. From the WINDBG Run menu, select Go. You'll see a message in the WINDBG command window saying that WINDBG is waiting to connect.

4. Reboot the target machine with the Kernel's debug client enabled. As the system boots, you'll see it trying to make a connection with the debugger on the host. When the systems connect, there will be a lot of activity in WINDBG's command window.

Once you've established a connection between the host and target machines, you have a wide range of commands available to you. For the most part, the interactive WINDBG commands are a superset of the ones you use to analyze a crash. You also have the added capability of setting breakpoints on the target and single-stepping through target code.

After you've completed a debugging session, you should follow these steps to disconnect the host and the target:

1. If you've set any breakpoints in your driver, pause the target system by typing CTRL+C in the WINDBG command window. (Alternatively, you can press the SYSREQ key on the target itself.)

2. From the Debug menu, choose Breakpoints. When the breakpoint dialog appears, click on Clear All and OK.

3. From the Run menu, choose Go (or use the toolbar button) to let the target machine continue.

4. From the File menu, choose Exit.

After WINDBG has exited, the target machine may pause for 30 seconds or so the first time it hits a **KdPrint** macro. This delay is the time it takes the Kernel's debug client to realize there's no debugger to talk to. It occurs only once.

Setting Breakpoints

One of the great things about WINDBG is its ability to set source-code breakpoints in a driver. This can be immensely helpful for figuring out the exact nature of a bug. To set a breakpoint with WINDBG, do the following:

1. If the target machine is currently running, type CTRL+C in the WINDBG command window to pause the target. (Alternatively, you can press the SYSREQ key on the target.) You can't set breakpoints if the target is running.

2. From the File menu, choose Open. The Open File dialog box will appear. Navigate to the directory containing your driver's source code. Double-click on a source file to open it.

3. Move the cursor to the source code line where you want to set the breakpoint. If you're breaking on a multiline C statement, make sure you position the cursor on the line containing the semicolon.

4. Click on the breakpoint button in the toolbar. (It's the one that looks like a little hand.) If your driver is currently loaded in memory, the source-code line will turn red; if it hasn't been loaded yet, the source line will turn magenta.

5. Click on the Go button in the toolbar to let the target machine continue. When the target machine hits the breakpoint, it will stop and the source-code line in WINDBG will turn green.

To remove a breakpoint, simply pause the target machine, select the source code line containing the breakpoint, and click on the toolbar's breakpoint button. You can also use the Debug Breakpoints menu item to remove multiple breakpoints.

Breakpoints highlight another of WINDBG's little quirks. If you set several breakpoints in a driver that hasn't been loaded yet, WINDBG won't be able to resolve the first one that it hits. Instead it will display a dialog box asking you how it should handle the breakpoint. You should select the Defer option. This will cause WINDBG to instantiate all the breakpoints in the driver and proceed. When WINDBG hits the next breakpoint, it will work correctly. (In fact, even if it hits the first breakpoint again, it will work properly.) Breakpoints that you set after the driver is loaded don't seem to have this problem.

This odd behavior can make it difficult to set breakpoints in the DriverEntry routine. The easiest solution is just to set an extra (dummy) breakpoint somewhere at the beginning of DriverEntry. This one will cause the others to behave properly.

Setting Hard Breakpoints

With WINDBG, there aren't too many compelling reasons for putting hard breakpoints into your driver. If you do find such a need, you can use the following two calls:

```
VOID DbgBreakPoint( VOID );
VOID KdBreakPoint( VOID );
```

KdBreakPoint is just a macro that wraps a conditional compilation directive around **DbgBreakPoint**. **KdBreakPoint** becomes a no-op if you build a free version of your driver.

Beware: NT will crash with a KMODE_EXCEPTION_NOT_HANDLED error if your driver hits a hard-coded breakpoint and the Kernel's debug client isn't enabled. If your driver hits a breakpoint and there's no debugger on the other end of the serial line, NT will hang the target machine. You can recover from the hang by starting up WINDBG on the host machine.

Using Print Statements

Debugging code by peppering it with **printf** statements has a long and honorable history. You can continue the tradition by calling either **DbgPrint** or **KdPrint**. Both allow you to send a debug string from your driver (on the target system) to the WINDBG command window (on the host machine). These calls have the following syntax:

```
ULONG DbgPrint( FormatString, arg1, arg2... );
ULONG KdPrint(( FormatString, arg1, arg2... ));
```

DbgPrint and **KdPrint** take the same arguments as the standard **printf** function. Since **KdPrint** is actually a macro (defined in **NTDDK.H**), you have to include an extra set of parentheses in order to pass it a variable-length list of arguments. **KdPrint** also becomes a no-op in free builds of a driver.

17.7 WRITING WINDBG EXTENSIONS

One of WINDBG's strengths is that you can expand its capabilities by writing extension commands for it. This can be very helpful, particularly for printing out the contents of driver-defined data structures. Unfortunately, the documentation and sample extension code that come with the NT DDK are incorrect. This section explains how to add extension commands to WINDBG.

How WINDBG Extensions Work

A WINDBG extension is just a user-mode DLL that exports various commands in the form of DLL functions. The extension DLL also contains several support routines that perform initialization and version-checking operations.

One of the tricky aspects of writing a WINDBG extension is gaining access to memory in the target system (whether it's a crash file or a live machine). To make this easy, WINDBG supplies a set of callback routines that the extension DLLs use to touch the debug target. This means the DLL has the same view of the target system's memory as WINDBG itself. In particular, extension commands can't access anything that is paged out at the time a crash or breakpoint occurs.

Initialization and Version-Checking Functions

When you write an extension DLL for WINDBG, there are two required initialization functions that you must include. At your option, you can also include a third version-checking function. These are described in the following subsections.

WinDbgExtensionDllInit   WINDBG calls this function when the user loads the extension DLL. Its job is to save the address of the callback table so that other parts of the DLL can use it. This function (shown in Table 17.2) is required.

Table 17.2   Function prototype for WinDbgExtensionDllInit

VOID WinDbgExtensionDllInit

Parameter	Description
PWINDBG_EXTENSION_APIS lpExtensionApis	Address of table containing pointers to WINDBG callback functions
USHORT MajorVersion	• 0xF for free build of NT
	• 0xC for checked build of NT
USHORT MinorVersion	Build-number of NT
Return value	(None)

ExtensionApiVersion   WINDBG calls this function when you try to load an extension DLL. Its job is to convince WINDBG that the extension DLL has the same version as WINDBG itself. It does this by returning a pointer to the version structure associated with the extension DLL. This function (shown in Table 17.3) is required.

Table 17.3   Function prototype for ExtensionApiVersion

LPEXT_API_VERSION ExtensionApiVersion

Parameter	Description
VOID	(None)
Return value	Address of the DLL's EXT_API_VERSION structure

CheckVersion　Each time WINDBG executes a command in the DLL, it calls this function before calling the command routine. CheckVersion's job is to make sure that the version of the extension DLL is compatible with the version of NT being debugged. If not, it should complain loudly (and perhaps set a global DLL variable to inhibit command execution). This function (shown in Table 17.4) is optional.

Table 17.4　Function prototype for CheckVersion

VOID CheckVersion

Parameter	Description
VOID	(None)
Return value	(None)

Writing Extension Commands

Each command in your extension DLL is implemented as a separate function. Define these command functions using the DELCARE_API macro, like this:

```
DECLARE_API( command_name )
{
    //
    // Your code...
    //
      :
}
```

DECLARE_API gives your command function the prototype shown in Table 17.5. Be sure the names of your commands are entirely lower-case, or WNDBG won't be able to find them.

Table 17.5　Commands declared with DECLARE_API have this prototype

VOID *command_name*

Parameter	Description
IN HANDLE hCurrentProcess	Handle of current process on target machine
IN HANDLE hCurrentThread	Handle of current thread on target machine
IN ULONG dwCurrentPc	Current value of program counter value
IN ULONG dwProcessor	Number of current CPU
IN PCSTR args	Argument string passed to the command
Return value	(None)

These extension commands can perform any sort of operation that will make debugging easier. Their most common use is to format and print the contents of various driver-defined data structures, like the Device Extension.

Finally, if one of your extension commands is going to take a long time to execute, or if it's going to generate a lot of output, it should periodically check to see if the WINDBG user has typed CTRL+C. Otherwise, the user won't have any way to abort the command until it completes. One of the WINDBG helper functions described next lets you make this check.

WINDBG Helper Functions

Your extension DLL gains access to the system being debugged by calling various helper functions exported by WINDBG itself. These functions also give your DLL access to the WINDBG command window for input and output. Table 17.6 contains a brief description of these helper functions.

Table 17.6 A WINDBG extension DLL can call these helper functions

WINDBG helper functions

Function	Description
dprintf	Print formatted text in WINDBG command window
CheckControlC	See if WINDBG user has typed CTRL+C
GetExpression	Convert a C expression into a DWORD value
GetSymbol	Locate name of symbol nearest a given address
Disassm	Generate string representation of machine instruction
StackTrace	Return stack-trace of current process
GetKDContext	Return current CPU number and count of CPUs
GetContext	Return CPU context of process being debugged
SetContext	Modify CPU context of process being debugged
ReadControlSpace	Get platform-specific CPU information
ReadMemory	Copy data from system virtual space into buffer
WriteMemory*	Copy data from buffer to system virtual space
ReadIoSpace*	Read I/O port
WriteIoSpace*	Write I/O port
ReadIoSpaceEx*	Read I/O port on specific bus-type and number (Alpha only)
WriteIoSpaceEx*	Write I/O port on specific bus-type and number (Alpha only)
ReadPhysical	Copy data from physical memory into buffer
WritePhysical*	Copy data from buffer to specific physical addresses

*These functions can only be used during an interactive debugging session.

The only complete documentation on these helper functions is in the WINDBG online help. To find it, do the following:

1. From the WINDBG help Contents screen, click on the KD button.

2. Click on the "Creating Extensions" topic.

3. Scroll about halfway down this topic and you'll find a list of helper functions.

4. Click on the name of a function to see its prototype and a description.

Building and Using an Extension DLL

Although a WINDBG extension is just a user-mode DLL, you still need to compile and link it using the BUILD utility. This is because it incorporates the DDK header files, and it needs all the compile-time symbol definitions provided by BUILD. Consequently, using Visual C++ projects to create an extension DLL isn't easy. The example in the next section contains a **SOURCES** file that builds one of these DLLs.

To use an extension DLL, you first load it using WINDBG's **!load** command. Then you execute one of its functions with a command of the form !*function*. The **!unload** command allows you to unload an extension DLL.

WINDBG allows you to have up to 32 extension DLLs loaded at one time. When you execute a !*function* command, WINDBG searches the list of currently loaded extensions, starting with the most recently loaded and going back to earliest.

17.8 CODE EXAMPLE: A WINDBG EXTENSION

This example shows how to write a simple WINDB extension DLL. You can find the code for this example in the **CH17\XXDBG** directory on the disk that accompanies this book.

XXDBG.C

All the code for this extension DLL is in a single file. The following subsections break it into easily digestible pieces.

Headers This part of the code contains all the headers and definitions needed to make everything work. Warning: There is some odd stuff going on here. Don't change the sequence of anything between ❶ and ❸.

```
#include <ntddk.h>❶
#include <windef.h>

#define LMEM_FIXED 0x0000 ❷
```

```
#define LMEM_MOVEABLE 0x0002
#define LMEM_NOCOMPACT 0x0010
#define LMEM_NODISCARD 0x0020
#define LMEM_ZEROINIT 0x0040
#define LMEM_MODIFY 0x0080
#define LMEM_DISCARDABLE 0x0F00
#define LMEM_VALID_FLAGS 0x0F72
#define LMEM_INVALID_HANDLE 0x8000

#define LPTR (LMEM_FIXED | LMEM_ZEROINIT)

#define WINBASEAPI

WINBASEAPI
HLOCAL
WINAPI
LocalAlloc(
    UINT uFlags,
    UINT uBytes
    );

WINBASEAPI
HLOCAL
WINAPI
LocalFree(
    HLOCAL hMem
    );

#define CopyMemory RtlCopyMemory
#define FillMemory RtlFillMemory
#define ZeroMemory RtlZeroMemory

#include <wdbgexts.h> ❸

//
// Other header files...
//
#include <stdlib.h>
#include <string.h>

#include "..\driver\xxdriver.h" ❹
```

❶ This is the beginning of some magic. The problem is that we're trying to build a Win32 user-mode DLL, but we need access to things defined in **NTDDK.H** and **XXDRIVER.H**. It takes a little trickery to get all the header files to live together.

❷ The various definitions that follow are taken from **WINBASE.H** in the Win32 SDK. The WINDBG extension definitions from **WDBGEXTS.H** won't work without them. Unfortunately, **NTDDK.H** and **WINBASE.H** can't coexist in the same source file. The only solution is to cut the required pieces from **WINBASE.H** and include them here.

❸ Now it's safe to bring in the WINDBG extension definitions. This header is located in **MSTOOLS\H** in the Win32 SDK. Here ends the magical sequence of headers and definitions.

❹ Finally, bring in the driver-specific data structures and definitions.

Globals   These global variables are necessary for the proper operation of the extension library.

```
static EXT_API_VERSION
  ApiVersion = { 3, 5, EXT_API_VERSION_NUMBER, 0 }; ❶

static WINDBG_EXTENSION_APIS ExtensionApis; ❷

static USHORT SavedMajorVersion; ❸
static USHORT SavedMinorVersion;
```

❶ This structure identifies the version of WINDBG that this particular extension library works with. WINDBG won't allow you to load an incompatible extension DLL.

❷ This will hold a pointer to the table of WINDBG callback functions. The access macros defined in **WDBGEXTS.H** assume that this pointer is called **ExtensionApis**, so don't change the name.

❸ These variables will hold information about the version of NT that is being debugged. You can use this information to verify that your library is compatible with that version.

Required functions   These functions perform various kinds of initialization and version-checking.

```
VOID
WinDbgExtensionDllInit(
  PWINDBG_EXTENSION_APIS lpExtensionApis,
  USHORT MajorVersion,
  USHORT MinorVersion
  )
{
  //
  // Save the address of the WINDBG callback
  // table and the NT version information
  //
  ExtensionApis = *lpExtensionApis;

  SavedMajorVersion = MajorVersion;
```

```
   SavedMinorVersion = MinorVersion;

   return;
}
VOID
CheckVersion(
  VOID
  )
{
  //
  // Replace this with your
  // version-checking code
  //
  dprintf(
        "CheckVersion called... [%1x;%d]\n",
        SavedMajorVersion,
        SavedMinorVersion
        );
}

LPEXT_API_VERSION
ExtensionApiVersion(
  VOID
  )
{
  return &ApiVersion;
}
```

Command routines   Here is the code for a command that formats and prints the contents of the Device Extension. It illustrates how to access memory on the system being debugged.

```
DECLARE_API(devext)
{
  DWORD dwBytesRead;
  DWORD dwAddress;

  PDEVICE_OBJECT pDevObj;
  PDEVICE_EXTENSION pDevExt;

  if(( pDevObj = malloc(
             sizeof( DEVICE_OBJECT ))) == NULL )  ❶
  {
        dprintf( "Can't allocate buffer.\n" );
        return;
  }
```

```
dwAddress = GetExpression( args ); ❷

if( !ReadMemory(
            dwAddress,
            pDevObj,
            sizeof( DEVICE_OBJECT ),
            &dwBytesRead )) ❸
{
    dprintf( "Can't get Device object.\n " );
    free( pDevObj );
    return;
}

if( (pDevExt = malloc(
            sizeof( DEVICE_EXTENSION ))) == NULL ) ❹
{
    dprintf( "Can't allocate buffer.\n" );
    free( pDevObj );
    return;
}

if( !ReadMemory(
            (DWORD)pDevObj->DeviceExtension,
            pDevExt,
            sizeof( DEVICE_EXTENSION ),
            &dwBytesRead )) ❺
{
    dprintf( "Can't get Device Extension.\n " );
    free( pDevExt );
    free( pDevObj );
    return;
}

dprintf( ❻
        "BytesRequested: %d\n"
        "BytesRemaining: %d\n"
        "TimeoutCounter: %d\n"
        "DeviceObject: %8x\n",

        pDevExt->BytesRequested,
        pDevExt->BytesRemaining,
        pDevExt->TimeoutCounter,
        pDevExt->DeviceObject
        );

free( pDevExt ); ❼
free( pDevObj );
}
```

❶ Allocate memory for a copy of the Device object.

❷ Get the address of the Device object from the command line using a WINDBG callback function.

❸ Use another WINDBG callback function to get a copy of the Device object from the system being debugged.

❹ Allocate another buffer to hold the Device Extension.

❺ Get the address of the Device Extension (on the target system) from the Device object. Copy the Extension from the target system into the buffer.

❻ Display some interesting values from the Device Extension.

❼ Remember to clean everything up before leaving.

XXDBG.DEF

Here's the Linker definition file for the extension library.

```
LIBRARY XXDBG

EXPORTS
  WinDbgExtensionDllInit  ❶
  CheckVersion
  ExtensionApiVersion
  devext  ❷
  printargs
```

❶ You need to export the required functions so that WINDBG can access them.

❷ Here are all the extension commands exposed by the DLL. Again, the command names must be exclusively lowercase.

SOURCES file

This is the BUILD control file that creates the extension DLL. Since it's creating a user-mode DLL, it uses some BUILD keywords that don't show up in the SOURCES files for drivers.

```
TARGETNAME= xxdbg
TARGETPATH= .
TARGETTYPE= DYNLINK

INCLUDES= $(BASEDIR)\inc;.

USE_CRTDLL= 1

DLLBASE= 0x1000000

SOURCES= xxdbg.c

UMTYPE= console
```

Sample Output

Here is a sample of the output generated by the **XXDBG** extension DLL.

```
KDx86> !load xxdbg  ❶
Debugger extension library [xxdbg] loaded

KDx86> !devext ff58bc40  ❷
 CheckVersion called... [f;1057]
BytesRequested: 0
BytesRemaining: 0
TimeoutCounter: 0
DeviceObject: ff58bc40

KDx86> !unload  ❸
Extension dll xxdbg unloaded
```

❶ The **!load** command brings **XXDBG** into memory and makes it the default extension library. For this to work, **XXDBG.DLL** must be in one of the directories where the system looks for DLLs.

❷ To execute a command, just prefix the command name with an exclamation point.

❸ The **!unload** command unloads the current default extension library. To unload some other extension DLL, specify the name of library as an argument to the command.

17.9 MISCELLANEOUS DEBUGGING TECHNIQUES

Often the main problem in correcting driver bugs is just getting enough information to make an accurate diagnosis. This section presents a grab bag of techniques that may help.

Leaving Debug Code in the Driver

In general, it's a good idea to leave debugging code in place, even when you think the driver is ready for release. That way, you can reuse it when you have to modify the driver at some later date. Conditional compilation makes this easy to do.

The BUILD utility defines a compile-time symbol called **DBG** that you can use to conditionally add debugging code to your driver. In the checked BUILD environment, **DBG** has a value of one; in the free environment it has a value of zero. Several of the macros described below use this symbol to suppress the generation of extraneous debugging code in free versions of drivers. If you're adding your own debugging code to a driver, you should wrap it in **#if DBG** and **#endif** statements.

Catching Incorrect Assumptions

As in real life, making unfounded assumptions in kernel-mode drivers is a dangerous practice. For example, assuming that some function argument will always be non-NULL, or that a piece of code will only be called at a specific IRQL level can lead to disaster if these expectations aren't met.

To catch unforeseen conditions that could lead to driver failure, you need to do two things. First, you have to document the explicit assumptions made by your code. Second, you need to verify that these assumptions are actually true at runtime. The **ASSERT** and **ASSERTMSG** macros will help you with both these tasks. They have the following syntax:

```
ASSERT( Expression );
ASSERTMSG( Message, Expression );
```

If *Expression* evaluates to FALSE, **ASSERT** writes a message to WINDBG's command window. The message contains the source code of the failing expression, plus the file name and line number where the **ASSERT** macro was called. It then gives you the option of taking a breakpoint at the point of the **ASSERT**, ignoring the assertion failure, or terminating the process or thread in which the assertion occurred.

ASSERTMSG exhibits the same behavior, except that it includes the text of the *Message* argument with its output. Don't try getting too fancy with the *Message* argument; it's just a simple string. Unlike the debug print functions described earlier, **ASSERTMSG** doesn't allow you to include any **printf**-style substitutions.

Several things are worth mentioning here. First, both assertion macros compile conditionally and disappear altogether in free builds of your driver. This means it's a very bad idea to put any executable code in the *Expression* argument.

Another little twist is that **RtlAssert** (the underlying function used by these macros) is a no-op in the free version of Windows NT itself. So, if you want to see any assertion failures, you'll have to run a checked build of your driver under the checked version of Windows NT.

Finally, a warning is in order: The checked build of Windows NT will crash with a KMODE_EXCEPTION_NOT_HANDLED error if an assertion fails and the Kernel's debug client isn't enabled. If the debug client is enabled, but there's no debugger on the other end of the serial line, the target machine will simply hang when an assertion fails. You can recover from the hang by starting up WINDBG on the host machine, but you won't see the text of the assertion that failed.

Using Bugcheck Callbacks

A bugcheck callback is an optional driver routine that gets called by the Kernel when the system begins to crash. These routines give you a convenient way to capture debugging information at the time of a crash. You can also use them to put a piece of hardware in a known state before the system goes away. Here's how they work.

1. In **DriverEntry**, call **KeInitializeCallbackRecord** to set up a KBUG-CHECK_CALLBACK_RECORD structure. The space for this opaque structure must be nonpaged, and must be left alone until you call **KeDeregisterBugCheckCallback**.

2. Also in **DriverEntry**, call **KeRegisterBugCheckCallback** to request notification when a bugcheck occurs. The arguments to this function include the bugcheck-callback record, the address of a callback routine, the address and size of a driver-defined crash buffer, and a string that will be used to identify this driver's crash buffer. As with the bugcheck-callback record, memory for the driver's crash buffer must be nonpaged and can't be touched until the driver calls **KeDeregisterBugCheckCallback**.

3. Call **KeDeregisterBugCheckCallback** in your driver's Unload routine to disconnect from the bugcheck notification mechanism.

4. If a bugcheck occurs, the system will call the driver's bugcheck-callback routine and pass it the address and size of the driver's crash buffer. The job of the callback routine is to fill the crash buffer with any information that would not otherwise end up in the dump file (like the contents of device registers).

5. When you analyze the crash with WINDBG, use the **!bugdump** command to view the contents of the crash buffer.

There are some restrictions on what a bugcheck callback is allowed to do. When it runs, the callback routine can't allocate any system resources (like memory). It also can't use spin locks or any other synchronization mechanisms.[9] It is allowed to call Kernel routines that don't violate these restrictions, as well as the HAL functions that access device registers.

Catching Memory Leaks

A memory leak is one of the nastier kinds of driver pathology. Drivers that allocate pool space and then forget to release it may just degrade system performance over time, or they can lead to actual system crashes. You can use NT's built-in pool-tagging mechanism to determine if your driver leaks memory. Here's how it works.

1. Replace calls to **ExAllocatePool** with **ExAllocatePoolWithTag** calls. The extra 4-byte tag argument to this function will be used to mark the block of memory allocated by your driver.

---

[9] Synchronization shouldn't be a problem, though, since nothing else is allowed to run while the bugcheck callback is executing.

2. Run your driver under the checked build of NT. Keeping track of pool tags is an expensive activity, so it only works under the checked version of NT.[10]

3. When you're analyzing a crash, or when your driver is at a breakpoint, use the **!poolused** or **!poolfind** commands in WINDBG to examine the state of the pool areas. These commands sort the pool areas by tag value and displays various memory statistics for each tag.

One easy way to use pool tagging is to replace the **ExAllocatePool** function with **ExAllocatePoolWithTag** with conditional compilation. This way, you can turn tagging on and off without too much trouble. Add something like the following to your driver's header file:

```
#if DBG
#define ExAllocatePool( type, size )    \
  ExAllocatePoolWithTag( (type), (size), 'DCBA' )
#endif
```

The tag argument to **ExAllocatePoolWithTag** consists of four case-sensitive ANSI characters. Because of the way things work on little-endian machines, you need to specify the characters in reverse order. Hence, the DCBA in the example will become ABCD in the pool tag display.

In this example, we used the same tag value for all the allocations made by a single driver. For some situations, you might also want to use different tag values for different kinds of data structures, or for allocations made by different parts of your driver. These kinds of strategies might help you see exactly what's been leaking out of your driver.

The POOLMON utility that comes with the NT DDK also lets you look at the pool tags dynamically, without the need for WINDBG. You run this command-line utility on the target machine and it outputs a continuously updated display of the pool tags. See Chapter 6 of the DDK *Programmer's Guide* for details on running POOLMON.

Using Counters, Bits, and Buffers

There's no question that interactive driver debugging is a wonderful thing. Unfortunately, some kinds of bugs are time-dependent, and they disappear when you use breakpoints or single step through the code. This subsection presents several techniques that may help you catch these bugs.

---

[10] Chapter 6 of the DDK *Programmer's Guide* claims that you can enable this feature in the free build of NT by ORing the FLG _POOL_ENABLE _TAGGING bit into the **GlobalFlag** value of the **HKEY_LOCAL_MACHINE\System\CurrentControlSet\Control\SessionManager** key of the Registry. Unfortunately, none of the currently available documentation or header files defines what this value is.

Sanity counters   You can use pairs of counters to perform several kinds of sanity checks in your driver. For example, you might count how many IRPs arrive at your driver and how many you send to **IoCompleteRequest**. Or, in a higher-level driver, you could track the number of IRPs allocated versus the number released. Checks like these can help you find subtle inconsistencies in the behavior of your driver. The only disadvantage of sanity counters is that they don't necessarily tell you where the problem is occurring.

Implementing a counter is very simple. Just declare a ULONG variable in your Device Extension for each counter and then add appropriate code to increment the counters throughout your driver. As with all debugging support, it's a good idea to wrap sanity-counter code in conditional compilation statements that depend on the **DBG** symbol.

If you're feeling really ambitious, you can write a WINDBG extension to display the counters. As a simple alternative, your driver can force a bugcheck after it has collected enough data, and simply use a bugcheck callback to save the counter values.

Event bits   Another useful technique is to keep a collection of bit flags that track the occurrence of significant events in your driver. Each bit represents one specific event, and when that event happens, your driver sets the corresponding bit. Where sanity counters tell you about global-driver behavior, event bits can give you an idea of what parts of your code have executed.

One of the decisions you'll have to make is whether to clear the event variable during **DriverEntry**, during the Dispatch routine for IRP_MJ_CREATE, or when you begin processing each new IRP. Each of these options can be useful in different situations.

Trace buffers   The problem with event bits and counters is that they don't give you any idea of the sequence of execution of your code. To get around this limitation, you can add a simple tracing mechanism that makes entries in a special buffer as different parts of your driver execute.

Trace buffers can be very useful for tracking down unexpected interactions in asynchronous or full-duplex drivers. On the downside, this extra information isn't free. Trace buffers use more CPU time than counters or event bits, and this could have an effect on time-sensitive bugs.

Implementing a trace buffer mechanism takes a little more work than the other techniques we've looked at. Here are the basic steps you need to follow:

1. Add trace buffer data structures to your driver. Normally, you should put these structures in the Device Extension so you can trace things on a device-by-device basis. Every once in awhile, you might find some value in a global buffer that traces the entire driver.

2. Define a macro to make entries in the trace buffer. As with other pieces of debug code, it's a good idea to bracket the trace macro with conditional compilation statements.

3. Insert calls to the trace macro at various strategic places in your driver.

4. Write a debugger extension to dump the contents of trace buffer.

The trace buffer itself is just an array, coupled with a counter that keeps track of the next free slot. The following code fragment illustrates the structure of a basic trace buffer.

```
typedef _DEVICE_EXTENSION {
    :
#if DBG
  ULONG TraceCount;
  ULONG TraceBuffer[ XX_TRACE_BUFFER_SIZE ];
#endif
    :
} DEVICE_EXTENSION, *PDEVICE_EXTENSION;
```

Again, depending on what you're looking for, you can initialize the **Trace-Count** field once in your DriverEntry routine, each time you get an IRP_MJ_CREATE request, or with each new IRP.

Adding entries to the buffer is just a matter of storing an item in the array and incrementing the counter.[11] This code fragment shows how to implement a basic trace macro.

```
#if DBG
#define XXTRACE( pDE, Tag )                               \
   if( pDE->TraceCount >= XX_TRACE_BUFFER_SIZE )    \
        pDE->TraceCount = 0;                              \
   pDE->TraceBuffer[ pDE->TraceCount++ ] =           \
                              (ULONG)(Tag);         \
#else
#define XXTRACE( pDE, Tag ) while( FALSE ) {}
#endif
```

Notice that this implementation ignores all the synchronization issues that arise when you call **XXTRACE** from multiple IRQL levels (potentially on multiple CPUs). Since the whole purpose of using trace buffers is to catch errors that are sensitive to timing, putting synchronization mechanisms into **XXTRACE** would probably make it useless. So, just how do you prevent the trace macro from trashing itself?

One solution is to call **XXTRACE** only from places in your driver where synchronization won't be a problem. For example, if you call **XXTRACE** from DPC routines, synchronization is already being handled as part of the larger structure of the driver itself. Similarly, if you call it from an ISR and a SyncCritSection routine,

---

[11] If you have a large enough trace buffer and an accurate idea of how many events will be traced, you can save some time by eliminating the test for a full buffer. This is a very dangerous optimization, so use it with care.

synchronization is already guaranteed. If you can't live with these restrictions, you'll have to add explicit synchronization to **XXTRACE**.

17.10 SUMMARY

When you write a driver, very few limits are placed on what you can do to the system. With all this power comes the heavy burden of making sure that your driver doesn't compromise system integrity. You need to correct not only overt, catastrophic errors, but also subtle problems that may over time damage the system. This chapter has presented some techniques you can use to diagnose and eliminate bugs, both early in the development cycle, and later when the driver is out in the world.

But suppose bugs aren't the problem. Suppose the driver works, but it just isn't fast enough. The next chapter examines the important area of driver performance.

Driver Performance

*T*here's a certain feverish look — a kind of glassy stare — that comes into the eyes of a programmer about to start *tuning* a piece of code. You can almost hear their thoughts: "If I just squeeze out a few cycles here and there, make this loop a little tighter, optimize the code by hand, maybe even use some *assembly language...*" Through some kind of magic, everything will run twice as fast.

Unfortunately, the results seldom meet these expectations, and after a lot of effort, the code runs only a few percent faster. The problem is that no amount of optimization or tuning will make up for an inherently slow design. Performance is something you have to think about all the way through the development cycle. If you've done that, then you can use the techniques described in this chapter to verify that your driver meets its performance goals.

18.1 GENERAL GUIDELINES

Acceptable driver performance can mean different things in different situations. As a result, the guidelines given in this section are necessarily a little fuzzy. Hopefully, they'll act as a springboard for your own thinking on the subject.

Know Where You're Going

You have to know where you're trying to go or else you won't know when you've gotten there. In the case of driver tuning, this means you should have some specific performance targets in mind when you start. These targets can be the result of a number of things:

- The device itself may have some timing needs. For example, it might need to be serviced within a certain minimum interval, or it may generate data at some particular rate. Understanding your device and how it will be used are important factors in setting performance targets.

- Application programs may have expectations of how quickly the device will respond, or how many transactions per second it should be able to handle.

- The user's perception may be the determining factor in choosing performance targets. The drivers of video cards, sound boards, and even pointing devices are judged by how they feel to the user more than anything else.

Very early in the design process, formulate your performance goals in the most concrete terms possible. Come up with numbers if you can. Then look at your overall driver design and see where these performance needs will have the biggest impact.

Get to Know the Hardware

Learn as much as you can about the hardware your driver is managing. Does it have any weird quirks that might impact driver performance? Are there any specific sequences of operations that make things go faster or slower? Are you making the most of any built-in processing capabilities of the device itself? If you're working with a multiunit controller, does it support overlapped operations on several devices at the same time? The more you know about the hardware you're driving, the better you'll be able to see what your options are.

Explore Creative Driver Designs

Some of the most powerful optimizations come, not from tweaking code, but from looking for a whole different approach to the problem. NT has a very well-defined driver architecture, but it may not always be suitable for what you're trying to do.

For example, look at the way video and display drivers work. Display speed would be abysmal if Win32 went all the way through the I/O Manager every time it touched the video hardware, so the drivers use a nonstandard architecture. In some cases, it may make sense to map device registers or device memory into user space if that's the only way to achieve acceptable performance. Real-time device control might demand this kind of design.

The mouse class and port drivers provide another example of nonstandard interfaces. In this case, the class driver gives the mouse port driver a pointer to a function that it should call when mouse events arrive. This allows the port driver to pass data using a common buffer and greatly reduces the system's overhead in processing large numbers of events.

The downside of all this is that you may end up compromising system integrity. Don't abandon the standard NT driver architecture right off the bat, but if it's clear that nothing else will give you good performance, go for it.

Optimize Code Creatively

This is where everyone wants to look first, when in fact it's probably the last place to focus your attention. It's worth repeating that no amount of clever optimization will make up for an inherently bad design. If you do need to squeeze more performance out of your code, here are some things to think about.

First, be very clear about what you're trying to accomplish. Your goal should be to find new ways of doing things, not just ways to tweak existing code. Most decent C compilers do a wonderful job of tweaking code. Your advantage as a human is that you know the context in which the code will run. This allows you to look for entirely different ways of accomplishing a particular task. Don't waste this gift by turning yourself into a glorified peep-hole optimizer.

Also, focus your attention on the relatively small areas of code that really determine overall performance. It's often the case that one or two tiny subroutines, comprising maybe 10 percent of your overall driver, will be the gate that controls the speed of the driver. Try to find those hot spots or critical code paths and make them as fast as possible. The code paths through your driver's most frequently executed operations are a good place to look.

Finally, don't assume that an optimization will have the same impact on all NT platforms. Some kinds of optimizations may work only on a specific type of CPU. If you plan to support your driver on more than one CPU or bus architecture, be sure that improvements work equally well everywhere. At the very least, make certain that an optimization on one configuration doesn't degrade performance anywhere else.

Measure Everything You Do

Concrete measurement forms the basis of all good science. It's amazing how much faster a piece of code can seem just because you've put several hours of work into optimizing it. Don't get caught in the trap of wishful thinking; measure the impact of everything you do. If you don't have any quantitative data to go by, you won't know if you're helping or hurting.

Later in this chapter, you'll see one way to analyze a driver's behavior using the PERFMON utility. You can also measure the speed of specific routines using the profiling timer available in NT. The only limitation is that this counter's resolution on 80x86 machines is only one microsecond, and on a 100 MHz Pentium, a lot of instructions can flow by in that time.

18.2 PERFORMANCE MONITORING IN WINDOWS NT

One of your options for observing a driver's behavior is to tie into NT's performance monitoring system. The advantage of this technique is that you or anyone else can use the PERFMON utility to collect and display data about your driver. This section presents the overall architecture of NT's performance monitor system.

Some Terminology

Like other parts of NT, the performance system uses an object-based model to describe its operation. Before we look at the actual steps involved in using the performance system, it's a good idea to define some of the terms appearing in the discussion.

Performance object   This is any object that makes performance data available through the Registry. System components, drivers, and services can all export various performance objects. For example, the system exposes objects like memory and CPU, and drivers can expose separate performance objects for each device they support.

Performance counter   Data about a given performance object takes the form of *counters*. Although the name seems to imply the summing of discrete events, these counters can actually represent a wide variety of measurements: an absolute number of events, a rate of occurrence, a ratio of quantities, the average availability of a resource, and so forth. For example, NT's Memory object exposes counters representing the number of available bytes and the number of page faults per second.

Object instance   There may be more than one *instance* of some kinds of objects on the system. For example, there can be several CPUs and several disk drives. To distinguish among members of a set of identical objects, performance monitoring components usually represent these objects as separate instances of the object type. CPU performance data would show up as information about CPU0, CPU1, CPU2, and so on.

Counter instance   When a performance object supports multiple object instances, each instance will have its own complete set of counters. Referring back to the CPU object, there are separate interrupt rate counters for each CPU object instance.

How Performance Monitoring Works

Windows NT provides a common set of interfaces that drivers and application programs can use if they want to participate in performance monitoring operations. Figure 18.1 shows how these interfaces work.

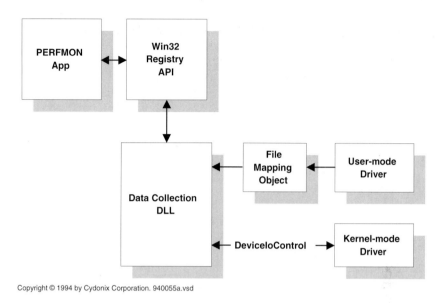

Copyright © 1994 by Cydonix Corporation. 940055a.vsd

Figure 18.1   NT performance monitoring components

The following describes what happens when you run the PERFMON utility (located in the Administrative Tools program group). The process would be the same for any application program curious about system performance data.

1. The PERFMON utility uses the Win32 **RegQueryValueEx** function to access the **HKEY_PERFORMANCE_DATA** key.

2. The Registry API scans **HKEY_LOCAL_MACHINE\...\Services** for drivers and services with a **Performance** subkey. Having this subkey marks a driver or service as a performance monitoring component. Values contained in the **Performance** subkey identify a data-collection DLL that acts as an interface between the Registry API and the objects being monitored.

3. The Registry API maps these interface DLLs into the process requesting performance data. It then calls the **Open** and **Collect** functions in each DLL to determine what objects and counters the DLL supports.

4. Each time PERFMON wants updated performance information, it calls the **RegQueryValueEx** again. This results in calls to the **Collect** function in each performance component's data-collection DLL. The **Collect** function gets a raw data sample from the object being monitored and sends it back to PERFMON.

5. When PERFMON closes the **HKEY_PERFORMANCE_DATA** key with **Reg-CloseKey**, the Registry API calls the DLL's **Close** function to do any necessary cleanup. It then unmaps the DLL from the process.

You can see from this description that performance information isn't actually stored in the Registry in the same way that hardware or software configuration data is. Rather, the Win32 Registry API calls gather performance data at the time someone asks for it.

How Drivers Export Performance Data

Drivers that support monitoring have to maintain performance data about themselves. They make this data available to their data-collection DLL using either of two different techniques:

- **IOCTLs** — Kernel-mode drivers make their performance data available through a privately defined IOCTL function.

- **File Mapping objects** — User-mode drivers expose performance data through a File Mapping object (i.e., shared memory) that has a well-known name.

The example appearing later in this chapter shows how to implement a data-collection DLL for a kernel-mode driver. A similar example in the NT DDK illustrates how to set up monitoring for a user-mode system component.

18.3 ADDING COUNTER NAMES TO THE REGISTRY

One of the goals of NT's performance monitoring architecture was to make the display names of performance objects and counters independent of any particular national language. If you have the American version of NT installed, performance monitoring tools should display counter names in English, while the French version of NT should use French names.

To accomplish this, both the data-collection DLL and the PERFMON utility refer to performance objects and counters using index numbers rather than names. These index numbers are assigned when a driver is installed on a given machine, and they are globally unique on that system. These object and counter indexes are stored in the Registry along with their corresponding display names. Tools like PERFMON use this area of the Registry to convert an object or counter index into text. A similar mechanism allows PERFMON to display help text (in the appropriate language) about a given counter.

Counter Definitions in the Registry

As you can see from Figure 18.2, individual counter definitions are stored under the **Perflib** key, grouped according to their language ID. This scheme allows you to support counter names and help text in multiple languages without having to modify your driver.

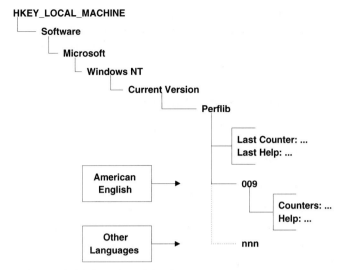

Copyright © 1994 by Cydonix Corporation. 940057a.vsd

Figure 18.2 Counter definition area in the Registry

Look at Table 18.1 for a more detailed view of the individual Registry entries. As you can see, each performance object or counter is coupled with a unique, even integer. These pairs are stored under the **Counters** subkey for each language. Help text for a given counter has an odd-numbered index one greater than the index for the counter itself. Help text definitions are stored under the **Help** subkey of each language.

Although you could do something disgusting such as using REGEDT32 to add your counter definitions to the Registry, there is an easier way. The NT DDK

Table 18.1 Registry entries that define counter names and help text

Perflib Registry entries

Entry	Contents	Example
nnn	Names and help text for a specific language ID	009 is the language ID for American English
nnn \Counters	REG_MULTI_SZ string composed of index / name	2 \0 System \0 4 \0 Memory \0 6 \0 % Processor time \0 \0
nnn \Help	REG_MULTI_SZ string composed of index / help text	3 \0 The System object type... \0 5 \0 The Memory object type... \0 7 \0 % Processor time is... \0 \0
Last Counter	Highest assigned name index	0x330
Last Help	Highest-assigned help index	0x331

contains two utilities, LODCTR and UNLODCTR, that add and remove counter definitions for you. In order to add counters with LODCTR, you need to do the following:

1.   Write a LODCTR command file.

2.   Write a counter-offset header file.

3.   Add a subkey called **Performance** to your driver's Registry service key.

4.   Run the LODCTR utility to install the counter definitions.

Writing LODCTR Command Files

To use the LODCTR utility, you first need to write a command file describing the objects, counters, and help text you want to add to the Registry. The command file is divided into three sections and can contain the keywords listed in Table 18.2.

Table 18.2   Section names and keywords in a LODCTR command file

LODCTR command file

Section	Keywords	Description
[info]	**DRIVERNAME=***DriverName*	Name, if driver
	APPLICATIONNAME=*ProgName*	Name, if service
	SYMBOLFILE=*FileName.H*	Counter-offset definition file
[languages]	*langid=LanguageName*	IDs of languages in this file (*LanguageName* is ignored)
[text]	*symbol_langid_***NAME=***Name text*	Name of one object or counter
	*symbol_langid_***HELP=***Help text*	Single line of explanatory text

The LODCTR utility uses the Win32 profile functions to parse its command file, so it should come as no surprise that these files usually have the extension INI. Let's look at an example of the command and header files needed to define some performance counters.

COUNTERS.INI   The following example of a LODCTR command file adds one object with two counters to the Registry. It supports only American English versions of the counters.

```
[info]
drivername=XXDRIVER
symbolfile=COUNTERS.H

[languages]
009=English
```

```
[text]
XXDEVICE_009_NAME=XX Device
XXDEVICE_009_HELP= The Xx Device does whatever it does.

INTERRUPTS_009_NAME=Interrupts/sec
INTERRUPTS_009_HELP=Measures the interrupt rate.

OPERATIONS_009_NAME=Operations/sec
OPERATIONS_009_HELP=Measures device activity.
```

COUNTERS.H You also need to write a header file containing the relative index values of each object and counter that you plan to add to the Registry. This header file defines relative offsets for the XXDEVICE object and its two counters.

```
#define XXDEVICE        0
#define INTERRUPTS      2
#define OPERATIONS      4
```

These indexes must be even numbers starting at zero. The names in the header file have to match the names in the **[text]** section of the LODCTR command file, and they are case-sensitive. This header file will also be included in your data-collection DLL.

Using LODCTR and UNLODCTR

To add your counter names to the Registry, run LODCTR from the command line and give it the name of the command file, like this:

```
LODCTR COUNTERS.INI
```

When you run LODCTR, it uses the **Last Counter** and **Last Help** values in the **Perflib** Registry key to assign absolute index numbers to your objects, counters, and help text items. It also stores the first and last counter and help indexes assigned to your driver in the **Performance** subkey of the driver's Registry service key.

A single command file can contain object and counter definitions in more than one language. However, LODCTR will only install counter definitions for language IDs already listed under the **Perflib** Registry key.

To remove all the objects, counters, and help text associated with a particular driver or service, run the UNLODCTR utility. Its only argument is the name of the driver or service that you specified in the **[info]** section of the INI file.

```
UNLODCTR XXDRIVER
```

If you want to modify the object and counter names associated with a particular driver, you have to remove the existing counter definitions for the driver with UNLODCTR and run LODCTR again. LODCTR performs only minimal error checking, and if you run it twice for the same driver, the results are unpredictable.

18.4 THE FORMAT OF PERFORMANCE DATA

When the Registry API calls your data-collection DLL, it expects you to return counter information in a very specific format. This data format is one of the more Byzantine things in NT, so it deserves a little motivating explanation.

Along with the goal of language-independent object and counter names, the NT architects also wanted to make performance data totally self-descriptive. This means that programs like PERFMON should be able to process and display a block of performance data using only the contents of the block itself. This open-ended, extensible architecture allows standard tools to monitor objects that they know nothing about.

Unfortunately, data that's totally self-descriptive is also very complicated. The following subsections describe the Registry's performance data format.

Overall Structure of Performance Data

Figure 18.3 illustrates the overall structure of the information returned by your data-collection DLL. For each performance object in the DLL, you have to provide

- Information about the object itself
- Definitions for each counter the object exposes
- A header for all the counter data
- A block containing the counters themselves

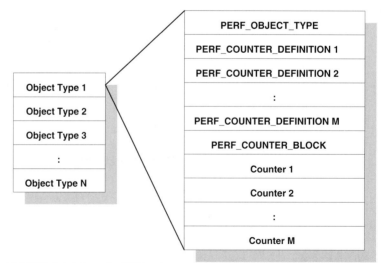

Copyright © 1994 by Cydonix Corporation. 940054a.vsd

Figure 18.3   Structure of performance data for objects with single instances

The following subsections describe these structures in more detail. You can find additional information in the **WINPERF.H** header file that comes with the Win32 SDK.[1]

PERF_OBJECT_TYPE This structure acts as a header for information about a single object type. You must provide one of these structures for each object being exposed by your performance DLL. Table 18.3 lists the fields in this structure.

Table 18.3 Contents of a PERF_OBJECT_TYPE structure

PERF_OBJECT_TYPE, *PPERF_OBJECT_TYPE

Field	Contents
DWORD TotalByteLength	sizeof(PERF_OBJECT_TYPE) + NumCounters * sizeof(PERF_COUNTER_DEFINITION) + sizeof(PERF_COUNTER_BLOCK) + sizeof(allCounters)
DWORD DefinitionLength	sizeof(PERF_OBJECT_TYPE) + NumCounters * sizeof(PERF_COUNTER_DEFINITION)
DWORD HeaderLength	sizeof(PERF_OBJECT_TYPE)
DWORD ObjectNameTitleIndex	Index of this object's name in the title database
LPWSTR ObjectNameTitle	NULL
DWORD ObjectHelpTitleIndex	Index of object's description in the help database
LPWSTR ObjectHelpTitle	NULL
DWORD DetailLevel	Complexity level of information • PERF_DETAIL_NOVICE • PERF_DETAIL_ADVANCED • PERF_DETAIL_EXPERT • PERF_DETAIL_WIZARD
DWORD NumCounters	Number of counters in each counter block
DWORD DefaultCounter	Default to display, or –1
DWORD NumInstances	Number of instances of this object, or –1 if no separate instances
DWORD CodePage	0 for drivers
LARGE_INTEGER PerfTime	Current value, in counts, of the high-resolution performance counter
LARGE_INTEGER PerfFreq	Current frequency, in counts per second, of the high-resolution performance counter

---

[1] This header also contains a great deal of descriptive commentary. I recommend reading it if you're going to be working with the performance subsystem.

Table 18.4　Contents of a PERF_COUNTER_DEFINITION structure

PERF_COUNTER_DEFINITION, *PPERF_COUNTER_DEFINITION

Field	Contents
DWORD ByteLength	sizeof(PERF_COUNTER_DEFINITION)
DWORD CounterNameTitleIndex	Index of this counter's name in the title database
LPWSTR CounterNameTitle	NULL
DWORD CounterHelpTitleIndex	Index of this counter's description in the help database
LPWSTR CounterHelpTitle	NULL
DWORD DefaultScale	Scaling factor for display, expressed as a power of 10
DWORD DetailLevel	Complexity level of information • PERF_DETAIL_NOVICE • PERF_DETAIL_ADVANCED • PERF_DETAIL_EXPERT • PERF_DETAIL_WIZARD
DWORD CounterType	(See below)
DWORD CounterSize	Size of counter in bytes
DWORD CounterOffset	Offset from start of PERF_COUNTER_BLOCK structure to the first byte of this counter

PERF_COUNTER_DEFINITION　You must supply a separate counter definition for each counter in your DLL. This block (described in Table 18.4) pinpoints the size and position of the counter data itself, as well as defining the type of information the counter represents.

PERF_COUNTER_BLOCK　This block (described in Table 18.5) is simply a header for all the raw counter data itself. The counters come immediately after it.

Table 18.5　Contents of a PERF_COUNTER_BLOCK structure

PERF_COUNTER_BLOCK, *PPERF_COUNTER_BLOCK

Field	Contents
DWORD ByteLength	sizeof(PERF_COUNTER_BLOCK) + sizeof(allCounters)

Types of Counters

The **CounterType** field of the counter definition block specifies the kind of information represented by the counter. **WINPERF.H** contains a number of pre-defined types, most of which are listed in Table 18.6. Your choice of a counter type

Table 18.6 Use these values for the CounterType field of a PERF_COUNTER_DEFINITION

Predefined CounterType values

Counter type	Description	Suffix
PERF_COUNTER_COUNTER	32-bit event rate **ΔCount / ΔTime**	/sec
PERF_COUNTER_TIMER	64-bit Timer **ΔCount / ΔTime**	%
PERF_COUNTER_QUEUELEN_TYPE	Average queue length **ΔCount / ΔTime**	—
PERF_COUNTER_BULK_COUNT	64-bit event rate **ΔCount / ΔTime**	/sec
PERF_COUNTER_TEXT	Unicode text	—
PERF_COUNTER_RAWCOUNT	32-bit counter No time averaging	—
PERF_SAMPLE_FRACTION	% Busy counter numerator 1 or 0 on each sampling interrupt **ΔCount / ΔTime**	%
PERF_SAMPLE_BASE	% Busy counter denominator Directly follows numerator counter.	—
PERF_SAMPLE_COUNTER	Sampled counter **ΔCount / ΔTime**	—
PERF_COUNTER_NODATA	Label only; no data	—
PERF_COUNTER_TIMER_INV	64-bit Timer inverse Measure % idle but display % busy **100 – (ΔCount / ΔTime)**	%
PERF_AVERAGE_BULK	A bulk count which, when divided (typically) by the number of operations, gives (typically) the number of bytes per operation. **Count / Base**	—
PERF_AVERAGE_TIMER	A timer which, when divided by an average base, produces a time in seconds which is the average time of some operation. This timer times total operations, and the base is the number of operations. **Timer / Base**	sec
PERF_AVERAGE_BASE	Denominator of time or count averages Directly follows numerator counter.	—

Table 18.6   (Continued)

Counter type	Description	Suffix
PERF_100NSEC_TIMER	64-bit Timer in 100 nsec units **ΔCount / ΔTime**	%
PERF_100NSEC_TIMER_INV	64-bit Timer inverse **100 − (ΔCount / ΔTime)**	%
PERF_COUNTER_MULTI_TIMER	64-bit multi-instance Timer **ΔCount / ΔTime** Result can exceed 100%	%
PERF_COUNTER_MULTI_TIMER_INV	64-bit multi-instance Timer inverse **100 * MULTI_BASE** **− (ΔCount / ΔTime)** Result can exceed 100% Followed by a MULTI_BASE. Counter	%
PERF_COUNTER_MULTI_BASE	Number of instances to which the preceding _MULTI_..._INV counter applies	—
PERF_100NSEC_MULTI_TIMER	64-bit multi-instance 100 nSec Timer **ΔCount / ΔTime** Result can exceed 100%	%
PERF_100NSEC_MULTI_TIMER_INV	64-bit Timer inverse **100 * _MULTI_BASE** **− ΔCount / ΔTime** Result can exceed 100%. Followed by a MULTI_BASE counter	%
PERF_RAW_FRACTION	Counter is a fraction of base **Count / Base** No time averaging	%
PERF_RAW_BASE	Base for the preceding counter	—

will determine not only the data you have to supply, but also how the Performance Monitor displays that data.

Objects with Multiple Instances

If your data-collection DLL reports data separately for each instance of an object, you need to use a slightly different data format. As you can see from Figure 18.4, the main change is that you have to supply a name for each object instance and separate instances of each counter.

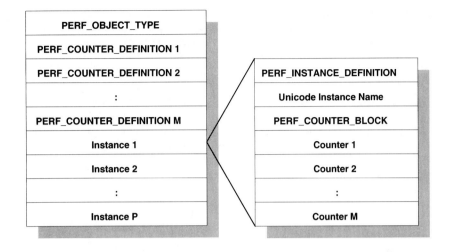

Figure 18.4   Modified structure of performance data for objects with multiple instances

You need to calculate slightly different values for two fields in the PERF_OBJECT_TYPE if you're using multiple object instances. Table 18.7 lists these changes.

The other new item for multi-instance objects is a block that describes each object instance. See Table 18.8 for the contents of this block. Notice that you can identify an instance either by a Unicode name or by a number. If you use a name, the name string immediately follows the instance definition block. Keep in mind that, since this Unicode name string is embedded in the data, it won't be translated into the local language.

Table 18.7   These fields of PERF_OBJECT_TYPE are different for multi-instance objects

PERF_OBJECT_TYPE fields

Field	Contents
TotalByteLength	sizeof(PERF_OBJECT_TYPE) + NumCounters * sizeof(PERF_COUNTER_DEFINITION) + NumInstances * sizeof(PERF_INSTANCE_DEFINITION) + sizeof(allInstanceNames) + NumInstances * sizeof(PERF_COUNTER_BLOCK) + NumInstances * sizeof(allCounters)
NumInstances	Value ‡ 1

Table 18.8   Contents of a PERF_INSTANCE_DEFINITION structure

PERF_INSTANCE_DEFINITION, *PPERF_INSTANCE_DEFINITION

Field	Contents
DWORD ByteLength	sizeof(PERF_INSTANCE_DEFINITION) + sizeof(InstanceNameString)
DWORD ParentObjectTitleIndex	Index in the title database of object type which is this object's parent or 0 if no hierarchy
DWORD ParentObjectInstance	Index, starting at 0, into the instances being reported for the parent object type
DWORD UniqueID	Zero-based numerical identifier used in place of a name; PERF_NO_UNIQUE_ID if none
DWORD NameOffset	sizeof(PERF_INSTANCE_DEFINITION)
DWORD NameLength	sizeof(InstanceNameString) or 0 if no name

18.5 WRITING THE DATA-COLLECTION DLL

As we've already seen, the data-collection DLL acts as an interface between the driver and the Registry API. This section describes the contents of the DLL and explains what you have to do to make the DLL visible to the system.

Contents of the Data-Collection DLL

The data-collection DLL consists of three major functions. You can call these routines anything you like, since their names will be recorded in the **Performance** subkey of your driver's Registry service key. The following subsections describe each of these functions.

Open   The Open function queries the Registry to determine the proper index values for each object and counter exported by the DLL. It also initializes the static versions of PERF_OBJECT_TYPE and PERF_COUNTER_DEFINITION structures used by the DLL's Collect function. Finally, it establishes a connection with the specific devices being monitored. Table 18.9 contains the prototype for the Open function.

Table 18.9   Prototype for data collector's Open function

DWORD XxPerfOpen

Parameter	Description
IN LPWSTR lpDeviceNames	Unicode strings naming each device managed by this driver or NULL
Return value	• ERROR_SUCCESS — function succeeded • ERROR_XXX — some Win32 error code

Table 18.10 Prototype for data collector's Collect function

DWORD XxPerfCollect

Parameter	Description
IN LPWSTR lpwszValue	Unicode string identifying requested data • **Global** — data about all objects • *index 1 index 2...* — data about specific objects • **Foreign** *ComputerName* • **Foreign** *ComputerName index1 index2...* • **Costly** — data that's expensive to collect
IN OUT LPVOID *lppData	IN: Pointer to buffer pointer for returned data OUT SUCCESS: Updated pointer OUT ERROR: Unchanged from input input
IN OUT LPDWORD lpcbBytes	IN: Pointer to DWORD containing buffer size OUT SUCCESS: Number of data bytes in buffer OUT ERROR: 0
OUT LPDWORD lpcObjectTypes	OUT SUCCESS — Count of ObjectTypes OUT ERROR: 0
Return value	ERROR_MORE_DATA — buffer too small ERROR_SUCCESS — all other cases

Collect The Collect function (described in Table 18.10) is called once when the DLL is opened to get a list of all the objects supported by the DLL. From then on, it is called periodically to retrieve current counter values from each object being monitored.

The first argument to this function is a NULL-terminated Unicode string describing the kind of data that the caller wants to receive. This argument can either be a specific keyword (like **Global**), or it can be a list of index numbers that identify particular object types. Your Collect function will need to parse this string to see if it can provide data about any of the objects the caller is interested in.

Close This function is called when it's time to close the connection with the monitored devices and release any resources held by the DLL. The prototype for this function appears in Table 18.11.

Table 18.11 Prototype for data collector's Close function

DWORD XxPerfClose

Parameter	Description
VOID	—
Return value	ERROR_SUCCESS

Error Handling in a Data-Collection DLL

It's a good idea for your data-collection DLL to record any problems it encounters in the Event Log. That way, you or a system administrator can poke around with the Event Viewer utility if your driver's performance objects aren't showing up in PERFMON for some reason.

Since a data-collection DLL is running in user mode, it doesn't use the kernel-mode event-logging interface described in Chapter 13. Instead, it works with the Win32 event logging functions, **RegisterEventSource**, **ReportEvent**, and **DeregisterEventSource**. The code example that accompanies this chapter shows how to use these functions.

Another implication of the data-collection DLL's user-mode environment is that you have to record its error message file (which is usually the DLL itself) in a slightly different part of the Registry. Rather than dangling beneath **...Services\EventLog\System**, the DLL's message file is recorded in **...Services\EventLog\Application**.[2] Figure 18.5 shows how this works.

It's also polite behavior to give system administrators the ability to control the amount of event logging your DLL performs. One way to do this is to put a REG_DWORD value called **EventLogLevel** under the **Parameters** subkey of the driver's Registry service key. The DLL's Open function retrieves this value from the Registry and uses it as a logging threshold. The higher the number, the more event-logging detail the DLL generates.

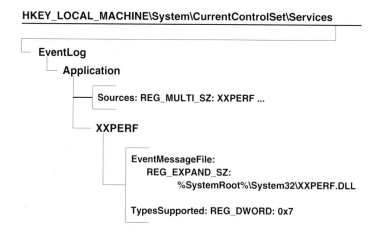

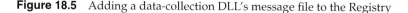

Copyright © 1996 by Cydonix Corporation. 960026a.vsd

Figure 18.5   Adding a data-collection DLL's message file to the Registry

---

[2] This also means the DLL's event messages will show up in the Application log rather than the System log when you use the Event Viewer utility.

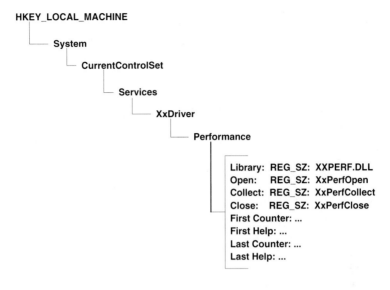

HKEY_LOCAL_MACHINE
  └─ System
      └─ CurrentControlSet
          └─ Services
              └─ XxDriver
                  └─ Performance
                      Library: REG_SZ: XXPERF.DLL
                      Open: REG_SZ: XxPerfOpen
                      Collect: REG_SZ: XxPerfCollect
                      Close: REG_SZ: XxPerfClose
                      First Counter: ...
                      First Help: ...
                      Last Counter: ...
                      Last Help: ...

Copyright © 1994 by Cydonix Corporation. 940056a.vsd

Figure 18.6   Contents of a driver's Performance subkey

Installing the DLL

Once you've built the data-collection DLL itself, you need to move it to the **%SystemRoot%\SYSTEM32** directory. To make NT aware of your DLL, you have to add several values to the **Performance** subkey of your driver's Registry service key. Figure 18.6 shows the structure of these Registry entries, and Table 18.12 describes them in detail.

The **First Counter**, **Last Counter**, **First Help**, and **Last Help** values were put there by LODCTR. The data-collection DLL retrieves the two **First** values and uses them to calculate the proper index numbers for each of its objects, counters, and help text items. You only need to add the values that identify the DLL and its entry points.

Table 18.12   Values in a driver's Performance subkey

Performance subkey values

Value	Description	Example
Library	Full path name of data-collection DLL	XXPERF.DLL
Open	Name of DLL's (optional) Open function	XxPerfOpen
Collect	Name of DLL's Collect function	XxPerfCollect
Close	Name of DLL's (optional) Close function	XxPerfCollect

18.6 CODE EXAMPLE: A DATA-COLLECTION DLL

This example shows how to set up a data-collection DLL. It also illustrates the modifications you'd need to make to a kernel-mode driver in order to retrieve performance data from it.

It takes a fair amount of code to implement all the pieces of this example. Unfortunately, not all of it will fit here. The complete code for all the components can be found in the **CH18** directory on the disk that accompanies this book. In this directory, you'll find three subdirectories:

- **Driver** — This directory contains a version of XXDRIVER that supports a IOCTL_XX_GET_PERF_DATA I/O control code. The driver itself is just a stub that illustrates how to pass performance data back to the collection DLL. The performance measurements generated by the driver are all bogus.

- **Ioctl** — The only file in this directory is **XXIOCTL.H** which contains the IOCTL definitions and structures used by both the driver and the collection DLL.

- **Library** — The files in this directory implement the data-collection DLL itself. This includes support for event logging, parsing the argument string of the DLL's Open function, and gathering and formatting performance data.

Again, because of space limitations, only selected portions of the data-collection DLL will appear here.

XXPERF.C

This file of the example contains the Open, Collect, and Close functions that interface with the Win32 Registry API calls.

Preamble area   This section of the data-collection DLL's source code contains header files, data definitions, and function prototypes necessary to the proper operation of the DLL.

```
//
// All-inclusive header file
//
#include "xxperf.h"  ❶

//
// Data global to this module  ❷
//
static HANDLE hDevice;
```

```
static DWORD dwOpenCount = 0;
static BOOL bInitialized = FALSE;
//
// Initialized object header defined
// in data.c
//
extern XX_HEADER_DEFINITION XxObjectHeader;  ❸

//
// Forward declarations of routines  ❹
//
PM_OPEN_PROC        XxPerfOpen;
PM_COLLECT_PROC     XxPerfCollect;
PM_CLOSE_PROC       XxPerfClose;
```

❶ The master header file includes **WINPERF.H** from the Win32 SDK. This Win32 header defines all the performance data structures.

❷ Multiple functions in this source module need access to the device handle, the count of threads using the library, and the initialization flag. The easiest way to deal with this is to make the variables global.

❸ The modules **DATA.C** and **DATA.H** contain a single copy of all the static parts of the object-type and counter-definition data.

❹ The three exported functions in the DLL must be identified using these specific forward declarations if you want everything to work properly.

XxPerfOpen   This function sets up the DLL. This includes getting a handle to the target device and calculating the absolute index values for each object and counter exported by the DLL. To simplify the collection process, the DLL keeps a single, statically initialized copy of the data header information in a global structure defined in **DATA.C** and **DATA.H**.

```
DWORD
XxPerfOpen(
  LPWSTR lpDeviceNames
  )
{
  HKEY hKeyDriverPerf;
  DWORD dwFirstCounter;
  DWORD dwFirstHelp;
  DWORD dwType;
  DWORD dwSize;
  DWORD dwStatus;

  if( dwOpenCount == 0 )  ❶
  {
```

```
        XxOpenEventLog();❷

        hDevice = CreateFile❸
                        XX_WIN32_DEVICE_NAME,
                        GENERIC_READ,
                        FILE_SHARE_READ |
                                FILE_SHARE_WRITE,
                        NULL,
                        OPEN_EXISTING,
                        FILE_ATTRIBUTE_NORMAL,
                        NULL );
        if( hDevice == INVALID_HANDLE_VALUE )
        {
            dwStatus = GetLastError();
            XxLogErrorWithData(
                LOG_LEVEL_NORMAL,
                XXPERF_CANT_OPEN_DEVICE_HANDLE,
                &dwStatus, sizeof( dwStatus ) );
            XxCloseEventLog();
            return dwStatus;
        }

        //
        // Open the Performance subkey of the driver's
        // service key in the Registry.
        //
        dwStatus = RegOpenKeyEx(❹
                        HKEY_LOCAL_MACHINE,
                        "SYSTEM\\CurrentControlSet"
                            "\\Services\\XxDriver"
                                "\\Performance",
                        0L,
                        KEY_ALL_ACCESS,
                        &hKeyDriverPerf );

        if( dwStatus != ERROR_SUCCESS )
        {
            XxLogErrorWithData(
                LOG_LEVEL_NORMAL,
                XXPERF_CANT_OPEN_DRIVER_KEY,
                &dwStatus, sizeof( dwStatus ));

            CloseHandle( hDevice );
            XxCloseEventLog();
            return dwStatus;
        }
```

```
//
// Get base index of first object or counter
//
dwSize = sizeof (DWORD);
dwStatus = RegQueryValueEx(
                    hKeyDriverPerf,
                    "First Counter",
                    0L,
                    &dwType,
                    (LPBYTE)&dwFirstCounter,
                    &dwSize);

if( dwStatus != ERROR_SUCCESS )
{
      XxLogErrorWithData(
            LOG_LEVEL_NORMAL,
            XXPERF_CANT_READ_FIRST_COUNTER,
            &dwStatus, sizeof( dwStatus ));

      RegCloseKey( hKeyDriverPerf );
      CloseHandle( hDevice );
      XxCloseEventLog();
      return dwStatus;
}
//
// Get base index of first help text
//
dwSize = sizeof (DWORD);
dwStatus = RegQueryValueEx(
                    hKeyDriverPerf,
                    "First Help",
                    0L,
                    &dwType,
                    (LPBYTE)&dwFirstHelp,
                    &dwSize );

if( dwStatus != ERROR_SUCCESS )
{
      XxLogErrorWithData(
            LOG_LEVEL_NORMAL,
            XXPERF_CANT_READ_FIRST_HELP,
            &dwStatus, sizeof( dwStatus ));

      RegCloseKey( hKeyDriverPerf );
      CloseHandle( hDevice );
      XxCloseEventLog();
```

```
              return dwStatus;
          }

          //
          // Don't need Registry handle anymore
          //
          RegCloseKey( hKeyDriverPerf );

          //
          // Initialize PERF_OBJECT_TYPE struct❺
          //
          XxObjectHeader.XxDevice.
                    ObjectNameTitleIndex =
                          dwFirstCounter + XXDEVICE;

          XxObjectHeader.XxDevice.
                    ObjectHelpTitleIndex =
                          dwFirstHelp + XXDEVICE;

          //
          // Initialize 1st PERF_COUNTER_DEFINITION
          //
          XxObjectHeader.Interrupts.
                    CounterNameTitleIndex =
                          dwFirstCounter + INTERRUPTS;
          XxObjectHeader.Interrupts.
                    CounterHelpTitleIndex =
                          dwFirstHelp + INTERRUPTS;

          //
          // Initialize 2nd PERF_COUNTER_DEFINITION
          //
          XxObjectHeader.Operations.
                    CounterNameTitleIndex =
                          dwFirstCounter + OPERATIONS;
          XxObjectHeader.Operations.
                    CounterHelpTitleIndex =
                          dwFirstHelp + OPERATIONS;

          //
          // Mark DLL as successfully initialized
          //
          bInitialized = TRUE;
      }

  //
  // One way or another, there's one more
  // thread using the DLL.
```

```
    //
    dwOpenCount++;

    return ERROR_SUCCESS
}
```

❶ If the DLL is being called by SCREG from a remote computer, there may be multiple threads accessing it at the same time. Therefore the DLL needs to keep a count of how many times it's been opened. The first call causes the DLL to initialize itself; the rest simply bump the count.

❷ Any errors that occur will go to the Event Log. This helper function (defined in **EVENTLOG.C**) manages the details of setting up the connection.

❸ The kernel-mode driver will give performance data to the DLL in response to a special IOCTL code. To issue that IOCTL, the DLL needs a handle to the device. This handle is stored in a global variable (hDevice) where the rest of the DLL can get to it.

❹ This next section of code gets a handle to the **Performance** subkey below XXDRIVER's Registry service key. Then it recovers the base index number for XXDRIVER's objects and counters (from the **First Counter** value), and the base index number for help text (from the **First Help** value).

❺ Once the base index values are recovered, it's necessary to calculate the index number of every object, counter, and help text item supported by this DLL. The resulting indexes are put into the various **...TitleIndex** fields of the statically initialized object header defined in **DATA.C**.

XxPerfCollect   The Collect function retrieves one sample of data from the object being monitored. After copying the static data header into the caller's buffer, it uses an IOCTL to put the current counter values there as well.

```
DWORD
XxPerfCollect(
  IN LPWSTR lpValueName,
  IN OUT LPVOID *lppData,
  IN OUT LPDWORD lpcbTotalBytes,
  IN OUT LPDWORD lpNumObjectTypes
  )
{
  DWORD dwQueryType;
  DWORD dwStatus;
  DWORD dwBytesReturned;
  PPERF_COUNTER_BLOCK pPerfCounterBlock;
  PXX_HEADER_DEFINITION pXxObjectHeader;

  if( !bInitialized ) ❶
  {
```

```
        *lpcbTotalBytes = (DWORD) 0;
        *lpNumObjectTypes = (DWORD) 0;
        return ERROR_SUCCESS;
}

dwQueryType = XxGetPerfQueryType( lpValueName ); ❷

if( dwQueryType == PERF_QUERY_TYPE_FOREIGN )
{
        //
        // Can't service foreign requests.
        //
        *lpcbTotalBytes = (DWORD) 0;
        *lpNumObjectTypes = (DWORD) 0;
        return ERROR_SUCCESS;
}

if( dwQueryType == PERF_QUERY_TYPE_ITEMS )
{
        if( !XxIsNumberInList(❸
                    XxObjectHeader.
                        XxDevice.
                            ObjectNameTitleIndex,
                    lpValueName ))
        {
            *lpcbTotalBytes = (DWORD) 0;
            *lpNumObjectTypes = (DWORD) 0;
            return ERROR_SUCCESS;
        }
}

if( *lpcbTotalBytes < ❹
            ( sizeof( XX_HEADER_DEFINITION ) +
                sizeof( XX_PERF_DATA )))
{
        *lpcbTotalBytes = (DWORD) 0;
        *lpNumObjectTypes = (DWORD) 0;
        return ERROR_MORE_DATA;
}

pXxObjectHeader = ❺
            (PXX_HEADER_DEFINITION) *lppData;

memmove(
        pXxObjectHeader,
        &XxObjectHeader,
        sizeof( XX_HEADER_DEFINITION ));
```

```
    pPerfCounterBlock = ➏
         (PPERF_COUNTER_BLOCK) &pXxObjectHeader[1];

    if( !DeviceIoControl(
               hDevice,
               IOCTL_XX_GET_PERF_DATA,
               NULL,
               0,
               (LPVOID)pPerfCounterBlock,
               sizeof( XX_PERF_DATA ),
               &dwBytesReturned,
               NULL ))
    {
         dwStatus = GetLastError();
         XxLogErrorWithData(
               LOG_LEVEL_NORMAL,
               XXPERF_CANT_READ_PERF_DATA,
               &dwStatus, sizeof( dwStatus ) );

         *lpcbTotalBytes = (DWORD) 0;
         *lpNumObjectTypes = (DWORD) 0;
         return ERROR_SUCCESS;
    }

    *lppData = ➐
         (PUCHAR)pPerfCounterBlock +
                  sizeof( XX_PERF_DATA );

    *lpNumObjectTypes = XX_NUM_OBJECT_TYPES;

    *lpcbTotalBytes =
         sizeof( XX_HEADER_DEFINITION ) +
               sizeof( XX_PERF_DATA );

    return ERROR_SUCCESS
}
```

➊ If for some reason the DLL didn't initialize itself properly, just exit gracefully from this call.

➋ The DLL may be asked to provide a number of different kinds of data. The **XxGetPerfQueryType** helper function (defined in **PARSE.C**) scans the Unicode argument string and decides what kind the caller is asking for.

➌ The caller apparently passed an explicit list of object-type indexes. Use the **XxIsNumberInList** helper function (defined in **PARSE.C**) to determine whether the only object type we support was among the items in the list. If not, then do nothing. If this DLL supported multiple object types, it would need to call **XxIsNumberInList** for each one.

❹ Figure out how much space we'll need in the caller's buffer for all the objects we're going to return. If the buffer is too small, signal an error and don't return anything. ERROR_MORE_DATA is the only error condition signaled by the DLL. All other conditions (good or bad) return ERROR_SUCCESS.

❺ pXxObjectHeader points to the static PERF_OBJECT_TYPE and PERF_COUNTER_DEFINITION structures that were set up by **XxPerf-Open**. Copy this header information into the caller's buffer.

❻ Get a pointer to the place in the caller's buffer where the PERF_COUN-TER_BLOCK is going to go. This is the start of the counter data itself. Then call the kernel-mode driver to dump raw counter data into the caller's buffer. This IOCTL also fills in the **ByteLength** field of the PERF_COUNTER_BLOCK.

❼ Finally, update the caller's arguments.

XxPerfClose   This function decrements the use-count for the DLL. If it hits zero, **XxPerfClose** frees any resources being held by the DLL. Here, this simply means closing the target device handle and the Event Log.

```
DWORD
XxPerfClose( )
{
  //
  // One less thread is using the DLL
  //
  if( --dwOpenCount <= 0 )
  {
      //
      // When the last thread goes,
      // shut everything down
      //
      CloseHandle( hDevice );

      XxCloseEventLog();
  }
  return ERROR_SUCCESS;
}
```

Building and Installing this Example

Because this example is rather involved, a little explanation of how to set it up is probably a good idea. Follow these steps to build and test the data-collection DLL and its kernel-mode driver.

1. Use the BUILD utility to create **XXDRIVER.SYS**. Move the driver file to the **%SystemRoot%\SYSTEM32\DRIVERS** directory.

2. Use BUILD to generate **XXPERF.DLL** and move the DLL to the **%System-Root%\SYSTEM32** directory.

3. Create a service key in the Registry for XXDRIVER using REGEDT32.

4. Create a **Parameters** subkey beneath XXDRIVER's service key and add a REG_DWORD value called **EventLogLevel** to this key. Set **EventLogLevel** to 3 (maximum information).

5. Create a **Performance** subkey beneath XXDRIVER's service key and add REG_SZ values called **Library**, **Open**, **Collect**, and **Close**. Set these values up so that they match the examples listed in Table 18.12

6. Under **...\Services\EventLog\Application** in the Registry, create a subkey called **XXPERF**. Add **EventMessageFile** and **TypesSupported** values to this subkey. (See Chapter 13 if the details are fuzzy.) Also add "XXPERF" to the list of event-logging sources stored in the REG_MULTI_SZ **Sources** value under **...\Services\EventLog\Application**.

7. Run the LODCTR utility to add the object and counter names to the Registry. The command file is called **COUNTERS.INI** and it's in the **CH18\LIBRARY** directory.

8. Reboot the system and start XXDRIVER using the Devices applet in the Control Panel.

9. Run the Performance Monitor application (located in the Administrative Tools program group). When you select Add to chart from the Edit menu, you should see "Xx Device" as one of the object types.

If "Xx Device" doesn't show up in the Performance Monitor, start up the Event Viewer utility. Fatal error messages contain a Win32 status code that will help track down the problem.

18.7 SUMMARY

That finishes our look at driver performance. The techniques you've seen in this chapter will allow you to monitor the operation of your driver and decide what, if anything, you need to improve. Once again, don't wait until your driver is written before you start thinking about performance; it's an issue that you should be thinking about all through the design process.

The Development Environment

A.1 HARDWARE AND SOFTWARE REQUIREMENTS

Although it's possible to develop drivers using only a single machine, you really need two systems if you plan to do any serious debugging. You connect these machines (referred to the *host* and the *target*) using a null-modem serial cable. A network link between the machines isn't required, but it's a very good idea. Assuming the host and target have the same CPU architecture, you configure them as follows.

Host system   You use the host system to compile and link your driver and to run the WINDBG Kernel debugger. If you have to make a choice, this should be the machine with the most powerful hardware. Here is a list of the things that live on the host system:

- Windows NT retail build
- Visual C++
- Win32 SDK tools
- Windows NT DDK
- Symbol files from target
- Driver source code

Target system   The target system provides the environment for actually running your driver. Since you don't run the development tools on this system, it doesn't need as much power as the host. These are the things to keep on the target:

- Windows NT retail and checked build with debugging enabled
- Driver executable
- Driver's hardware
- Crash dump file
- Miscellaneous tools from the SDK (WINOBJ.EXE)
- Hardware compatibility tests from the NT DDK

You should install both the retail and checked versions of NT on the target machine. The checked version of NT performs a lot of sanity checking that's bypassed in the retail version, at the cost of reduced system performance. This sanity checking is very helpful when you're debugging a driver. However, before you send your driver out into the world, you'll also have to verify that it works with the retail version of the operating system.

Connecting the Host and Target

To debug your driver interactively with WINDBG, you need to connect the COM ports on the host and target machines using a standard, commercially available null-modem serial cable. For DB9 and DB25 connectors, the cable has these connections:

- Transmit Data connected to Receive Data (pin 2 to pin 3)
- Receive Data connected to Transmit Data (pin 3 to pin 2)
- Ground connected to Ground (pin 7 to pin 7)

WINDBG and the NT debug client don't use any of the other serial control lines. However, if you run into problems using a standard null-modem cable, you might try connecting jumpers from Data Terminal Ready to Data Set Ready and from Request To Send to Clear To Send. Make these modifications to the connectors on both ends of the cable:

- On a DB9 connector, add a jumper from pin 4 to pin 6 and a jumper from pin 7 to pin 8.
- On a DB25 connector, add a jumper from pin 20 to pin 6 and from pin 4 to pin 5.

You have a certain amount of flexibility when it comes to connecting the host and target systems. By default, WINDBG uses the host's COM2 port, but you can override this value. For Intel 80x86 targets, the default debug port is COM2 if you have multiple communications ports, or COM1 if you have a serial mouse attached to COM2. You can override these values by editing **BOOT.INI** (described below). RISC-based targets use COM1 as the default debug port.

A.2   DEBUG SYMBOL FILES

Along with the development software, you also need to put copies of the target system's debug symbol files on the host. These symbols are necessary if you plan to do any symbolic debugging or crash-dump analysis. Follow these steps to set up the symbol directories on the host:

1. Under the directory where you installed NT, create subdirectories called **...\SYMBOLS\FREE** and **...\SYMBOLS\CHECKED**.

2. From **\SUPPORT\DEBUG**<*platform*>**\SYMBOLS** on the NT distribution CD, copy various symbol files to **...\SYMBOLS\FREE** on the host. At a minimum, you'll need **EXE\NTOSKRNL.DBG, DLL\NTDLL.DBG**, and **DLL\HAL.DBG**.

3. Copy the checked versions of the same symbol files from **\CHECKED\SUPPORT\DEBUG**<*platform*>**\SYMBOLS** on the NT distribution CD to **...\SYMBOLS\CHECKED** on the host. You'll need these symbols when you run your driver under the checked build of NT.

4. Each time you rebuild your driver, copy the driver's symbol file into these directories. Refer back to Chapter 16 for an explanation of creating the driver's debug symbol file.

One thing to watch out for: Installing an NT service pack changes all the symbol information. So, if you've upgraded NT on the target system with a service pack, you have to get the operating system symbol files from the service pack CD. The symbols on the standard distribution CD won't work. The symbol directory paths on the service pack CD are the same as those on the NT distribution disk.

A.3   ENABLING CRASH DUMPS ON THE TARGET SYSTEM

Crash dump files can be very helpful when you're tracking down bugs in a kernel-mode driver. Refer back to Chapter 17 for information on reading these files. Follow these steps on the target system if you want Windows NT to dump crash information after a bugcheck.

1. In the Control Panel, double-click on the System applet.

2. Click on the Recovery button. The Recovery dialog box will appear.

3. Select the Write Debugging Information To check box. You can enter a path and filename for the crash file in the test box, or accept the default value (**%SystemRoot%\MEMORY.DMP**).

4. Select the Overwrite Any Existing File check box if you want new crashes to overwrite an existing dump file with the same name. If this check box is clear, you won't get any crash information if a dump file with the same name already exists.

5. Reboot the system to have these options take effect.

When a crash occurs, the system copies an image of physical memory into the paging file located on the system root partition. During the reboot after a crash, NT copies the crash image from the paging file to the target file specified in the Recovery dialog.

If You Don't Get Any Crash Dump Files

Several things can prevent the system from creating a dump file after a crash. If you're having troubles, here's what to look for.

Premature reboot   Make sure you don't hit the reboot switch until NT has finished dumping memory into the crash file. If you reboot before the dump is complete, you won't get any crash information. You can tell when NT has finished by looking at the message at the bottom of the blue screen display.

Paging file issues   NT can only use the paging file on the system root partition for storing the crash image. If you don't have a paging file there, NT won't be able to save crash information.

Also, make sure there's enough space in this paging file. It must be big enough to hold all of physical memory plus one additional megabyte. If the file is too small, you won't get any crash information.

Lack of disk space   There has to be enough space on the system root partition to hold the dump file itself. Although you can specify any target directory for the dump file, NT initially creates it in the **%SystemRoot%** directory and then copies it to its final destination. If there isn't enough free space, NT won't be able to create the file.

Hardware issues   Certain specific hardware configurations have problems generating crash files. Most of them (though not all) involve SCSI disk controllers. If you search the Knowledge Base section of the Microsoft Developer CD for a title containing the name of your system (or SCSI controller) and **MEMORY.DMP**, you may find a bug report helpful. Other than getting some new hardware, there's not much you can do in this case.

Even if your system isn't one of the ones with known problems, the lack of a dump file may indicate that you're using an out-of-date driver for your system disk. See if there's a newer version available.

A.4   ENABLING THE TARGET SYSTEM'S DEBUG CLIENT

Both the retail and checked versions of Windows NT include a debugging client that allows NT to communicate over a serial line with the WINDBG debugger. However, you have to enable this debugging client on the target system if you want to debug the target system interactively with WINDBG.

Depending on the CPU architecture, you follow different procedures to enable kernel-mode debugging on the target system. On RISC machines, you need to modify the **OSLOADOPTIONS** environment variable in the ARC firmware. See your system documentation for an explanation of how to do this.

To enable the debugger on 80x86-based machines, you edit the BOOT.INI file located in the root directory of the boot partition. This is a hidden system file that tells the NT loader what operating systems are available for booting. Follow these steps to modify BOOT.INI:

1. Remove the read-only, hidden, and system attributes from the file using this command:

   ```
   attrib -r -h -s BOOT.INI
   ```

2. Open **BOOT.INI** for editing with your favorite text editor.

3. In the **[operating systems]** section, add appropriate options to the boot command line for the free and checked versions of Windows NT.

4. Save the changes and close the file.

5. Use the following command (or its File Manager equivalent) to restore the file's original attributes:

   ```
   attrib +r +h +s BOOT.INI
   ```

Regardless of the machine architecture, you can specify the options listed in Table A.1. Keep the following things in mind when you're selecting bootstrap options.

- If you specify NODEBUG, then DEBUGPORT, BAUDRATE, and CRASH-DEBUG are ignored.

- If you specify BAUDRATE, kernel debugging is enabled; you do not also have to specify DEBUG. Select the highest baud rate that works for both machines.

Table A.1   Debugging options for BOOT.INI files or OSLOADOPTIONS

BOOT.INI options

Options	Description
DEBUG	Enables kernel-mode debugging.
NODEBUG	Disables kernel-mode debugging. This is the default.
DEBUGPORT=*PortName*	Specifies debug serial port used by target machine.
BAUDRATE=*BaudRate*	Specifies baud rate used by target machine.
CRASHDEBUG	Causes debugger to activate only when the system bugchecks.
MAXMEM=*SizeInMB*	Specifies the amount of memory to be made available to the system.
SOS	Displays the name of each module being loaded during system bootstrap

- On 80x86 machines, COM2 is the default debugger communications port, if it exists and if it isn't being used. In all other cases, COM1 is the default.
- The MAXMEM option can be useful for stress testing your driver in a low-memory environment. For example, you can limit a 24-megabyte machine to using only 12 megabytes.

The following example of a BOOT.INI file offers three choices at boot time: a nondebugging, free version of NT; a free version of NT with the debugger enabled; and a checked version of NT with debugging enabled. The checked version is also restricted to a 12 MB environment.

```
[boot loader]
timeout=30
default=c:\

[operating systems]
multi(0)disk(0)rdisk(0)partition(1)\winnt="NT Free"
multi(0)disk(0)rdisk(0)partition(1)\winnt="NT Free" /DEBUGPORT=COM1
multi(0)disk(0)rdisk(0)partition(1)\wntchk="NT Check" /DEBUG=COM1 /MAXMEM=12
```

Common Bugcheck Codes

B.1   GENERAL PROBLEMS WITH DRIVERS

A variety of driver errors can produce the bugchecks in Table B.1. The accompanying notes may help you locate the source of the problem.

Table B.1   General errors

Bugchecks caused by general driver problems

Code and parameters	Description

IRQL_NOT_LESS_OR_EQUAL (0x0A)
1 — Address that was referenced
2 — IRQL at time of reference
3 — Type of access
  • 0 — Read
  • 1 — Write
4 — Address where reference occurred
	CAUSE: A driver touched paged memory at or above DISPATCH_LEVEL IRQL.
	ACTION: The driver may be using a bogus pointer. Use the fourth bugcheck parameter to find the offending source code line.

KMODE_EXCEPTION_NOT_HANDLED (0x1E) 1 — The exception code[1] 2 — Address of the failing instruction 3 — First exception parameter 4 — Second exception parameter	**CAUSE:** A driver generated an exception. **ACTION:** Use the second bugcheck parameter to locate the offending source code line.

Table B.1   (Continued)

Code and parameters	Description
UNEXPECTED_KERNEL_MODE_TRAP (0x7F) 1 — Code number of trap[2]	**CAUSE:** On Intel platforms, this means the CPU generated a trap that it can't handle in kernel mode. **ACTION:** From WINDBG, find the trap frame address with **kb**. Use **!trap** to format the frame.[3] The contents of EIP will show where the trap was taken.
PANIC_STACK_SWITCH (0x2B)	**CAUSE:** The kernel-mode stack has overflowed. This can mean other operating system data structures have been damaged. **ACTION:** In the stack trace, look for a driver that's using too much stack space.[4]
PAGE_FAULT_WITH_INTERRUPTS_OFF (0x49)	Same as 0x0A (above).
IRQL_NOT_DISPATCH_LEVEL (0x08) **IRQL_NOT_GREATER_OR_EQUAL (0x09)** **IRQL_GT_ZERO_AT_SYSTEM_SERVICE (0x4A)**	**CAUSE:** Miscellaneous problems with IRQL level. **ACTION:** Use the stack trace to locate the code causing the crash.
INVALID_SOFTWARE_INTERRUPT (0x07) **SYSTEM_SERVICE_EXCEPTION (0x3B)** **INVALID_DATA_ACCESS_TRAP (0x04)** **NO_EXCEPTION_HANDLING_SUPPORT (0x0B)** **TRAP_CAUSE_UNKNOWN (0x12)** **LAST_CHANCE_CALLED_FROM_KMODE (0x15)**	**CAUSE:** Miscellaneous problems with exceptions. **ACTION:** Use the stack trace to locate the code executing at the time of the crash.

[1] You can determine what kind of exception it is by searching **NTSTATUS.H** for this number. A common exception code is 0x80000003. This means the system hit a hard-coded breakpoint or ASSERT while it was booted with the /NODEBUG switch. Connect a debugger and reboot with the /DEBUG switch to locate the problem.

Another popular error is 0xC0000005, which is an access violation. In this case, argument 4 (the second exception parameter) is the address your driver was trying to touch.

[2] See the *Intel486 Processor Family Programmer's Reference* (listed in the bibliography) for a list of CPU trap codes.

[3] On Intel platforms, the frame will be associated with a procedure called **NT!KiTrap**.

[4] Keep in mind that the driver whose stack operation generated the bugcheck is not necessarily the driver that's using too much stack space.

B.2   SYNCHRONIZATION PROBLEMS

The bugchecks in Table B.2 are caused by improper use of various NT synchronization mechanisms.

Table B.2   Synchronization problems

Bugchecks caused by synchronization problems	
Code and parameters	**Description**
SPIN_LOCK_INIT_FAILURE (0x81) **SPIN_LOCK_ALREADY_OWNED (0xF)** **SPIN_LOCK_NOT_OWNED (0x10)** **NO_SPIN_LOCK_AVAILABLE (0x1D)**	**CAUSE:** Misuse of spin locks. **ACTION:** Use the stack trace to locate the code executing at the time of the crash.
MAXIMUM_WAIT_OBJECTS_EXCEEDED (0x0C) **THREAD_NOT_MUTEX_OWNER (0x11)** **SYSTEM_EXIT_OWNED_MUTEX (0x39)**	**CAUSE:** Improper use of Mutexes in kernel mode. **ACTION:** Fix the driver logic error causing the problem.
MUTEX_LEVEL_NUMBER_VIOLATION (0xD) 1 — Current thread's Mutex level 2 — Mutex level of requested Mutex	**CAUSE:** A driver thread has requested ownership of a Mutex that violates the level number sequence. **ACTION:** Use the stack trace to identify the driver. Use the level numbers to identify the Mutexes.[1]

[1] If the Mutexes belong to NT, use **EXLEVELS.H** to figure out which ones they are.

B.3   CORRUPTED DRIVER DATA STRUCTURES

The bugchecks in Table B.3 are caused by problems with various I/O Manger data structures. In general, these problems indicate some kind of serious logic error in a driver.

Table B.3   Driver data structure problems

Bugchecks caused by data structure problems

Code and parameters	Description
DEVICE_REFERENCE_COUNT_NOT_ZERO (0x36) 1 — Address of Device object	**CAUSE:** A driver has called **IoDeleteDevice** with a Device object that still has a nonzero reference count. **ACTION:** Locate the driver logic error leading to this situation.
NO_MORE_IRP_STACK_LOCATIONS (0x35) 1 — Address of the IRP	**CAUSE:** A higher-level driver has tried to pass an IRP to a lower-level driver using **IoCallDriver**, but there are no more stack locations in the IRP.[1] **ACTION:** If your driver allocated the IRP, examine how you're calculating the number of stack slots. If the IRP is being passed to you, your Device object's **StackSize** field is too small.
INCONSISTENT_IRP (0x2A) 1 — Address of the IRP	**CAUSE:** The I/O Manager has found an IRP with fields that are not internally consistent.[2] **ACTION:** Make sure your driver isn't writing over the contents of the IRP.
MULTIPLE_IRP_COMPLETE_REQUESTS (0x44) 1 — Address of the IRP	**CAUSE:** A driver has called **IoCompleteRequest** with an IRP that's already been completed. Either one driver is trying to complete the same IRP twice, or two drivers both think they own the IRP.[3] **ACTION:** The **DeviceObject** field of the IRP's stack locations will show you who was using the IRP. This may help.

Table B.3   (Continued)

Code and parameters	Description
CANCEL_STATE_IN_COMPLETED_IRP (0x48) 1 — Address of the IRP	**CAUSE:** A driver has called **IoCompleteRequest** with an IRP that still has a cancel routine. **ACTION:** This is a driver logic error. Take the IRP out of the cancelable state before you try to complete it.
DEVICE_QUEUE_NOT_BUSY (0x02)	**CAUSE:** A Device Queue object is in an inconsistent state. **ACTION:** The Device Queue object is probably getting corrupted by inappropriate access or because of bogus use of pointers.

[1] This is really a disaster, since the higher-level driver thinks it has filled in the IRP parameter fields for the lower-level driver. However, there was no room in the IRP for these parameters, so the higher-level driver has actually written off the end of the IRP and mangled some unrelated piece of memory.

[2] For example, an IRP that was being completed but was still marked as being attached to a driver's Device Queue object.

[3] Finding the two drivers is difficult, since the identity of the first one has already been covered up by the time the second driver makes the failing call to **IoCompleteRequest**.

B.4   MEMORY PROBLEMS

The bugchecks in Table B.4 are caused by driver memory problems. Drivers can cause many subtle (and not so subtle) system failures through improper use of memory.

Table B.4   Memory problems

Bugchecks caused by memory problems	
Code and parameters	**Description**
NO_MORE_SYSTEM_PTES (0x3F)	**CAUSE:** There are no system page table entries left. This often means a driver isn't cleaning up after itself. **ACTION:** The **!sysptes** command may give some insight.
TARGET_MDL_TOO_SMALL (0x40)	**CAUSE:** A driver has called **IoBuildPartialMdl** and passed a target MDL that isn't large enough to map the entire range of addresses requested. **ACTION:** Locate the call to **Io-BuildPartialMdl** in the stack trace. Its arguments identify the bad MDL. Also use the stack trace to see who called this function.
MUST_SUCCEED_POOL_EMPTY (0x41) 1 — Size of unsatisfied request 2 — Number of pages used of nonpaged pool 3 — Number of too large PAGE_SIZE requests from nonpaged pool 4 — Number of pages available	**CAUSE:** There isn't enough memory to satisfy a request from one of the **XxxMustSucceed** pool areas. **ACTION:** Look for a driver that's leaking memory.
NO_PAGES_AVAILABLE (0x4D) 1 — Number of dirty pages 2 — Number of physical pages in machine 3 — Extended commit value in pages 4 — Total commit value in pages	**CAUSE:** The system has run out of free pages. **ACTION:** Look for processes or drivers that are leaking memory.
PFN_LIST_CORRUPT (0x4E) 1 — 1 2 — ListHead value that was corrupt 3 — Number of pages available 4 — 0 **– OR –** 1 — 2 2 — Entry in list being removed 3 — Highest physical page number 4 — Reference count of entry being removed	**CAUSE:** A driver has probably corrupted an MDL. **ACTION:** Trace backward on the stack from the system routine that detected the error to the driver routine that passed the MDL. This may be the driver that corrupted the MDL.

Table B.4   (Continued)

Code and parameters	Description
PROCESS_HAS_LOCKED_PAGES (0x76) 1 — Process address 2 — Number of locked pages 3 — Number of private pages 4 — 0	**CAUSE:** A driver hasn't released some locked pages at the end of an I/O operation. **ACTION:** Look for a driver that isn't cleaning up after an I/O.
BAD_POOL_HEADER (0x19) **MEMORY_MANAGEMENT (0x1A)** **PFN_SHARE_COUNT (0x1B)** **PFN_REFERENCE_COUNT (0x1C)** **PAGE_FAULT_IN_NONPAGED_AREA (0x50)** **INSUFFICIENT_SYSTEM_MAP_REGS (0x45)**	**CAUSE:** Miscellaneous memory errors. **ACTION:** Look for drivers active at the time of the crash. One of them may be corrupting memory.

B.5   HARDWARE FAILURES

The bugchecks in Table B.5 are the result of various hardware failures. Try to locate and correct the problem.

Table B.5   Hardware problems

Bugchecks caused by hardware problems

Code and parameters	Description
KERNEL_STACK_INPAGE_ERROR (0x77) 1 — 0 2 — 0 3 — PTE value at time of error 4 — Address of Kernel stack signature — OR — 1 — Status code 2 — I/O status code 3 — Page file number 4 — Offset into page file	**CAUSE:** A page of the kernel-mode stack couldn't be read because of a bad block in the paging file or a disk controller error. **ACTION:** If the first two parameters are zero, there is a hardware error. Else, look at the status code: • C000009C or C000016A: bad block • C0000185: SCSI cable or termination problem • C0000009A: insufficient nonpaged pool

KERNEL_DATA_INPAGE_ERROR (0x7A)
1 — Lock type that was held:
  • Value 1, 2, 3
  • PTE address
2 — Error status
	CAUSE: A page of kernel-mode data couldn't be read because of a bad block in the paging file or a disk controller error.

Table B.5   (Continued)

Code and parameters	Description
3 — Current process 4 — Virtual address that could not be read	**ACTION:** See error 0x77 (above)
DATA_BUS_ERROR (0x2E) 1 — Virtual address that caused the fault 2 — Physical address that caused the fault 3 — Processor status register (PSR) 4 — Faulting instruction register (FIR)	**CAUSE:** Either there is a parity error in system memory or a driver is accessing a nonexistent system-space address. **ACTION:** If a memory test succeeds, then use stack trace to locate the driver making the reference.
MULTIPROCESSOR_CONFIGURATION_ NOT_SUPPORTED (0x3E)	**CAUSE:** NT has detected that all the CPUs in a multiprocessor system are not identical. This is not a supported configuration. **ACTION:** Correct the asymmetry.
INSTALL_MORE_MEMORY (0x7D) 1 — Number of physical pages found 2 — Lowest physical page 3 — Highest physical page 4 — 0	**CAUSE:** There isn't enough memory available to boot the system. **ACTION:** Install more memory.
NMI_HARDWARE_FAILURE (0x80) **INSTRUCTION_BUS_ERROR (0x2F)** **DATA_COHERENCY_EXCEPTION (0x55)** **INSTRUCTION_COHERENCY_EXCEPTION (0x56)**	**CAUSE:** Miscellaneous hardware failures. **ACTION:** Use hardware diagnostics to locate and correct the problem.

B.6   CONFIGURATION MANAGER AND REGISTRY PROBLEMS

The bugchecks in Table B.6 result from problems with crucial Registry information. If the failure occurs only when your driver is running, you may be able to trace the problem back to bad calls to Registry functions. Since the Registry is mapped into system space, drivers can also corrupt the Registry by using bogus address pointers.

Table B.6   Registry problems

Bugchecks caused by Registry problems

Code and parameters	Description
CONFIG_INITIALIZATION_FAILED (0x67) 1 — 5 2 — Location where failure occurred	**CAUSE:** Configuration Manager couldn't get enough paged pool for the Registry.[1] **ACTION:** Get a stack trace and call Microsoft.
CONFIG_LIST_FAILED (0x73) 1 — 5 2 — 2 3 — Index of hive 4 — Pointer to UNICODE_STRING containing filename of hive	**CAUSE:** One of the core system Registry hives (SOFTWARE, SECURITY, or SAM) is unreadable or corrupted. **ACTION:** Get a stack trace and call Microsoft.
BAD_SYSTEM_CONFIG_INFO (0x74)	**CAUSE:** Either the SYSTEM hive is corrupted, or various crucial keys and values are missing. **ACTION:** Try booting from the Last Known Good configuration. If that fails, use the emergency repair disk. If that fails, reinstall NT.
CANNOT_WRITE_CONFIGURATION (0x75)	**CAUSE:** There is no room on the disk to increase the size of the SYSTEM hive files. **ACTION:** Free up space in the system partition.
REGISTRY_ERROR (0x51) 1 — Indicates where error occurred 2 — Indicates where error occurred 3 — Pointer to hive 4 — Internal error return code	**CAUSE:** Something is seriously wrong with the Registry. It may be the result of an I/O error or file system corruption. **ACTION:** Try rebooting using the Last Known Good option or the emergency repair disk.

[1] This error should never occur, since Registry setup happens early enough during system initialization that there should always be enough pool space.

B.7   FILE SYSTEM PROBLEMS

The bugchecks in Table B.7 result from failures in a file-system driver or a related component. Since Microsoft doesn't currently support customer-written FSDs, there is little you can do to diagnose these problems.

Table B.7   File system problems

Bugchecks caused by file system problems	
Code and parameters	**Description**
CACHE_MANAGER (0x34) FILE_SYSTEM (0x22) FAT_FILE_SYSTEM (0x23)	**CAUSE:** Internal problems with a Microsoft-supplied file-system driver.
NTFS_FILE_SYSTEM (0x24) NPFS_FILE_SYSTEM (0x25) CDFS_FILE_SYSTEM (0x26) RDR_FILE_SYSTEM (0x27) MAILSLOT_FILE_SYSTEM (0x52) PINBALL_FILE_SYSTEM (0x59) LM_SERVER_INTERNAL_ERROR (0x54)	**ACTION:** Get a stack trace and call Microsoft.
APC_INDEX_MISMATCH (0x01)	**CAUSE:** This internal error could be the result of file system problems. **ACTION:** Get a stack trace and call Microsoft.
KERNEL_APC_PENDING_DURING_EXIT (0x20) 1 — Address of pending APC 2 — The thread's APC disable count 3 — The current IRQL	**CAUSE:** This indicates a logic error in a file system driver. **ACTION:** See if any third-party file system drivers were installed at the time of the crash. Be suspicious of them.

B.8   SYSTEM INITIALIZATION FAILURES

The bugchecks in Table B.8 occur only during system initialization. Some of them are the result of mismatched software components, while others indicate problems that can only be diagnosed by Microsoft.

Table B.8   Bootstrap and initialization failures

Bugchecks caused by bootstrap problems

Code and parameters	Description

MISMATCHED_HAL (0x79)
1 — 1 (Release levels don't match)
2 — Release level of Kernel
3 — Release level of HAL
   – OR –
1 — 2 (Build types don't match)
2 — Kernel build type
   • 0 — Free multiprocessor-enabled build
   • 1 — Checked multiprocessor-enabled build
   • 2 — Free uniprocessor build
3 — HAL build-type
   – OR –
1 — 3 (MCA HAL required)
2 — Machine type detected at bootstrap
   • 2 means MCA
3 — HAL type
	CAUSE: The HAL revision level and HAL configuration type do not match those of the Kernel or the machine type.[1]
	ACTION: Make sure the proper versions of the HAL and NTOSKRNL are installed.

FTDISK_INTERNAL_ERROR (0x58)	**CAUSE:** The system is trying to boot from the wrong copy of a mirrored partition. **ACTION:** Reboot from the shadow copy of the partition.
INACCESSIBLE_BOOT_DEVICE (0x7B) 1 — Pointer to boot Device object – OR – 1 — Pointer to UNICODE_STRING structure containing ARC name of volume that can't be mounted.	**CAUSE:** Either the device driver for the boot device failed to initialize, or the file system driver for the boot device didn't recognize the file structures on the volume. **ACTION:** Be sure the right device driver is installed for the boot device, and that the system is trying to boot from the correct location.

Table B.8   (Continued)

Code and parameters	Description
PHASE0_EXCEPTION (0x78)	**CAUSE:** Failure during initialization of a system component. **ACTION:** Get a stack trace and call Microsoft.
SESSION1_INITIALIZATION_FAILED (0x6D) **SESSION2_INITIALIZATION_FAILED (0x6E)** **SESSION3_INITIALIZATION_FAILED (0x6F)** **SESSION4_INITIALIZATION_FAILED (0x70)** **SESSION5_INITIALIZATION_FAILED (0x71)** 1 — NT status code at time of failure	**CAUSE:** Failure during initialization of a system component. **ACTION:** Get a stack trace and call Microsoft.
PHASE0_INITIALIZATION_FAILED (0x31) **PHASE1_INITIALIZATION_FAILED (0x32)** **HAL_INITIALIZATION_FAILED (0x5C)** **HEAP_INITIALIZATION_FAILED (0x5D)** **OBJECT_INITIALIZATION_FAILED (0x5E)** **SECURITY_INITIALIZATION_FAILED (0x5F)** **PROCESS_INITIALIZATION_FAILED (0x60)** **HAL1_INITIALIZATION_FAILED (0x61)** **OBJECT1_INITIALIZATION_FAILED (0x62)** **SECURITY1_INITIALIZATION_FAILED (0x63)** **SYMBOLIC_INITIALIZATION_FAILED (0x64)** **MEMORY1_INITIALIZATION_FAILED (0x65)** **CACHE_INITIALIZATION_FAILED (0x66)** **FILE_INITIALIZATION_FAILED (0x68)** **IO1_INITIALIZATION_FAILED (0x69)** **LPC_INITIALIZATION_FAILED (0x6A)** **PROCESS1_INITIALIZATION_FAILED (0x6B)** **REFMON_INITIALIZATION_FAILED (0x6C)** 1 — NT status code describing the failure 2 — Indicator of location where failure occurred **WINDOWS_NT_BANNER (0x4000007E)**	**CAUSE:** Failure during initialization of a system component. **ACTION:** Get a stack trace and call Microsoft.

[1] This error probably means that someone has manually updated either **NTOSKRNL.EXE** or **HAL.DLL**. It can also result from mixing a uniprocessor HAL with a multiprocessor Kernel, or vice versa.

B.9　Internal System Failures

The bugchecks in Table B.9 all come from fatal errors within a Microsoft-supplied software component. For the most part, there's little you can do to track these errors.

Table B.9　Internal system errors

Bugchecks caused by internal system problems	
Code and parameters	**Description**
PORT_DRIVER_INTERNAL (0x2C) **SCSI_DISK_DRIVER_INTERNAL (0x2D)** **FLOPPY_INTERNAL_ERROR (0x37)** **SERIAL_DRIVER_INTERNAL (0x38)** **ATDISK_DRIVER_INTERNAL (0x42)**	**CAUSE:** Miscellaneous errors from a system-supplied driver. **ACTION:** Get a stack trace and call Microsoft.
STREAMS_INTERNAL_ERROR (0x4B) **NDIS_INTERNAL_ERROR (0x4F)** **XNS_INTERNAL_ERROR (0x57)**	**CAUSE:** Internal errors from system-supplied networking components. **ACTION:** Get a stack trace and call Microsoft.
CORRUPT_ACCESS_TOKEN (0x28) **SECURITY_SYSTEM (0x29)**	**CAUSE:** Internal security sub-system errors. **ACTION:** Get a stack trace and call Microsoft.

Bibliography

Books about Software Development

Hatley, Derek J., and Pirbhai, Imtiaz A. *Strategies for Real-Time System Specification.* New York, NY. Dorset House Publishing, 1988. Device drivers are complex pieces of real-time software. The techniques in this book can help in their design.

Kaner, Cem, et al. *Testing Computer Software*, 2nd ed. New York, NY. Van Nostrand Reinhold, 1993. This book gives a good overview of the software testing process. If you're responsible for finding and fixing the bugs, this is a good place to start.

Books about Windows NT and Win32

Custer, Helen. *Inside Windows NT.* Redmond, WA. Microsoft Press, 1993. This book (although getting rather long in the tooth at this point) contains a good high-level overview of the original Windows NT architecture. Unfortunately, it's somewhat lacking in specific implementation details.

Microsoft Corporation. *Windows NT 3.5 Resource Kit.* Redmond, WA. Microsoft Press, 1994. These volumes have been updated for NT 3.51 and presumably will be for NT 4.0 as well.

Richter, Jeffrey. *Advanced Windows NT.* Redmond, WA. Microsoft Press, 1994. This book will give you a good background in Win32 user-mode programming.

Books about Bus Architectures

Anderson, Don. *PCMCIA System Architecture*, 2nd ed. Reading, MA. Addison-Wesley Publishing Company, Inc., 1995. I can't say enough good things about this series of hardware books from Shanley and Anderson. They're accurate, readable, and detailed enough to give driver writers a comprehensive introduction to various bus and system architectures. To top it all off, they're not even terribly expensive.

Bowlds, Pat A. *Micro Channel Architecture*. New York, NY. Van Nostrand Reinhold, 1991. If you're in the unenviable position of writing a driver for an MCA device, this is one of the few sources of information available. It's a little bit fluffy.

Schmidt, Friedhelm. *The SCSI Bus and IDE Interface*. Reading, MA. Addison-Wesley Publishing Company, Inc., 1995. This provides a good introduction to the SCSI bus. It's worth reading before you dive into the ANSI SCSI specification itself.

Shanley, Tom. *Plug and Play System Architecture*. Reading, MA. Addison-Wesley Publishing Company, Inc., 1995.

Shanley, Tom and Anderson, Don. *ISA System Architecture*, 3rd ed. Reading, MA. Addison-Wesley Publishing Company, Inc., 1995.

Shanley, Tom and Anderson, Don. *EISA System Architecture*, 2nd ed. Reading, MA. Addison-Wesley Publishing Company, Inc., 1995.

Shanley, Tom and Anderson, Don. *PCI System Architecture*, 3rd ed. Reading, MA. Addison-Wesley Publishing Company, Inc., 1995.

Shanley, Tom and Anderson, Don. *CardBus System Architecture*. Reading, MA. Addison-Wesley Publishing Company, Inc., 1996.

Books about CPU Architectures

Heinrich, Joe. *MIPS R4000 User's Manual*. Englewood Cliffs, NJ. Prentice Hall Inc., 1993.

Intel Corporation. *Intel486 Processor Family Programmer's Reference*, Beaverton, OR. Intel Corporation, 1992.

Shanley, Tom. *PowerPC 601 System Architecture*. Reading, MA. Addison-Wesley Publishing Company, Inc., 1994.

Sites, Richard and Witek, Richard. *Alpha AXP Architecture Reference Manual*, 2nd ed. Newton, MA. Digital Press, 1995.

Books about Miscellaneous Hardware

Campbell, Joe. *Programmer's Guide to Serial Communications*, 2nd ed. Indianapolis, IN. SAMS Publishing, 1994. 1993. This is an incredibly comprehensive source of information about the operation of UARTs and related devices.

Ferraro, Richard. *Programmer's Guide to the EGA, VGA, and Super VGA Cards*, 3rd ed. Reading, MA. Addison-Wesley Publishing Company, Inc., 1994. This is probably the most comprehensive source of information about PC video hardware and how to program it.

Intel Corporation. *Intel Peripheral Components Handbook*, Beaverton, OR. Intel Corporation, 1993. This handbook has information about common peripheral interface chips such as the programmable interrupt controller and DMA controller.

About the Author

Art Baker has spent over twenty-five years in the computer industry, where he's worked on everything from compilers to real-time data gathering software. In 1984, he changed the focus of his career and began writing and teaching technical training classes for Digital Equipment Corporation. His broad technical background and good communication skills made him a consistent favorite with students and won him several awards for instructor excellence. After leaving Digital, Mr. Baker founded Cydonix Corporation, a Washington, DC training and consulting firm.

In his spare time, Mr. Baker is an accomplished classical pianist, and an avid collector of old science fiction movies. He lives in Washington, DC.

INDEX

LICENSE AGREEMENT AND LIMITED WARRANTY

READ THE FOLLOWING TERMS AND CONDITIONS CAREFULLY BEFORE OPENING THIS DISK PACKAGE. THIS LEGAL DOCUMENT IS AN AGREEMENT BETWEEN YOU AND PRENTICE-HALL, INC. (THE "COMPANY"). BY OPENING THIS SEALED DISK PACKAGE, YOU ARE AGREEING TO BE BOUND BY THESE TERMS AND CONDITIONS. IF YOU DO NOT AGREE WITH THESE TERMS AND CONDITIONS, DO NOT OPEN THE DISK PACKAGE. PROMPTLY RETURN THE UNOPENED DISK PACKAGE AND ALL ACCOMPANYING ITEMS TO THE PLACE YOU OBTAINED THEM FOR A FULL REFUND OF ANY SUMS YOU HAVE PAID.

1. **GRANT OF LICENSE:** In consideration of your payment of the license fee, which is part of the price you paid for this product, and your agreement to abide by the terms and conditions of this Agreement, the Company grants to you a nonexclusive right to use and display the copy of the enclosed software program (hereinafter the "SOFTWARE") on a single computer (i.e., with a single CPU) at a single location so long as you comply with the terms of this Agreement. The Company reserves all rights not expressly granted to you under this Agreement.

2. **OWNERSHIP OF SOFTWARE:** You own only the magnetic or physical media (the enclosed disks) on which the SOFTWARE is recorded or fixed, but the Company retains all the rights, title, and ownership to the SOFTWARE recorded on the original disk copy(ies) and all subsequent copies of the SOFTWARE, regardless of the form or media on which the original or other copies may exist. This license is not a sale of the original SOFTWARE or any copy to you.

3. **COPY RESTRICTIONS:** This SOFTWARE and the accompanying printed materials and user manual (the "Documentation") are the subject of copyright. You may <u>not</u> copy the Documentation or the SOFTWARE, except that you may make a single copy of the SOFTWARE for backup or archival purposes only. You may be held legally responsible for any copying or copyright infringement which is caused or encouraged by your failure to abide by the terms of this restriction.

4. **USE RESTRICTIONS:** You may <u>not</u> network the SOFTWARE or otherwise use it on more than one computer or computer terminal at the same time. You may physically transfer the SOFTWARE from one computer to another provided that the SOFTWARE is used on only one computer at a time. You may <u>not</u> distribute copies of the SOFTWARE or Documentation to others. You may <u>not</u> reverse engineer, disassemble, decompile, modify, adapt, translate, or create derivative works based on the SOFTWARE or the Documentation without the prior written consent of the Company.

5. **TRANSFER RESTRICTIONS:** The enclosed SOFTWARE is licensed only to you and may <u>not</u> be transferred to any one else without the prior written consent of the Company. Any unauthorized transfer of the SOFTWARE shall result in the immediate termination of this Agreement.

6. **TERMINATION:** This license is effective until terminated. This license will terminate automatically without notice from the Company and become null and void if you fail to comply with any provisions or limitations of this license. Upon termination, you shall destroy the Documentation and all copies of the SOFTWARE. All provisions of this Agreement as to warranties, limitation of liability, remedies or damages, and our ownership rights shall survive termination.

7. **MISCELLANEOUS:** This Agreement shall be construed in accordance with the laws of the United States of America and the State of New York and shall benefit the Company, its affiliates, and assignees.

8. **LIMITED WARRANTY AND DISCLAIMER OF WARRANTY:** The Company warrants that the SOFTWARE, when properly used in accordance with the Documentation, will operate in substantial conformity with the description of the SOFTWARE set forth in the Documentation. The Company does not warrant that the SOFT-

WARE will meet your requirements or that the operation of the SOFTWARE will be uninterrupted or error-free. The Company warrants that the media on which the SOFTWARE is delivered shall be free from defects in materials and workmanship under normal use for a period of thirty (30) days from the date of your purchase. Your only remedy and the Company's only obligation under these limited warranties is, at the Company's option, return of the warranted item for a refund of any amounts paid by you or replacement of the item. Any replacement of SOFTWARE or media under the warranties shall not extend the original warranty period. The limited warranty set forth above shall not apply to any SOFTWARE which the Company determines in good faith has been subject to misuse, neglect, improper installation, repair, alteration, or damage by you. EXCEPT FOR THE EXPRESSED WARRANTIES SET FORTH ABOVE, THE COMPANY DISCLAIMS ALL WARRANTIES, EXPRESS OR IMPLIED, INCLUDING WITHOUT LIMITA-TION, THE IMPLIED WARRANTIES OF MERCHANTABILITY AND FITNESS FOR A PARTICULAR PUR-POSE. EXCEPT FOR THE EXPRESS WARRANTY SET FORTH ABOVE, THE COMPANY DOES NOT WARRANT, GUARANTEE, OR MAKE ANY REPRESENTATION REGARDING THE USE OR THE RESULTS OF THE USE OF THE SOFTWARE IN TERMS OF ITS CORRECTNESS, ACCURACY, RELIABILITY, CUR-RENTNESS, OR OTHERWISE.

IN NO EVENT, SHALL THE COMPANY OR ITS EMPLOYEES, AGENTS, SUPPLIERS, OR CONTRACTORS BE LIABLE FOR ANY INCIDENTAL, INDIRECT, SPECIAL, OR CONSEQUENTIAL DAM-AGES ARISING OUT OF OR IN CONNECTION WITH THE LICENSE GRANTED UNDER THIS AGREE-MENT, OR FOR LOSS OF USE, LOSS OF DATA, LOSS OF INCOME OR PROFIT, OR OTHER LOSSES, SUSTAINED AS A RESULT OF INJURY TO ANY PERSON, OR LOSS OF OR DAMAGE TO PROPERTY, OR CLAIMS OF THIRD PARTIES, EVEN IF THE COMPANY OR AN AUTHORIZED REPRESENTATIVE OF THE COMPANY HAS BEEN ADVISED OF THE POSSIBILITY OF SUCH DAMAGES. IN NO EVENT SHALL LIABILITY OF THE COMPANY FOR DAMAGES WITH RESPECT TO THE SOFTWARE EXCEED THE AMOUNTS ACTUALLY PAID BY YOU, IF ANY, FOR THE SOFTWARE.

SOME JURISDICTIONS DO NOT ALLOW THE LIMITATION OF IMPLIED WARRANTIES OR LIABILITY FOR INCIDENTAL, INDIRECT, SPECIAL, OR CONSEQUENTIAL DAMAGES, SO THE ABOVE LIMITATIONS MAY NOT ALWAYS APPLY. THE WARRANTIES IN THIS AGREEMENT GIVE YOU SPECIFIC LEGAL RIGHTS AND YOU MAY ALSO HAVE OTHER RIGHTS WHICH VARY IN ACCOR-DANCE WITH LOCAL LAW.

ACKNOWLEDGMENT

YOU ACKNOWLEDGE THAT YOU HAVE READ THIS AGREEMENT, UNDERSTAND IT, AND AGREE TO BE BOUND BY ITS TERMS AND CONDITIONS. YOU ALSO AGREE THAT THIS AGREE-MENT IS THE COMPLETE AND EXCLUSIVE STATEMENT OF THE AGREEMENT BETWEEN YOU AND THE COMPANY AND SUPERSEDES ALL PROPOSALS OR PRIOR AGREEMENTS, ORAL, OR WRITTEN, AND ANY OTHER COMMUNICATIONS BETWEEN YOU AND THE COMPANY OR ANY REPRESENTA-TIVE OF THE COMPANY RELATING TO THE SUBJECT MATTER OF THIS AGREEMENT.

Should you have any questions concerning this Agreement or if you wish to contact the Company for any reason, please contact in writing at the address below.

Robin Short
Prentice Hall PTR
One Lake Street
Upper Saddle River, New Jersey 07458